A History of Cookbooks

CALIFORNIA STUDIES IN FOOD AND CULTURE
Darra Goldstein, Editor

A History of Cookbooks

From Kitchen to Page over Seven Centuries

Henry Notaker

UNIVERSITY OF CALIFORNIA PRESS

University of California Press, one of the most distinguished university presses in the United States, enriches lives around the world by advancing scholarship in the humanities, social sciences, and natural sciences. Its activities are supported by the UC Press Foundation and by philanthropic contributions from individuals and institutions. For more information, visit www.ucpress.edu.

University of California Press
Oakland, California

Library of Congress Cataloging-in-Publication Data

Names: Notaker, Henry, author.
· Title: A history of cookbooks : from kitchen to page over seven centuries / Henry Notaker.
Description: Oakland, California : University of California Press, [2017] | Series: California studies in food and culture ; 64 | Includes bibliographical references and index. | Description based on print version record and CIP data provided by publisher; resource not viewed.
Identifiers: LCCN 2017009465 (print) | LCCN 2017012224 (ebook) | ISBN 9780520967281 (Ebook) | ISBN 9780520294004 (cloth : alk. paper)
Subjects: LCSH: Cookbooks—Europe—History. | Manners and customs in literature.
Classification: LCC TX723.5.A1 (ebook) | LCC TX723.5.A1 N68 2017 (print) | DDC 641.5—dc23
LC record available at https://lccn.loc.gov/2017009465

Manufactured in the United States of America
25 24 23 22 21 20 19 18 17
10 9 8 7 6 5 4 3 2 1

CONTENTS

ILLUSTRATIONS

Cookbooks have a long history, at least as long as many other types of texts we encounter in our daily lives. But these culinary texts have very rarely been studied with the methods used in most histories of literature. This has partly to do with the development of the concept of literature, which started in the eighteenth century. Before that time, "literature" was a term for most kinds of what we now call fiction and nonfiction, but gradually the concept was narrowed to include only fiction and occasionally certain forms of nonfiction that had traditionally been considered to have a higher literary value—like personal essays, for example. Literature was specified as beautiful or artistic, a view expressed through designations such as *belles-lettres* in French, *schöne Literatur* in German, and *khudozhestvennaia literatura* in Russian.

This does not mean that nonfiction works were ignored, but they were not studied in the same way as belles-lettres. When they were discussed in histories of literature, it was because of their scientific, philosophical, or historical value. But entirely excluded from histories of literature were most handbooks with practical contents, as they were considered far less important than theories and ideas. Starting in the mid-twentieth century, however, these books—cookbooks and household books included—were met with ever greater interest. Scholars from various fields—historians, sociologists, anthropologists, linguists, and others—have found these books to be important sources of information about mentalities, customs, ideas, daily life, technical developments, and more. But they have not been interested in the texts of these works per se; rather, they see these books only as possible sources for the subjects they are investigating, such as food history, culinary development, table manners, and social distinction.

This study takes a different approach: it outlines a literary history and book history of European and Western cookbooks, describing their text as well as their subjects. The period examined stretches from the Middle Ages up to the present, and I have made a special effort to give a broad picture by including references to cookbooks from various European cultures and languages. In making this book, I have profited from studies written about particular cookbooks or authors and from descriptions of particular periods or countries. I have also greatly benefited from the rapid progress being made during the past decades within the field of book history. New developments in the long-established science of bibliography have led to a deeper understanding of the book as a material object, while new studies of the transition from orality to print and the role of print culture in the shaping of society have shed new light on the history of the cookbook. And finally, I have drawn on research published in recent years on nonfiction text and text cultures, research that gives us a better grasp of the characteristics of different nonfiction genres.

A cookbook—written or printed on parchment or paper—is the final merger of many different traditions, primarily cooking and writing, but also editing, design, binding, printing, and photography. But when considering the process of producing a finished cookbook, two characters stand out: the one who invents or develops the recipes and the one who gives them a written form—in other words, the cook and the writer. These characters are the subjects of the chapters in part 1.

Parts 2 and 3 examine the form and contents of the text of cookbooks. A cookbook is basically a collection of recipes for the preparation of food. But cookbooks contained a mix of recipes, household advice, cultural background information, anecdotes, reminiscences, and personal commentaries since long before the advent of printing. And, like all other books, cookbooks included dedicatory letters, introductory prefaces, and other forms of paratexts. This makes it necessary to distinguish between the cookbook as a whole and the recipe text, its most important element. Chapters 3 through 10 will look into different aspects of the recipe, the basic text in most cookbooks, and the cookbook as an entity.

Part 2 looks at the origin of the recipes, how they are transformed from oral tradition to script, and how they are collected and organized. The relationship between creativity and plagiarism is explored, as well as the pedagogical ideas and didactic methods applied in the presentation and structuring of recipes. Finally, the question of the recipe as a particular text type will be raised, and I will investigate whether it is possible to define the cookbook as a literary genre.

Part 3 discusses the different values and ideas governing cookbook text: social and economic considerations, religious taboos and ideological convictions, national and regional attitudes, medical and nutritional theories, and aesthetic and artistic aims.

An important aspect to remember is that these culinary works, like all forms of literature, have to be explained and understood as part of general historical development (social, economic, cultural, political). This is why references will continually be made to events and ideas in Western society.

ACKNOWLEDGMENTS

This study is based on material published in Norwegian in *Kokken og skriveren* (Oslo: Aschehoug, 2012). Certain conclusions from this book have been further discussed and elaborated in my article "Printed Cookbooks: Food History, Book History, and Literature," published in *Food and History* 10, no. 2 (2013). I am grateful to Brepols Publishers for letting me use parts of the text, which I have substantially expanded, particularly in the sections treating the literary genre and book history.

My work with cookbooks started in the 1980s, after meetings and conversations with Alan Davidson and Rudolf Grewe, and continued with contributions to the journal *Petits Propos Culinaires* and later an inspiring collaboration with the Institut Européen d'Histoire et des Cultures de l'Alimentation and with the journal *Food & History*. Many scholars working within the field of food and culinary history have contributed to my research, and I expressed my gratitude to them in my book *Printed Cookbooks in Europe 1470–1700: A Bibliography of Early Modern Culinary Literature* (New Castle: Oak Knoll Press, 2010).

My work on that book led to the idea of writing a literary history of cookbooks. When I presented my first version to Karin Becker, she gave it a critical reading and suggested new ideas and angles. With her keen eye for detail and her broad knowledge spanning several academic disciplines, she eliminated many errors and ambiguities, and I am extremely grateful for her enthusiastic support. I also owe many thanks to Ken Albala, Gilly Lehmann, and Barbara Santich for important commentaries, which helped me improve the text.

A key moment was the immediate positive reception of my text by Darra Goldstein, editor of the Food and Culture series. The active encouragement and efficient and competent administration of the project by Kate Marshall at the University of

California Press have been invaluable. Bradley Depew has guided me through necessary processes, solving problems and answering questions precisely, patiently, and kindly. The same is true for the project editor, Dore Brown, with whom I have had fascinating conversations about the mysterious science of indexological organization. My copyeditor, Genevieve Thurston, has challenged me with a flood of queries about points needing clarification and has struggled through a jungle of norvagisms to clear the path for readers. I am also extremely grateful for the positive attitudes I have been met with by everybody at UCP who in one way or another have been involved in the promotion of this book.

Finally, I want to thank Marita Aksnes, Zsuzsanna Kiss, Beatrix Koll, Roar Lishagen, Hallvard Notaker, Hans Henrik Olsen, Jan Pařez, Bendik Rugaas, Jon Smidt, Göran Ternebrandt, Laura Terragni, and Johan L. Tønnesson for their ideas, help, and support, and last but not least, Marit Notaker for her patience with my nerd-like interest in these books and for the valuable contributions she was able to make to the text due to her long experience in publishing and editing.

PART ONE

Food and Text—Cook and Writer

Prologue

A Rendezvous

Behind the first printed cookbook in Europe we find two people, a professional cook and a professional writer, who contributed each in his own way to the final product. We will start with the writer, who grew up as Bartolomeo Sacchi, although his family name was later changed to Platina, the Latin name for his birthplace, Piádena, a small town on the wide plains north of the river Po between Carmona and Mantua. Platina left his hometown early and fought for four arduous years in the light infantry under the general Francesco Sforza, a soldier's illegitimate son who later became Duke of Milan, an example of social mobility that dramatically outshone Platina's own.[1]

In 1449, Platina enrolled in one of the first and most prestigious schools of the Italian Renaissance, Casa Giocosa in Mantua, where both rich aristocrats and young talents without economic resources were introduced to the classics. Casa Giocosa was built on the property of the princely family of the Gonzagas, with whom Platina soon became acquainted, and he gained the marquis's confidence to such an extent that Platina was entrusted with the education of the nobleman's children. The young intellectual may have been first introduced to the culinary arts in the elegant, palatial rooms of the Gonzaga's estate, but more important to Platina at this stage was the help the marquis gave him in obtaining admission to the Accademia Platonica in Florence. The academy had been established by Cosimo, the almighty head of the Medici family, who built his power on political sagacity combined with a shrewd handling of banking and finance, but who nevertheless was an intellectual with a genuine interest in all aspects of cultural life. In addition to being exposed to the Greek language and philosophy in Florence, Platina made many friends, and at the fashionable dinners he attended he became

3

known as an affable and charming gentleman, even if people were sometimes provoked by his comments and temper.

Platina moved to Rome in 1462 and was soon introduced to a circle of intellectuals who took a particular interest in the history and culture of antiquity. Thanks to recommendations from friends in high places—and a certain amount of money—he was employed in the papal chancellery, the Abbreviatori del Parco Maggiore, one of the offices responsible for documents issued by the Vatican. The pope at the time was the humanist Pius II. In 1464, Paul II was elected, and he dismissed Platina and the other members of the group of learned humanists. After a conflict with the new pope, Platina spent three months in the prison Castel Sant'Angelo. Sometime after he was released, he must have met the professional cook Maestro Martino de' Rossi, the other character in our story.

Martino had practiced his art of cooking at the ducal court of Milan for the same Sforza under whom Platina had served as a soldier in his youth. Martino, who hailed from one of the valleys in the north of Italy that is now part of Switzerland, would go on to become one of the most influential cooks in Italy during the Renaissance, having a long and successful career as a chef for prelates, princes, and a pope. He was a culinary inventor, and he created a completely new type of Italian cuisine, which is known from later manuscripts written by professional scribes. Bruno Laurioux, who put together biographies of Platina and Martino by studying material from Italian archives of the fifteenth century, thinks it is possible and even plausible that Platina not only wrote his own cookbook, *De honesta voluptate et valetudine* (On right pleasure and good health), but was also directly involved in the elaboration of Martino's text *Libro de arte coquinaria* (Book of culinary art). He finds it too much of a coincidence that Platina's and Martino's books, "innovative in their tone, their style, and their conception, while sharing a great part of the contents," were created independently at the same time. He believes that it was a "four-handed creation" (création à quatre mains) that resulted in two versions of essentially the same work: a "practical" one in Italian and a "theoretical" one in Latin.[2]

This collaboration took place in the 1460s, when only one small printing office existed in Italy, so both cookbooks were in manuscript form. We know that copies of Platina's work circulated among his friends. Martino may have used his notes as an aide-memoire during his career as chef. To judge from the existing manuscripts attributed to him, he continually reworked his recipes. Between the various manuscripts, some recipes were left out, others were modified, and new ones were added. The different versions constitute "a veritable museum " (un véritable conservatoire) of Italian cuisine during that period, and they also serve as a perfect testimony of the culinary cosmopolitanism of the late fifteenth century.[3] Gillian Riley, who translated the Martino manuscript kept at the Library of Congress, calls his text "a modern work covering the New Gastronomy and the oldfashioned, but then current, International Cuisine of the ruling classes of Europe."[4] Martino never saw a printed version of his book and could not have had any idea of the success early sixteenth-century publishers would win when they printed his text repeatedly with other titles and other names and without giving any acknowledgement to Martino.

Platina's book was printed in the early 1470s, when he was once again imprisoned in Castel Sant'Angelo, accused this time of having participated in a conspiracy against the pope. We will probably never have the final and complete answer as to how serious the conspiracy was or whether Platina really was guilty. He was released after about a year with injuries caused by torture, but soon another humanist acceded to the papacy. Sixtus IV became famous for his *renovatio urbis*, a policy that made the somewhat backward Rome into an international metropolis by restoring antique monuments and commissioning prestigious projects of Renaissance art, among them the Sistine Chapel, named after the pope himself. The upgrading and reorganization of the Vatican library—founded by pope Nicholas V—became part of this process, and Platina was given the position of head librarian. His inauguration is immortalized in a painting in the Vatican, originally a fresco by Melozzo da Forli, in which the pope, surrounded by his powerful nephews, is sitting on his throne in front of a kneeling Platina, depicted as a fifty-four-year-old with a relatively youthful appearance, alert nut-brown eyes, thick greyish bobbed hair, and a blue-gray gown draped over his rust-colored suit.[5] When he died in 1481, he was interred in the Santa Maria Maggiore church, where his tombstone bears a strange inscription: "Whoever you are, if you are righteous, don't disturb Platina and his [family]. They are lying tight and want to be alone" (Quisquis es si pius Platynam et suos ne vexes anguste iacent et soli volunt esse). In this church, his friends bade him farewell in a solemn ceremony, but until he died, he held a prominent position in Roman society, symbolized by a fine villa in an attractive part of the city.

Platina's legacy is a solid collection of books. When he was appointed as head librarian, he had already written thirty works of different sizes and content. The book most often referred to is his history of the popes, which was a source for both Calvin's and Luther's attacks on the Vatican. But his very first manuscript to be printed was the cookbook from the 1460s: *De honesta voluptate*. Platina would certainly have been greatly surprised if he had been told of the fame this book would bring him inside and outside of academic circles in many countries and for many centuries.[6] But was this fame completely deserved? Nobody asked such questions until the 1930s, when the American chef Joseph Vehling discovered Martino's then unknown fifteenth-century manuscript, which bore a strong similarity to Platina's book.[7] While the learned writer had obtained great and everlasting celebrity, the cook behind the recipes had been forgotten by everybody for centuries and had never been considered worthy enough to be portrayed either in a fresco or on a canvas.[8]

The cook and the writer are not always two different people. We should think instead of these being two different roles. The role of the cook demands creativity and intuition in the preparation of food; a sense of balance between different ingredients; an understanding of the nuances of taste; and, to reach the desired result, experience with the choice of temperature and cooking times. The writer transforms the food into words, names the culinary processes and dishes, and makes the cooking techniques understood and accessible. But he or she is not only the person who puts the recipes on paper or types them on a computer; the role of writer covers everyone involved in the publishing process, including editors, printers, translators, booksellers, and publishers.

But even if these roles are somewhat interchangeable—there are, of course, cooks who write and writers who cook—the general truth is this: cooks who produce food and writers who produce books belong to separate professional traditions, and they have experienced very different working conditions and social status through the centuries.

1

The Cook

Today, many celebrity chefs have acquired a status that places them on par with stars of film, pop, and sports, the descendants of royals in the—not always firm—firmament of celebrity. The Michelin Guide distributes stars to restaurants, and each year various magazines name one lucky individual the World's Best Chef. The Bocuse d'Or is the Oscar of cooking, and in the courtyard of Paul Bocuse's Lyon restaurant, the names of the winners are engraved in a culinary Walk of Fame. But these top chefs are as far from the average cook as were the *maîtres queux* in princely courts during the Renaissance and the Baroque and the master chefs who won their fame within the new restaurant culture of the nineteenth century. Throughout history, ordinary cooks have suffered from a low status in society.[1]

MANUAL WORK, BLOOD, DIRT, AND VICES

In the Middle Ages, when guilds were important in defining social rank, cooks were members of the less prestigious ones. In thirteenth-century Genoa, cooking was among the least well-remunerated trades. In fourteenth-century Florence, cooks belonged to the minor guilds, along with butchers, bakers, innkeepers, tanners, smiths, leatherworkers, and other humble tradesmen, while the more prestigious Arte dei Medici, Speciali e Merciai was the guild for doctors, apothecaries, and merchants who sold spices, dyes, and medicines.[2]

This low status is explained partly by the fact that cooks were recruited from the inferior social strata but also, to a certain extent, by the strenuous physical work the job entailed, which was not highly regarded by the elite responsible for maintaining the established value system. The aristocratic elite was physically active, but their bodily exercise was limited by the codes of the warrior caste; the ideal pursuits were riding, fencing, and hunting. Hunting was considered not only entertainment for the nobles but also a serious preparation for military duty, an idea that goes all the way back to Aristotle and was repeated in the Renaissance by Machiavelli.[3] And if the proud counts and barons contributed at all in the dining hall, it was by carving up the big roasts, an art carried out with tools resembling well-known weapons. But this was very far from handling bloody carcasses in cramped kitchens thick with heat and smoke (figure 1).

Blood was associated with cooking well into the twentieth century. Cooks—professionals as well as housewives—were responsible for the slaughtering of animals. Cookbooks had instructions on such work, some of which expressed empathy for the animals—"humane ways of slaughtering at home," as it is phrased in one Danish cookbook from the late 1800s[4]—and how to pluck poultry. In fact, the descriptions were not too different from what we find in an English recipe from the Middle Ages: "Cut a swan in the rofe of the mouth toward the brayn of the hed, & let hym blede to deth."[5]

Further back in antiquity, Greek society had *mageiroi*, religious officials who killed sacrificial animals for the rituals preceding big banquets, but *mageiroi* also sold meat at markets and prepared dinners for people wealthy enough to hire professional cooks with a more sophisticated culinary range than ordinary slave cooks.[6]

Heat and smoke were constant problems in kitchens. In 2010, French historian Patrick Rambourg, who was trained as a professional cook, described with great sensitivity how cooks discover that the fire—such an important ally in cooking—suddenly becomes an enemy "when it is not properly controlled."[7] Two centuries earlier, the celebrated culinary artist Antonin Carême presented a lamentation that probably expressed the feelings of many of his colleagues: cooks working in drafty, humid subterranean kitchens would develop painful rheumatism, while cooks above ground had to inhale the mortal fumes from burning charcoal. Even the arbiter of taste under the First French Empire, Grimod de la Reynière, who probably spent more time in the dining hall than in the kitchen, was concerned about the health of cooks and pointed out the dangers they were exposed to when faced with steam, smoke, and fire.[8]

The danger created by filth and dirt is another recurrent theme in many cookbooks throughout history; the concern with cleanliness and hygiene in these books almost amounts to an obsession. And this was of vital importance long before the nineteenth and twentieth centuries, when domestic science teachers gave it top priority. Around 1600, Francisco Martínez Montiño, chef at the Spanish court, opened his *Arte de cocina* (Culinary art) with these words: "In this chapter I plan to treat cleanliness, which is the most necessary and important." In his list of priorities, he put cleanliness (*limpieza*) first, taste (*gusto*) second, and speed (*presteza*) third. A similar stress on perfect cleanliness is found in books written at several European

Einnew Kochbuch/
Das ist/

Ein Gründtli,
che Beschreibung / wie man recht vnd
wol/ nicht allein von vierfüssigen/ heymischen vnd wilden Thie,
ren / sondern auch von mancherley Vögel vnnd Federwildpret / darzu von allem
grünen vnd dürren Fischwerck/ allerley Speiß/ als gesotten/ gebraten/ gebacken/ Presolen/Carbonaden/mancher,
ley Pasteten vnd Füllwerck/ Gallrat/etc. auff Teutsche/Vngerische/ Hispanische/ Italianische vnd Frantzö,
sische weiß/ kochen vnd zubereiten solle: Auch wie allerley Gemüß/Obs/Salsen/Senff/
Confect vnd Larwergen/ zuzurichten seye.

Auch ist darinnen zu vernemmen/ wie man herrliche grosse Pancketen/sampt
gemeinen Gastereyen / ordentlich anrichten vnd bestellen soll.

Allen Menschen hohes vnd nidriges Standes/ Weibs vnd Manns Personen/ zu nutz jetzundt zum
ersten in Druck gegeben/ dergleichen vor nie ist außgegangen/
Durch
M. Marren Rumpolt/ Churf.Meintzischen Mundtkoch.

Mit Röm. Keyserlicher Maiestat special Priuilegio.

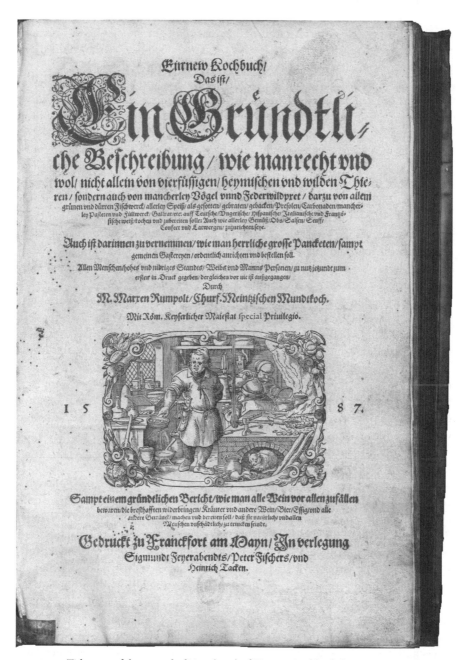

1 5   8 7.

Sampt einem gründtlichen Bericht/wie man alle Wein vor allen zufällen
bewaren/die bresthafften widerbringen/ Kräuter vnd andere Wein/Bier/Essig/vnd alle
andere Getränck/ machen vnd bereiten soll/ daß sie natürlich/ vndallen
Menschen vnschädlich/ zu truncken seudt.

Gedruckt zu Franckfort am Mayn/ In verlegung
Sigmundt Feyerabendts/Peter Fischers/vnd
Heinrich Tacken.

FIGURE 1. Title page of the second edition (1587) of *Ein new Kochbuch,* by Marx Rumpolt, private cook to the prince-elector of Mainz, first published in 1581 in Frankfurt am Main. The woodcut by Jost Amman shows a busy cook in the kitchen. Nasjonalbiblioteket, Oslo, qLib.rar. 1065.

courts. In Poland, an administrator for a prince wrote in the preface of his cookbook that a cook must be clean and shaven, have combed hair, washed hands, and
pared nails, and wear a white apron.[9]

If we are to believe authors of literary fiction, lack of hygiene is often the reason
for low status among cooks. Roger "Hogge" in Geoffrey Chaucer's *Canterbury
Tales,* who was not a court cook but rather a professional known for his skill in
preparing tasty dishes—*blancmanger,* for example—has a skin eruption on his leg,
suggesting an absence of personal hygiene.[10]

Drunkenness and greed are other vices often attributed to cooks. There is a
tendency in food histories to mention northern Europe first in discussions of
excessive alcohol intake, but there are sources that clearly demonstrate that this
was also a problem in the southern part of the continent. In his household book
from 1668, the Italian Francesco Liberati emphasized that cooks must not drink
too much. He followed this assertion with a list of the damaging effects drunkenness will have on one's cooking. The list is so specific that the author undoubtedly
had experience with such bad habits.[11]

"Greedy glutton" was a frequent expression in the fifteenth century. For example, it was used in the most popular book in German before the Reformation,
Sebastian Brant's 1494 moralist satire *Das Narrenschiff* (*Ship of Fools*). Brant also
linked greed to dishonesty, claiming that when their masters were out of the house,
cooks ate and drank the best victuals to be found.[12] Some books directly accused
cooks of stealing provisions or of helping themselves to more than they were enti-
tled to in situations when board and lodging were part of their salary. The author
of a 1584 Italian book about the duties of the chief steward noted that he needed to
watch over the servants so they didn't steal supplies.[13]

COOKS AND COOKERY JUDGED BY THE MORALISTS

In Plato's dialogue *Gorgias,* Socrates is of the opinion that people who prepare food
and drink for the citizens should not consider their activity important work, and
Socrates mentions with evident disgust three representatives of these activities: a
baker, a wine merchant, and Mithaikos, who wrote a book about Sicilian cuisine.
Earlier, in one of his letters, Plato had written about how shocked he was when he
discovered the gluttonous food culture in Sicily. The word he used for "cuisine" or
"cookery" was *opsoniía,* which means preparation of *opson. Opson* had originally
referred to what was served in a meal in addition to bread, and it included both
fish and meat, but the word gradually took on a wider meaning as something delicious and dainty. In Greek texts from antiquity, terms such as "*opson*-lover" and
"*opson*-eater" are used to describe people we would now call gourmets. The word
opson comes up in a discussion in another dialogue by Plato, the *Republic.* In this
work, Socrates describes what food should be served in the ideal state, and when

asked about *opson,* he mentions vegetables, fruits, and cheese. When Glauco—
Socrates's conversation partner—wants more refined *opson,* Socrates immediately
tries to discredit such pleasure by comparing it to promiscuous sexual pleasure.[14]

In *Gorgias,* Socrates says that culinary art, just like rhetoric, has nothing to do
with art (*techne*) but is only experience and practice, and that cookery, also like
rhetoric, is false—it is flattery (*kolakeia*).[15] The pleasure argument was taken up by
the Roman moralists, especially the Stoics and Cynics. When Cicero presented his
arguments about the value of different occupations, the bottom level was reserved
for fishmongers, butchers, poulterers, and cooks, who shared the same status as
perfumers and dancers. The common denominator of these trades was that they
catered to sensual pleasure (*voluptas*).[16]

Early in the Middle Ages, the Catholic Church declared gluttony (*gula*) to be
one of the seven capital sins, and cooks—masters of good food, exquisite ingredients, and dainty dishes—could thus easily be considered dangerous tempters, lur-
ing people down the broad road to hell. Numerous paintings of hell, such as those
by Hieronymos Bosch, make Carême's description of subterranean kitchens seem
like an amusement park. These works portray demons acting as cooks, sadistically
enjoying roasting sinners on skewers, piercing them with iron forks, or letting
them boil in large black cauldrons—that is, if they aren't beating them with mon-
strous wooden ladles.[17] The gluttons are literally stewed in their own juices, and the
cooks are, to quote Sebastian Brant, the devil's *braeters,* or rôtisseurs.[18]

There are also writings describing cooks in hell. *Le songe d'Enfer* (The dream of
hell), a French text written in 1215, relates a dream of a visit to Inferno, where the
narrator is served a menu of tasty dishes prepared by enthusiastic cooks. In this
account, the gluttonous cooks are not alone in their suffering. There are stuffed and
fried usurers, murderers marinated in garlic, pimply and wrinkly harlots prepared
as game, baked heretics, and pies filled with tongues from liars and chatterboxes,
and, as in Dante's travelogue of the same region, not even the church representatives are excused: black monks are served with herbal sauce.[19] In an English sermon
written in the same century, a Dominican preacher blamed cooks directly for trans-
forming cuisine from the simple bread and water that was present at "the begyn-
nynge of the worlde" to food that was more for the pleasure of the body than for the
sustenance of mankind, made "with grete busyness and with craft of cokys."[20]

The view of gluttony as a capital sin has its origins in the eastern Christian tradition of hermits and monks, which was influenced by the dualism in Hellenistic
syncretistic religions, where contempt for the body was strong. Evagrios Pontikos
(also known as Evagrios the Solitary), who lived in the fourth century, put gluttony
first in his list of eight vices. Eating too much was only one aspect of gluttony as it
was later defined by Johannes Cassianus, Pope Gregor the Great, and others; even
worse was a passion for refined dishes, which were exactly what the best cooks were
preparing.[21] This was also the main point made by the Cistercian abbot Bernard of

Clairvaux when, with verbal wit and moral indignation, he criticized the food habits among the Benedictines in Cluny, decrying the new spices and foreign sauces they were using. One of the moralist attacks on gluttony from 1495 even mentioned specific dishes: partridges, quails, hazel grouses, capons, and geese, served with cameline sauce. The author may have leafed through a recently published book, *Le viandier* (The victualer), the first printed cookbook in France, which included recipes for all these birds and a special chapter about *sauce cameline*. The title page attributes the book to the "great chef of the King of France."[22]

THE COMIC COOK IN LITERATURE

Paintings of kitchen devils can easily create an impression that cooks are threatening figures, and as Ann Henisch documents, there are numerous stories about cooks using cleavers and flesh-hooks as weapons in scary situations.[23] In literary works, however, examples of cooks as clowns are more frequent. In comedies of the late Middle Ages, humor was created by associating cooks with bodily functions related to appetite: slurping, gulping, dribbling, slobbering, belching, burping, and what was generally referred to by the euphemism "wind"—all of which were behaviors that had earlier been common to all social groups but had from the Renaissance onward gradually became disapproved of by the elite. According to the sociologist Norbert Elias's theory of the civilization process, this was part of a more universal pattern, a development toward a stronger control over one's own body. Repugnance at touching greasy and sticky food led to the introduction of the individual fork as an indispensable part of the cutlery in daily use.[24] The comic effect in the late medieval plays was created by the contrast between the new table manners of the elite and the vulgar conduct of cooks and other common people. In seventeenth-century France, the rules of the classical drama (*la doctrine classique*), with its ideals of decency and decorum (*bienséance*), banned all references to bodily acts (*le bas corporel*) on the stage.

Also comical were the carnivalesque characters depicted in paintings (and allegorical dialogues), particularly popular during the Dutch and German Renaissance, of the great battle between Carnival and Lent, where the weapons were enormous ladles and forks, and the combatants wore pots on their heads instead of helmets. Peter Burke found it difficult not to interpret this as a way of ridiculing knights, as carnival was the period when the established order of society was turned upside down.[25] But why was this considered ridiculous? Perhaps it was because the paintings compared the noble estate to a group that was often exposed to mockery. There was a long tradition of using cooks, peasants, and other "simple" tradespeople linked to bodily work as stock characters in farces.

In comedies from antiquity, a different element brought about the humor. The Greek *mageiros* often appeared as a pompous, verbose, talkative person. In *The*

Boastful Chef, a study of the existing fragments of comic literature from the classical period, John Wilkins made the point that the boasters exaggerate their theoretical knowledge and philosophical mentality. In the conversations between the cook and the host, the cook speaks at length about his insights into art and academic disciplines, while the host, bored with his prattle, tries to get the cook back to the kitchen to do the waiting tasks.[26]

Even Platina's *De honesta voluptate* contains a trace of irony or at least ambiguity in the praise it bestowed on the cook Martino de' Rossi, the original creator of Platina's recipes. To be sure, Platina wrote in a list of requirements for good cooks that they ought to be like Martino, who had taught him all the methods of food preparation. But he included the phrase "the prince of cooks of our age," which sounds in Platina's pen like a witty paradox or oxymoron, considering the social position of cooks at that time. In another chapter, he opened his praise with even more glorifying words, "Oh, immortal gods, what a cook you have brought to me. If you had heard him lecture extempore about these subjects, you would have called him another Carneades."[27]

Famous in Rome after his lectures in 156–155 BCE, the founder and leader of the Third Academy in Athens, Carneades of Cyrene, had shown independence, critical sense, and systematic order, qualities emphasized in modern comments about Martino's talents.[28] But is it absolutely certain that this is the reason Platina mentioned the Greek thinker? Might it be just another of his ironic remarks? We know that Platina admired Cicero, who frequently used jokes and puns in his speeches and writings, and Platina admitted in a letter that his book had much wit and sarcasm.[29] The way Platina praised Martino seems a bit too exaggerated to be completely sincere, similar to when, in his 1736 poem "Le Mondain," Voltaire called a cook "un mortel divin," and when King Frederick the Great flattered his French cook Noël with these words: "He is the Newton of the cooking pot, / A real Caesar of the dripping pan."[30]

Platina's amusing and often ironic digressions in the recipes in *De honesta voluptate* were directed to his friends in his intellectual circle. They would have understood the subtext and humor when he quipped that an elderberry pie was good for Caelius, "who is more melancolic than Saturn," or when he completed a recipe with a line not belonging to a cookbook at all: "When it is cooked, serve it to your enemies, there is nothing good in it." This last remark, coming as a comment after Martino's original recipe, does not exactly express admiration. Platina also dismissed one of Martino's recipes by calling it a silly invention, a form of nonsense typical of cooks.[31] All this probably reveals, in my opinion, that there was a difference in attitude to humor between representatives of two social groups. This is even more evident in the way the two men described a medieval dish in which the cooked meat of a peacock is put back inside the skin and feathers and the whole bird is then put on the table to look as if it were alive. Martino wrote that "if you want him [the peacock] to blow fire from the beak" you may put cotton and camphor soaked in aqua vitae or wine in the mouth of the bird and light it on fire.[32] Platina wrote, "There are people who for fun [*ad ludum et risum*] put camphor and cotton in the mouth [of the peacock]," and so on, as in Martino.[33] It seems that Platina tried to keep his distance from such vulgar behavior; he described it from the outside, as an entertainment he would never participate in himself.

Much of this indicates that Platina intended for the book to be tongue-in-cheek, something different from his other, more academic, works. When, in the letter to Ammannati, he mentioned the use of wit and sarcasm, he added that there may be more than "foods seem to require" in the book—in other words, it contained more literary eloquence than would have been expected in the treatment of such a common subject. He also called the work "that poor little book," which could not have been just a modest remark. Laurioux observed that Platina did not mention his cookbook in a list of what was worth remembering from his life ("ce qu'il fallait retenir de sa propre vie").[34] A poem written by a contemporary bishop made fun of Platina and ridiculed the lowly subject matter of the book and the even more lowly class of people it attracted.[35]

A LOWLY SUBJECT

Of course, descriptions of cooks in comedies cannot be taken as a general characterization of a whole group of people. These cooks are stock characters, just as protagonists in most comedies are. John Wilkins wrote of the Greek comedy cooks: "They probably reflect a special reality to some extent, but are mainly used by the comic poets to bring together the heat of the kitchen with the rhetoric and brilliance of the dining room."[36] And Henisch compared the cooks in medieval comedies to the other staple characters of comedy and concluded that the depiction "has a grain or two of truth in it, but it is a likeness slanted to catch laughter, not to show truth."[37]

But even if these descriptions were more literary than historical, and the characters more stereotypical than typical, there is still no doubt that cooks were looked down on by the social groups represented in the audience. The practical work of cooks was outranked over and over again by more theoretical treatments of food. In a learned book from 1563, *Ars magirica* (Culinary art), which includes both gastronomic information and practical recipes, the philologist—the person who names all things—tops the list of different specialists within the arts and sciences who treat the subject of food. Then follows the scientist, who has knowledge about all animals and plants. Next comes the physician, who understands the principles of nutrition, and after him is the theologian, who knows the laws regulating diet. At the very bottom, we find the cook, who must modify his practice according to the advice of the theoreticians above him.[38] *Ars magirica* was written in Latin. In many ways, it is interesting that the Renaissance, when humanists were looking back to the classical beauty of the Latin language, was also the period when the expressions *Küchenlatein* and *latino maccheronico* gained ground as terms for a Latin that was crammed with neologisms and vernacular words.[39]

To understand the work of cooks and other artisans, it may be useful to apply the distinction Peter Burke made between two different forms of knowledge: practical, useful, and specialist knowledge, on the one hand, and theoretical, liberal, and general knowledge, on the other. The latter, known as *scientia superior,* was the knowledge of the humanists, whose background was in university studies and *artes liberales,* a system of seven disciplines elaborated in Late Antiquity that dominated thinking in the Middle Ages. *Artes mechanicae,* however, was the name given to the different forms of practical work. Even if the title gave the practical professions a certain status, they were quite clearly put on a lower level than the liberal arts of the elite, as they were not concerned with intellectual dimensions of life but only with the materialistic. Their task was to satisfy the needs of the body and create the necessities of daily life. They were consequently defined as lower and less important: *leviores, minores, inferiores.*[40]

The condescending attitude toward the art of cookery—and the profession of cooks—is a recurrent theme in the history of cookbooks. It was sometimes expressed by the professionals themselves, as in the case of Domingo Hernández de Maceras, the cook at a college in Salamanca around 1600. In his introduction to *Libro del arte de cozina* (Book of culinary art), which he dedicated to a bishop, he made an apology for writing such a small book on such a lowly and humble subject, a type of excuse that was characteristic of the prefaces within this genre.[41]

A similar attitude toward the subject was evident when John Evelyn, a learned gardener and horticulturalist, published a book about salads in 1699. The first part was a botanical and dietetic description of different plants; the second part contained practical recipes. Evelyn was a secretary of the scientific Royal Society, and in the dedicatory letter in his book, addressed to the influential Baron Somers of Evesham, he apologized "to usher in a Trifle, with so much Magnificence." But as a justification, he explained that this subject, "as low and despicable as it appears, challenges a part of Natural History,"[42] which is true of the scientific section of the book. The recipe section was added as an appendix, printed in a different typeface and without pagination—in other words, it was clearly separated from the main text. Nevertheless, Evelyn excused the subject matter by noting that learned men before him, such as Plinius, Athenaeus, and Bacon, had treated the same material. And to be on the safe side, he pointed out that he had gotten the recipes from an experienced housewife. The truth was that he collected recipes himself, and some of the recipes that were printed in the salad book are more polished forms of recipes from his personal collection. It is possible that the puritan in Evelyn had problems showing interest in good food, but he also displayed a trace of contempt for the subject when he mockingly called himself a "saladmaker" and a "planter of colewort."[43] To prove how persistent this attitude to food was, at least in certain circles, it is worth mentioning a warning that the American Marion Harland, who had won a certain literary reputation for her novels, short stories, and essays, received from a critic when she published a cookbook in 1871. The critic cautioned her that whatever she wrote "after this preposterous new departure would be tainted, for the imaginative reader and reviewer, with the odor of the kitchen."[44] This is probably also the reason for the low rank art historians through the ages have given to still life depictions of the life of the table, or as Norman Bryson put it, "the basic creaturely acts of eating and drinking." Bryson pointed out that when academics mentioned still life in theoretical accounts of painting, "they did so disparagingly: still life was always at the bottom of the hierarchy, unworthy of the kind of superior attention reserved for history painting or the *grande manière*."[45]

COOKS WITH DIFFERENT RANKS

Professional cooks could exercise their skills in many different venues, some of which were more distinguished than others. In the Middle Ages, many of them belonged to various branches of guilds. Some had their own shops where they sold take-away food, and there were cooks who specialized in sausages, pies, sweets, or similar products. Other cooks worked in institutions, such as monasteries or hospitals. Along the roads between towns and cities, inns and stands provided food to travelers. The cooks at these establishments did not always have a good reputation. They were ridiculed in many forms of literature, and they were despised by court cooks. Marx Rumpolt, private cook at a German court, wrote in his 1581 *Ein new Kochbuch* (A new cookbook) that the remains of a certain dish should be thrown away because it "tastes of the inn" (schmeckt nach der Herberg). The chef Charles Carter, who worked for many English aristocrats, poured scorn on the tavern cooks. In 1730, he expressed his contempt for aristocrats who, to save money, "reject a thorough-pac'd Artist, and suffer a Raw, and perhaps Tavern-bred Dabbler in the Science." William Verral, who had trained under a French chef in the kitchens of the Duke of Newcastle and then became master chef of a Sussex hotel, the White Hart Inn, complained in the preface of his 1759 cookbook that he was "no more than what is vulgarly called a poor publican."[46]

In several countries, the authorities repeatedly tried to regulate the activities of the different guilds, which often quarreled among themselves over who had the right to produce and sell certain products. In 1734, Munich established a guild system that regulated competence for bakers, butchers, and the so-called *Gar-Köche,* caterers of ready-made dishes.[47] In France, different guilds prepared roasted meat dishes (*rôtisseurs*), smoked and salted foods (*charcutiers*), and pies and casseroles (*traîteurs*). When new groups appeared in the eighteenth century trying to break down the partitions in this system and claiming the right to serve dishes such as bouillons that were hot and nourishing (these restorative foods were called *restaurants* in French), one of the decisive steps was taken toward what would become modern restaurant culture.[48]

Starting in antiquity, there were many people preparing food in all the ways described above, but from very early on, a few professional cooks stood out from the rest, known in England as chief cooks or master cooks. They headed the kitchens in princely palaces, and many of them were given honorary titles and substantial salaries. Bruno Laurioux detected a radical change—an improvement—in the social position of cooks at the end of the Middle Ages. He argued that this was partly due to a new promotion of cuisine as science or art.[49] But this promotion seems to have been ambiguous at best, and at any rate, it is valid only for a few top performers employed by princely courts. Several among them wrote cookbooks, including Guillaume Tirel (better known as Taillevent), at the court of the French King Charles VI; Bartolomeo Scappi, at the papal court in Rome; and Francisco Martínez Montiño, at the court of King Philip III in Madrid. It is quite natural that conditions for the fine art of cookery were good at a court, where there was an excellent supply of necessary victuals and interesting ingredients combined with access to the best technology of the time. But in this environment, social distinctions prevailed between the servants responsible for food. There was an intricate hierarchy with many levels and regulated duties.

Bartolomeo Stefani, cook at the court of Mantua in the seventeenth century, mentions four categories in the kitchen: *capo cuoco* (head cook), *sotto cuoco* (assistant cook), *garzone* (apprentice), and *guattero* (unqualified handyman or scullery boy). The head cook had to be a good organizer with a comprehensive view of what was needed for everything to function properly. He needed to keep an eye on the fire and make sure the utensils were clean, the cutlery was polished, and the victuals were delivered at the right time.[50] But most head chefs were under the orders of an even higher administrator. In many of the books on how banquets ought to be arranged, there is a chief steward on top, called *Hofmeister* in German, *maître d'hôtel* in French, and *scalco* in Italian. Bartolomeo Stefani's book stated that a *maggiordomo* occupied the highest position in the house; under him was a *maestro di casa*, followed by a *scalco*, who gave orders to the head chef. At around the same time Stefani published his book, a German book, written at a monastery in Alsace in 1671, listed the responsibilities of the head chef, known in German as a *Kuchen-Meister* or *Speiss-Meister*: he needed to maintain "diligent supervision" (fleissige Aufsicht) over the cooks so the food was prepared correctly and served on time.[51] Servants at these upper echelons were sometimes recruited from aristocratic families, but those who had managed to climb all the way up the ladder from the position of kitchen apprentice also ranked high above ordinary cooks.

Even if cooks were generally placed in the lower ranks, in certain cases a cook could acquire a special position that did not correspond to his normal place in the hierarchy. To get an idea of how this functioned, it is worth considering the American sociologist and economist Thorstein Veblen's observations about servants. He wrote that those activities that were by right the proper employment of the leisure class (e.g., government, fighting, hunting) were considered noble, while those that properly fell to the industrious class (e.g., handicrafts, menial services) were seen as ignoble. But he added that "a base service performed for a person of very high degree may become a very honorific office."[52] He mentioned as examples the King's Master of the Horse and the Queen's Lady in Waiting, but in our case a suitable example might be the personal cook in princely courts in the Middle Ages and the early modern period. In France, an ordinance was enacted in 1285 that mandated the separation of the kitchen that cooked for the king and his guests from the kitchen that prepared meals for the entire staff. A 1668 Italian book about court administration included a special chapter about the private cook of the prince, who was called *il cuoco segreto*, and it was noted that this was the person who had the responsibility and the privilege of serving food to the prince himself. The book pointed out that it was common for this cook to have at his disposal a kitchen separated from the kitchen for the palace staff.[53] A special relationship might be established between the prince and his personal cook. The German term for this position, *Mundkoch*, directly translated as "mouth cook," is a reminder of a time when the cook had to taste all food before the prince touched it to make sure it was not poisoned. To put a more positive spin on it, the job entailed taking good care of the prince, for those who didn't might be accused of being the prince's murderer, wrote Marx Rumpolt, *Mundkoch* for the prince-elector of Mainz in the sixteenth century.[54]

Some of the cooks recruited from the lower social strata were introduced to a food culture that was completely different from the one they had grown up with. They had to adapt to carry out their work in the kitchens of the wealthy. But Alberto Capatti and Massimo Montanari, in their history of Italian cuisine, suggested the possibility that cooks acted as "key points" (punto-chiave) in the exchange between two different cultures. They brought their own food cultures with them to court, modified the dishes according to the demands of this new setting, and then brought the resulting products back with them to their own social environment.[55]

WOMEN AND PROFESSIONAL COOKING

The cooks described in this chapter have been exclusively men, although women are in an absolute majority as cooks throughout the history of mankind. Their work has not been thought of as a profession, however, because most women have carried out daily cooking in the home. But starting in the Middle Ages, women were employed as cooks in inns and institutions, and they also privately produced food for sale. This work sometimes violated the rules of the guilds, which often restricted women because they lacked the recognized skills and qualifications men had.[56] The French guilds, which were abolished in 1791, required both masters and apprentices to be male.[57] For hundreds of years, women also worked as cooks and household servants in families that could not afford to pay for male cooks. The aristocracy normally preferred male cooks, but more and more female cooks were employed in wealthy families during the eighteenth century.[58] This became the rule in bourgeois households, which employed fewer servants, but these female cooks had less prestige than cooks in palaces and mansions. Generally, female cooks also received smaller salaries than male cooks. In France, it was reported that male cooks earned up to three times as much as their female counterparts.[59]

Following the great social transformations of the nineteenth century, particularly in northern Europe, women cooks became increasingly common in ordinary middle-class families, where they often combined cooking with other household tasks—if the housewife did not cook herself (figure 2). Many of these cooks had not been properly prepared for their work. Eliza Acton stated in her 1855 cookbook that very few cooks are "really trained to a knowledge of their duties," and she therefore welcomed "the establishment of well-conducted schools for the early and efficient training of our female domestic servants."[60]

Cooking schools go back a long time, particularly in England and Scotland, but the modern form of education that includes cooking as part of "domestic science" or "household economy" emerged in nineteenth-century Europe and the United States. By the end of the nineteenth century, this education was not oriented exclusively to domestic servants but also to young women who would become housewives with a responsibility for cooking themselves. This was quite a different situation compared with that of a lady who only supervised the household's cook or even simply let an appointed housekeeper take care of that task.

Historically, men have often referred to female cooks with little respect. When the successful eighteenth-century French cookbook writer Menon, after publishing a series of great works for the professional chefs of the aristocracy, was persuaded to write a book for female cooks in bourgeois households, *La cuisinière bourgeoise,* he demonstrated a rather patronizing attitude by giving easy recipes for simple dishes.[61] The German gourmet writer Karl von Rumohr was full of contempt in his 1822 description of female cooks, who, in his opinion, lacked the necessary thoroughness for the trade, had a penchant for fashion and decoration, and demonstrated unyielding resistance to his many good suggestions for improvements.[62] The folklorist and amateur cook P. Chr. Asbjørnsen was just as merciless in 1859 when scolding Norwegian housewives, who, according to him, did not have the required knowledge about the new and scientifically based cookery that he had picked up from German cooks who followed the nutritional ideas of the chemist Justus von Liebig.[63]

When women enrolled in professional cookery courses in France in the later years of the nineteenth century, one male specialist had an indignant and choleric reaction and accused the women of usurping a profession that did not belong to

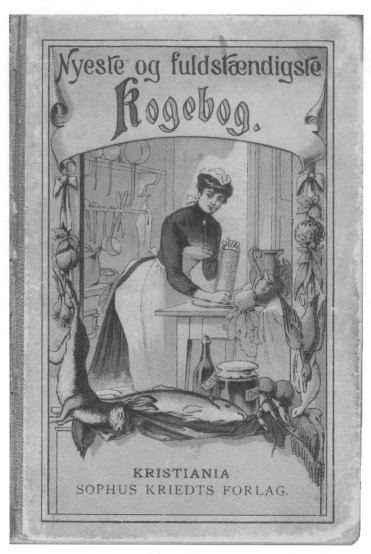

FIGURE 2. Title page of *Nyeste og fuldstændigste kogebog* (The newest and most complete cookbook), published in the Norwegian capital, Kristiania (present-day Oslo), in 1894. In the late nineteenth and early twentieth centuries, most middle-class families had a maid, who also served as cook if the housewife did not prepare the food herself.

them. He was aware that women were immersed in cooking from birth and had no objection to women who made traditional dishes at home, but he claimed that they had no right to enter what he called "our work," which he considered too fatiguing for the female constitution and also too extensive for their flimsy knowledge. "The result will in any case be nothing more than a deficient, I will even say a bad, imitation," he asserted.[64] These are exactly the same arguments that have always been made when women have tried to enter new arenas previously reserved for men.

In turn, women expressed strong criticism of male cooks, accusing them of being spendthrifts with no concern for health. This was a topic in many English books of the eighteenth century that discussed the value of French cooks. In Italy, the first cookbook written by an Italian woman, published in 1900, claimed that male cooks had no care for the stomach or the purse of the person who paid him: "For [the male cooks] it is enough to pose as artist, these cooks are seeking a name for themselves, and they want glory and laurels, even at the risk of spoiling other people's digestion." She wrote that they cooked for the epicures and the gluttons rich enough to pay, while the female cooks were satisfied if the food was healthy, tasty, and did not cost "a mint of money" (un occhio della testa).[65] In the early twentieth century, the German Mary Hahn compared the male cook to a general (*Feldherr*) who was not afraid of spending and waste, whereas "the housewife to her kitchen herd is as the mother hen who carefully selects the best morsels and grains for her fledglings and makes sure that nothing is wasted."[66] It took a long time for female restaurant and hotel cooks to become firmly established, and they remain a minority in the profession even today. A few pioneers have had great influence. Eugénie ("Mère") Brazier, for example, received three Michelin stars in 1933 and took in Paul Bocuse as a young commis in 1946. But very few women have participated in the Bocuse d'Or—the world's most prestigious culinary competition—and among the forty-eight medalists between 1987 and 2015, there is only one female chef.

COOKS, SERVANTS, AND PATRONS

The big differences between rich and poor cooks and between famous celebrities and unknown toilers cannot hide the fact that most cooks were, until recently, servants. Even the cooks with lofty reputations and many privileges had a duty: to serve their masters, their princes, or their patrons. A Polish cookbook from 1682 made clear that the job of the cook was to understand his master's intentions when preparing a banquet and to make sure the food was served at the right time so that his master would not get worked up. In his list of qualifications for a cook, he added the word *pokorny,* which means "humble" or "submissive." The Italian chief steward Giovanni Battista Rossetti wrote in 1584 that the most important quality in a cook was fidelity and reliability, and as late as 1801, the cook was hailed by the French poet Joseph Berchoux as "a faithful servant" (un serviteur fidèle).[67]

Most important of all for the cook was to honor and respect the taste of his patron, a view expressed as early as antiquity, when, in one of his epigrams, Martial said that he didn't want to accommodate his palate to that of his cook; a cook ought to have the same taste as his patron ("domini debet habere gulam").[68] Martino repeatedly stressed that the taste of his patron was what decided the amount of spices and other details in his cooking. The same attitude can be found in many cookbooks and works written about the household. The author of the late fifteenth-century manuscript *Cuoco napoletano* expressed explicitly that a cook had to be a glutton (*ghiotto*), not for himself, but for his *patrone*.[69] Bartolomeo Scappi, private cook at the papal court in the sixteenth century, often stressed in his writings that a cook must take taste into consideration, not his own taste or some neutral palate but rather the personal taste of whoever had ordered the meal.[70] Several hundred years later, in 1853, the Milanese cook Giovanni Felice Luraschi wrote almost the same thing: a cook must have a good palate in order to study the taste of his master because "the cook must have the same palate as his master."[71] A German chef went as far as saying that the taste of the master must be holy (*heilig*) for the cook and that the cook must not be permitted to act against it.[72] Even those cooks who worked as freelancers and were admired for their art had to follow guidelines from their employers.[73]

To get a better understanding of the relationship between the cook and the patron, it is worthwhile to compare cooks to another group of servants: artists. Artists were often treated as working men. As Johan Huizinga pointed out in his study of forms of life, thought, and art in the fourteenth and fifteenth centuries, all art during this period was more or less applied art, and therefore the distinction between free visual art (*vrij beeldende kunst*) and handicraft (*kunsthandwerk*) was in practice wiped out, and consequently there was no difference between artists and craftsmen. Huizinga gave several examples of great court painters who colored chairs, painted shields, and repaired mechanical apparatuses.[74] In Florence, Botticelli had to paint wedding chests and banners. In Ferrara, most painters were paid per day or by surface area, a master potter earned more than a sculptor, and a tapestry weaver or a skilled tailor could earn four times as much as an architect. In Spain, King Philip IV put Velázquez on the payroll as an upholsterer. In Peter Burke's words: "Renaissance artists generally did more or less what they were told. The constraints on them are part of their history."[75]

With examples covering hundreds of painters, sculptors, and others, Burke demonstrated that the attitude the elite had toward artists varied: "Three social prejudices against artists retained their power in this period [the Renaissance]. Artists were considered ignoble because their work involved manual labor, because it involved retail trade [just like cobblers and traders] and because they lacked learning [they were trained in guilds and not at universities]."[76]

The situation began to change during the sixteenth century, when the Italian art critic Giorgio Vasari began to distinguish between "craft" and "art," especially painting, sculpture, and architecture. In his analysis of Italian courts in sixteenth century Italy, Guido Guerzoni wrote, "It should be remembered that the debate on the alleged superiority of certain expressive genres (such as painting) over other arts was late in developing and limited to specific intellectual circles. It became more generally accepted from the late 1570s in Ferrara."[77] But Italy was perhaps more advanced in this respect than other parts of Europe. In a 1506 letter to the German humanist Willibald Pirckheimer, the painter Albrecht Dürer wrote about his positive experience in Italy: "Here I am a gentleman, at home a sponger" (Hie bin ich ein Herr, doheim ein Schmarotzer).[78]

When artists worked in courts rather than within guilds or in workshops, they were often better paid and able to obtain a higher status. Some of them were even knighted in their old age, just like certain Italian cooks and scalcos. But this improved status did not immediately lead to artistic independence. The main task of artists was to entertain the prince, and this was not so different from that of other servants, such as cooks.

The sociologist Norbert Elias described the situation at a court where Mozart's father was employed as a musician in the eighteenth century, and he equated the rank and status of musicians in a princely household with that of cooks and confectioners (Zuckerbäcker).[79] In an indignant letter to his father in 1781, Amadeus himself complained about the bad treatment he received at the court of the archbishop in Salzburg. At dinner, he was seated with the servants, among them the cooks ("bej die herrn köche")[80] But he was not the only one who suffered such humiliation. Great artists such as Johann Sebastian Bach and Joseph Haydn were kept on a tight leash by their protectors. Haydn grumblingly wrote to his friend Marianne von Genzinger that he didn't know if he was "Capellmeister oder Capelldiener" (music director or music servant). According to the cultural historian Tim Blanning "the dependent culture fostered by the representational worlds of the courts could bring security, wealth, and even status, but it also involved subservience to the patron, whether individual or institutional."[81]

From the later part of the eighteenth century, a bourgeois public sphere emerged, leading to the gradual liberation and independence of artists. In his well-known analysis of the transformation of the public sphere, the philosopher Jürgen Habermas pointed out that in the case of music, performance was no longer exclusively something that took place at courts and churches, with their appointed composers and musicians. People paid for admission to concerts, and music became a commodity, but at the same time, music became zweckfrei—not tied to a purpose. The earlier Gebrauchsmusik—music for special occasions—was replaced by music chosen according to what one preferred.[82]

If we try to apply Habermas's ideas to the art of cooking, we can easily imagine that restaurants—public dining rooms—which appeared more or less at the same time as public concerts, represented the emergence of a new bourgeois public for gastronomy. Gourmet food became a commodity people could buy and not only a part of the representation and self-presentation of the courts. But if this comparison is valid for the change of audience—the guests—it is more doubtful that it applies to the culinary artists.

There was indeed a growing esteem for some of the most successful new restaurateurs in Paris in the early nineteenth century. This was partly due to the fact that in the new restaurant culture, competition, and consequently reputation, became important. The historian Jean-Paul Aron, a specialist on French "eating culture" in the nineteenth century, considered chefs to be different from employees in the general meaning of the word. Chefs were practitioners and artists, and they had the same aim as restaurant owners; some of them even owned their own restaurants. And they commanded a brigade.[83] But this was not necessarily true for all cooks in all European countries. One of the Parisian restaurateurs, Antoine Beauvilliers, who owned a tavern before the French Revolution, summarized his experiences in 1814 and claimed that Spanish gastronomy had seen little progress as a result of the general contempt toward people who prepared food for others—in other words, cooks. His statement clearly implied that this was not the case in France.[84] This is in line with what the British writer Launcelot Sturgeon claimed a few years later: "Whatever may be the praises bestowed on a dinner, the host never thinks of declaring the name of the artist who produced it; and while half the great men in London owe their estimation in society to the excellence of their tables, the cooks on whose talents they have risen, languish 'unknown to fame' in those subterraneous dungeons of the metropolis termed kitchens. In France, on the contrary, a man's cook is his pride."[85]

This was in 1822, and there seems indeed to have been a certain development in the valuation of cooks in France over the course of the Napoleonic period and the Bourbon Restoration. This development can be traced in texts by the French writer Grimod de la Reynière. In 1803, in the preface to the first volume of his *Almanach des gourmands,* Grimod explained how the journal would be important for gourmands with ignorant cooks who didn't know how to make good food with little money. The next year, in the second volume, he contended that it was not enough for a host to have a lot of money and a good cook, claiming that he would never be able to eat and dine well if he depended only on his servants. Contrary to what Sturgeon would write fifteen years later, Grimod regretted—in the 1807 edition of the *Almanach*—that the name of the cook was too often unknown to the guests at a dinner.[86] In his handbook for hosts, *Manuel des amphitryons,* published in 1808, Grimod wrote that although the cook ought to present suggestions for the menu each day, it was the host who made the decisions, and he might often give a very capable cook the most brilliant ideas.[87] But then, in the 1812 edition of his *Almanach,* he observed that chefs had acquired a greater importance, noting that hosts had started to work with their cooks in the same way princes worked with their ministers. The cooks were no longer only chefs, they had become true artists, and in this process, they had acquired more respect and a higher salary.[88] But, as their salaries indicated, they were after all still servants.

If a few of the great gourmets understood the creativity and originality of culinary chefs in early nineteenth-century Paris, cooks in general did not enjoy more respect from the public. In 1821, the playwright Eugène Scribe made theater audiences laugh when he presented the comedy *Le sécretaire et le cuisinier,* which was about a secretary and a cook starting new jobs in a big mansion. The employer mistakes one for the other, and the comical effect is created by the contrast between conversations belonging to two very different spheres, similar to the method used in Greek comedies from antiquity. And in order to further underline how the cook was perceived, Scribe gave him the ridiculous name Soufflé, a word that is not only a culinary term but also means "inflated," as in "pompous."

In the eighteenth and nineteenth centuries, an exclusive group of French cooks became famous, and many of them had successful careers abroad. But this did not mean that they achieved the same independence as artists. Their job was to serve food that satisfied the expectations of the guests. Cooks who tried to break away by making their own experiments risked running into problems. The French-born cook Alexis Soyer made his career in Victorian England, where he was honored by princes and gourmets, but he quit his assignment as chef in London's Reform Club because—at least as he explained it—he disagreed with certain plans the management wished to implement. He gained fame for his books, his charitable work, his technical inventions, and his culinary genius. But although the writer George Augustus Sala declared at Soyer's funeral in 1858, "He was my dear and good friend," he prefaced this by saying, "He was but a Cook." This was the same expression Helen Morris used in her biography of Soyer eighty years later: "He was only a cook." And in 1860, Soyer himself wrote with a certain bitterness that "cookery, in our era, has been thought beneath the attention of men of science" and that a cook was "in the opinion of almost every one, a mere menial."[89]

During the nineteenth century, there are numerous examples from France of how the status of cooks remained low, as expressed in the book *Hygiène alimentaire* (Food hygiene), published in 1868 by the physician Auguste Debay: "In France as in most civilized nations cooking is exclusively a task for women and for men from a lower social class and without education."[90] Even the great French cook Auguste Escoffier, the innovator of international hotel cuisine, said that when he started as an apprentice in 1859, the profession of cooks had very low esteem in high society.[91] When, at the end of his career, in 1928, he became an Officier in the Légion d'honneur, he was the first cook in French history to receive this mark of distinction.

In the first half of the twentieth century, great cooks established themselves in restaurants in France and became an inspiration for the generation of chefs in the provinces who launched the so-called *nouvelle cuisine* in the 1960s. According to two American writers, "They blended new and old styles, exotic and common-place ingredients, familiar and foreign cuisines. They emphasized a richness of taste derived from the freshest ingredients."[92]

This brought great fame to some chefs, but the real change in social status occurred, according to Paul Bocuse, when cooks became owners of their own restaurants. Then they were their own masters and had a say not only in the kitchen but also in the dining room.[93] Bocuse was a special case. After working in various restaurants, he returned to his father's auberge in 1958 and took over when he died. But his point of view was confirmed by the experience the Catalan chef Ferran Adrià had with the restaurant elBulli, where he was chef from 1984. He and the director Juli Soler appreciated the freedom given by the owners, but they also knew that this freedom had its limits; in important matters, they depended on approval from the owners. This changed when Adrià and Soler bought the restaurant in 1990.

Ownership also favored promotion. Paul Bocuse, for example, started a whole industry, using his name as a brand not only for new restaurants and culinary courses around the world but also for all sorts of products, such as wine coolers and pepper mills. His genius, observed Pankhurst Ferguson, "lay in his ability to promote at one and the same time himself, his cuisine, and his profession."[94]

In addition to greater commercial creativity, cooks from the generation after the emergence of *nouvelle cuisine* also represent something new in the way they apply science in their culinary work. Edouard de Pomiane, a biologist at the Pasteur Institute, launched his "gastrotechnology" in the 1930s, and in 1984, the writer Harold McGee published his book *On Food and Cooking*, in which he explained to a broad public the chemical processes taking place during food preparation. McGee's book was influential for Heston Blumenthal, the English chef and TV star known for, among many other things, the show *Kitchen Chemistry*. The French chemist Hervé This called this new scientific approach to food "molecular gastronomy," a term first used at a workshop in 1992 called Molecular and Physical Gastronomy, which This codirected with the influential Oxford physicist Nicholas Kurti, who worked with food from a scientific point of view.

Ferran Adrià has referred to his cooking as "deconstructivist" because he breaks down the ingredients of known dishes and puts them together in new ways. In 2006, Adrià, Blumenthal, and McGee wrote a manifesto about what they called the "new cookery," in which they emphasized the value of innovation but not novelty for its own sake: "We may use modern thickeners, sugar substitutes, enzymes, liquid nitrogen, sous-vide, dehydration, and other non-traditional means, but these do not define our cooking. They are a few of the many tools that we are fortunate to have available as we strive to make delicious and stimulating dishes."[95]

Parallel to this elevation of the scientific knowledge of prominent cooks was an increased recognition of their work as true art. In the 1980s, the French minister of culture, Jack Lang, promoted forms of expression that until then had not been considered art, such as sport, fashion, design, and cuisine. In 2010, UNESCO added the French national meal to its Representative List of the Intangible Cultural Heritage. All of this has brought the world's top chefs greater fame than any court cook in history could have imagined, particularly because of the extra push given by modern mass media. Their restaurants have long waiting lists, and reservations have to be made months in advance. They participate in celebrity events of all kinds, and they publish best-selling cookbooks.

But just as in the past, these chefs are a small elite within the profession. Most cooks do not reach such summits. Even if cooks have obtained a more independent status through contracts with their employers, which give them rights in addition to duties, they are still faced with manual and physically strenuous work. And few among them, even in the combined ranks of professional and domestic cooks, are the authors of cookbooks.[96]

2

Writer and Author

Who should be considered the author of a work? When we know that almost half of Platina's *De honesta voluptate* originates from another person, for example, wouldn't it be fair to put both names on the title page?

And what is an author exactly? The answer is simpler to determine today than it was in the past. Even if there are discussions about sources, references, and plagiarism (increasingly so these days because of the existence of the Internet), the author of a printed work is generally identified through the contract he or she makes with a publisher. The text is corrected and modified by editors and copyeditors, but the author is the one responsible for the manuscript. Most of us think of a book as a collection of letters printed in a certain typeface. One example relevant to cookbook history is the page from the first dated edition of Platina's *De honesta voluptate,* published in Venice in 1475, represented in figure 3. But words are not only *printed* words. When Platina met Martino in the mid-1460s, printing in Italy was in its infancy, so the word "book" still referred to a manuscript, which literally means "handwritten."[1]

THE SCRIBE

If we take a closer look at scribal culture before Gutenberg, we will find several different people behind the creation of a manuscript. The best-known definition of their roles is the precise—albeit somewhat rigid—version given by the monk Bonaventura in the thirteenth century. He distinguished between four roles or professions, which represented different ways to write a book. Someone who copied out the work of another (either from an existing manuscript or via dictation) was

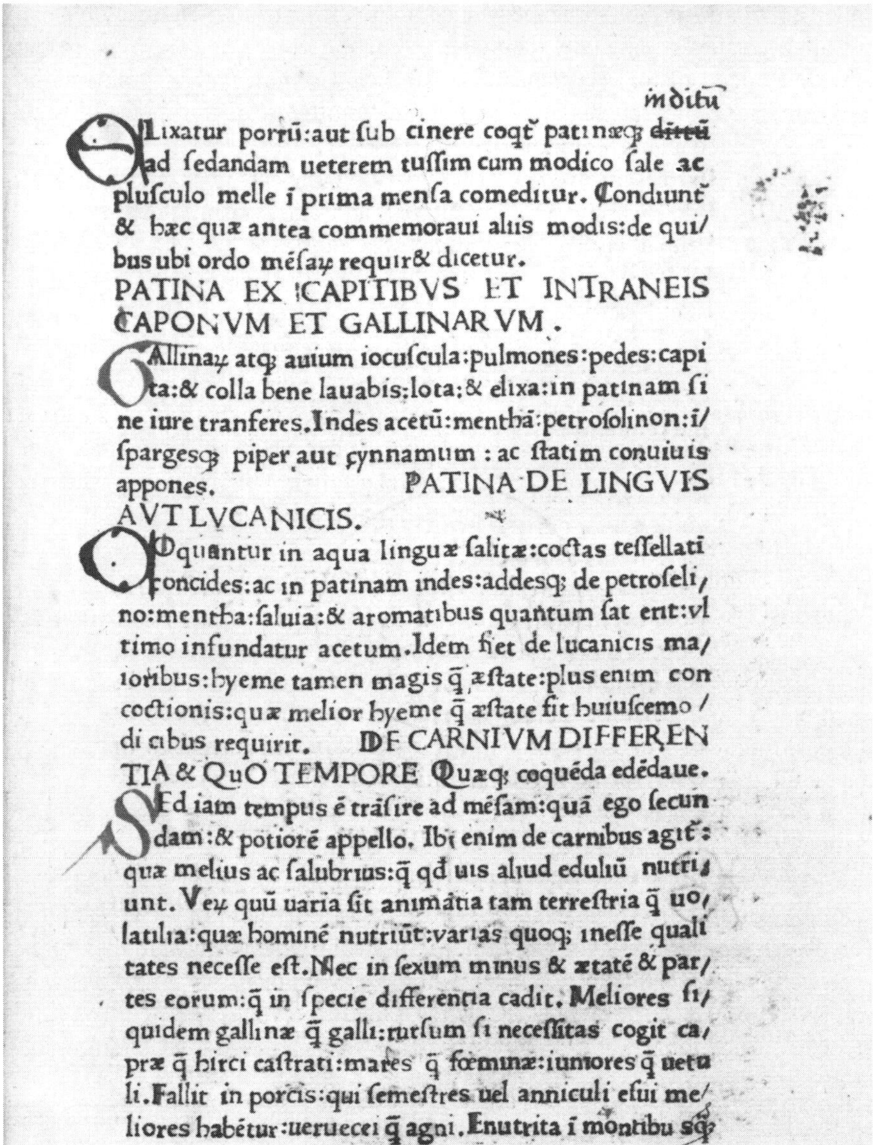

Lixatur porrū:aut ſub cinere coqť patinæꝗ ditū
ad ſedandam ueterem tuſſim cum modico ſale ac
pluſculo melle ĩ prima menſa comeditur. Condiunť
& hæc quæ antea commemoraui aliis modis:de qui/
bus ubi ordo méſaꝗ requir& dicetur.

PATINA EX ¡CAPITIBVS ET INTRANEIS
CAPONVM ET GALLINARVM.

Allinaꝗ atꝙ auium iocuſcula:pulmones:pedes:capi
ta:& colla bene lauabis;lota;& elixa:in patinam ſi
ne iure tranſferes.Indes acetū:menthā:petroſolinon:ĩ/
ſpargesꝗ piper aut ſynnamum : ac ſtatim conuiuis
appones. PATINA DE LINGVIS
AVT LVCANICIS.

Oquantur in aqua linguæ ſalitæ:coctas teſſellati
oncides:ac in patinam indes:addesꝗ de petroſeli/
no:mentha:ſaluia:& aromatibus quantum ſat erit:vl
timo infundatur acetum.Idem fiet de lucanicis ma/
ioribus:hyeme tamen magis ꝗ æſtate:plus enim con
coctionis:quæ melior hyeme ꝗ æſtate fit huiuſcemo /
di cibus requirit. DE CARNIVM DIFFEREN
TIA & QuO TEMPORE Quæꝗ coquéda edédaue.

Ed iam tempus é traſire ad méſam:quā ego ſecun
dam:& potioré appello. Ibi enim de carnibus agit :
quæ melius ac ſalubrius:ꝗ qd uis aliud eduliū nutri/
unt. Veꝗ quū uaria ſit animātia tam terreſtria ꝗ uo/
latilia:quæ hominé nutriūt:varias quoꝗ ineſſe quali
tates neceſſe eſt.Nec in ſexum minus & ætaté & par/
tes eorum:ꝗ in ſpecie differentia cadit. Meliores ſi/
quidem gallinæ ꝗ galli:rurſum ſi neceſſitas cogit ca/
præ ꝗ hirci caſtrati:mares ꝗ fœminæ:iuniores ꝗ ueta
li.Fallit in porcis:qui ſemeſtres uel anniculi eſui me/
liores habétur :ueruecei ꝗ agni.Enutrita ĩ montibu sꝗ

FIGURE 3. A page from the first dated edition of Bartolomeo Platina's *De honesta voluptate et valetudine,* printed in Venice in 1475. Württembergische Landesbibliothek, Stuttgart, Inc. fol. 13051.

called a *scriptor* (scribe); someone who combined texts from more than one manuscript was called a *compilator* (compiler); someone who copied one or more texts and then added his own explanation was called a *commentator* (commentator); and someone who wrote his own text but quoted other texts to support his statements was called an *auctor* (author).[2]

None of these roles involved exclusively writing one's own text. Originality was not an aim in itself; it was more important to imitate and transmit the work of one's predecessors. In other words, what counted was intertextuality with the old texts. For the theologian Bonaventura, the original text was the Holy Scripture—God was the ultimate *auctor,* because he was the ultimate *auctoritas* (authority). In his essay about the ancient art of rhetoric, Roland Barthes wrote that the people we anachronistically call writers in the Middle Ages were essentially mediators who passed on material from antiquity and "combinateurs" who edited and reorganized material.[3]

The first of Bonaventura's categories, the scribe, has been represented since antiquity by his spiritual brothers—and sisters, as there were also nuns who were scribes—in monasteries all over Europe. Gradually, other people also took on this role, starting with scholars in learned institutions and at courts. Then, beginning in the High Middle Ages, professional scribes emerged to work in commercial establishments. The ideal scribe meticulously copied, word by word, up to two hundred lines a day.[4] Sometimes, the result was elaborate calligraphy with gilded ornamental initials and details, as in one of the oldest Platina manuscripts, which is probably from before 1468, where the illuminated borders in red, blue, green, and gold are filled with drawings of birds and game, serving as tempting appetizers to the contents.[5] But there were also manuscripts marked by sloppiness and inaccuracies.

In the process of copying, the danger of textual corruption was great, and many errors have been documented.[6] Some scribes had difficulty understanding certain words, particularly if they had no competence in the subject treated. One such example is found in a German cookbook from the fourteenth century, *Daz Buoch von guoter Spise* (Book of good food). One of the ingredients given in the original is an herb, *reynevan,* but in a later version, the word *rainfal,* a type of sweet wine, was used instead. According to the cultural historian Hans Wiswe, this kind of error happened often, but it was more frequent in less prestigious literature, such as cookbooks, than in books about law and theology.[7]

Errors could lead to meaning being changed, but changes were not only a result of errors. Many of the well-trained and educated *scriptores* in the Middle Ages consciously altered language and content. They skipped material they had no interest in or did not find worth copying and added comments that eventually became a part of the text because in reality, the boundaries between Bonaventura's four categories were less distinct than in his rigid definition.[8] In fact, it is not a question of four different professions but rather of four different roles that sometimes blended into one another. As Malcolm Parkes, one of the specialists of medieval palaeography and codicology, put it, "Inside many a scribe there lurked a compiler struggling to get out."[9] This is why certain scholars of medieval literature have seen the philological emphasis on "original texts" as anachronistic and have proposed more investigation into the variations and mobility of texts. *Mouvance* and *variance* are concepts coined by French authors who are more focused on the total scribal tradition of a work than of finding an original "authorial" text.[10]

LITERACY AMONG COOKS

If we try to use Bonaventura's model to define Platina's role in the creation of *De honesta voluptate,* it is evident he was the scribe, compiler, commentator, and author of his own texts. But what about Martino? Which part did he play? Did he write his own texts, or was he simply an authority in cooking who had no writing skills? How literate were cooks before schooling became a right and a duty for everybody in society? How direct is the connection between the culinary ideas of these cooks and the language chosen when their ideas were written down as reci- pes? As recently as 2011, the historian Pascal Ory wrote in his introduction to Auguste Escoffier's memoirs that this literate chef was an exception because a book with the name of a cook on the title page was often partly or completely written by a ghostwriter—and this is still true.[11]

Traditionally, the art of cooking, like other mechanical arts, was passed on from the master to the apprentice orally without the use of books. Bruno Laurioux checked the identity of known owners of culinary manuscripts in the late Middle Ages, as identified by inscriptions in manuscripts or from catalogs of provenance in libraries. He found no cooks among them, and the culinary manuals written at the time did not address cooks. He also repudiated as a fantasy the idea that there were learned cooks during that era.[12] But the lack of books on the subject was due at least in part to a strategy: cooks' recipes, methods, and techniques were part of the professional secrets they had to protect from people outside their own guilds or other similar organisations.

As described in chapter 1, there were substantial differences in princely house- holds between the chief cooks and the multitude of kitchen assistants of various ranks. It is worth noting that the cooks named on the title pages of early cook- books were always kitchen chefs at royal or aristocratic courts. Most books written before 1500 are anonymous, so we don't know the identity of the actual authors, but even when an author's name is given, we don't really know what part he played in the process. Taillevent, so famous in France that François Villon mentioned him (albeit ironically) in some of his verses, was at most responsible for only a few of the recipes attributed to him.[13] One of the manuscripts of an old English cook- book—*Forme of Cury* (Method of cooking)—claims to have been compiled by the chief cooks of King Richard II and controlled by his royal physicians, who knew the accepted medical theories, but we don't know who gave the recipes the written form they have in this particular copy of the work.[14] An untitled German manuscript dated 1460 is attributed to Meister Hans, who was private cook (*koch zer kamer*) to a count in Württemberg. But the cookbook is a compilation of older recipes, and the text was produced by a professional scribe.[15] The recipes in the 1393 French household manuscript *Le menagier de Paris* (The Parisian householder), written by an anonymous Parisian bourgeois for his young wife, were taken from earlier manuscripts.[16]

Du fait de cuysine (On cooking), a French cookbook manuscript that originated at the court of Duke Amadeus VIII of Savoy, was dictated to a scribe by the duke's chef, Maître Chiquart. But the one surviving copy of the book is not the original manuscript. Consequently, we don't know which changes were made to the text by scribes in the intervening editions. Certain traces of orality can be detected in the text, and it is interesting that Chiquart remarked in the preface that he was not able to consult books: "I have no books or notes concerning this."[17] Does this remark imply that he had reading skills but no access to books? Or that he was illiterate and therefore unable to consult what other people had written about the subject? Was his culinary knowledge based only on the experience he had gained during his apprenticeship and later while directing the ducal kitchen?

Court kitchens were veritable schools in the art of cooking, where apprentices were first introduced to necessary basic techniques and then gradually rose in the ranks until they qualified to learn more refined preparations. But this training did not equip cooks with the tools to adequately express their experience in written form. It is even possible that cooks were different from other artisans in this respect. According to Elizabeth Eisenstein, the printing revolution brought out a new type of author, tradespeople who worked in practical professions. These individuals wrote about their trades in a simple way and in their own national languages (instead of in Latin). Their texts were based on their own practical experiences, and they lacked the respect for tradition and authorized models that many academics had. Eisenstein gives as examples the potter Bernard Palissy, the midwife Louise Bourgeois, and the barber-surgeon Ambroise Paré.[18]

These artisans may have had different backgrounds than the average cook, or even cooks of high rank. In the 1590s, when the court cook Frantz de Rontzier was asked by his employer, the Duke of Brunswick, to write a cookbook, he made it quite clear that the recipes were dictated, "ad pennam dictiret," since he could not write.[19] Ronzier's spoken language was Low German (*niederdeutsch*), and there are many traces of this in the text, which is written in High German.[20] In another sixteenth-century text, this one by the papal cook Bartolomeo Scappi, the lexical and semantic forms used point to a person from Veneto, far from Scappi's birthplace in northern Varese. In her biography of the cook, June di Schino reproduced a recipe written in Scappi's own hand, so he definitely knew how to write, but even if the plan of the book and the collection of recipes can be attributed to Scappi himself, the actual writing and formulation of phrases, "la messa in bello," must have been left to a professional scribe or editor.[21]

The lack of proficiency in writing among cooks was probably the reason so many court administrators in the fifteenth and sixteenth centuries became "authors"—in other words, the ones putting the recipes on paper. In Italy, several books were written by chief stewards, who compiled recipes along with other information necessary for court administration.[22] The only Polish cookbook published in the seventeenth century signals immediately in its Latin title, *Compendium ferculorum*, that it was written by someone of a higher rank than a cook, although a translation is given in the Polish subtitle, *Zebranie potraw* (Collection of dishes). The title page explained that the author Stanislaw Czerniecki was "secretary of his Princely Highness." He was an administrator for an aristocrat married to a close relative of the king, and he described in detail the tasks and duties of a cook and the correct organization of a banquet, but he probably received the recipes from the professionals in the kitchen.[23]

In Germany, the oldest cookbook manuscript is part of a *Hausbuch* written by Michael de Leone, protonotary to the bishop of Würzburg,[24] and he probably based the recipes on information from cooks at the court. In another cookbook, also originating in a German court, the person behind the text was presented as a *Küchenschreiber*, a position with responsibility for accounts and other tasks demanding pen and paper. In the preface, he explained that he had "collected and described" (zusammen getragen und beschrieben), which may indicate that he wrote down recipes that were circulating in the kitchen of the prince-elector.[25]

In the eighteenth century, there was certainly a difference in literacy between higher-ranking cooks and kitchen apprentices. In one beautifully illustrated Austrian cookbook, *Neues Saltzburgisches Koch-Buch* (New Salzburg cookbook), the author, Conrad Hagger, made an important point concerning the special value of the illustrations in his work (figure 4). He wrote that they were meant for young cooks, particularly those who didn't know how to read. By looking at the engravings of pastry work, they would be able to manage without the help of the text.[26]

In the nineteenth century, cooks were expected to take simple notes, and this became a more common practice as literacy among the general population increased. In a book about household management and cookery printed in Germany in 1829, the author, a former *Küchenmeister* at a court in Saxony, wrote that the cook in every big household should deliver a menu (*Speise-Zettel*) to his patron daily with the dishes he planned to serve. Similar advice was given in an Italian cook's handbook, *Manuale del cuoco*, from around the same time, in which the author recommended that a cook give his patron "the menu of the meal in writing" every day.[27] But this level of literacy was far lower than what would be demanded of an author of a cookbook. There were also parts of Europe—tsarist

FIGURE 4. Presentations for pâté in *Neues Saltzburgisches Koch-Buch* (New Salzburg cookbook), by Conrad Hagger, published in Augsburg in 1719. Universitätsbibliothek Salzburg, R 2.890 I.

Russia, for example—where a very high degree of illiteracy lasted into the twentieth century. In 1901, in the twenty-second edition of Elena Molokhovets's classic cookbook, *Podarok molodym khoziaikam* (Gift to young housewives), the author drew attention to how Russian cooks had to be instructed in detail.[28]

In France, the given authors of important seventeenth-century cookbooks held leading positions in court households, and this was also true throughout the eighteenth century. Some chief stewards were recruited from aristocratic families and may have been able to write with proficiency. A few authors were physicians. Unfortunately, we know nothing about the prolific Menon, who published numerous books during the 1700s. To judge from his work, he had experience with the culinary arts, but he almost definitely belonged to a higher social group than most cooks.[29] He made an interesting comment in his 1755 court cookbook, *Les soupers de la cour:* he noted regretfully that some cooks seemed to be embarrassed if they were discovered reading a cookbook and asked, "Would a physician, a lawyer, an architect blush if reading the works concerning his profession?" This appears to indicate that there actually were cooks in court circles who knew how to read, even if Menon called them "craftsmen with second-rate knowledge" (artisans d'un sça-voir médiocre).[30] But among cooks in the lower ranks, illiteracy may have been more common. In a French collection of recipes in verse set to popular melodies, the author informed readers (supposed to be ladies): "Singing, you can, Mesdames, teach your employees to make the ragoûts and sauces that will please you."[31]

An increasing number of female cooks worked in bourgeois households in eighteenth-century France, and many of these women are said to have been literate, as they often took care of bookkeeping as well,[32] but this knowledge did not necessarily translate into a proficiency in writing books. Women did not publish any cookbooks in France before the Revolution.

In northern Europe and Great Britain, however, literacy was higher, particularly in Protestant areas, where reading had been encouraged among men and women. In Germany in 1597, Anna Wecker became the first woman to have her name appear on the title page of a printed cookbook. During her life, Wecker collected recipes, many of them for sick people. After Wecker's death, her daughter and son-in-law published the recipes as a book, and to give the book more authority, they added, after Anna Wecker's name: "Widow of the famous physician Johann Jacob Wecker." But the increasing number of women authoring cookbooks in England and Germany did not signify an increased literary activity among cooks in general. The authors were ladies and housewives who commanded cooks, and housekeepers drawn from the impoverished gentry, who were likely to be literate.[33] Several authors had worked as teachers in cooking schools, many of them in cities other than London, such as Edinburgh and Newcastle.[34] Women related to men in the publishing trade were often the real compilers of recipe books. Take, for example, the wife of the publisher of a 1691 German book, the sister-in-law of the publisher of a 1772 Dutch book, and the printer's wife of an 1887 Norwegian book.[35]

The first American author of a printed cookbook, Amelia Simmons, was not illiterate, but she admitted in 1796 that she was without "an education sufficient to prepare the work for the press" and therefore entrusted another person to prepare her recipes for publication.[36] African-American slaves working in kitchens on big plantations in the South had even less formal education than Simmons. In his memoir, one of Thomas Jefferson's slaves recalled that Mrs. Jefferson would come to the kitchen with a book in her hand and read out of it to the pastry cook to explain how to make cakes, tarts, and so on.[37] When housewives on Southern plantations began to publish cookbooks, they used recipes from European works, but they also picked up dishes their cooks had adapted from African and Caribbean cuisines. These cooks got no credit in antebellum books; it is only very recently that they have been hailed for the creativity they demonstrated when meeting new realities and new demands. The first of these former slave cooks to see her name on a title page was Abby Fisher. She was illiterate, but her recipes were written down and edited by others and published in 1881.[38]

For a long period, women authors were limited to certain geographical areas. Before 1800, cookbooks by women were published only in German-speaking Europe, England, Scotland, Scandinavia, and the United States. In the nineteenth century, women authors also published in French, Russian, Polish, and Czech. But in Portugal, Spain, Italy, and Greece, there were no women authors of printed cookbooks before 1900.[39]

During the twentieth century, most European cooks—men as well as women—learned to read and write. In France, there was even a group of male cooks who frequented intellectual circles. They were editors of magazines, bibliophiles and collectors, students of dietetics, and authors of books that became classics in the genre. Among them were Joseph Favre, Jules Gouffé, Charles Durant, Édouard Nignon, and Prosper Montagné.[40] But these men were still exceptions. As Pascal Ory pointed out above, many cooks still did not have the professional capabilities to put together a workable cookbook and thus relied on ghostwriters. In several countries, the active editing of recipes was taken over by a new professional group, the mostly female teachers of home economics, who were educated in practical housework and also in accounting and other fields of modern household management. Many of them published their own books, like Fannie Farmer, known for her *Boston Cooking-School Cookbook* of 1896.

WHY PEOPLE WROTE COOKBOOKS

What were the motivations behind all these books? From the fifteenth and sixteenth centuries, there were princes taking the initiative to have recipes written down. This was the case with Duke Amadeus VIII of Savoy, who had his kitchen chef, Maître Chiquart, write a cookbook in 1420. The duke went on to become the last of the antipopes during the Papal Schism, but when the cookbook was written, he was still the head of a principality with worldly ambitions. In his preface, the chef Chiquart pointed out that the duke himself had ordered him to pass on his knowledge. Allegedly, the duke's intention was to give future cooks access to the reservoir of experience and expertise stored in Chiquart's brain, but Bruno Laurioux suspects that the duke may have had the ambition of showing other princes how resplendent banquets were in Savoy.[41] Foods served in noble households were admired in the same way as other manifestations of power and status—such as palaces, vehicles, furniture, paintings, clothes, and jewelery—but because food is ephemeral, a cookbook could serve as a visible and solid documentation of the food culture at a court.

A desire to show off was probably also the reason the Duke of Brunswick in 1594 asked his private cook Frantz de Rontzier to make an inventory of dishes served at his banquets. The duke was a well-educated intellectual but nevertheless spent enormous resources on maintaining a luxurious court at the Wolfenbüttel palace, where he hosted magnificent banquets. It is possible that the cookbook was meant for the duke and his friends rather than for a wider audience, a theory supported by the fact that the book was not distributed in the usual way. After Rontzier dictated his preface, probably when the manuscript was finished, four years passed before the book was finally printed, and this in the duke's own newly established printing office. The book was printed only in this edition.[42]

The first printed cookbook in Spanish, published in 1525, was likewise the result of a princely initiative. The author, a man named Ruberto de Nola, according to the title page, served as master cook at the court of King Ferdinand II of Naples. In the preface, Ruberto mentioned that the king asked him several times to write down the principles of his cooking. The Spanish book is a translation from the original Catalan, but the oldest known Catalan edition, from 1520, where the author is given as Mestre Robert, says nothing about the king's request, so either there was an older edition of this book or the reference to the king's wishes was a later editorial addition.[43]

Another way to judge the motivation behind books like these is to look at other types of text collections. There was a great interest in cataloging encyclopedic knowledge, and it was not always necessary for the resulting texts to have any practical use. This was true in many fields, including several branches of science.[44]

There are without doubt authors who published their recipes with pure motives, such as a desire to enlighten, educate, or help people make better use of their resources. Recipes were often referred to as "secrets," as cooks and other specialists had earlier kept them hidden. The anonymous author of Le pastissier françois (The French pastry cook, 1653) presented the recipes in his book as having been "kept secret by the court and Parisian pastry chefs."[45] Several other cookbook authors made a point of revealing their secrets for the public.[46] But such authors were controversial and risked criticism from members of the guilds. In the preface of his cookbook, first printed in 1661, William Rabisha admitted that many in "the Fraternity of Cooks" would attack him because he was making knowledge available to "every Kitchen wench," but he retorted that the same accusation could be made against "all other Arts and Sciences," and he mentioned astronomers, mathematicians, navigators, physicians, and surgeons, all of whom published books divulging their knowledge.[47] As late as 1866, the preface of an anonymous French cookbook divided cookbook authors into two groups: the charlatans who speculated in the simplicity of the public and the practicioners who didn't want to reveal their secret recipes because they were afraid of the guilds of cooks, which were like a sort of Freemasonry.[48]

Many of the reasons authors gave for publishing cookbooks were idealistic, but an important motivation certainly was the possibility of profit, particularly from the late fifteenth century, when the new printing press made copying quicker and easier and consequently more profitable. Barbara Ketcham Wheaton suggested that with increased literacy, secrecy may have become less valuable than fame, because when "more people could read, the cook gained economically through the fame brought by published recipes."[49]

Before Gutenberg's invention, being an author was not a good business. Authors depended on patrons who were willing to pay a scribe or support them in other ways. With printing and a trade in printed books, this gradually changed. The elite considered earning money from writing disgraceful, but writers from other social classes made a profit by writing books, and there are particularly many stories about women who provided an income for themselves by compiling recipe collections. In England, the playwright Aphra Behn is generally mentioned as the first woman to earn a living by writing, but the first female cookbook author did the same at around the same time. Hannah Woolley published her cookbooks during the periods when she was unprovided for, after the deaths of her first and second husbands. This was in the late seventeenth century, but several women found themselves in similar situations in the following centuries. Harriet Beecher Stowe, who cowrote a household book with her sister, the educator Catherine Beecher, had a number of motives for writing, but an important one was no doubt to supplement her husband's modest salary.[50] A study of Norwegian women who wrote cookbooks between 1830 and 1870 showed that the authors were almost all single or widows and without a regular income.[51] During the same period, Anne Marie Mangor, a Danish fifty-six-year-old author and widow, published her first cookbook and gave this explanation of why she started writing: "I had lost my husband and did not know how to manage. Then the idea struck me that I might start collecting recipes for all sorts of dishes, cakes, and salads, even if—as the good Lord knows—I could not afford to eat them."[52]

But even if authors slowly received better remuneration for their work, they had few rights in their negotiations with publishers or printers, who wanted to be reimbursed for their investments of capital, labor, and material. For a long time, authors shared costs with publishers and received a number of copies of their books as compensation. Sometimes, a publisher would buy the rights to the text for a fixed price, or author and publisher agreed on a fifty-fifty split of the profit (profit was defined by the publisher after deducted costs). Copyright laws developed gradually, but it was only with the advent of the royalty system—which originated in the United States—that authors became fairly compensated for their work.[53]

PUBLISHERS AND COMPILERS

With the modern printing techniques developed in the late fifteenth century, the commercial aspect of creating books became increasingly important. Printers, publishers, and booksellers discovered that recipes were valuable commodities, and these groups enjoyed most of the profits from early book production. Many of them were extremely active and creative. They picked up old manuscripts and encouraged qualified people to edit and translate them, if they did not do it themselves. The first printed cookbooks in English, Dutch, Czech, and Hungarian were most likely initiated by prominent men such as Richard Pynson in London, who later became King's Printer; Thomas vander Noot in Brussels, who had studied printing in Paris and Lyon; Pavel Severin in Prague, who was mayor of the city from 1534 to 1537; and Miklos Tótfalusi Kis in Cluj, who was renowned in Western Europe under the name Nicholas Kis as the inventor of many fonts. Hieronymus Vietor in Cracow, and formerly Vienna, printed a Polish translation of the first Czech cookbook around 1540, and Salomon Sartorius in Copenhagen printed a compilation of recipes translated from German in 1616.[54]

Some of these professionals were well-educated personalities who frequently socialized with learned humanists. They obtained international reputations, and some of the most beautiful cookbooks of the era were their products. In 1581, Sigmund Feyerabendt in Frankfurt am Main published a big folio volume by the court cook Marx Rumpolt with woodcuts and copper engravings by acknowledged artists. One of the most attractive books produced by the Dutch printers Louis and Daniel Elzevier in Amsterdam was the 1655 edition of the pastry cookbook *Le pastissier françois.*

But according to Elizabeth Eisenstein, such characters represented a minority; although the "romantic figure of the aristocratic or patrician patron" overshadowed the capitalist entrepreneurs, the latter were actually in the majority.[55] The absence of regulations within the trade "encouraged the unqualified and the unscrupulous, the mere adventurers and the speculators, to enter the field of printing and publishing."[56] There were commercial motives behind all kinds of books, even religious propaganda. Johann Eberlin von Günzburg, known for the Protestant pamphlets he produced during the Reformation, complained about printers who thought only of profit and switched to printing for papists if they did not find reformist literature profitable enough.[57]

It is probably fair to say that many printers who published cookbooks had more knowledge of the market than of cuisine. Some printers published a single text in different guises over long periods; others compiled and combined various texts in almost endless combinations to create new products. One example from Germany illustrates some of the possibilities available to printers. In 1597, Anna Wecker's cookbook *Ein köstlich new Kochbuch* (An exquisite new cookbook) was published in the small German town Amberg. The book was a success, and the local printer produced new editions in 1598 and 1600. In 1605, the powerful publisher Ludwig König in Basel discovered the book and had it printed in a new format, but he used the same title and the name Wecker, which was a well-known Basel family name due to the fame of Dr. Johann Jacob Wecker, Anna's husband. Two years later, the small Amberg printer published another edition that included a new chapter with recipes for pâtés. König saw this, and in his next edition, released in 1609, he added an extra chapter with pastry recipes. Nothing new happened with the book until 1620, when König suddenly published Wecker again, but this time with a slightly revised title, *New köstlich und nutzliches Kochbuch* (New exquisite and useful cookbook). In this edition, only half of the recipes were from Wecker's original. König had added the greater part of another cookbook, *New kunstreich und nützliches Kochbuch* (New ingenious and useful cookbook, 1611), by Johann Deckhardt, a cook who had worked in a princely household in Dresden, Saxony. But Deckhardt's name does not appear on the title page or anywhere else in the book; Wecker is still named as author, probably for publicity reasons. After the Thirty Years War, when French influence was very strong in Germany, a new edition was printed by the König family printing office, with an appendix called *Parisische Küchenmeister* (Parisian chef), which was actually a translation of the classic French *Les délices de la campagne* (Rural delights), by Nicolas de Bonnefons, originally published in 1654. But the Königs had not discovered the French book and provided a translation. They just used a translation by Georg Greflinger that had been published in Germany two years earlier.[58]

PUBLICITY AND AUTHORS' NAMES

The increasing commercial interest in book publishing strengthened the need for publicity and marketing. This lead to the emergence of title pages. Many old manuscripts just started at the top of a page (or sometimes even in the middle of a page), and the first words were later referred to as the work's title. At the end of the book, the author or scribe often put his name and sometimes also the place and the date the manuscript was finished. Over the years, this information was gradually expanded—particularly after the introduction of modern printing—and eventually moved to a separate leaf at the beginning of the book. A short title was sometimes put on the first leaf, but titles were soon enlarged with more details and functioned in many ways as advertisements. At the bottom of the page were the name of the printer and the address of the bookshop where the book could be purchased.

With these developments, the name of the author became a potentially important factor, as a famous name gave authority to the work and promoted sales. Although the names of some cooks appeared in late medieval cookbook manuscripts, the majority of them were anonymous. But from the sixteenth and seventeenth centuries, the names of authors became more important, and the authors of many cookbooks were introduced as court cooks or prominent administrators. This element increased the sales potential of cookbooks to such an extent that it became part of the marketing, even if the claims that were being made were not true. There are no documents, for example, confirming that Meister Sebastian was private cook for an emperor, that Joseph Cooper was "chiefe Cook" to King Charles I, or that Maestro Giovanni had worked in the kitchens of the Vatican.[59]

This admiration for experience at royal and princely courts was taken to a comical extreme when the publisher of a small, old German cookbook presented Platina as the author and even gave the intellectual librarian the title of chief steward for Pope Pius II. In another edition of this book, the text was presented (falsely) as the work of several authors: Platina; Apicius, the alleged author of the only known Roman cookbook; Varro, a Roman politician who wrote about agriculture; and Baptista Fiere, an Italian physician who analyzed the nature of foodstuffs.[60]

Court cooks and administrators with experience as cooks were popular as authors through the seventeenth and eighteenth centuries. As late as 1846, a small cookbook printed in Norway was presented as having been written by a cook for Karl Johan, the king of Sweden and Norway. Documents in the palace archives in Stockholm, however, show that the cook in question was a mere *apprenti de cuisine* in the kitchens of Queen Désirée, who had her own household administration, separate from the king's.[61]

One way to emphasize the importance of an author was to print his portrait in the book. In the sixteenth and seventeenth centuries, we find such portraits only in Italy and England, but later, prominent authors from several countries had their portraits on frontispieces (figure 5).

In the nineteenth century, many cookbooks credited famous restaurant chefs, but not necessarily because they were the real authors. The value publishers placed on this profession at the time is demonstrated in a story told by the Italian Pellegrino Artusi, author of *La Scienza in cucina e l'arte di mangiar bene* (Science in the kitchen and the art of eating well), published in 1891. When more than fifty thousand copies of this bestseller had been printed, he revealed that the book had initially been rejected by publishers. When he first presented his manuscript, he was just an unknown author of obscure literary studies, and one of the publishers he approached said that he would have printed the book if the author had been Dancy, one of the most popular restaurateurs in Florence.[62] This was the start of the era of celebrity restaurant chefs and maîtres d'hôtel, such as August Escoffier in London and Paris, Karl Šroubek in Prague, Charles Ranhofer and Oscar

FIGURE 5. Portrait of Swedish physician and writer Charles-Emil Hagdahl in the 1891 edition of his cookbook, *Kokkonsten som vetenskap och konst* (Cooking as science and art). The idea of a portrait was probably suggested by the publisher.

Tschirky in New York, and Victor Hirtzler in San Francisco—all of whom were cookbook authors.

ANONYMITY AND PSEUDONYMITY

The interest in famous names runs parallel to a tradition of anonymity and pseudonymity. There were writers outside the culinary profession who did not wish to reveal their identities. Prominent examples from the seventeenth century are the French horticulturalist and courtier Nicolas de Bonnefons, the Alsatian abbot Bernardin Buchinger, and the Antwerp church official Frans van Sterbeeck. Sterbeeck, known for a botanical work on mushrooms, *Theatrum fungorum* (1675), had also contributed a selection of mushroom recipes to a cookbook. He was very unhappy when his name was made known because he did not want to be seen as a cookbook author.[63] We are, in other words, back to the "lowly subject" of cooking described in the preceding chapter. When the Norwegian celebrity Peter Chr. Asbjørnsen—a folklorist, scientist, and public forester—published a cookbook pseudonymously, word quickly spread about the true identity of the author. A Swedish translation was printed, and a reviewer in Stockholm wrote, "When it was published in Norway, it caused a certain stir because people found it difficult to understand that a man, and an esteemed scholar at that, could devote his time to something as ordinary as cooking."[64]

In his discussion of anonymity, Gérard Genette mentioned Boileau, La Rochefoucauld, La Bruyère, and Madame de La Fayette and described them as anonymities of convenience, used by persons of high estate who would have thought it demeaning to sign so common a work as a book in prose.[65] A similar attitude was possibly the reason many of the French intellectuals in the eighteenth century who wrote prefaces in cookbooks did not sign them.

The German art historian Karl Friedrich von Rumohr published his 1822 cookbook under the name of his private cook, Joseph König. In the preface, which he signed with his own name, he pointed out the low status cookery had at the time. Scientists, poets, and economists have been interested in the improvement of agriculture, he wrote, "but they are shamefully silent about cookery, which in fact is the preparation of the products they are so eager to promote. These noble philanthropists would never dare to appear as inventors of soups for the poor."[66]

When so many people tried to hide their involvement with the lowly subject of cookery, the logical question is why they contributed at all. The most obvious answer is money, because it is reasonable to imagine that not all of them had a satisfactory personal economy, and they were likely remunerated by publishers for their work. There may of course have been other factors—perhaps some authors contributed as a form of jest within a circle of friends—but we will probably never get the full answer to this intriguing question.

Women cookbook authors—with a few exceptions—only hesitantly entered their names on title pages of works published during the closing years of the seventeenth century and the beginning of the eighteenth. Women authors were often identified simply by their initials or by expressions such as "By a Lady." The title page of the 1697 culinary appendix to the Countess of Troppau and Jägerndorff's medical recipe book had only "Von einer Hoch-adelichen Persohn" (by a member of the high nobility).[67] At around the same time, Maria Sophia Schellhammer published a cookbook under the label "Von einer Vornehmen Dame" (by a distinguished Lady). In the second edition, this was substituted for the initials M. S. S. G. C., which stood for Maria Sophia Schellhammer née (*Geboren*) Conring. Only in a later book did she admit to the authorship.[68] In the eighteenth century, Susanna Egerin, Maria Elzberg, E. Smith, and Hannah Glasse—a German, a Swede, and two Englishwomen—hid themselves in the early editions of their books behind the initials S. E., M. E. B., E-S-, and the phrase "By a Lady."[69] In Denmark, the first cookbook compiled by a woman was called simply *En høyfornemme madames kaagebog* (A most distinguished lady's cookbook), published in 1703.[70]

It should be pointed out that the authorial designation "By a Lady" was not limited to cookbooks, at least not in Great Britain. Between 1750 and 1830, the majority of English novels were published without attribution, and three-quarters of them were labeled "By a Lady" or "By a young Lady."[71] A common interpretation of this anonymity is that it was imposed. Elizabeth Ezell writes that this has been seen as "a direct response to gender conflicts within a culture, an authorial device which acts as a disguise for the protection of the writer, a masking device which indeed creates the physical space on the title page for her to be a poet or an essayist within the pages of a published text."[72] But Ezell demonstrated that this was not necessarily the case, because if women authors had wanted to hide their gender, they could have opted for full anonymity or a male pseudonym, such as Mary Ann Evans did when she published her novels under the pen name George Eliot in the nineteenth century. The phrase "By a Lady" may have been used in some cases as a commercial strategy, a theory supported by the fact that many of the novelists using this expression were actually men.

On the other hand, some cookbooks with the names of men on the title page might in fact have recipes originally written by women. In the preface of a book from 1577 by the schoolteacher Georgius Mayr, the author mentioned that he got the recipes from ladies in Augsburg.[73] The recipes are very similar in language and style, so Mayr probably decided or was instructed by his publisher to edit them according to a uniform system and orthography. Similar editing was done by Gervase Markham in *The English Housewife* (1615), where the medical and culinary recipes were taken from various sources, among them a manuscript allegedly written by a woman.[74]

It seems that certain male elites had problems accepting that women might be authors of culinary works. During a conversation at a dinner in London in 1778, the subject of cooking was introduced, and Dr. Samuel Johnson—according to his biographer, James Boswell—uttered the famous words: "Women can spin very well, but they cannot make a good book of Cookery."[75] A publisher present at the dinner remarked that Hannah Glasse's *The Art of Cookery* had actually been written by Dr. Hill, a male physician, a false statement that was later repeated by other learned Englishmen.

In the nineteenth century, female writers were held in high esteem, especially in the growing bourgeoisie, where housewives were household managers and wanted recipes adapted to their situation. Many housewives didn't trust men when it came to instruction in daily cooking; they felt women were more experienced with the sort of dishes they needed to prepare. This was probably the reason the title of *Il cuoco bolognese,* which was published in 1857, was changed to *La cuciniera bolognese* when it was reprinted in 1874. *Cuoco* means male cook, and *cuciniera* means female cook.[76]

Just as had been the case in British fiction, male authors who wrote cookbooks in the nineteenth century pretended to be women. The most extraordinary example is the English actor Charles Selby, who published a cookbook in 1860 under the name Tabitha Ticklecloth and even appeared in drag in a photograph on the frontispiece.[77] But there were many others. The French writer Horace Raisson, who had published *Code gourmand* for the male gourmets, used the alias Mademoiselle Marguerite for *Le Cordon Bleu, ou Nouvelle cuisinière bourgeoise;* the German publisher Carl Ferdinand Philippi used the pseudonym Regine Hofmann; the Danish bookseller Søren Fredrik Helm-Petersen printed cookbooks under the female name Laura Adeler; and in Norway, Johan Halmrast, a successful author of popular stories, chose the name Marie Larsen, very much an ordinary housewife's name, for his compilation of recipes (all of which had been printed previously).[78] All these male authors probably thought their books would have a better chance of selling if people believed they were written by women. This practice was taken a step further when compilers of recipes used pseudonyms with the obvious intention of making customers believe that the books were written by famous authors. In Sweden, where one of the most popular cookbook authors in the nineteenth century was Gustafva Björklund, there were suddenly books published under names such as Gustafwa Berglund and Gustafa Björkström.[79] In Russia, after Elena Molokhovets published the successful *Gift to Young Housewives* in 1861, a flood of plagiarisms followed. She had published the first edition anonymously, but to protect herself, she started to use the initials of "E. M . . . ts" on later editions. But this did not stop the copycats. Shortly thereafter, a book with the title *Contemporary Gift to Young Housewives* came out signed "E. M . . . n." When she started to give her whole name on the title page, books followed with titles such as *Precious Gift to Young Housewives, New Gift to Young Housewives,* and *Complete Gift to Young Housewives,* with authors such as Morovich, Malkovets, and Morokhovtsev, printed with a similar typography.[80] In Germany, where Henriette Davidis had great success, cookbooks that she had not written were published under the name H. Davitis and H. Davithis.

The plagiarists described in the previous paragraph were in many ways the successors of the seventeenth-century Grub Street tradition, the pejorative term the English gave to hack writers for hire, so named after the street in London where many of them lived.[81] But the plagiarists were not only English. Full of disgust, Voltaire called French representatives of this profession "the riff-raff from the attics of literature who barked to gain a penny."[82] An eighteenth-century German critic labeled them "word hackers" and described their work as "factory writing" and "scrawl cookery."[83] In the nineteenth century, they made money in the culinary genre all over Europe.

Cookbooks are often collections of recipes that have been compiled and edited rather than creative works written by single individuals. Many family cookbook manuscripts were expanded and revised through generations with new recipes added from relatives and friends, primarily women. There is a rich material of this sort in archives and libraries, not least in Great Britain, where manuscripts have been digitized and studied during the last decades by scholars such as Margaret Ezell, Sara Pennell, Wendy Wall, and others.[84]

For the printed literature—the main focus in this study—the contributors represent a wider variety of experiences and backgrounds. They include printers, editors, publishers, booksellers, household managers, professional cooks, housewives, householders, restaurateurs, innkeepers, and domestic science teachers but also gardeners, farmers, physicians, scientists, scholars, social reformers, and professional writers, not only of nonfiction but also of novels, poetry, and short stories. Apart from trained cooks and restauranteurs, few of these—if any—were qualified as professionals. They had different degrees of knowledge and expertise, and many of them were more writers than cooks. The texts of their cookbooks came into existence as a result of various processes that we will take a closer look at in the following chapters.

PART TWO

The Text and Its Form

3

The Origin and Early Development of Modern Cookbooks

The history of the modern European (or Western) cookbook goes back to the end of the thirteenth and the beginning of the fourteenth centuries, when manuscripts with predominantly short and condensed recipes appeared in several languages.[1] Between 100 and 150 recipe collections have survived from the late Middle Ages, and they do not seem to have been directly influenced by earlier cookbooks. Consequently, these books may be seen as a new form of culinary literature.

The oldest known collections of written culinary recipes were found on three Mesopotamian clay tablets from 1700 BCE, inscribed in the Akkadian language in cuneiform script.[2] Although the thirty-five recipes on the tablets are the only examples from this period, they prove that such recipes, with instructions for food preparation, have a long history and also tell us that recipe collections were made at a very early time.[3] More than a millennium later, Greek authors wrote technical cookbooks in prose and gourmet recollections of tasty dishes in verse. Some fragments from these books have survived through quotes in later literature, primarily in *Deipnosofistae* (The sophists' dinner), the "anthology" by Athenaeus from the late second century CE.[4] From Roman antiquity, we have one cookbook traditionally attributed to a man by the name of Apicius, but we don't know anything about the real author (or authors) or when the final version was completed; the book is known today through two manuscripts from the ninth century.[5] There are various recipes in several household and agricultural books from antiquity, mainly on how to store and preserve agricultural products, how to make wine and olive oil, and how to prepare sauces and relishes.[6] Certain recipes are also found in Anthimus's dietetic work from the sixth century and in the medieval "health rules" that followed the *Regimen sanitatis* tradition, but these are generally considered to belong to a different genre than cookbooks.[7] Recipes for the preservation of foodstuffs were included in certain medieval texts, such as the Greek *Geoponika* from tenth-century Byzantium[8] and Pier de' Crescenzi's book on agriculture from around 1200.[9] But the French scholar Bruno Laurioux considered the culinary texts of the fourteenth century to have a form that was completely new compared to that of earlier recipes.[10] Laurioux also found that these works showed very little influence from the Arab texts that were circulating in southern Europe at the same time the first manuscripts in European languages appeared, even if a diffusion of certain Arab culinary practices has been documented in the late medieval period and the names of certain dishes—particularly in Spanish cuisine and early Spanish cook-books—have clear Arabic roots.[11]

EARLY MANUSCRIPT RECIPE COLLECTIONS

The more than one hundred surviving medieval recipe collections have important differences. Most of them—with some notable exceptions—are anonymous and do not mention the author's intentions. Some of the manuscripts are luxuriously elaborated, while others are simple copies in bad handwriting and without ornamental elements. There is a wide variation in how the material is organized and in the use of paratexts. The overwhelming majority of them are in codex form, what we would call a book today. Used for letter-writing, record-keeping, and note-taking at school, the codex became popular during the last centuries of antiquity, particularly for Christian texts, and established itself as the dominant book form during the early Middle Ages.[12] It replaced the earlier papyrus roll (scroll), but the roll did not disappear completely in the medieval period. Three of the surviving cookbook manuscripts from that time were actually written on parchment rolls (papyrus was no longer in use): two copies of the English text *Forme of Cury* and one copy of the French *Le viandier*.[13] A few of the other codices may originally have existed in the form of rolls.[14]

The number of recipes in the existing manuscripts varies from one to more than two hundred, but 60 percent have more than fifty recipes. The manuscripts are all compilations copied from earlier texts or recorded from oral communications by cooks; some recipes probably go back to culinary practices in the thirteenth century or even earlier. Certain manuscripts originating in the same geographical area use the same source or texts, which can be traced back to the same source; consequently, it is possible to group certain manuscripts in each language into "families" or "traditions" with similarities in vocabulary, technical expressions, and ingredients.[15]

The manuscripts in German and English dominate, with each making up more than one third of the total, while those in French, Italian, and other languages are less numerous. Even if certain geographical differences can be pointed out—for example, more lard is used in the north of Germany, and more oil is used in the south of France—one can hardly consider the manuscripts as representative of national or regional cuisines. But how international or cosmopolitan the recipes are and how strong the similarities are across borders is a subject open for discussion.[16]

In addition to the culinary recipes, some of the manuscripts contain other types of material, such as recipes for confections and medical remedies, instructions for the service at table, suggestions for menus, and practical hints for householders and chief stewards on big estates and in princely courts. This broadening of the contents was a tendency that became much more pronounced in the sixteenth and seventeenth centuries.

THE INCREASING IMPORTANCE OF LITERARY MODES

Why did this new culinary literature surface at that particular time? There does not seem to be a direct link to earlier culinary literature, so we must search for the explanation in the important developments that took place in the preceding centuries, relating to economy, demography, literacy, book production, and court culture.

During the High Middle Ages, towns and cities emerged and grew all over Europe, commerce flourished, and there was a tendency toward a greater specialization in public administration and in production of material goods. In this new context, a shift in modes of communication began. From around 1100, there was a move away from oral modes and toward literary modes, or as historian Michael Clanchy put it, "from memory to written record."[17]

Oral and memorial modes were still important in church sermons and liturgy, in university lectures, and even in business and public administration, and it is worth keeping in mind Brian Stock's observation that the change in this period "was not so much from oral *to* written as from an earlier state, predominantly oral, to various combinations of oral *and* written."[18] The main point, however, is there was an increased production of documents of all sorts during the twelfth and the thirteenth centuries; in France, for example, there was "an astonishing acceleration in book production in the thirteenth century."[19] German scholar Michael Giesecke pointed out that a change in the balance between the communication forms occurred no later than the thirteenth century, when an expansion in the use of written form (skriptographische Medien) occurred in social contexts.[20]

The general tendency to rely increasingly on written records was evident in many fields. In business and commerce, this happened because transactions gradually became more complex, and the same was true for public administration and legal matters. On big estates, where new systems of accountable management were introduced, the use of script became a necessity. In England, more than thirty medieval treatises have survived from the thirteenth and fourteenth centuries with texts on husbandry, accountancy, and conveyancing. In Germany, city doctors had handbooks demonstrating the treatment of wounds and other medical and surgical practices. In several European countries, there were special works for the growing number of artisans in towns that gave recipes for new colors for dyers and the latest models of clothes for tailors. The written record even found its way into the day-to-day affairs of daily life for certain more privileged groups.[21]

During this period, book production became established as a commercial enterprise. Beginning in the fifth century, the greater part of book production was monastical, but by the twelfth century, as the appetite for books grew, the monastic scribes were no longer able to keep up with the demand. As early as the end of the eleventh century, there is evidence that monasteries farmed out piecework to scribes outside the community, and in the mid-thirteenth century, there were more scribes in commercial enterprises than in monasteries. By 1400, a separate commercial book production was in place, and it was soon accompanied by an organized book trade.[22]

Some of the medieval crafts could not be taught or developed within monasteries. Consequently, from the twelfth century, instructional handbooks were produced by royal and princely courts, which were in possession of both wealth and professional expertise. At the courts, there were various specialists, such as hunters, falconers, physicians, surgeons, astrologists, chief cooks, and kitchen administrators, who could write or translate books on particular subjects.[23] Quite a few early cookbooks are allegedly products of such a court culture, where a greater refinement—not least in the cuisine—developed after 1100. The tasks of the different kitchen officials became diversified, and these employees were organized in a hierarchy within the household, as described in chapter 1. Cooks began to use a greater variety of spices and other ingredients as a consequence of a greater diversity in preparations and cooking techniques. This was typical in the palaces and big estates of the royalty and aristocracy, who were beginning to take more pleasure from food and drink. This attitude suffered many attacks from moralists, who stressed that gluttony was one of the seven capital sins in the church doctrine. Nevertheless, the new culinary refinement continued in the palaces of secular as well as ecclesiastical princes and dignitaries. And this refinement was not limited to royalty and the high nobility. The ideas spread to the lower regional gentry and to an expanding and wealthy urban patriciate, which not only had beautiful residences but also represented a new cultural elite.[24] Some German cookbooks may have come from such groups as landed gentry and urban bourgeoisie, although it is impossible to identify the social environment of all the manuscripts.[25]

The move toward a society where literary modes were increasingly dominant would not have been possible without qualified work by literate laymen. From the sixteenth century, individuals in urban centers used the written word for testaments, correspondence, family history, and more. Even if literacy was still limited to a small segment of the population at this point, it was increasing. This was accompanied by an increase in the number of books in the vernacular compared to works written in Latin. In European cities, schools were established that gave education not only in Latin and liberal arts but also in calculation and writing in local languages.[26] By the seventeenth century, book learning had spread from the clerical elite to both the aristocracy and the expanding middle class. More and more laypeople owned books, and these texts were on subjects not only within their professional spheres but also within their domestic spheres.[27] The great majority of new practical handbooks were written in the vernacular.[28]

Increased literacy did not imply that people from different social or professional groups read the same books. Malcolm Parkes proposed a distinction between three kinds of literacy.[29] The first is that of the "professional" reader, the scholar. Universities in the thirteenth century, beginning with Bologna, Oxford, Cambridge, and Salamanca, followed by many others all over Europe, were relying more and more on written texts for education and research. Even primary schools, where young boys learned to read and write, became dependent on books, particularly on the reading primer, one of the most common and simple books in production in England during the High Middle Ages and into the age of printing.[30] Parkes's second group of literacy was that of the "cultivated" reader—in other words, the literacy of recreation. There was a growth in the production of literary works, such as poetry and romances, but also of prayer books, like the books of hours that were particularly favored by the ladies of the aristocracy. Finally, Parkes listed the literacy of the "pragmatic" reader, who had to read or write in the course of transacting business. Books in this group included medical books for doctors, legal works for lawyers, nautical manuals for seafarers, books on commerce and bookkeeping for merchants, and management treaties for administrators of big households.[31] All these types of works belong to the literature of *artes mechanicae*, classified by certain scholars as one of the groups of medieval literature, beside those of *artes liberales* and *artes magicae*.[32] Some of these works were in recipe form, which Gerhard Eis called the primary form (*Grundform*) of medieval prose.[33] Medical recipes in Latin have been documented in Germany as early as around 800, but from the eleventh century onward, most of these recipes were written in the vernacular. In other words, the recipe genre was already established when the first cookbooks appeared, around 1300. The growth of all the different types of practical handbooks, which shared knowledge normally taught orally in the workshops and ateliers of craftsmen and other professionals, was probably indicative of the need for written texts that emerges whenever things become more complex.

Did the written recipe represent a step forward, a sign of progress when compared to oral knowledge? This question is part of a discussion that goes back to antiquity, when, according to Plato, Socrates expressed his lack of belief in, and even his distrust of, writing.[34] The question has been commented on in numerous cookbooks through the centuries, which reveals that there was an awareness of the difficulty of putting practical knowledge into words. As recently as the mid-nineteenth century, the talented Norwegian autodidact Hanna Winsnes, who taught the art of cookery to young girls in her own kitchen, found it necessary to emphasize her point of view on the matter in the introduction to her household book: "I certainly know that written communication can not make up for personal instruction."[35] In the seventeenth century, an English cooking school teacher pointed out the same in a book on confectionery: "For, as the Old Saying is, it is Use that makes Perfectness, and no Person can do that with a Pen, that your seeing and observing shall do; for, if so, then all Arts would be easily obtained." But then she added that the main aim of the book was "to help your memories."[36]

Books—handwritten or printed—are no doubt mnemonic aids, an important point that has been observed in several professions outside of the culinary. In his study of quantification in the West, Alfred W. Crosby quoted sergeants, who saw a need to be literate, "For it is harde by Memorie to discharge so many things wel as he shall be charged withal."[37] This is confirmed by the botanist Otto Brunfels, who in the sixteenth century considered books to be a help for the memory and found that written or printed knowledge ("Verschriftung des Wissen") was better suited to transmitting cultural experiences to the next generations than oral communication.[38] Music saw a similar shift in the late Middle Ages. Written notation to indicate rhythmic patterns was introduced in the thirteenth century, and as the musicologist Anna Maria Busse Berger noted, over "the next two centuries, as musical culture gradually evolved from one that was largely oral to one that was written, more precise rhythmic notations were developed to accomodate the increasingly complex polyphonic innovations of musicians."[39]

COOKING INSTRUCTION, FROM ORAL TO SCRIPT

If the emergence of modern European cookbooks can be explained as a need to put knowledge into written words in the increasingly literate climate of the High and Late Middle Ages, an important question is: How did this transfer of practical knowledge into script happen? Before recipes were written down, the knowledge existed as plans for culinary preparation in the heads of the people responsible for cooking. Most of this knowledge was probably the result of trial and error, like so many steps forward in the history of human civilization. The culinary use of fire—which was fundamental in the development of the human art of cooking[40]—has gone through several technological stages, from the first mixtures of water and crushed grains cooked on embers to today's focaccia, its name based on the Latin *focus,* meaning "fireplace." Many similar dishes have their origins thousands of years ago; simple preparations evolved more or less spontaneously, independent of one another, and passed through various forms of refinement before becoming lefse, chapatti, pita, and tortilla.

The next step, into spoken words, came with culinary instruction, where oral tradition has always been fundamental. We tend to forget that words are not only *written* words. As Thomas Hobbes wrote in the chapter "On Speech" in *Leviathan,* "The Invention of Printing, though ingenious, compared with the invention of Letters, is no great matter. . . . But the most noble and profitable invention of all was that of SPEECH."[41] Before the first letters or symbols were carved in stone, cut in wood, or drawn in clay, words were exchanged between people in daily conversations and oral word constructions were developed for various purposes: religious hymns and cosmological myths, ethical laws and regulations, entertaining songs and stories. Famous historical figures are known for texts they did not write down themselves. Socrates never wrote anything, nor did Buddha, Jesus, or Muhammed.

In practical professions, instructions were passed on from master to apprentice, and in the case of home cooking, from mother to daughter. The techniques of cooking were imparted by the fire and over the kitchen pot. What happened during this instruction? We have no sources that describe such activities in prehistoric times, but, just as it is in the present, it was probably a combination of words and acts. The advantage of this kind of instruction is that the words accompany the acts and explain them. It is of course possible to imagine such instruction being nonverbal, but then the reasons behind the acts would be absent, and the reasoning is a very important didactic element, both for understanding and remembering. On the other hand, the words used for instruction would not by themselves be enough to explain a culinary preparation. If they were written down exactly as they were spoken in the kitchen, with interruptions, questions, and repetitions, they would probably not have the same pedagogical effect as they had when accompanied by acts and would certainly not constitute a recipe as we know it. "Writing," Jack Goody stated, "is not simply added to speech as another dimension, it alters the nature of verbal communication."[42]

The written recipe is normally produced at a desk rather than by the fire (even if it is later used in the kitchen). More important is that the writer who records the recipe, if he is not documenting it only as a personal aide-memoire, must position himself in relation to another addressee, not a pupil or a daughter by his or her side, but rather a reader or readers, who are invisible to the writer. Therefore, the writer must bring into the recipe all the things and acts a pupil would be able to observe directly but that cannot be seen by the reader, such as utensils, ingredients, and the physical actions necessary to handle them. We are talking about two different "utterances" in Mikhael Bakhtin's terms, as set forth in his essay about speech genres.[43] Both utterances, the oral and the written, have the same goal—that is, instruction— but only the written utterance has a form that corresponds to our conception of what a recipe is like. Two German Romanists described the difference between oral and written communication as a difference between a near and a distant language.[44] The difference is characterized by opposite pairs, such as dialogue versus monologue, spontaneity versus reflexion, affective participation versus objectivity, and less versus more complexity. The philologist Trude Ehlert studied early German culinary texts from this point of view, and she concluded that none of them express orality, which in her opinion is proof that the cooks themselves did not write the recipes down; she believed that physicians probably did the writing. But even if her observations of the actual manuscripts are correct, we don't know what happened between the kitchen and the writing desk. Is there really an insurmountable gap between oral instruction and script? "Each utterance," Bakhtin wrote, "is filled with echoes and reverberations of other utterances in which it is related by the communality of the sphere of speech communication."[45]

Perhaps this may be understood also as a form of link between oral and written utterances. As a matter of fact, a study of early written recipes reveals certain features that are possible to interpret as "echoes" of the original oral instruction. One example is the syntactic structure, where main clauses follow each other in an additive way, a sequence corresponding to the step-by-step progression of a culinary preparation in a kitchen. Another characteristic element of early recipes—which still exists in several languages—is the use of verbs in the second person indicative or imperative, which is typical for a communicative function, a dialogue. This is a possible vestige of situations where a teacher says to a pupil, "Do this!" or, "You can do that." But even with oral echoes, the recipe formula already represented a literary elaboration compared with the words uttered in the kitchen. And in fact, Ehlert dismissed the use of the second person as oral because it was already the standard in medical recipes. This means that people who put early culinary recipes on paper may have used medical recipes as a model. However, the use of the second person may have been established in oral instruction in the kitchen before the first medical recipes were written down. Laurioux actually suggested that culinary recipes circulated orally before physicians wrote down their dietetic advice.[46]

Is it possible to imagine intermediary stages between oral instruction and written recipes? We know that cooks—just like other craftsmen—needed to keep many details in mind, and this required a good memory. Adam Fox observed that when such professionals did not have the means to store information on written records, "there were many alternatives available. Rhyming was one device which provided an aid to memory in innumerable contexts (prayers, spells and charms, moral advice, practical guidance)."[47] And Linda Voigts found examples of texts in bound form as a mnemonic aid in medieval medical literature: "Verse is often preferred for the communication of lists, as, for example, enumeration of the common thirty-two bloodletting veins."[48] This was a useful method for the practitioner in his work as well as in his instruction of others, and verses have also been used in old household books.[49]

There were other repetitive and fixed formulaic patterns used as mnemonic devices as well. One such text form in the Middle Ages were *sententiae*. These were brief proverb-like expressions, originally quotations from antique literature. As

Bruno Laurioux observed, some early medical and culinary recipes had similarities to *sententiae*. He explained the oral style of such texts in these words: "The basic process is the repetition: The uniform succession of stages, the stereotypical formulas, and the reiteration of ingredients in the same order further without doubt the memorization of the recipes, and the first recipes that were written down kept a trace of their usual mode of transmission."[50]

Some early recipes were little more than lists of ingredients, and they may first have been scribbled down on separate scraps of paper, the way housewives and others have done to this day. Notes of various kinds have also been found on other types of writing material. Besides (and before) the use of papyrus, parchment, and paper, notes were written on pieces of bark or wood, stone (slate), clay (both dry and wet), and above all on wax tablets, which were wooden or ivory boards with waxed writing surfaces.[51]

One interesting aspect relating to clay tablets used in the mid-second millennium BCE in Mesopotamia is that the writing on them was often for pedagogical use. Most traditions in this society (in religion, law, and practical professions) were transmitted orally, but texts were written down to facilitate memorization, which gave the tablets an ephemeral function. We don't know if this practice also applied to culinary recipes, because the recipes documented in Mesopotamia were not necessarily thought of as part of cookbooks but perhaps as religious instruction; the dishes were served to the gods in holy temples.[52]

Wax tablets were used in Rome during antiquity, a time when most important texts—legal and literary—were written on papyrus scrolls. There is a fresco from the first century CE in Pompeii showing a baker and his wife, he with a scroll of papyrus, she with a pair of wax tablets. The fresco aimed to show what a high status in society the couple had acquired, but Cornelia Roemer interpreted the different writing materials as an example of the different social roles of scrolls and wax tablets. The scroll demonstrated the education and position of the man (who at that point had become a magistrate), while the wax tablet was a symbol of the wife's responsibilty for household records. The tablets were more ephemeral and were thus used for accounts and other notes that might eventually be removed and substituted by others.[53] Athenaeus (who lived around 200 CE) wrote that it was custom at dinner parties for the host to be offered a little tablet (*grammateídion*) with a list of the dishes the cook planned to serve.[54] Whether such tablets were also used to note ingredients for a dish is possible, but we have no direct documentation of that. What we know from antiquity is that texts were used as an aid for oral activity; a written record was necessary to provide rhetoric patterns for orators, even if the speeches themselves were performed without a manuscript.[55]

Wax tablets did not disappear at the end of antiquity; they continued to be used into the Middle Ages. Michelle Brown called them the missing link in the history of writing. It seems that they were sometimes used to record texts that needed to

be memorized, such as liturgical formulae, another example of how orality continued to take precedence over script.[56]

But these notes also functioned as "drafts" in the production of books during
the Middle Ages. Paul Saenger pointed out that some authors had assistants who
"worked from an authorial text written on wax tablets or scraps of parchment."[57] In
other words, it is possible to envisage lists of ingredients being written down by
persons with a certain level of literacy—chief stewards in palaces and on big
estates, for example—who wanted to have them available as a form of aide-memoire for later use, when they could inform first the head of provisions and then the
(illiterate) cooks not of the preparation methods but of the ingredients needed for
a particular occasion. Laurioux called attention to a revealing passage in one of the
oldest French manuscripts, which probably had been copied from an original in
scroll form. The text stated that whoever wanted to serve in a respectable house
"ought to have everything on this scroll written down in his heart or in writing. If
he has not, he cannot work to the satisfaction of his master."[58]

An interesting passage in an early fifteenth-century Italian text by Agnolo Pandolfini about management of the family may also contribute to understanding the
origin of recipes. Pandolfini advised ladies hiring cooks for banquets to watch how
they work, question them, learn, and remember so that they knew what to do when
no cooks were available.[59] This may have resulted in literate ladies taking notes on
bits of paper or tablets. Sabina Welserin's manuscript cookbook from the mid-six-
teenth century contained a recipe that may have been based on such a note, written
down by Welserin after a conversation with a cook. The heading of the recipe reads:
"Anno domini 1548 the 25th day of January Kochmaister Simon, cook for the count
of Leuchtenberg, has taught me to make *sultzfisch* the following way."[60] The way
linguistic features gradually change in this note gives an idea of how certain recipes
may have found their form. The beginning is like a report: "He has first taken a pike
of 2 pounds." In the middle of the recipe, we find expressions such as "then one
makes" and "one must," but in the last phrases of the recipe, Welserin used the
imperative—the common form in sixteenth-century culinary recipes.

Isolated notes of this kind may well have circulated among housewives, householders, and chief stewards long before they were compiled into books.

MANUSCRIPT AND PRINT—CODIFICATION AND INNOVATION

Written recipes may have been used as aides-memoire, but did they lead to a codification that stopped culinary development? Simon Eliot and Jonathan Rose
stated, in their introduction to *A Companion to the History of the Book,* that
embodying the text may have had two contrary effects: "It becomes fixed, unlike
most oral performances. It can also be copied, though copying opens up the pos-

sibility of variations, intended or accidental."[61] There are, in fact, cookbook authors who suggest that the written word is valuable, not just as a mnemonic aid, but also as inspiration for new experiments. In the eighteenth century, the prolific French cookbook writer Menon acknowledged the importance of books for the cook: "His memory does not always provide him—at the moment when he needs it—with all the dishes he knows how to prepare." But Menon went a step further. Although he admitted that books couldn't replace experience in the kitchen, he stated that not only could they help cooks remember preparations but they could also give them new ideas: "Often a book will give inspiration to invent dishes one never had thought of."[62] In an essay on food and popular culture in the region around Bologna during the late nineteenth and early twentieth centuries, the historian Piero Camporesi pointed out that cookbooks in bourgeois homes were a means of innovation, which is in contrast to the preservation and reproduction of established dishes among the masses, who depended on oral tradition.[63] This corresponds to Walter J. Ong's suggestion that when knowledge is stored in a written text and one does not need to remember it, the mind gains a greater freedom for more original thought and new speculation.[64]

Scholars who have studied old culinary manuscripts have observed how they are in many ways "open books." Original recipes could be changed by copyists and compilers, who suggested variations and different combinations of ingredients and spelled out procedures with more pedagogical precision. It was a question not only of additions, however, but also of abbreviations and omissions. These modifications could be either intended or accidental, the result of ignorance or lack of attention or the result of inspiration from new oral traditions that in turn may have had their roots in other written texts. In this way, recipes are the result of a "textual makeshift job" (bricolage textuel).[65] But it is important to remember that every text was open to being rewritten because the idea of intellectual property did not yet exist.

The embodiment of texts is an even more important concept when discussing the printed books and leaflets that became so successful starting in the second half of the fifteenth century. Printing with movable type was a completely new way to copy texts; Lotte Hellinga described it as "a new technique that allowed books to be manufactured at a rate that caused amazement and delight."[66] The technology was an answer to the growing demand from an increasingly literate public. Nobody denies the obvious effects printing had; from the 1450s, books were available in far greater numbers than before. This was true for all kinds of books, including culinary recipe collections. The first cookbooks in Latin were printed in the 1470s; in Italian, French, and German in the 1480s; in English in 1500; in Dutch around 1510; in Catalan and Spanish in the 1520s; and in Czech and Polish in the 1530s. There has been much discussion about the importance of printing, particularly since Elizabeth Eisenstein's 1979 study of print as an "agent of change," in which she asked if the increase in the output of old texts after the advent of printing may have led to the formulation of new theories—for example, because printing created a greater possibility for cross-referencing.[67] The French book historians Lucien Febvre and Henri-Jean Martin had a more critical attitude and found that printing seemed to constitute an obstacle to new knowledge and new theories because it popularized traditional ideas and strengthened old prejudices.[68]

How does this apply to culinary literature? Early cookbooks were printed from old manuscripts and therefore in no way represented a new culinary development. If we look at the first hundred years of printing, it is correct that there were more copies of cookbooks available than previously, but until the 1540s, they were all based on a few old manuscripts. In Italy, one original text was the basis for three different titles; in Germany, only one of the existing fifty-five manuscripts by the end of the fifteenth century, *Küchenmeisterei*, was printed first in 1485 and then reprinted at least thirty-five times before new cookbooks appeared in print in the 1540s.[69] Consequently, the printed book did not constitute a development of culinary ideas. In fact, there had been a much more significant culinary development in fifteenth-century manuscripts, which introduced a new cuisine compared with that of the previous century. If there was a "Renaissance cuisine," it was established before the invention of printing. This is why book historians increasingly tend to point out that printing did not imply a sharp break with the scribal culture of the past. As David McKitterick put it, "The boundary between manuscript and print is as untidy chronologically as it is commercially, materially or socially."[70]

It is possible to see a process toward uniformity in the development of early printed cookbooks—a codification of certain traditions. It took a long time before new culinary texts were printed. However, it is necessary to see the bigger picture because, as Stephen Colclough noted, there was a "complex interweaving of manuscript and print culture in an age that we usually associate with the fixity of print."[71] First of all, the "open book" aspect did not disappear completely with printed texts. Many readers continued this tradition from the scribal culture into the sixteenth and seventeenth centuries; they made annotations in the margins of their printed books and filled in new information adapted to their personal situations and experiences. Some printed genres actually encouraged such comments; from the late seventeenth century, almanacs, for example, included blank pages for the reader to fill in,[72] a feature later adopted by cookbook publishers (figure 6). Readers of printed texts also picked out sentences and paragraphs that caught their special interest and copied them into their own notebooks, commonplace books, letters, diaries, and in the case of recipes, in their handwritten cookbooks.

Important to bear in mind is that the manuscript culture did not die out with printing, particularly not for collections of culinary recipes. Sabina Welserin's German manuscript is dated 1553; Ellinor Fettiplace's English manuscript, 1604.[73] And the collectors were not only women. John Evelyn, John Locke, and Kenelm Digby

No. 203. Cold Chili Sauce

One peck ripe tomatoes, chopped fine and drained, two cups chopped onions, two cups chopped celery, two cups brown sugar, three green peppers (use seeds from only one), one tablespoonful mustard seed, one-half cup salt, one quart vinegar.

1 Peck Tomatoes
2 Cups Onions
2 Cups Celery
2 Cups Brown Sugar
3 Green Peppers
1 Tablespoonful Mustard Seed
½ Cup Salt
1 Quart Vinegar

No. 204. Cucumber Relish

Pare large cucumbers (not ripe), cut them in halves and take out the seeds; then cut in thin slices and chop, using Cutter No. 1; strain off the water, season to taste with salt and paprika, and add a very little sugar and the same measure of vinegar as of cucumbers. Store in jars closely sealed.

No. 205. Cucumber Sauce

Take three dozen cucumbers, chop and put some salt over them; drain in a colander until the water is out; chop six onions and put with them one-half ounce each of black and white mustard seed, little salt and pepper, vinegar enough to make a little moist; no cooking required.

36 Cucumbers
6 Onions
½ Ounce Black Mustard Seed
½ Ounce White Mustard Seed

No. 206. Cucumber Pickles

Chop twelve large cucumbers without seeds or skins, four large green peppers and four large onions; add one-half cup salt, mix well and let it stand over night; in the morning drain and add one cup of chopped horseradish, one cup sugar, one teaspoonful celery seed, one tablespoonful mustard seed; mix all with cold vinegar.

12 Cucumbers
4 Green Peppers
4 Onions
½ Cup Salt
1 Cup Horseradish
1 Cup Sugar
1 Teaspoonful Celery Seed
1 Tablespoonful Mustard Seed
Vinegar

Grape-nuts Baked Custard. (June)

MEMORANDA (Served)

2 eggs, slightly beaten, 2 cups milk, scalded
¼ cup sugar — ½ tsp. vanilla
⅛ tsp. salt — ¾ cup grape-nuts

Combine eggs, sugar + salt. Add milk gradually, mixing thoroughly; add vanilla. Put about 1 tbs. grape-nuts in each custard cup; fill with custard. Place cups in pan of hot water. Bake in a slow oven (325°) 40–45 min., or until silver knife inserted comes out clean. Or bake in greased baking dish. Place dish in pan of hot water + baked at 325° about 1 hr. Serve plain with cream, or with sweetened crushed fruit sauce.

Grape-nuts Stuffed Egg Plant.
1 large eggplant — ⅔ cup grape-nuts
1 lb. chopped onions — ¼ " tomato pulp
½ tsp. salt — ¼ " chopped broiled bacon
⅛ " pepper — 1 egg, slightly beaten
2 tbs. bacon fat — ¼ tbs. grated Parm cheese

Parboil eggplant 5 min. Cut in halves lengthwise, scoop out center leaving shell 1" thick. Chop removed portion (about 4 c.) saute with onion, salt + pepper in bacon fat 10 min. Add the mix well then all remaining ingredients. Refill shells, sprinkle with a few additional grape-nuts, bake in hot oven 30 min. (Serves 6.)

were three prominent male recipe collectors in seventeenth-century England.[74] The manuscript cookbook tradition seems to have been most widespread in Germany, Scandinavia, Great Britain, and eventually North America. A Russian compiler and translator of cookbooks wrote around 1800 that unlike Europe, Russia had no tradition in writing down recipes, and there was therefore very little knowledge about old national dishes.[75]

Starting in the eighteenth century, recipe collecting was increasingly taken over by women. Handwritten cookbooks actually became a fashion within the upper classes at that time. A German culinary manuscript from 1785 informed readers that women should not be without such a work.[76] Many young girls prepared handwritten cookbooks before they got married and took charge of their own households. Those who didn't want to write one themselves could pay someone else to do it, just as was the habit before the arrival of printing.

But manuscript cookbooks were not always the result of one person's collecting or compiling. When Helle Schrøder sat down in the Danish town of Ringsted on June 13, 1692, and started her *Kaage-baag* (Cookbook), she had likely borrowed a manuscript from another person and probably copied it page by page.[77] Research has demonstrated that there exist two other similar manuscripts and that many of the recipes in Schrøder's book were printed in a cookbook published in Copenhagen in 1703.[78] However, a closer study of the four existing variants shows that none were directly copied from any of the others.[79] This implies the existence of one or more earlier manuscripts, or an urtext.

We know that manuscript cookbooks were the basis for several of the first printed books, but after the Gutenberg revolution, many handwritten books took recipes from printed books. This practice started early, a fact that has been demonstrated by the cookbook *Küchenmeisterei*. This book was printed in more than a dozen editions before 1500, and these printed copies coexisted with manuscripts of the same "family." An interesting question would be whether one of the manuscripts is the basis for the printed versions, but as a matter of fact, it may easily be the other way round. At least one early manuscript, now located in Zentralbibliothek Solothurn, in Switzerland, was copied from one of the incunabula editions.[80]

There are also manuscript cookbooks that were translated from printed cookbooks in other languages. There are several examples of these from language communities where few or no cookbooks had been printed. In Russia, the first printed cookbooks are from the end of the eighteenth century, but there is a Russian manuscript from the seventeenth century that is a translation of the Polish *Compendium ferculorum* (1682).[81] A Hungarian culinary manuscript from 1680—which is before the first cookbook was printed in this language—is a translation from a printed German cookbook.[82] In Poland, only one cookbook was printed between 1550 and 1700, but there is a manuscript cookbook from the seventeenth century based on an Austrian printed book that was first published in 1686.[83] A Norwegian

L'ÉCONOMIE DOMESTIQUE

Journal de la Cuisine

ET DE LA VIE PRATIQUE

A LA VILLE ET A LA CAMPAGNE

FIGURE 7. Title page of *Journal de la cuisine,* a culinary journal that was published by restaurant and hotel organizations in Brussels, Belgium, from 1891 to 1894. The culinary director of the journal was Jean de Gouy, a cookbook author.

manuscript from seventeenth-century Oslo was based on a German cookbook from 1598.[84]

The tradition of housewives making handwritten recipe collections for personal use continued into the nineteenth and twentieth centuries. Sources were still a mixture of printed books and handwritten recipes from friends, but an increasing number of recipes were taken from periodicals. The first culinary weekly was published in Stuttgart, Germany, in 1748,[85] and it was followed by journals edited by professional organizations of cooks and restaurateurs (figure 7). Gradually, recipes were also printed in weekly or monthly magazines aimed at female audiences.

Housewives used private, handwritten cookbooks in part to introduce more variation to their daily diet but mostly to help them surprise and impress guests when festive meals were given. However, there were handwritten books with a more traditional outlook. The German artist Ernst Barlach wrote about a recollection of the cookbook his mother made in 1899, when she wanted to transmit old family recipes to the next generation: "She wants no clinking royalty nor a publisher for her work, she will not think of new editions and tea table talk about it or that what she has written should be filtered through the press."[86]

There is no doubt that printed cookbooks became essential in the diffusion of culinary recipes. They were not only copied into handwritten books but also plagiarized, adapted, and translated, and they inspired new ideas and experiments within the genre. During the first five hundred years of printing, cookbook publishing grew from a minor business into a mass-market industry.

4

Printed Cookbooks

Diffusion, Translation, and Plagiarism

Starting in the 1460s, there was a sharp rise in the number of books after Gutenberg's invention of typographic printing spread from Mainz to the rest of Europe, so sharp that the number of books printed in the incunabula period (1450–1500) was much higher than the total number of known manuscripts produced before this date. However, cookbooks did not become an important part of the book industry during the first centuries of printing. The early history of printed books in fact reveals how insignificant the genre was. In 1480, more than a hundred cities and towns in Europe had printing presses, but only three of them had published a cookbook. Cookbooks represent less than 0.1 percent of the total number of (known) editions before 1500 and 0.15 percent in the sixteenth century.[1]

The spread of recipes in Europe began before the era of modern printing, but printed cookbooks make it easier to follow their geographical development. We don't always know if the recipes in these books express a real diffusion of new cooking—in other words, whether the recipes were actually tried out. For this reason, we ought to distinguish between diffusion of texts and diffusion of culinary practice. When foreign dishes were added to a cookbook, it may have been because they had already entered the country's national cuisine, but it could just as well have to do with the curriculum vitae of the author. Cooks traveled from country to country and picked up new preparations along the way. The Spanish court cook Martínez Montiño included many Portuguese recipes in his cookbook because he had been employed at the court in Lisbon. Marx Rumpolt in Mainz often referred to cooking in Central and Eastern Europe, where he grew up.[2] Foreign dishes also entered cookbooks in the form of translations of foreign books.

THE GEOGRAPHICAL DIFFUSION OF COOKBOOKS

Geographically, the first steps in the diffusion of printed culinary texts go from Italy to other countries in Europe. Platina's Latin book, *De honesta voluptate,* first printed in Rome (ca. 1470), Venice (1475), and Cividale del Friuli (1480), soon went to the presses in Leuven, Strasburg, Paris, Cologne, and Basel. Translations were published in Italian, French, and German, and part of the text was included in a Dutch book. Martino's recipes were never printed under his own name, but beginning in the early sixteenth century, they were used—almost unchanged—as the basis for printed cookbooks with the names of other authors on the title page. Most of these books were published by two enterprising Venetians who specialized in popular literature, romances of chivalry, and love stories but obviously also noticed the awakening interest in culinary literature among the wealthy Italian bourgeoisie. One of their books was translated into English in 1598 under the Italian title *Epulario,* but with the subtitle *The Italian Banquet.* The prominence of Italian cookbooks continued into the sixteenth century, when recipes from the impressive *Opera* (Work), by Bartolomeo Scappi—private cook to the pope—were published in Spanish and Dutch versions.

The Italian influence in the first period of printing had to do with the high position Italian culture generally occupied during the Renaissance. In France, the papal court in Avignon had been a gateway to Italian art, literature, and finance since the fourteenth century. Lyon, the second largest French city during the early modern period, was an international cultural center for merchants and bankers, many of them from Florence. In Paris, an important colony of Lombardians had settled and made themselves known within commerce and the arts. Even King Francis I employed prominent Italian artists, such as Leonardo da Vinci.[3]

A similar influence can be traced in other European countries, such as Hungary and Poland. In Bohemia, Italian food was so highly regarded that it became a target for moralists, who felt that foreign food habits undermined the old, local, and less extravagant traditions of the region. The Lutheran pastor Štelcar Želetavsky criticized "nobles, squires and burghers who now won't eat the old Czech way, but the Italian way ... [with] fifty or a hundred dishes or more ... on silvery and gilded plates."[4]

Yet despite the significant Italian impact on culinary culture, the first printed recipe books in Central and Eastern Europe seem more influenced by German cuisine than Italian, and the same is true for Denmark, where the first cookbooks were translations from German books. The reason for this may have been that publishers were more interested in a market among the growing bourgeoisie, which was generally more attached to German culture.

In the Netherlands, there were early influences from Italy as well as from Germany and France, but the foreign dishes referred to in cookbooks were primarily

Spanish. Strong commercial links were established between Dutch and Spanish merchants after King Philip II of Spain became the ruler of the Dutch provinces in 1556. In one manuscript from the late sixteenth century, a recipe was even named after the king's brutal military commander at that time, the Duke of Alba. Spanish dishes continued to be popular after the Dutch rebellion and the independence of the northern provinces in the seventeenth century.[5]

The overall cuisine in Europe was rather diversified until the mid-seventeenth century, when a new pattern appeared: influences began to arrive from France in courts and cities all over the continent. This new French cuisine, developed in the early seventeenth century, was first documented in England in the 1620s by John Murrell, who had visited France. He published a cookbook in which he presented twenty-two dishes with the epithet "French Fashion."[6] In France itself, the new cuisine was introduced in *Le cuisinier françois* (*The French Cook*), written by the chef La Varenne, who had experience working at the court of the Marquis of Uxelles. The book was published in 1651, and after a hundred years of nothing but reprints of old texts in France, its success was immediate, with seven editions produced during the first three years.[7]

THE FRENCH HEGEMONY

Le cuisinier françois was published in translation in England (*The French Cook,* 1653) and in an abridged version in Sweden (*Then frantzöske-kocken,* 1664), and other popular French books were published with similar titles in German (*Der Französische Becker, Koch und Confitirer,* 1665) and Italian (*Il cuoco francese,* 1680). In the eighteenth century, more translations—of the French authors Massialot, Menon, and Marin—followed in Poland, Russia, Holland, Scandinavia, England, and Italy. It is remarkable that during the seventeenth and eighteenth centuries, when several British and German philosophical works were published in French (including writings by Locke, Hume, and Kant), no foreign cookbook was translated into French.[8]

French cuisine dominated European cooking for centuries, and royalty and aristocracy in England, Prussia, and Italy employed French cooks. How can this hegemony be explained?[9] At the dawn of the 1600s, France was just emerging from a century of war and internal strife. But the country was the politically dominant power in Europe, with the largest army in the seventeenth century. And it was rich. By 1700, France's economy was twice that of England's, and the population was three times as big. The royal government, in the hands of powerful ministers, first Cardinal Richelieu and then Cardinal Mazarin, encouraged and patronized the arts during the seventeenth century. The Académie française (French Academy) was founded fifteen years before La Varenne's book was published. The apex of military, economic, and cultural strength was reached in the period after 1661, when King Louis XIV secured absolute power and the Château de Versailles became a symbol of French glory. The new French cuisine can be considered a part of the classicism that made its impact everywhere during the *siècle classique,* which was also a *siècle d'or.*

In Sweden, where close contact with France had been established during Queen Kristina's reign (Descartes moved to Stockholm on her invitation), three of the four cookbooks published in the seventeenth century were adaptations or translations of French works. In Portugal, the only cookbook of the eighteenth century was written by Lucas Rigaud, a French cook established at the royal court in Lisbon after thirty years of experience in courts in Paris, London, Turin, and Madrid.[10] In Italy, several French books were published in adapted translations with titles and subtitles such as "The Piedmontese cook perfected in Paris" and "The new Italian cook according to French taste."[11] The continuing influence of French cuisine can be easily detected by a look at the tables of contents in later Portuguese and Italian cookbooks.

The strong French presence is also documented in criticism and satire expressed in contemporary literature. The Danish scholar and playwright Ludvig Holberg made fun of the Francophiles in his comedy about a man named Hans Frandsen, who called himself Jean de France and said that he would have died of hunger if there hadn't been a French cook in Copenhagen.[12] In the comedy *Brigadir* (*The Brigadier*), written by Denis Fonvizin, a young man says that he wishes he had a wife with whom he could speak only French.[13] In Russia, as in several other countries, French was the preferred language of conversation among the elites during the eighteenth and nineteenth centuries. Several of the first cookbooks published in Russian were translations from French. One of the most prolific translators, the writer V. A. Levshin, was ridiculed by Pushkin, who called young epicures with their love for French food "fledglings of the Levshin school."[14] But Levshin's six-volume dictionary of cooking not only introduced French and other foreign dishes but also included a Russian cookbook with traditional recipes. He was well aware of the strong foreign influence in the aristocratic cuisine of the period, and in 1807, he published a pamphlet, a "message" or "letter" to the Francophiles, expressing his anti-French sentiment.[15]

France became a model for many German states after the Thirty Years' War ended in 1648. The nobility in Germany got a new lease on life; some historians talk of a "refeudalisation," with Germans imitating French court culture and etiquette. King Frederick the Great of Prussia boasted that he had not read one German book, and he even wrote a poem in French to his cook André Noël. French travelers in Germany had no problems with communication, Voltaire said, because only soldiers and horses spoke German.[16]

French influence in England was strong even before the Restoration and the return of the royal family from French exile after the Cromwell period. When Robert May finished the preface of his big cookbook, *The Accomplisht Cook,* at Englefields Manor in Leicestershire on January 24, 1659, he did not hide his knowledge of and experience with the most popular culinary tradition of that time: "As I lived in France and had the language, and have been an eye-witness of their Cookeries, as well as a peruser of their Manuscripts and printed Authours, whatsoever I found good in them I have inserted in this Volume."[17] French cooks were hired by English aristocrats, and French books were translated into English, but just as significantly, original French recipes were adapted by English women writers. They were skeptical about what they saw as expensive extravagance by the imported cooks, a point of view illustrated by the often-quoted Hannah Glasse: "If gentlemen will have French Cooks, they must pay for French tricks."[18] But in spite of the vitriolic nature of many of their comments, these women nonetheless contributed to the diffusion of French cuisine in England by simplifying the dishes and preparing them with less expensive ingredients.

In periods of war between the two countries, French influence in Britain met with difficulties, but the reputation of French cuisine never collapsed totally. After the Napoleonic Wars, the French delegation to the peace conference in Vienna demonstrated through the excellent dinners organized by the foreign minister Talleyrand that the French superiority in the culinary art was still evident. The famous chef Carême was hired by English and Russian monarchs, and the Paris restaurateur Antoine Beauvilliers proudly wrote in his 1814 cookbook *L'art de cuisinier* (The cook's art): "The French prided themselves when they saw the taste of their cuisine rule over the opulent states in Europe, from north to south, with the same majesty as their language and their fashion."[19]

In London, an essay was published the same year that described European cuisine from a historical perspective. The anonymous author regretted the lack of acknowledgment English authors gave to French works: "As it is common justice that every country should have the merit which is its due, we shall endeavour to restore to France her proper literature, and to recover for her artists an acknowledgement for those divine delicacies, of which the plagiarists of other countries would so unfairly deprive her."[20]

A persistent and growing interest in French culinary works (as well as the new gastronomic literature that was focused more on the pleasure of consumption than on production) was evident in Britain in the early nineteenth century. Margaret Dods opened her chapter on French cooking simply, with these words: "It will save much trouble to admit at once, that the French are the greatest cooking nation on earth."[21] French cuisine was regarded as more artistic than the cooking of other countries. John Ruskin, who had a high reputation as an art critic in the Victorian period, made a distinction in the culinary field between "the thoroughness of England" and "the art of France."[22]

In the second half of the nineteenth century, Auguste Escoffier turned modern restaurant cuisine—particularly in grand international hotels—into a culinary system that lasted into the twentieth century and inspired restaurant culture in all

FIGURE 8. Illustration from the 1891 edition of Charles-Emil Hagdahl's *Kok-konsten som vetenskap och konst.* The title of the dish is given in both Swedish (*kalfhufvud*) and French (*tête de veau*). The illustration is probably copied from a nineteenth-century French cookbook.

countries. The French stamp was seen very clearly on restaurant menus and in cookbooks, where the French names of dishes were used or put alongside the local names (figure 8). A new boost for French cuisine started in the 1970s with the emergence of *nouvelle cuisine,* supported by restaurant guides such as *Gault et Millau* and *Guide Michelin.* Most of the new celebrity cooks, such as Paul Bocuse, Michel Guérard, Roger Vergé, and Raymond Oliver, also published cookbooks, which were later translated into foreign languages.

This French hegemony, which started in the seventeenth century, has more recently met with competition from cuisines in other parts of Europe and the world, and French restaurant culture is no longer the sole star in international cuisine.

INCREASED COOKBOOK PRODUCTION
IN EUROPE AND ABROAD

By the end of the seventeenth century, a rich culinary literature existed in French, English, German, and Italian. Cookbooks in these languages made up 75 percent of the titles and 85 percent of all editions published before 1700. The rest consisted of a few books in Catalan, Czech, Danish, Dutch, Hungarian, Polish, Portuguese, Spanish, Swedish, and Latin. After the turn of the century, production increased constantly and exponentially, and 75 percent of the books published in the 1700s appeared in the second half of the century. This development must also be seen in light of the population growth in Europe, which was much stronger between 1750 and 1800 than between 1700 and 1750. The market was still totally dominated by the great Western powers at this time. English, German, and French books made up more than 80 percent of the total output of some 300 titles in 1200 editions published in the eighteenth century. The first Russian cookbooks were published in the late eighteenth century.[23] In the nineteenth century, cookbooks were published in Greek, Finnish, Icelandic, Norwegian, Slovak, Romanian, Bulgarian, Croatian, and Serbian as a part of the struggle for independence by nationalist groups in the old empires of the continent. Before this, the elites within these nations or national minorities had to resort to foreign books when they wanted to prepare dinners that were suitable to their social and economic status. These elites, however, were not particularly interested in local traditions, which consequently were almost invisible in the new cookbooks, where foreign-inspired dishes dominated.[24]

The European cookbook tradition spread to colonies established by the great European powers in America, Asia, Africa, and Australia.[25] Colonists brought books with them and subsequently had books sent to them from the mother country, but because the recipes often had to be adapted to local conditions and foodstuffs, many families had their own handwritten recipe collections, which were generally the responsibility of the housewife. We know of several such manuscripts in English from eighteenth-century North America (from the Penn, Washington, and Jefferson families, among others), and in Dutch and English from the nineteenth-century Cape Colony in the south of Africa.

North American printers had been active for more than a hundred years before they published the continent's first cookbook, in 1742, an edition of an English bestseller, *The Compleat Housewife*,[26] and editions of other English cookbooks followed.[27] But the import of English books continued, and after the American Revolution, "the new nation's publishing trade originated primarily in reprints of familiar works, not in the production of new books written by Americans."[28] This was also true for cookbooks,[29] and twenty years passed after the Declaration of Independence before a book was published with recipes for corn and dishes typical in the United States.[30]

The first cookbooks printed in Canada were, like those in the United States, imported titles. *La cuisinière bourgeoise* (1825) was a new edition of a French bestseller from the eighteenth century. *The Cook Not Mad* (1831) was originally published south of the border the year before. The first cookbooks written in Canada were *La cusinière canadienne* and *The Frugal Housewife's Manual*, both published in 1840, which also happens to be the year scholars now tend to define as the end of the early period of the book in Canada and the start of a new era.[31] But the American influence was still very strong; among the many cookbooks published up to 1877, only three were clearly local. That year, the situation changed with *The Home Cook Book* (1877), the best selling Canadian cookbook in the nineteenth century, and *Directions diverses données par La Rev. Mère Caron* (1878), the "signal event for French-language Quebec cookbooks in the last quarter of the nineteenth century."[32]

South of the Rio Grande, new Latin American states emerged from the former Spanish and Portuguese colonies, and these events were accompanied by a print revolution that involved "the disappearance of the printing monopolies, the end of the Inquisition, and the lifting of restrictions on the import of foreign books and printing presses."[33] Cookbooks from Europe had been common among the elites, but during the nineteenth century, the new republics printed their own cookbooks. The first Spanish-language cookbooks in Latin America were printed in Mexico in 1831, and they represented an important step in the process of national identity.[34] In Brazil—which was declared an empire in 1822—the first printed cookbook was published in 1843 with the title *Cozinheiro imperial* (The imperial cook). The recipes were basically from Portugal and other European countries. The text was attributed to R. C. M., who has never been identified, and there is a possibility that the recipes were compiled and edited by the publishers, two printers from Germany who ran a business in Rio de Janeiro producing mainly almanacs and all sorts of different handbooks.[35]

What is considered Australia's first cookbook had a title that clearly indicated the mother country of the colony: *The English and Australian Cookery Book* (1864). Many of the recipes were taken from other books, but this was the first cookbook to use native ingredients, such as kangaroo. The author, Edward Abbott, was born in the new continent, and he served as a member of the parliament of Tasmania, where the book probably was written.[36]

Cookbooks with Anglo-Indian cuisine, a combination of adapted Indian recipes and recipes the colonial elite brought with them to the subcontinent from Britain, were published in Calcutta, Madras, Bombay, and Allahabad before 1900. In Holland's Asian colonies, books were published in the mid-nineteenth century in Dutch and in the native languages of the Javanese centers Semarang and Batavia (present-day Jakarta).[37] The first printed cookbooks in South Africa are from the last decades of the nineteenth century, some of them containing recipes from England and Holland and others featuring adaptations of European cuisine to local conditions. The first book in Afrikaans was the 1890 *De Suid-Afrikaanse Kook-Koek-en-Recepteboek* (The South African cook, cake, and recipe book), by Elizabeth J. Dijkman, an immigrant from England who learned the Afrikaans language and compiled recipes she collected from the wives of Cape farmers.[38]

COOKBOOK TRANSLATIONS

Translations played an important part in the geographical diffusion of cookbooks, but before 1600, many translated books were published without professional editing. There were inevitably errors and misinterpretations, particularly when the translators did not know or understand the details of culinary practice.

There were also other difficulties. Platina discovered this when he translated Martino's Italian recipes into Latin. He wanted to write in the classical language of Cicero, but one of the problems he encountered was that many fish species were not described in the relevant literature from antiquity. He therefore often had to be content Latinizing the names used by common Italian people. What Martino called *lactarini,* Platina chose to refer to as *lacteolini,* explaining that it was because of the fish's milky white color. In other words, he defended his choice by giving an etymological explanation. When Martino called a certain crab *lione di mare* (sea lion), Platina described it as having the color of a lion and other similar traits and consequently gave it the Latin name *Leo marinus.*[39]

There is one dish that Martino simply called *salsicce* (sausages). In Platina's text, this became *Lucanicae* (a classical Roman sausage, allegedly from Lucania). Translations of the work published in the sixteenth century found different solutions. A Dutch translator called them *Ytaliaensche woorsten* (Italian sausages), which gives them a foreign air. But a German translator called them *Schibling,* the name of an established type of sausage in southern Germany. In other words, the German translator made the dish appear less foreign by changing its name, but he kept exactly the same text of the recipe and the original seasonings, fennel and black pepper.[40] In the French translation, the sausage recipe has the heading "Pour faire saulcisses." In fact, the French translators at the Saint Maurice monastery in Montpellier, led by the prior Desdier Christol, did much more than simply translate the Latin into French. They expanded and amplified the material, particularly the dietetic information, but they also included new recipes that originated in the south of France, where the monastery was located.[41]

Another example of this kind of adapted translation is a small cookbook published in Dutch in 1612 in Leuven (in present-day Belgium).[42] Of the 170 recipes in the book, 141 were based on Bartolomeo Scappi's *Opera,* originally published in 1570 in Italy, which contains more than a thousand recipes. But the author, known only by his pseudonym Antonius Magirus, made his personal selection and adaptation. He changed some of the recipes to make them more suitable for people in Flanders, where many of the Italian ingredients were unavailable.[43]

Magirus's adaptation contrasted strongly with the Spanish version of Scappi's book, translated by Diego Granado. Granado took 587 recipes from Scappi, 40 from another Spanish book, and 125 from other sources or his own experience.[44] He kept Scappi's references to Italy and did not try to adapt the recipes to Spanish conditions; for example, he did not revise the choice of meat and fish, even though Italy and Spain seem to have had different preferences.[45]

These examples demonstrate how translation was often a form of editing. The decision to select certain recipes from a foreign book and leave out others may have indicated important differences in the cuisine of two countries or cultures, but it may also have had to do with culinary changes over time, especially when the original was an old book.

One particular difficulty in translation concerns special technical terms. From the mid-seventeenth century, the French culinary terms tended to establish themselves in various countries. The Scottish cookbook writer Margaret Dods, who, unlike so many English authors, showed a positive attitude toward French cuisine, observed, "There is already much French cookery blended with our own, and of late we are taking to the names as well as the dishes."[46] The names of French dishes such as *soupe, sauce, compote, escalope, bouillon, omelette, vinaigrette, mousse, entrecote,* and many others have been integrated into most European languages and can be found in cookbooks all over the continent. But there are also examples of French names that did not stick. In his culinary dictionary, the Russian Levshin introduced terms such as *aladob, aliumeti, amureti, dariol,* and *frikando,* but they did not go on to find their way into national Russian dictionaries.[47]

The French language did not make an impact only in names of dishes. Several French terms for cooking methods, such as *sauter, passer, mijoter, braiser, mariner,* and *blanchir,* spread to Germanic, Romance, and Slavic languages in the eighteenth and nineteenth centuries. In a German book we find *blanchiren, mitonniren, grilliren, panniren,* and *glassiren;* in an Italian book, *bardare, farsire, passare,* and *bianchire;* and in a Slovak book, *sautírovať, mijotírovať, brajzírovať, marinovať,* and *blanžirovať.*[48]

The wider question of what happens when a work is translated from one cultural context to another is a subject that has not been satisfactorily analyzed. An interesting starting point is the theory and method developed by the German scholar Andrea Wurm. She studied German cookbooks translated from French in the seventeenth and eighteenth centuries and compared her results to cookbooks originally written in German in the same period.[49] One interesting observation she made was about the part played by the translator. Translation is not a mechanical or automatic process, Wurm contended; rather, the translator is an "independently acting person," a fact that is necessary to take into consideration when a translated work is studied.[50]

ORIGINALITY, COPYING, AND PLAGIARISM

In a rather straightforward way, two cookbook authors from the mid-twentieth century confessed that their recipes were "partly borrowed, partly stolen, and partly invented" and "begged, borrowed and inherited."[51] For hundreds of years, authors have read foreign cookbooks and created new (or not so new) texts in their own languages.[52] In the 1550s, Gheeraert Vorselmann, a Dutch medical practitioner, must have spread out in front of him on his desk Platina's Latin work, the French *Le viandier,* the first printed Dutch cookbook, and probably an old Dutch manuscript. At least this is how we can imagine it from the way he distributed recipes from these works into chapters following his own system in his cookbook, *Eenen nyeuwen coock boeck* (A new cookbook).[53]

In other cases, authors first tried recipes and then adapted them to conditions in their own societies. Such was the case with the Norwegian Henriette Schønberg

Erken. In her small study in the provincial town of Hamar, which has been left unchanged since she died in 1953, the shelves are lined with culinary classics from Scandinavia, Germany, England, and France. In the preface to her bestselling cookbook, published in 1914, she admitted her debt to "the most modern foreign works."[54] The Danish author Louise Nimb had included a similar line in her cookbook, which she published a few years earlier.[55] Both women were probably inspired by Isabella Beeton and her *Book of Household Management* (1861), the most famous cookbook in Victorian Britain. Today we know that Beeton herself compiled recipes from various contemporary books. The promotional material for Beeton's book claimed, "No recipe will be given which has not been tried or tested by the Editress herself or by her confidential friends and correspondents." But as her biographer clearly demonstrated, "Isabella didn't know the first thing about cookery." Beeton was only twenty-three years old when the first installment of her cookbook was published by her husband, who promoted the work through his *Englishwoman's Domestic Magazine,* and no more than twenty-five when the complete *Book of Household Management* appeared in 1861. An experienced cook had advised Mrs. Beeton to pick recipes from other books because, as she put it: "Cookery is a Science that is only learnt by Long Experience and years of study which of course you have not had."[56]

But what young Mrs. Beeton was lacking, the forty-eight-year-old Erken and the forty-six-year-old Nimb had plenty of when they published their classic books. Nimb learned to cook from her mother and had worked as a professional chef since the age of eighteen, when she had married a restaurateur in Copenhagen's popular Tivoli Park. Erken had taught the subject in schools for twenty years after studying domestic economy in Edinburgh and Berlin. These ladies were just two examples of female cookbook authors who flourished in northern and central Europe. Others were the Czech Dobromila Rettigová, the Russian Elena Molokhovets, the German Henriette Davidis, and the Austrian Katharina Prato, to mention only a few of those whose works became national classics. Most of them depended to a certain degree on recipes from earlier books, but they also had the necessary experience to adapt these recipes to their respective cultural environments.

This kind of independent assessment is possible to detect in older manuscripts and books as well. In *A Queen's Delight* (1671), one of the recipes ends with a single word in italics—"approved"—obviously a comment added in the original manuscript by a person who had tested the recipe.[57] Eileen White pointed out how the domestic cookbook *The Queens Closet Opened* (1655) seems to have been edited by a person who was critical to parts of the original manuscript. A recipe for cheese recommends putting it in hay, but this is followed by a disagreement that must have been added by another person: "I seldom lay in Hay, I turne and rub them with a rotten cloth especially when they are old once a week least they rot."[58] Similarly, Hannah Glasse ended a recipe she took from another cookbook with a critical comment:

"This Dish I do not recommend; for I think it is an odd Jumble of Trash ... but such Receipts as this, is what you have in most Books of Cookery yet printed."[59] In other words, the author included what she considered to be a bad recipe only because she knew that it would otherwise be missed by her readers.

Not all recipes were taken directly from cookbooks; some were gifts from friends and acquaintances. Jane Austen once expressed in a letter that she would like to have the recipe for an orange wine she had once been served by the addressee,[60] and many cookbook authors certainly gave similar hints or asked directly for recipes. This is similar to the old scribal publications dating back to the Middle Ages, a tradition that is characteristic of many manuscript cookbooks, which contained recipes that circulated within more or less limited social circles. We find traces of this tradition in the early modern period, both in handwritten and printed works. In a manuscript by Sabina Welserin dated 1553, there are recipes from three named persons: a cook, a medical practitioner, and a bishop.[61] In some cases, Welserin credited them in a very direct way, such as in the reference to the cook Simon (see chapter 3). We can find the same in printed books because many of them were based on old personal manuscripts. In Balthasar Staindl von Dillingen's German cookbook from 1544, there are short commentaries attached to some of the recipes. One of them indicates that the author had gotten the recipe from a cook: "Per Maister Hans Schatzmeister koc."[62] A Czech cookbook from 1542 has a recipe for porridge "as Matús made it."[63] *A Booke of Cookerie* (1597) has a recipe called "The keeping of Lard after my Lady Marquesse Dorsets way," and in *The Compleat Cook* (1671), we find "The Lord Conway, his Lordships Receipt for the making of Amber Puddings."[64]

The authors of printed cookbooks also received recipes from their readers, which they sometimes used in revised editions. In the thirteenth edition of his work *La scienza in cucina*, the Italian Pellegrino Artusi introduced a new recipe, for banana ice, which had been sent to him from an enthusiastic reader, something we know from a letter kept in the local archives in Artusi's hometown, Forlimpopoli.[65]

Acknowledging sources has never been the rule throughout the history of cookbooks. The Spaniard Diego Granado and the Flemish Antonius Magirus— two authors we have no biographical data about—put their names on cookbooks that contained recipes mainly from Scappi's *Opera*.[66] In a Czech cookbook from 1591, *Kuchařství* (Cooking), the aristocrat and scientist Bavor Rodovský wrote a dedicatory letter implying that he was the author, but the work was actually an edited and expanded version of an anonymous Czech book that had been published in three earlier editions in Prague.[67]

For a modern reader, this practice of collecting recipes from earlier books brings up the question of plagiarism. Eliza Acton indicated this problem in revised editions of her work *Modern Cookery for Private Families*. Some of the recipes in these later editions carried a note with the remark "Author's Receipt" or "Author's

Original Receipt." In the preface, she explained this as self-defence, "in consequence of the unscrupulous manner in which large portions of my volume have been appropriated by contemporary authors, without the slightest acknowledgment of the source."[68] In this way, they had deprived her of both credit and profit, and she may have been supported in her criticism by her active and knowledgeable publishers, the Longman brothers, who had also been victims of such plagiarism.

Before the eighteenth century, about 20 percent of printed cookbooks were "plagiarisms," while another 20 to 30 percent were translations from various languages, often without the name of the original author. These practices continued during the next centuries, to such a degree that many writers pointed them out publicly. In the preface to *Domácý kuchařka* (Domestic cooking, 1831), Dobromila Rettigová emphasized that her cookbook was based not on other books but rather on a collection of recipes from her mother and grandmother.[69] Many books were simply cut-and-paste jobs; in 1855, a Russian commentator claimed that most household books were literally "cut out" from other books or magazines or translated from German or French.[70] In 1867, the French cook Jules Gouffé judged all cookbooks to be without any value because they just copied all the errors from earlier books.[71] A German author of a diet manual from 1871 claimed that it was unnecessary to read new cookbooks because "all the new ones are just copies of the old."[72]

There were compilers who stole lock, stock, and barrel without restraint, while others tried to hide that they were stealing by making small changes. As mentioned earlier, there are many examples of errors and incomprehensible expressions, proof that the copying had been done by people without culinary skills.[73]

When isolated recipes were copied, it was less of a problem. Yorkshire pudding, boeuf bourguignon, and paella are established dishes, and there are limits to how much originality can be applied before a dish changes qualitatively and must be given another name. Recipes for these and other well-known dishes are more or less considered part of a common cultural heritage. But many "authors" lifted entire chapters from other people's books, keeping the same ingredients, cooking techniques, measurements, and even wording. In some cases, compilers would steal only a selection of recipes, often with very unfortunate results; for example, a recipe may refer to the preceding recipe for part of the preparation, but the preceding recipe was not included.

Illustrations were also copied or plagiarized. The woodcut in figure 9 depicting a cook in his kitchen was originally used in the German cookbook *Von allen Speisen* (About all foods), published by the printers Egenolff and Steiner in the 1530s and 1540s. But the same image appeared in the 1542 German translation of Platina's cookbook and again in Marx Rumpolt's great cookbook, *Ein new Kochbuch,* printed in the 1580s.[74] Feyerabend, Rumpolt's publisher, also used other old woodcuts or engravings in the book. The woodcut by Jost Amman used on Rumpolt's title page (see figure 1) was, in turn, copied in Anna Wecker's cookbook

FIGURE 9. Woodcut from the 1587 edition of Marx Rumpolt's *Ein new Kochbuch*. Nasjonalbibli-oteket, Oslo, qLib.rar. 1065.

seventeen years later—possibly by one of Amman's pupils—but the male cook was replaced by a woman (see figure 24).

Plagiarism in art and literature is historically difficult to define. Élisabeth Louise Vigée Le Brun, the most prominent female painter in France during the eighteenth century, once asked Jacques-Louis David if copying works in the Louvre would be considered plagiarism. David had as a young man not hesitated in borrowing, or "shopping," from other painters. Simon Schama discovered a Raphael Madonna, a Rubens saint, and a Poussin leper in an altarpiece David made for a church in Marseille.[75] With this background, David's answer to Vigée Le Brun hardly comes as a surprise: "Do as Molière, take whatever you want wherever you want."[76] Molière took ideas from medieval farces and commedia dell'arte. Yet there was no discussion of plagiarism, as most works were independent artistic adaptations of old material; a work might well be considered "original" even if much of it was borrowed from others. This is true not only of Molière but also of the greatest names in world literature, Shakespeare included. During that period, originality actually consisted of a sort of imitation. The historian William Bowsma showed that imitation was important during the Renaissance and that it allowed a high degree of creativity. Ben Jonson, a contemporary of Shakespeare, took up the subject in *Discoveries*, explaining *imitatio*, and referred to Horace, who advised writers not to imitate servilely. To show what he meant he used a culinary metaphor: "Not as a Creature that swallowes, what it takes in, crude, raw, or undigested; but that feedes with an Appetite, and hath a Stomacke to concoct, devide, and turne all into nourishment."[77]

The concept of imitation can be applied to the study of cookbooks. Recipes have always needed to be adapted to new realities, new periods, new societies, and new tastes, such as in the cases of Magirus and Christol. Martha Bradley of Bath, author of *The British Housewife* (1756), took most of her recipes from other books, but she gave the descriptions a more pedagogical form, simplified procedures, and reduced the number of ingredients.[78] The Danish author and publisher K. H. Seidelin admitted in the preface to his 1801 cookbook that readers would probably find recipes they recognized from other books, but he assured them that his versions were always improved, thanks to advice from cooks.[79] Many authors were undoubtedly conscious of the need for culinary development. In the 1800s, Henriette Davidis wrote in her German bestseller that she would not pretend to have invented all the recipes herself but said that they had been "tried out, improved and composed by myself, and I have only included recipes I am convinced are the right ones."[80] The same attitude is found among authors of handwritten cookbooks; simply repeating the same procedures was not the norm. Studies have shown that women made changes in language, ingredients, and quantities. In Germany, manuscripts tended to use fewer foreign words than the printed texts did; foreign terms were often replaced by German ones. More local products were used; recipes were often adapted to local or regional cuisines.[81] In England, there was a clear tendency to simplify dishes but to elaborate the instructions; recipes were adapted to new social groups that were not familiar with expressions meant for professional cooks.[82] This process gives, perhaps, a new meaning to Eisenstein's hypothesis about how the increased output of old texts may have led to the formulation of new theories (see chapter 3). The printed cookbook seems to have been an important inspiration for experiments among women, who modified recipes and thereby made them new.

The French restaurateur Antoine Beauvilliers, who wrote the well-received cookbook *L'art de cuisinier* (1814), stated that a new dish is created when ingredients are added or removed.[83] A good example of a modification along these lines can be found in *Arte de cocina* (1611), by the Spanish royal cook Martínez Montiño. Instead of giving a recipe for the traditional stew *olla podrida*, Montiño offered his readers a new "olla podrida in pie."[84] The historian Piero Camporesi gave a more general evaluation of the relationship between originality and imitation in his introduction to the 1995 reprint of Pellegrino Artusi's Italian classic, *La scienza in cucina*. He pointed out several of Artusi's sources and models and concluded by stating that in cooking, combination is more important than invention, and variation more important than creation.[85]

But no matter how much a recipe is revised and developed, many people will still harbor the feeling that it is not a completely independent literary product. The Russian author Elena Molokhovets, who, in addition to her culinary masterwork, published several books about religious and social problems, noted, "The compiler of a cookery book is far removed from real writing."[86] The very last words in *The Alice B. Toklas Cookbook* come to mind: "As if a cookbook had anything to do with writing."

5

Organizing the Cookbook

RECIPE SELECTION

There are cookbooks with thousands of recipes, but irrespective of size, every cookbook is the result of a selection. One way that a selection can be made is by choosing to concentrate on a particular type of food—such as soups, vegetarian dishes, Italian cuisine, food for the sick, or banquet meals, to name a few. In the twentieth century, specialization became even more extreme, resulting in books such as *Manifold Destiny: The Only Guide to Cooking on Your Car Engine* (1989). But authors of general cookbooks are faced with the problem: What should be included and what may be dropped? Is it necessary to explain the simplest daily preparations, or is it better to leave them out to make room for something more exciting? This is a question that cookbook authors have been asking themselves since early on. The author (or scribe) of a French manuscript from the late Middle Ages mentioned that a few simple dishes made from roots and pork tripe were not included because "everybody knows how they are made," and he mentioned women in particular as experts in this field.[1] In some cases, this assumption was not expressed in words but rather implicitly understood. One of the first cookbooks in German explained that a certain almond dish should be boiled the same way as milk soup. But there is no mention of milk soup in the soup chapter.[2] The preparation must have been so common that a recipe did not seem necessary.[3]

A more critical attitude toward simple dishes is apparent in *Banchetti*, written by Christofaro di Messisbugo, the chief steward at the court of Ferrara in the sixteenth century. He openly stated that he would not spend time and effort on descriptions of dishes that any ordinary woman—"qualunque uile feminuccia"—

knew how to cook. He would instead concentrate on giving recipes for the most noble and important foods.[4] This is why the book gives far more recipes for meat than for vegetables. Even if the elite had the means to eat more meat than those lower down the social scale, other sources indicate that they consumed far more vegetables than this cookbook might suggest. But such dishes were common and thus not necessary to describe.

The cookbooks referred to above were for professional cooks or administrators at the courts and estates of princes and aristocrats, who were familiar with common dishes and were looking instead for extraordinary, exceptional, and spectacular recipes. In sixteenth- and seventeenth-century manuscripts intended for use in private families, a similar attitude may explain the difference between the selected recipes and the normal composition of meals in an elite household. Maria Angeles Pérez Samper, a Spanish historian, studied several manuscripts from this period and found that recipes for more festive foods, such as cakes, confectionary, dried fruits, drinks, and high-quality cured meats, were far more common than those for fish and meat dishes.[5] The same pattern has been documented in German and English manuscripts. In a Danish seventeenth-century text by Helle Schrøder (referred to in chapter 3), 90 percent of the recipes are for desserts and cakes. We can conclude from this that the writers and compilers of cookbooks had no intention of covering all the dishes that normally were served in a house; rather, they wanted to present dishes that were new and fashionable, prestigious, or intended for special occasions.

The high proportion of recipes for confections was less pronounced in printed cookbooks than in manuscripts. Still, it is evident when looking at most of these books that the authors were not trying to reflect what they knew was the ordinary diet among their readers; they wanted to offer more modern and attractive dishes. In 1555, Nostradamus, introducing his recipes for confections from Valencia and Genoa, stated that his book was intended to "satisfy the wishes and desires of several pleasant persons, even of the female sex, who are eager to know and understand new things."[6]

Machiavelli saw this "fury for the new" as something typical of human nature,[7] and a hundred years later, the English scholar Robert Burton claimed in *The Anatomy of Melancholy* (1621) that "mans nature is still desirous of news, variety, delights; and our wandring affections are so irregular in this kind, that they must change, though it bee to the worst."[8] Cultural historians today, however, tend to connect the passion for novelty in the early modern period with special social groups rather than with human nature.[9] It was commonly found within urban or elite culture, whereas the culture of the popular classes, particularly in the countryside, was known to be more traditional. They did not tend to look for "the new" as something valuable in itself, resorting to it only if circumstances made it necessary—for example, when scarcity of grain led to a more extensive use of potatoes and corn in Europe.

But the growing segment of the population that bought books in the sixteenth and seventeenth centuries probably welcomed cookbooks with titles such as *Libro*

*novo, Opera nova, Lo scalco alla moderna, Neu Kochbuch, Le nouveau cuisinier,
Traiteur à la mode, A propre new booke of cokery,* and *Eenen nyeuwen coock boeck.*[10]
Similar titles were used for other practical manuals and how-to books, but they
were also given to works by scientists such as Francis Bacon (*Novum organum*),
Johannes Kepler (*Astronomia nova*) and Galileo Galilei (*Due nuove scienze*). The
intention of these scientists was to make a break with old theories. Throughout the
patristic and medieval periods, the quest for truth was thought of as the recovery
of what was embedded in tradition rather than the discovery of new information.[11]
In the Middle Ages, progress was conceived of as a process of reaching higher by
standing on the shoulders of the ancient giants—or building on previous discoveries. However, starting in the 1600s, the concept of "news" became crucial; this was
the period when the first newspapers were published. In institutions of higher
education, intellectual invention—rather than the transmission of tradition—
became one of the major goals during the seventeenth and the eighteenth centuries.[12]

The use of the adjectives "new" and "modern" in early cookbook titles continued into the following centuries[13] and spread to other regions.[14] Even if these titles
represented a small part of the total, the authors—or their publishers—were without a doubt aware of the value of novelty. The expression "new cuisine" appeared
in regular intervals from the seventeenth century onward, and in 1735, Vincent La
Chapelle opened the preface of his book *Le cuisinier moderne* (The modern cook)
by referring to the everyday search for "une nouvelle délicatesse." He was aware of
the changing fashions and wrote that a meal served the same way as twenty years
ago would not satisfy guests.[15] At about the same time, an English cookbook author
expressed a similar attitude: "Variety and Novelty are no small Parte of the Cook's
Art."[16] In the nineteenth century, the French gourmet writer Brillat-Savarin summarized this sentiment in the following aphorism: "The discovery of a new dish
does more for human happiness than the discovery of a new star."[17] Later in the
same century, the prominent French cook Urbain Dubois published a cookbook
with the characteristic title *La cuisine d'aujourd'hui* (Today's cuisine), which
boasted of "innovation," "originalité," and "toutes les nouveautés culinaires."[18]

All of this interest in the new and fashionable should be interpreted in a context
of social aspiration. Presenting novel dishes has the same value as presenting luxury; it creates a distinction of taste that social inferiors imitate, and that creates the
continuous need for new dishes.

RECIPES AND COOKBOOKS ADAPTED TO NEW
TASTES, FOODS, AND TECHNOLOGIES

New recipes generally represented changing tastes, but they also reflected access to
new foodstuffs and new technology, as well as an awareness of new ideas about

diet and nutrition. Cookbook authors had to pay attention to such changes in fashions and trends. Auguste Escoffier was aware of this when he wrote in *Le guide culinaire* (1903) that he did not pretend to have written a complete guide. Even if it was complete today, he said, it would no longer be so tomorrow because "progress marches on and gives birth to new recipes every day."[19] This is why new cookbooks were written and old books were revised. In 1979, the food writer Elizabeth David admitted that she was not so interested in first editions of old cookbooks, which are so popular among collectors. She wanted to study later editions, where the authors have made changes, corrected errors, added new recipes, updated methods, and included new ingredients.[20] Food historians who have studied such changes in cookbooks have pointed out variations in the use of spices, sugar, and butter; in attitudes toward combinations of sweet and sour; in the status of offal; and so on.[21] The art of sauce making grew, step by step, into a refined specialty that was defined by the work of Carême, Escoffier, and others.

New technology in the nineteenth and twentieth centuries created a need for new recipes. New preservation techniques led to the use of canned soups and meats as shortcuts in long and complicated preparations. Electrical stoves, microwaves, and other kitchen machines expedited many tasks. Chopping and mincing meat was a tough job before the grinder made the work easier, and it became even simpler with the invention of the electric meat grinder. The Italian Pellegrino Artusi wrote in the eleventh edition of his cookbook, printed in 1907, that he had gotten a grinder: "I also have adopted in my kitchen this instrument that saves the tiresome work of mincing meat with a knife and pounding it in a mortar."[22] But changes did not happen overnight, and in the thirteenth edition of his book, issued four years later, Artusi still felt that it was necessary to explain in the recipe for *scaloppine di carne battuta*, "If you don't have a grinder, mince it [the meat] fine first with a knife, then with a mezzaluna."[23] In the United States, Sears and Roebuck launched a special chopper in the early twentieth century under their brand name Puritan and published a special cookbook to demonstrate how easily many dishes could be prepared with the use of the tool (figure 10).

Barbara Santich observed that technological changes could even lead to the modification of the language in recipes. She studied the verbs used in two cookbooks published two and a half centuries apart: *The Art of Cookery,* published in England in 1747, and *The Cook's Companion,* published in Australia in 1996.[24] She compared the chicken recipes in the books and pointed out that some old verbs completely disappeared: "Industrialization of chicken slaughtering and processing means that contemporary cooks no longer have to wash, singe, draw, and truss their chickens as was standard practice in the eighteenth century." These verbs were consequently not used at all in the 1996 recipe. But there was also a significant difference in the use of verbs for culinary preparation, such as "fry," "brown," "turn," "strain," and "stuff." There were eighty variations on these verbs in the mod-

FIGURE 10. Title page of *Improved Puritan Cookbook,* published by Sears, Roebuck and Co. to promote their Puritan food chopper.

ern cookbook, whereas the eighteenth-century book contained only thirty-two. The most important differences were found in the verbs used to describe processes involving heat. Santich explained these differences as a reflection of more precise terminology, a greater use of synonyms, and, significantly, a larger range of technical possibilities.[25]

New discoveries were not limited to methods of preparation and technological inventions. At certain times, completely new foodstuffs had to be adapted to existing local conditions. Good examples of how this adaptation took place are found in the period after 1492, when contact was established between Europe and the enormous continent that was eventually given the name America. No immediate break in European food culture followed, but during what is called the Columbian Exchange, foods that had previously been unknown in Europe gradually became a natural part of the European diet. These included potatoes, tomatoes, red and green peppers, avocados, string beans, chocolate, vanilla, and turkey.[26] The Europeans who were first confronted with these products had to figure out how to fit them into a food culture that until then had developed for centuries with basically the same ingredients. During the Middle Ages, sugar, spices from the Far East, and rice were among the most important novelties.

There was a great difference between the various products in the way they were integrated. When people were confronted with the new foods, they compared them to existing and well-known food categories. The product that was most easily accepted was turkey—at least for those who could afford to buy it. This animal was not too different from the other big birds that had traditionally been served at the tables of the European elite. Turkey could be used as a substitute for peacock or capon and was prepared the same way. Meat from birds was also considered to be healthy, so it did not risk being criticized by doctors, as many of the other new foods were.

It is consequently no surprise that cookbooks with recipes for turkey were published in the first century after Columbus arrived in the New World. In 1570, the Italian Bartolomeo Scappi suggested the same preparation for turkey pullets and ordinary pullets, and he compared the cooking of turkey with that of peacock. A decade later, the German Marx Rumpolt proposed twenty different ways to prepare turkey, all of them well-established methods for other meats (figure 11).[27] A taste for turkey soon spread from the aristocracy to the wealthy bourgeoisie, and prices went down. In France in 1538, turkey meat cost eight times more than meat from hens; in 1711, it was only twice as much.[28]

The tomato is an example of a new food that was slow to become part of European food culture. For a long time appreciated only as an ornamental plant, the tomato was mentioned as food around 1600 in an Italian botanical treatise. As was the case with turkey, the fruit was compared with well-known ingredients in the kitchen; the author of the text explained that tomatoes could be eaten the same way as eggplants—with salt, pepper, and oil.[29] But the first professional recipe for the food did not come until 1692, when Antonio Latini's Italian cookbook gave a preparation for *salsa di pomodoro, alla spagnuola* (tomato salsa, Spanish style).[30] In Spain, tomatoes were not included in any cookbooks published before 1611. After

FIGURE 11. Woodcut introducing recipes for turkey in the 1587 edition of Marx Rumpolt's *Ein new Kochbuch*. Nasjonalbiblioteket, Oslo, qLib.rar. 1065.

that year, there is unfortunately a period in which no new Spanish cookbooks were published that lasted until 1745, when we find a recipe for tomato sauces with garlic and oil, typical of the Mediterranean food culture we know today.[31]

Tomato recipes in Spanish and Italian cookbooks surprise nobody, since the fruit could be grown in these countries. The situation was completely different in northern Europe, where effective cultivation came only in the twentieth century. The first tomato recipes from this region were from the last decades of the nineteenth century, and they suggested using canned tomatoes in soups and sauces. One of the Russian cookbooks written by Elena Molokhovets called for tomato purée in soups in early editions published in the 1860s and only gradually introduced fresh tomato dishes.[32] As late as 1896, Charles-Emil Hagdahl wrote in his gourmet cookbook that he regretted that tomatoes in Sweden were mainly sold in the form of bottles of purée, imported from abroad.[33] In Norway, a cookbook from 1888 included a series of interesting tomato recipes, but the book actually demonstrates why general conclusions about diet never should be drawn on the basis of one cookbook.[34] The author had spent several years in Constantinople (modern-day Istanbul), where tomatoes were common by that point, and her book was the only one of its kind. A decade later, another Norwegian author did not give any tomato recipes in the first edition of her cookbook, published in 1897, and in a later edition, issued in 1912, she remarked that "tomatoes are seldom appreciated the first time they are tasted," and wrote that in Norway, "tomatoes are still very expensive."[35]

An example from more recent times is the banana, a rare and exotic fruit for Europeans until the beginning of the twentieth century, when fast ships with special storerooms made importing huge quantities of the fruit possible. In 1873,

Grand dictionnaire de cuisine, by Alexandre Dumas, had the following commentary in the entry about bananas: "It helps the poor peoples [in the places the fruit is grown] the same way potatoes helped working men in our country."[36] In Europe, many readers in the early 1900s did not know the fruit, so Pellegrino Artusi found it necessary to describe in detail what it looked like: "a large pod similar in appearance to a cucumber with green peel, smooth, triangular and curved."[37] In other countries, there was a more pronounced degree of uncertainty about the banana. In Germany, one of the first recipes for the new and unknown product appeared in a cookbook published in 1913, and it seems that the author associated the fruit's form not to cucumber but to sausage. The recipe is called "banana sausage,"[38] and it involves frying the banana in a pan with marjoram, one of the most common spices used with sausages in northern Europe. The first American banana recipes came earlier, as the fruit was imported from Jamaica to the United States starting in the 1870s, primarily to Boston, where it entered two successful cookbooks, *Mrs. Lincoln's Boston Cook Book* (1884), by Mary Lincoln, and *The Boston Cooking-School Cook Book* (1896), by Fannie Farmer. Lincoln included a small note about bananas served whole or "sliced and slightly sweetened or salted," while Farmer had recipes for banana cake, custard, fritters, ice cream, salad, and even baked and sautéed bananas.[39]

Banana importers published their own booklets with information and recipes as a way to introduce the new product. Special recipe collections concentrating on one product had already been published for potatoes and products that had a low status or had been met with prejudice in certain regions or among certain social groups, including rabbits, mushrooms, and even greens, which peasants in many regions in Europe described as grass or animal fodder.[40]

Special booklets were also produced when new drinks arrived from abroad in the sixteenth and seventeenth centuries, particularly coffee, tea, and chocolate, but these books gradually became superfluous when the new drinks became an integral part of people's daily lives. New recipes appeared suggesting distilled alcohol as an ingredient in cordials that had earlier been based on wine, and later as part of the eighteenth-century drinks punch and bishop. The twentieth century witnessed a vast outpouring of short books containing recipes for cocktails, the new and popular drink developed in the United States from the 1860s onward.

Revisions and new recipes seem to be especially common during periods of increased international contact and commerce, most recently the so-called era of globalization. These intervals also seem to encourage the greatest growth in cookbook production.

Recipe selection and revision are of special interest to food historians. Studying different editions of the same cookbook makes it possible to find out, for example, when baking powder started to be commonly used, when margarine became an accepted substitute for butter, when it became more common for people to buy ready-made sausages than to make them, and when instructions about how to kill and pluck a goose were no longer provided because poultry could be bought ready for the oven. Food historians can follow the revisions made in later editions of a cookbook and use them as a source to the history of culinary development, but it is necessary to proceed with care. Some revisions were based on recipes in foreign cookbooks and not yet observed in the author's country. Other revisions came only after a new practice had been established. It was not easy for an author to assess which trends would prove to be permanent. Therefore, it is not easy to answer the question of cause and effect: Did cookbooks reflect people's changing taste, or did they create it?

But, as Wendy Wall has demonstrated, the study of revisions may also be of interest to the book historian. In an essay at the crossroads between book history and household history, she studied the publication history of Gervase Markham's *The English Housewife* (1615) and found that the book "increasingly organised the reading experience so as to model methodical practice. . . . Convention of print and household practice partook of a shared and evolving system of knowledge."[41]

CHAOS AND ORDER

When many recipes are collected in a book, we tend to expect a certain organization. Already in the Roman *Apicius* cookbook—at least in the two known copies that have survived from the ninth century the recipes were divided into ten chapters: preservation of foodstuffs, minced meat, vegetables, casseroles and fricassees, pulses, birds, special delicacies, animals, seafood, and fish. Platina, who was familiar with *Apicius,* followed the pattern of ten chapters when he wrote *De honesta voluptate,* but he organized them differently. He took most of the recipes in the last five chapters from Martino's manuscript, which had a certain system—for example, a chapter with recipes for tarts. In the first five chapters, Platina described different products, such as vegetables, herbs, and spices and listed their medical properties, but only occasionally gave recipes.

Many of the oldest medieval manuscripts have no systematic organization at all, and the reason is probably that they were made up of recipes that were written down on different scraps of paper and then compiled. In some cases, there are signs of a certain plan. The English fourteenth-century text known as *Utilis coquinario* (Useful for the kitchen) has no real system, but certain recipes—for example, recipes for fowl and blancmange and recipes involving fruits and flowers—are grouped together.[42] A few manuscripts vaguely referred to sections in the text. The oldest known French culinary manuscript, *Enseignements* (Teachings), from around 1300, has one section for fish and one for meat, following the old medieval division between *gras* (fat) and *maigre* (lean) dishes in the religious calendar. All the same, the text makes only one reference to this structure, at the start of the fish chapter: "Here begin sea fish and freshwater fish."[43] This was clarified in a later copy of the manuscript, when ornamental initials were added to signal where a new section started.[44] Other manuscripts give no explanation for the order of dishes. For example, in the oldest German manuscript, from around 1350, a blancmange made with hen breast is followed by "Hen the Greek way" and then "Rice the Greek way." Historian Hans Wiswe pointed out a possible logic based on associations, but this can hardly be called a system. If this is the way the book was conceived, it does not seem particularly useful for readers.[45]

Lack of organization is not exclusively found in handwritten books; in some early printed books—which were often based on old manuscripts—recipes followed each other pell-mell. The English cookbook *A Propre New Booke of Cokery*, from 1545, for example, opens with "To dresse a crab" and "To make a stewed broth," followed by pies, roast venison, a fish sauce, and a custard.

Another special feature of handwritten books is also found in some of the printed texts: the same recipe occurs twice. There are various explanations for this. The recipes may have come from different sources, such as from a book or a friend, and they may even have had different headings (or recipe titles). If they were recorded a long time apart—in family manuscripts, for example, a recipe may have been written down first by a mother and later by her daughter—the first version of the recipe may easily have been forgotten. This is not of much importance in a private manuscript; in a printed book, however, one would expect better editing, but this was not always the case. Many unorganized manuscripts were definitely sent to printers without professional editing of the material. The results can be ridiculous. For example, in an English cookbook from the sixteenth century, one recipe stops abruptly with the following remark: "The rest wanteth."[46] The explanation is probably that a person looked through the manuscript, discovered the error, and wrote a note to the responsible editor, who did not notice it and just passed the text on to the printer. Such comments have also been found in manuscripts of other genres. In an Italian poem from the sixteenth century, for instance, the poetry suddenly breaks off with a note: "Here some stanzas are missing."[47]

In spite of all the examples of disorganization, there was a movement toward greater order and system in the presentation of texts. This shift had already started in scribal culture with the division of texts into sections and subsections, as Thomas Aquinas did in his works with *partes, questiones/distinciones,* and *articuli.* From the twelfth century onward, there was a growing—if inconsistent—use of chapter headings, ornamental initials, running titles, and other organizational devices.[48] In the fourteenth-century household book *Le menagier de Paris,* the material was divided into *distinctions* and *articles.* Some of the first printed cookbooks may have been inspired by the way the Bible was organized into chapters. In the editions of the German *Küchenmeisterei,* published before 1500, each of the five parts is divided into chapters, which are numbered with Roman numerals and each contain one recipe.

As book production became more professional, the need for order and system became increasingly important. This was also true in several areas of society, particularly in the scientific community. One example of a new science with an urge to classify was botany. Since antiquity, nature had been the subject of serious study, not only in natural philosophy but also in the practical sciences, some of which were relevant to cooking. Farmers were looking for the best methods of cultivating, harvesting, processing, and storing cereals, roots, vegetables, and fruits. Physicians and apothecaries studied nature to work out the best diets and remedies (including culinary remedies) to prevent or cure diseases. By the end of the fifteenth century, the herbal genre flourished, and several new treatises were published, some of them also containing dietetic information. The medical perspective can be seen in two books with titles that translate to "garden of health": *Gart der Gesundheit* (1485) and *Ortus sanitatis* (1491). These popular works were part of the foundation when botany developed into a proper science in the sixteenth century. The main purpose of plant descriptions was no longer simply to catalog practical uses; instead, accurate description became a goal in itself, and later it became part of an effort to systematize nature.[49]

Botanists and other scientists formed an international elite, often writing in Latin so they could be understood by colleagues in foreign countries. Cookbook authors took the opposite approach; with very few exceptions, they stuck to writing in local languages. However, cookbooks written during the 1600s began to adopt certain scientific terms in prefaces, titles, and chapter headings. Expressions like "treatise" and "doctrine" had been used in medieval manuscripts; Martino's tart chapter was called "Tractato de torte." These terms were later followed by "method," "discourse," and "compendium." "Method" had been used in scientific works before the 1600s, but it entered the culinary literature in the decades after Descartes published *Discours de la méthode* in 1637. One anonymous book was called *Le cuisinier méthodique,* and other French cookbooks used terms such as *doctrine, méthode, discours,* and *traité.* La Varenne's *Le cuisinier françois* had several chapters that included the words *méthode* and *discours,* for example, "Discours & méthode de servir le poisson" (presentation and method for serving fish).[50] The Italian cook Bartolomeo Stefani had chapters that used the terms *trattato, metodo,* and *discorso,* for example, "Metodo per far bianchi mangiari" (method of making blancmanger) and "Discorso de' pesci" (presentation of fish), and in one case he used the phrase *discorso del modo,* a clear echo of Descartes.[51] In England, books had titles and subtitles like *A New System* and *A Complete System,* while in Germany, terms such as *Ordnung* (order) and *Regeln* (rules) were found in several books.

But using these ambitious expressions taken from scientific literature—by the cookbook authors or their publishers—did not suffice to create a system out of the existing material. The basic challenge was deciding in what order to present the recipes. It is possible to find seemingly very different dishes grouped together following a certain logic, as Sandra Sherman observed from the eighteenth century: "Hannah Glasse logically featured a recipe for bread next to one for ale, since yeast rising off of one was necessary to produce the other."[52] But this was an exception. Most authors, including Glasse, followed a set pattern. In some books, the recipes were organized according to cooking methods: boiled, stewed, roasted, baked, and so on.[53] Another system arranged recipes by basic ingredients: domestic animals, game and birds, poultry, fish, and vegetables. Rumpolt's sixteenth-century German book was arranged this way, with many kinds of preparations under each foodstuff.[54] This system was based on medieval dietetic literature, where the central idea was that different foods had different medical properties and qualities, but it survived the old medicine and has been found in cookbooks ever since. A third system listed recipes according to the sequence in which the dishes were to be served, beginning with appetizers, soups, and entrées, followed by the main dishes of fish and meat, then vegetables and sauces, and finally desserts, cakes, and confectionery. In a few books, recipes were grouped by season or by month, the same way as in an almanac.[55] These systems were difficult to implement consistently. Grouping by foodstuffs, for example, meant that additional chapters were needed for pies with different ingredients; grouping by seasons meant that there had to be a lot of repetition. Consequently, cookbooks often used a combination of two or more systems. Today, cookbooks tend to open with appetizers and soups and finish with desserts, while the bulk of the recipes are for beef, veal, mutton, pork, game, fish, and so on.

Another system made a division between meat dishes and Lenten dishes. This system dates from the Middle Ages and survived until recently in areas with large populations of Catholic or Orthodox Christians because a great number of days during the year were fasting days.

In a few books, the organization seems to be an end in itself. A Polish book from 1682 has three parts, containing meat dishes, fish dishes, and pies, respectively. Each part is organized exactly the same way: first come one hundred recipes, numbered from from one to one hundred, which are followed by ten recipes, numbered from one to ten, and at the end, a special recipe is given called "the secret of the cook."[56] There are, in other words, 111 recipes in each part, making a total of 333 recipes, all organized in a symmetric order typical of the baroque period.

INDEXES AND HEADINGS

The kind of organization chosen for a cookbook is linked to what function the book is meant to perform for its readers. Some recipe collections are primarily reference works. Readers use these books to consult a recipe for a certain dish planned for a meal, and therefore the material must be arranged in a way that makes recipes easy to find. But whichever system is chosen, it takes a long time to go through an entire chapter to find a particular recipe. Within the world of the written word, this was not exclusively a problem for cookbooks. The reading practices of lawyers, preachers, and other professionals moved from gaining knowledge of a whole work to rapidly searching for quotations and references that were necessary to give authority. In order to obtain easier access to such references, new techniques were created: indexes and concordances, and of course pagination.[57]

Rudimentary "tables of contents"—consisting of a list of the first words in each chapter—appeared in certain books in the twelfth century. In the thirteenth century, this concept was further refined and used in many of the manuscripts written in the late Middle Ages. The more efficient alphabetical index was developed in the thirteenth century, but it took several centuries to become firmly established.[58] This was particularly true for cookbooks, and there wasn't a consistent progress toward an alphabetical index. For example, the first printed German cookbook, *Küchenmeisterei,* had alphabetical indexes from 1490 to 1529 but not in later editions.[59] The reason for this change may have been economical. The simple table of contents involved less work for the printer and was consequently cheaper to produce.

A few books used the alphabet as their basic organizational principle and arranged all the recipes from *A* to *Z* (or the last relevant letter). This system was used in a small anonymous Italian manuscript from the fourteenth century known as *Libro per cuoco* (Book for the cook),[60] but the first important printed cookbook to use it was *Le cuisinier royal et bourgeois* (1691), by Massialot, which started with *abattis* (giblets) and ended with *vives* (weevers). This was at a time when the first modern alphabetical encyclopedias had their breakthrough (figures 12 and 13), and even if the alphabetical cookbook never became the dominant form, there are important examples in many countries: in France, *Dictionnaire des alimens* (Food dictionary, 1750) and *Dictionnaire portatif de cuisine* (Portable dictionary of cooking, 1767); in Sweden, *Udaf adelig öfningh en liten hand*-book (A little handbook for aristocratic instruction, 1695);[61] in Russia, *Slovar' povarennyi* (Dictionary of cooking, 1795–97);[62] in Austria, *Neues Lexikon der Französischen, Sächsischen, Österreichischen und Böhmischen Kochkunst* (New dictionary for French, Saxon, Austrian and Bohemian cooking, 1785);[63] and in the United States, *The Cook's Own Book* (1832).[64] The system has also been used in some modern culinary reference works, for example, *Larousse gastronomique,* first published in France in 1938.

Obviously, an organized cookbook is a great help when one is looking for a specific recipe. But a successful search also depends on how a dish is singled out from other recipes. Today, we expect every recipe to begin with a heading that gives the name of the dish on a line separate from the rest of the text. There are early examples of such headings from as far back as the fourteenth century, but they were not firmly established until the eighteenth and nineteenth centuries. Before 1500, there

FIGURE 12. Frontispiece of Gottlieb Siegmund Corvinus's *Nutzbares, galantes und curiöses Frauenzimmer-Lexikon* (Useful, gallant, and curious encyclopedia for ladies), published in 1739. The book contains mostly recipes, although it also has a great deal of other information for women, arranged in alphabetical order. Universitetsbiblioteket, Oslo, UHS Mag 314 M 6 Cor.

Nutzbares, galantes und curiöses

Frauenzimmer-
LEXICON,

Worinnen der

Frauenzimmer geist- und weltliche
Orden, Aemter, Würden, Ehren-Stellen,

Profeſſionen, Rechte und Privilegia, Hochzeit- und
Trauer-Solennitäten, Gerade- und Erb-Stücken; die
Nahmen und Thaten der Göttinnen, Heroinnen, gelehrter
Frauenzimmer, Künſtlerinnen, und anderer merckwürdigen Perſonen
weiblichen Geſchlechts;

Dererselben Trachten und Moden, und was
zum Putz und Kleidung des Frauenzimmers, und
Auszierung der Gemächer gehöret; ihre häusliche
Verrichtungen, Ergötzlichkeiten, Redens-Arten, und
was ſonſt einem Frauenzimmer zu wiſſen nöthig,

ordentlich nach dem Alphabet kurtz und deutlich erkläret zu finden,

wie auch

ein auf die allerneueſte Art verfertigtes vollkommenes

Koch-Buch nebſt Küchen-Zetteln
und Riſſen von Tafel-Auffätzen.

Vermehrte und verbeſſerte Auflage.

Franckfurt und Leipzig,
bey Joh. Friedrich Gleditſchens ſeel. Sohn,
1 7 3 9.

FIGURE 13. Title page of Corvinus's *Nutzbares, galantes und curiöses Frauenzimmer-Lexikon.*

were manuscripts where the text was unbroken. If a dish had a name, it immediately followed the previous recipe, sometimes with a number, a special mark, or an ornamental initial letter. Occasionally, the name was written in red ink, which is why headings were called *rubrica*, a Latin word for a type of red-colored clay used for dyeing. This word is still used in several languages. Instead of a heading, many recipes had a special incipit phrase. In a German manuscript from around 1445, most of the recipes follow this pattern: "If you want to prepare stuffed crayfish, take a big crayfish . . ."[65] Each recipe begins on a new line, with the first letter outlined in black ink and decorated with gold leaf, but there are no headings.

The opening line "if you want to" is a construction found in many early recipe books. In a copy of the French cookbook *Enseignements,* for example, from the first decades of the fourteenth century, we find: "If you want to make a jelly with pike, take . . ." But a certain number of the recipes in this text are preceded by a sort of heading, for instance: "For blancmanger—If you want to prepare a blancmanger . . ."[66] This copy of *Enseignements* is probably not the original manuscript, and it is possible that the heading ("for blancmanger") was added by a scribe who wanted to make the text more systematic. It is an embryo of a heading, even if it is not typographically set apart from the rest of the text.

In an untitled Dutch manuscript from the fifteenth century, each recipe starts on a new line, with a short description of the dish—for example, "Amandeleyt" (almond milk) and "Appelmoes in de vastene" (apple mush during Lent). These are in fact headings, but they are written in the same script as the rest of the recipe, without any distinction.[67] There were separate headings in other manuscripts from the fourteenth and fifteenth centuries, however, such as in Martino's text ("Menestra de carne," "Per fare tomacelli") and in the English *Forme of Cury* ("Rauioles," "For to make blanc manger").[68] According to the linguist Ruth Carroll, this type of heading was a recurrent feature of medieval recipe collections in England.[69]

Early printed cookbooks from the end of the fifteeenth century and the beginning of the sixteenth century followed different patterns in European countries. The first cookbooks printed in Italian, English, Catalan, and Spanish had separate headings. The first printed Czech book had headings, but they were in the same typeface as the rest of the text, and there were no blank lines between the recipes. Real headings were introduced in the second edition. In other countries, headings took longer to become established. The first printed cookbooks in French and in Dutch had no headings in the first part of the text, but they were gradually introduced, although they did not always appear on separate lines. In Germany, the first editions of the cookbook *Küchenmeisterei* followed the old pattern, with recipe introductions such as "Wiltu ein gebaches machen von erbessen . . ." (If you want to bake a cake with peas . . .). But in editions published after around 1490, the recipes were numbered and an alphabetical index was added that referred to the name of the dish—for example, in the case of the aforementioned recipe, "Gebachens von erbssen"—and gave the part of the book in which the recipe appeared and the number of the dish within that part in Roman numbers.[70] There are headings in the 1516 edition, but they just give the number of the recipe: "Das XX Capitel," for example. It was not until 1530 that two prominent printers—Egenolff in Strasbourg (and later Frankfurt am Main) and Steiner in Augsburg—finally started using real headings in their editions of *Küchenmeisterei*.

In the course of the sixteenth century, cookbooks in most countries established the use of separate headings, but they had no common pattern. Headings might introduce the name of a dish by using a verb in the infinitive (e.g., "To make Pancakes," "A fare minestra di carne," "Gute Turten zu machen"). Some started with the adverb "how" or the preposition "about" or "of." Others referred to the "manner" in which a dish was prepared. Some headings consisted only of the "name" of the dish, and this style became more and more common.

A few notable cookbooks from the sixteenth and seventeenth centuries did not use headings in this way but rather had general headings for different foodstuffs (e.g., turkey or cod) or groups of dishes (e.g., salads or soups) under which all the different recipes in these categories would be presented without separate headings.[71]

What these examples clearly demonstrate is that the structure of cookbooks went through many stages in different countries before reaching the standard form we find in most culinary works today.

6

Naming the Recipes

In order to find a recipe in an index, particularly in an alphabetical index, the dish must be referred to in an unambiguous way, preferably by a name. As discussed in the previous chapter, such names appeared in the text in some cookbooks (e.g., *amandeleyt* and *blancmanger*), but in other cases, the names were found in headings or incipit phrases. From the phrase "If you want to prepare stuffed crayfish," it is easy to construct the name "stuffed crayfish." But rather early on, authors observed that different designations existed for the same dishes. In his 1607 cookbook, the Spaniard Hernández de Maceras gave a recipe for "how to make *bolos de clauonia*," although he then clarified, "These are also named *bollos maymones*."[1] The Italian Bartolomeo Scappi's *Opera* (1570) had a recipe with the heading "To make minestra of dried beans" that he concluded with a commentary indicating a regional name for the dish: "And in Lombardy this dish is called *Macco*."[2] The same can be found in the German cook Marx Rumpolt's *Ein new Kochbuch* (1581): in a recipe for boiled hen tripe, he writes that in Swabia, the name of the dish is *Kragel Magel*.[3]

Where do the names of dishes come from? Names for things and phenomena have always intrigued the human mind. In Genesis, God brought every animal he created to Adam, who named them. In one of Plato's dialogues, the discussion is about names: Are they just the result of local conventions, or do they express the nature of things? Hermogenes, who argues for the conventional point of view, observes—just like the three cookbook authors mentioned above—that names are different among different people, not only between Greeks and barbarians but also between different Greek tribes.[4]

Names of dishes were probably created locally as part of human communication, the same way other things—such as plants, animals, lakes, mountains, and stars—were named. When new dishes arrived from outside, their names were adapted to the local language or dialect. The three cooks named above recognized similarities between dishes with different names and took the first small step toward classification.

Bollos maymones, Macco, and *Kragel Magel* are fascinating names that are open to speculation and discussion of origin and etymology. But a study of the headings and names in cookbooks, taken in a long historical perspective, reveals that most of them are just simple constructions. The basic principle behind some of these constructions can be compared to binominal nomenclature, the formal naming of plants and animals by genus and species, even if the naming of dishes doesn't follow the systematic approach we find in botany and zoology. Such binominal culinary names may describe the main ingredient (a noun) and the preparation (an adjective derived from a verb that characterizes the cooking process): for example, *veau rosty* (roasted veal) and *leshch pechenyj* (baked bream).[5] Two nouns may be combined, and often one of them will refer to a special type of preparation used for many different ingredients, such as *ein Apfelmus* (an apple mush), *tartes of fysshe* (fish tarts), and *potaje de fideos* (bean soup).[6] Two ingredients may be combined with a preposition, such as in *ptáki s cibuli* (fowl with onion) and *høns met pebberrod* (hen with horseradish).[7] There are names based on one or more ingredients, including *risotto* (from rice) and *aïoli* (garlic and oil). But names may become detached from their original ingredients: names derived from specific ingredients may be used for dishes with other ingredients as a result of culinary development. The name of the Italian dish polenta comes from a Latin word for peeled barley, the ingredient the porridge was originally made from. But when corn was introduced to the country and substituted for barley in polenta, the name of the dish remained the same. Something similar happened in Romania, where the corn porridge is called *mămăliga,* after *malai,* a word for millet, and this is how we know what this porridge was originally made of.

Because color has long been an important element in cuisine, there are many names that combine a type of dish with a color, such as *sopa dorada* (golden soup), *torta bianca* (white cake), *hwitmoos* (white mush), *saulce verte* (green sauce), and black caps (baked apples).[8] Color may even have been indicated indirectly by the name *saracen* (which refers not to Arabic culinary tradition but to dark color of the dish). In a French recipe for *brouet sarasinois,* cinnamon, long pepper, and saffron are added "to give it color."[9]

Cooking methods have been the foundation for new dish names. Take, for example, the verb "boil" in different languages. There is the classical Spanish dish *cocido* (the past participle of *cocer*), the Scandinavian dishes *vælling* and *sod* (from old Norse *vella* and *sjóða),* the Russian *vareniki* (from *varit*), and the French dishes *bouillie, bouilli,* and *bouillon* (all from *bouillir*). The first part of *bouillabaisse* has the same root. The Italian *stufato* is a slowly cooked stew, after the verb *stufare;*

similar French dishes are *à l'estouffade, à l'étouffée,* and *à l'étuvée,* from the verbs *étuver* and *étouffer*. To this group, we can add names that indicate the heat source used to cook a dish, such as the Italian dishes *focaccia* (after the Latin *focus,* or hearth) and *carbonata* (after *carbone,* or coal).

The vessel used to prepare a dish is also the basis for many names. In French and English, *casserole* is the name for both the container and the dish. Something similar is true for *pot,* which in French is the root of the names for the dishes *potage* and *pot-au-feu* and in English, of pottage. In Spain, the word for "pot" is *olla* or *cazuela,* and both words are also the names of dishes. The name of the Valencian dish *paella* comes from the Latin word *patella,* meaning frying pan. The mortar inspired the names of several dishes that can be found in old cookbooks, including *morterol* (Catalonia), *mortellus* and *mortrews* (England), and *mortraeus* (Denmark).

There are countless names that refer to shape, such as roll, ball, timbale, wreath, croissant (crescent), bagel (from the Yiddish *beygel,* which comes from an old German word meaning ring), and strudel (whirl), not to mention all the names of different forms of pasta, including *orecchiette* (small ears), *conchiglie* (shells), *lingue di passero* (sparrow tongues), and *vermicelli* (small worms).

Some names have a surprisingly jocular ring, such as the German *Schuhsohlen* (shoe soles), the Spanish *borrachuelos* (small drunkards), the English "drunken rolls," the Sicilian *minni di vergini* (virgin breasts), and the Italian *palle de nonno* (granddad's balls). There are many sweets from the Iberian peninsula with Catholic-inspired names: *tocino de cielo* (bacon from heaven), *cabello de angel* (angel hair), and *hueso de santo* (saint's bone), to name a few. One might think that this kind of humor is of a recent date, but in 1651, La Varenne, in his great work *Le cuisinier françois*—which is not particularly humorous—had a recipe for small pastries called *pets de putain* (whore's farts).[10] These treats were known from French fourteenth-century manuscripts that contained recipes for *pets d'Espagne* (Spanish farts).[11] In his 1782 food history, Le Grand d'Aussy referred to the *beignets venteux* (wind cakes) in Platina's book and gave the following explanation: "They are probably what we call farts [*pets*]."[12] *Larousse Gastronomique* has no reference to "whore's farts" but contains entries for "nun's farts," to which it added the euphemism "nun's sighs."

There are many dishes with names that refer to the royal or aristocratic circles where so many elegant meals were served, a tactic that was probably intended to bring extra status to the food. These dishes use terms such as *à la Royale, à la Reine, dauphine, princesse, duchesse, cardinale, impériale,* and *régence*. But new trends also entered cuisine that were inspired by an interest in or a romantic admiration for the popular classes and the simple life of the countryside: *à la fermière, jardinière,* and *paysanne*.[13]

The names that have led to the most queries and the most questionable interpretations are those that refer to particular places and persons. These types of names are found in very early cookbooks, such as *Apicius*, which was compiled in Roman antiquity, at least in the oldest known copies of the book from the ninth century. The book has recipes for Numidian chicken, Parthian lamb, suckling pig Trajan style, and peas Vitellius style.[14] In his treatise on agriculture, Cato the Elder gives a recipe for Punic porridge, named after the powerful enemy in Carthage, which he fought all his life.[15]

GEOGRAPHICAL NAMES

Place names have been found in recipes from the late Middle Ages up until today. But what exactly do these names tell us? Were authors (or whoever was responsible for the headings) indicating that the dishes were typical for a particular area? With a few names, this is obviously *not* the case because they refer to the sites of specific historical events. *Marengo* is the French name for a chicken or veal sauté, which, according to legend, was first served to the emperor Napoleon in 1800 after his victory over the Austrians near the Italian town Marengo. The ingredients are reputedly what his cook had at his disposal in the field. The name *mayonnaise* is in the same category: the sauce was allegedly invented by or for the Duke of Richelieu after he conquered the port of Mahon in Menorca in 1756.

Most geographical names, however, seem to refer to culinary traditions in different countries, regions, localities, cities, and ethnic and religious communities. Some examples are French puffins, carp the High German way, salmon the Polish way, milk as in Gdansk, Italian sausage, Bohemian peas, Dutch dish, pike the Hungarian way, rabbit the Portuguese way, eggplant the Morisco way, and Turkish rice.[16]

But are these geographical indications to be trusted? It is necessary to point out, as the historians Capatti and Montanari have done, that local products that are consumed at a local level are devoid of geographical identity. The *mortadella* made in Bologna, for instance, is only called *mortadella di Bologna* when it leaves the city where it is produced.[17] The name, in other words, is given to the product by someone from the outside. But have cookbooks accurately used these designations? They were probably faithful to what the authors knew of such dishes. We have seen that some cooks, such as Marx Rumpolt and Martínez Montiño, traveled and brought back with them new ideas from foreign countries, the same way other craftsmen did, at a time when most people spent their entire lives in the village where they were born. It is also evident in the recipe for eggplant the Morisco way, referred to above, that the author was well aware of the ethnic background of the dish when he explained that sweet oil was used instead of pork fat because the Moriscos did not eat pork.[18]

One recurrent feature is that different cookbooks show important differences in recipes with the same place names. This is demonstrated in fish dishes in German cookbooks between 1500 and 1800 that include the adjectives "Polish" and "Hungarian" and contain onions and apples. One book describes a dish called Carp with

Onion or Polish.[19] But other books mention both onion and apples as ingredients.[20] In the only printed Polish cookbook from the period—edited by a court official— onion is used in many fish dishes, but not more than parsley, lemon, sugar, raisins, and many spices. Apples are found in only one of the hundred fish recipes in the book.[21] Fish recipes called "Hungarian" and containing onions and apples are found in one Italian book, one Czech, a few German books, and a cookbook in French from Liège (present-day Belgium).[22] In the only printed Hungarian cookbook from this period, there are examples of a few fish dishes with apples and onion, but there are also recipes that call for apples *or* onion.[23] In this book, apples are also used in meat dishes, sometimes combined with onion, sometimes with other ingredients. Many of the fish dishes called "Polish" or "Hungarian" in the German books have pike as the main ingredient. In a Hungarian manuscript from the seventeenth century, one dish with apple is called Pike in Yellow Polish Broth.[24] But even if apples appear more often in Hungarian recipes than in recipes in other countries, it is difficult to consider this a style that deserves to be called national.

One possible explanation for the use of these names in German cookbooks is that there was a direct diffusion of recipes from Polish and Hungarian kitchens and not via Polish and Hungarian cookbooks. There is in fact an interesting remark in an earlier version of the mentioned Czech cookbook. The recipe starts with a sentence in first person singular (instead of the usual imperative): "I saw a fish prepared the Hungarian way," with onion and apples.[25] But to verify a diffusion of this sort would demand other sources. In any case, one can hardly use this explanation for the recipes in *all* the books in Western Europe, so there is reason to believe that recipes spread from one book to others in the way described in chapter 4.

Another important consideration is that dishes evolve over time and the ingredients may change, as happened with polenta. It is therefore difficult to determine if dishes with geographical names really originated in the mentioned area or are representative of its cuisine. Such questions were not often discussed in cookbooks, even if some authors explained that the same dish could be found with different names. One author who repeatedly came back to names was Pellegrino Artusi, an Italian intellectual who stuffed his 1891 cookbook with personal commentaries of all kinds. He sometimes explained the name of a recipe; for example, he wrote that *lingua alla scarlatta* pointed to the red color of the dish, and that *pane de sabbia* crumbled like sand in the mouth. But he criticized many culinary terms, calling them strange or ridiculous and deriding them as pompous designations ("titoli ampollosi"). When discussing the English dish toad in the hole (in his book, he called it simply "reboiled meat the English way"), he said that the culinary art could be called "the art of bizarre and odd names" (l'arte dei nomi capricciosi e strani). Even if it is possible to trace the real origin of many dishes, Artusi demonstrates that names may be the result of chance, coincidence, or fantasy.

When describing a dish that is called Hungarian, he said that it could well be Span-ish or French but that the name was not important as long as the dish is good. He called one dish *maccheroni alla francese* because he found the recipe in a French cookbook.[26]

Another interesting example is that of Danish pastries, which are called *Kopen-hagener* by Germans and Austrians, but *wienerbrød* (Vienna bread) in Copenha-gen and the rest of Scandinavia.

In the study of cookbooks, one must also consider the possibility for errors in copying and translation. When the English Renaissance personality Hugh Plat gave a recipe for "sawsedges of Polonia," he was actually referring to a dish from Bologna.[27] In her commentaries to the Russian classic cookbook by Elena Molokhovets, Joyce Toomre demonstrated that the dishes in the book with French names do not include the traditional ingredients or have been changed in other ways, with the result that they have no reason to claim a French origin.[28]

A more recent dish whose origin has been much discussed is the hamburger. Today, the dish is prepared as a flat patty served in a bun, a form that seems to have been invented at the 1904 St. Louis World's Fair, but the name "Hamburg steak" had been known in the United States before then; there was a recipe for *hamborger beefsteg* (based on minced meat) in a Scandinavian cookbook printed in Chicago in 1884.[29] In Europe, beef from the German city of Hamburg had a special reputa-tion by the beginning of the nineteenth century, when Grimod de la Reynière and Brillat-Savarin wrote about how Parisian cuisine incorporates specialties from all over, mentioning "le boeuf de Hambourg" as one of these products.[30] In many northern European cookbooks in the nineteenth century, we find recipes for dishes calling for "Hamburg meat," but this is often smoked or salted. There is, however, a recipe for "Hamburger Beefsteak" in a cookbook published in Rostock in 1868, and fresh meat is used; there is even a variant with minced meat.[31] It is served with onion and a fried egg. *Neues Hamburger Kochbuch* (1858) has a recipe for a dish made from scraped (*geschabt*) beef with the addition of spices, egg, and onion that is fried at a high temperature, but it is called "tartare."[32] Onion and egg are also among the ingredients in a Russian recipe from the early 1870s for *bifshteks po-gamburgski*.[33] In 1896, Fannie Farmer's *The Boston Cooking-School Cook Book* had a recipe for Hamburg steaks. They are compared to ordinary meat steaks but are made with onion, a beaten egg, and nutmeg. Strangely enough, the recipe is exactly the same in the 1923 edition, even though the book was said to have been completely revised.[34] The conclusion in this case must be that there are two parallel and different traditions. One was developed in cookbooks in Europe and later in the United States, whereas the other was developed in North American restaurant culture and only entered cookbooks recently, after ordinary meat steaks or meat patties had lost their Hamburg connection.

PERSONAL NAMES: A SPECIAL TRADITION

The names of specific individuals have been used in the naming of plants, animals, and minerals to honor the person who discovered or identified them. Similarly, a dish that includes someone's name may refer to the person credited with inventing it, as was the case with Pellegrino Artusi's *panettone Marietta,* named after his cook, Marietta Sabatini. In this case, Artusi opened the recipe with an explanation, saying that Sabatini was a good and honest cook who deserved to have her name attached to the dish because she taught him to make it.[35] But this is an exception; dishes named after individuals are more often meant to honor people outside the league of cooks or to create an anecdote that stimulates interest for the dish (figures 14 and 15).

There are a few dishes from before 1800 that are named after people—for example, *béchamel* and *duxelles,* named after Marquis de Béchamel and Marquis d'Uxelles, two seventeenth-century aristocrats—but the practice became much more popular in the nineteenth and twentieth centuries. It is significant that in Manfred Höfler's dictionary of French culinary terms and expressions, more than 80 percent of the dishes named after individuals were "invented" during the past two centuries. These dishes were named after historical personalities as diverse as Lucullus, the Médicis, Henri IV, and Agnes Sorel; the composer Rossini; the writers Fontenelle and Chateaubriand; the financier Rothschild; the Russian aristocrats Romanoff, Orloff, Strogonoff, and Demidoff (all written here in the French transcription known from cookbooks); and the diplomat Nesselrode, made famous through Marcel Proust's masterpiece, *À la recherche du temps perdu.* There were even dishes named after mythological or literary persons, like the opera characters Carmen and Belle-Hélène. A few dishes were named after key actors in politics, like the French ministers Colbert and Talleyrand.[36] In the years after national unity was established in Germany and Italy, new popular dishes included *Kaiser Wilhelm Kartoffelsuppe, Bismarckhering, carciofi alla Cavour,* and *pizza Margherita.*

A boom for recipes named after individuals came with the growth of a new restaurant culture after the French Revolution, particularly during the second half of the nineteenth century. Cooks and restaurateurs coined names of recipes to honor artists, royalty, and celebrities who met at the fashionable hotels and restaurants. *Crêpe Suzette* was allegedly first served in a restaurant in Monte Carlo by a chef who wanted to flatter the mistress of the partying Prince Edward, while *pêche Melba* was the star cook Auguste Escoffier's homage to the Australian opera singer Nellie Melba.

These new names were entered into cookbooks only after they appeared on restaurant menus, where all the dishes of an establishment were listed. Menu cards had became more and more common in private dinner parties of a certain importance after the introduction of the Russian serving system (*service à la russe*) in the nineteenth century. In the earlier French system (*service à la française*), all the dishes

361. Posteier à la Mazarin.

Petits pâtés à la Mazarin.

FIGURE 14. Illustration for little pies named after Jules Mazarin, a French cardinal and politician of Italian origin. From *Kogebog* (Kristiania, 1895), by M. Schulze, who was the chef of a restaurant for Freemasons in the Norwegian capital.

712. Beafsteg à la Nelson.

Bifteck à la Nelson.

FIGURE 15. Illustration for a beefsteak dish named after Horatio Nelson, an English admiral. From M. Schulze, *Kogebog* (1895).

were placed on the table at once for the guests to choose, but only one dish was served at a time in the Russian system, which meant that the guests depended on an account of what was to come so they could regulate their intake according to appetite and taste.[37] In restaurants, a written or printed list of available dishes became absolutely necessary, whether people wanted to order from a set menu or à la carte.[38] But a long time before the individual menu cards and restaurant menus of the nineteenth century, cookbooks had printed lists of dishes composed for dinners or banquets. Some of these "menus" were suggestions made according to the religious calendar, for example: "Here followeth the order of meats how they must be serued at the Table, with their sauces for flesh daies at dinner."[39] Other books had menus listing what had actually been served at a specific meal. Bartolomeo Stefani, cook at the Mantua court of the Gonzagas, included in his recipe collection seven pages describing a banquet given in 1655 for the visiting Swedish Queen Kristina, who had abdicated the year before, but was received in Italy as a majesty and celebrated for her conversion to Catholicism: "Banchetto ordinato per la Maesta' della Regina Christina di Svecia dal Serenissimo di Mantova."[40] In the nineteenth and twentieth centuries, many ambitious cookbooks had menus for various occasions. In his book *The Epicurean* (1894), Charles Ranhofer, chef at Delmonico's in New York, dedicated several hundred pages to all sorts of different menus used in his restaurant since 1862, following both the Russian and French service systems and with special reference to breakfast and buffet menus common in the United States.[41]

How important were these elegant menus, filled with exotic names, to the guests and cooks? To answer this, the sociologist Jean-Pierre Poulain investigated the possible meanings of recipe names in the nineteenth century, when this genre really started to flourish.[42] He concluded that these names have a double function, one scientific and one poetic. The first function may be seen as a part of the emphasis cooks and cookbook authors from the eighteenth century onward have put on the scientific element in cooking ("la cuisine scientifique"). Inspired by Linnaeus and others who classified natural sciences, representatives of the culinary profession started to name dishes and recipes in a systematic way, a process culminating with Auguste Escoffier's codification of culinary nomenclature.[43]

To explain the other function of recipe designations, the poetry and fantasy ("poétisation, fantasmatisation") that maximizes the pleasure for the gourmand, Poulain refers to the three categories suggested in Jean-Paul Aron's classic work, *Le mangeur du XIXᵉ siècle* (The nineteenth century eater, 1973):

1. "La parole du monde." Geographical names that do not so much refer to national or regional culinary techniques as they do to the imagination and dreams of distant horizons. They have, in other words, a symbolic meaning for the consumer, or "le mangeur," as Aron calls him.
2. "La rhétorique du sublime." Names of royal, aristocratic, or other prestigious persons who do not necessarily have any relation to the dish but serve to lift it out of daily banality and into a higher sphere and to elevate the consumer into a culinary pantheon. Poulain supposed that the name of a celebrity or a nobleman may have given extra value to a dish: "For a parvenu searching legitimacy, to eat *riz Condé* means to be ennobled by consuming the attributes, the emblematic nutrition of one of the greatest aristocrats."[44]

3. "La metamorphose." Names with no direct connection to the food in question but which use the power of metaphors to create suggestive associations and allusions, for example, to mythical splendor: "Des turbans de filets de merlans à la royale" (turbans of whiting filets à la royale).[45]

These interpretations by Aron and Poulain are inspired by the gastronomic writers of the early nineteenth century, and by Grimod de la Reynière in particular. In the preceding centuries, most creators of dishes seem to have been more interested in the practical use of names and less in their symbolic value. Metaphors, when used, had a tendency to be more for entertainment—playful names, for example—but these were met with ambiguity in the nineteenth century. Grimod defended such names, claiming that they could create interest and curiosity. In his gastronomic journal from 1804, he mentioned the pot-au-feu dish *potage à la jambe de bois* (wooden leg soup), and in the next edition, he commented, "This name has aroused the curiosity of many people."[46] But others—among them cooks and cookbook authors—found such names coarse and vulgar. Louis Eustache Ude, cook to Napoleon's mother, later became a prominent chef in England and wrote in *The French Cook* (1822): "I confess there are some ridiculous names; for instance, *soup au clair de lune, soup à la jambe de bois, la poularde en bas de soie, les pets de nonne* &c. &c. and many other names still more ridiculous, which I omit to mention in my Treatise."[47] Carême condemned these "barbaric" terms; in his view, *potage à la jambe de bois* should be named *potage à la moelle de boeuf* (the dish was made with a whole leg of beef, but the marrow was the main point).[48] He also criticized *culs d'artichauts* (artichoke butts), *pets de nonne glacés* (glazed nun's farts), and *veau roulé en crotte d'âne* (veal in donkey turd), from the cookbook *Le cuisinier gascon*.[49] In his 1867 book, *Le livre de cuisine,* the French chef Jules Gouffé commented on the language in cookbooks and said that he had taken great care to avoid "les dénominations pompeuses ou bizarres."[50]

Carême discussed the names of dishes in several of his works. One of his basic beliefs was that names were important; he thought that they produced effects and ought to be decorative. Therefore, he recommended invoking royalty and the aristocracy as well as great chefs when naming dishes. Escoffier invented many special names for new dishes, including a whiting mousse with crayfish that he called Rêve de Katinka (Katinka's dream) and described as being "as light as the artistic steps of the famous dancer" (aussi légère que les pas artistiques de la célèbre danseuse). Escoffier was conscious of the artistic aspects of cuisine and the importance of relevant expressions. He believed that the names of dishes ought to sound to the ear like soft harmonies, in sympathy with the prepared dishes.[51]

Escoffier called the menu "une sorte de poésie." A French gourmet used a similar wording, "une poésie sublime," suggesting that reading the menu would bring ecstasy and transport the true gastronome to the promised paradise.[52] But this poetry may be deceptive, like all language in relation to sensations, an observation made by the French philosopher Henri Bergson in his 1889 doctoral thesis: "Not only does language make us believe in the unchangeableness of our sensations, but it will sometimes deceive us as to the nature of the sensation felt. Thus, when I partake of a dish that is supposed to be exquisite, the name which it bears, suggestive of the approval given to it, comes between my sensation and my consciousness; I may believe that the flavour pleases me when a slight effort of attention would prove the contrary."[53]

In other words, a catchy name is not necessarily an asset. Maybe this reflection was taken up by the protagonists of *nouvelle cuisine* in the 1970s when they advocated abandoning naming dishes after individuals and instead transferring the attention back to the ingredients and preparation methods.[54] Paul Bocuse, prominent representative of *nouvelle cuisine,* gave recipes for *tournedos Henri IV* and *beurre Bercy,* dishes with a long history, in his 1980 cookbook, *La cuisine du marché,* but most of his recipes have descriptive names, such as *brandade de morue aux truffes, croquettes de pommes de terre,* and *omelette aux fines herbes.*[55] Elizabeth David, who used the traditional names of her Mediterranean dishes, asked in an article, "What's, after all, in a name?"[56] It sounds immediately commonsensical: Why bother with a name instead of just concentrating on the preparation of a dish? But it is not as simple as that. When Heston Blumenthal served a crab ice cream to accompany a crab risotto, guests found it too sweet, but when he renamed it frozen crab bisque, people accepted it and found it less sweet.[57] There is, after all, a lot in a name.

NAMES OF DISHES AS METAPHORS

From what has been written above, it is evident that the names of dishes have a practical function as well as a symbolic one. But during the history of cuisine, the names of many dishes have been used in areas far from the kitchen and the dining room, a fact that illustrates how aspects of daily life have influenced the culture of European society. For example, hotchpotch (English), *insalata* (Italian), *salmigondis* (Spanish), and *labskovs* (Danish) are all names of dishes, but they are also words for mixtures of different things that do not necessarily have anything to do with food. The dishes are simple but appetizing, whereas the metaphors often have a negative value, as they refer to combinations of elements that don't belong together. Names of dishes have also been used—negatively and positively—in religious and political conflicts, humorous entertainment, and even descriptions of literary works. This last point is of course only one aspect of the important role culinary terms in general have played as literary metaphors since antiquity.[58]

When names of dishes have been used in a literary context, they sometimes take on a negative or at least a self-mocking tone, as in the words Montaigne chose when he evaluated (perhaps ironically) some of his essays: he wrote that he slapped together a *fricassée* and made a *galimafrée* of various ingredients.[59] But other writers are entirely positive when they resort to culinary metaphors. In letters to his friend the Count of Argental, Voltaire referred to the five acts of his tragedy *Irène* as "five pies" (cinq pâtés).[60] Honoré de Balzac praised Brillat-Savarin's *Physiologie du goût* for its variety by comparing it to an *olla podrida,* a Spanish dish made with a multitude of delicious ingredients.[61] In *À la recherche du temps perdu,* Marcel Proust described the expressions used by the character Madame de Guermantes as "as savory as the dishes possible to discover in the delicious books by Pampille," a cookbook author he later called a true poet.[62] In the final pages of the novel, the narrator conceives of the book he is writing as being made in the same way as his cook Françoise's *boeuf à la mode,* where the jelly is enriched by all the pieces of exclusive meats.[63]

A more systematic use of culinary terminology has been applied in certain forms of satiric literature,[64] particularly in sixteenth-century disputes and quarrels between Catholics and Protestants. *Satyres chrestiennes de la cuisine papale* (1560) is a famous Calvinist polemic in verse that attacked the pope and the Catholic Church by way of its cuisine. We find a criticism in these satires in line with contemporary views of intemperance and overindulgence among the clergy:

> The drunkenness among the priests
> The traitors with their gourmandizing.

But the rude rhetoric is not only directed against the lifestyle of the priests; it also critiques the Catholic liturgy and theology. The center of orthodox theology at the time was the Sorbonne University in Paris, which is alluded to in these lines:

> Tell me if you want carbonades,
> or do you prefer Sorbonades?

The satire, called "The Pope's Banquet," referred to the serving of meals in ways that allude to what takes place in the Eucharist: with "bread of lies and wine that of the falsehood stinks." Religious concepts and culinary terms were mixed in ways that must have felt blasphemous to most Catholics:

> Paternosters and rosaries
> are saffron, cinnamon and spices,
> miraculously appropriate
> to give taste to the soup.

Protestants gave their services in local languages, and they attacked the use of Latin in the Catholic Mass, and more particularly the Greek prayers, which few people understood, such as the Trisagion prayer. The first and last Greek words in this prayer appeared in the satire in a list of sausages and other dishes with mixed ingredients:

> *Agios* and *himas* are andouilles,
> sausages, saveloy, black pudding,
> *hâtereau* and salmagundis.

Andouille is made from pork chitterlings and tripe, *hâtereau* is a ball of pork liver, and all of the dishes mentioned are made with offal and blood, mixed together.[65] A mixture of various ingredients was intrinsically negative (a ragout is another example), as it represented confusion.

"Confusion" was one of the favorite words the Protestants used to describe the Catholic doctrine. This is the same expression John Calvin himself chose when he described how the Roman Church "disguised" Jesus: "The teachings of the gospel are mixed together as a confused soup." Another prominent Protestant, Philippe de Marnix de Sainte-Aldegonde, chose *capilotade* to indicate confusion. This is a form of ragout often made with leftovers.[66] There is no doubt that the decision to use culinary metaphors had to do with the low status kitchen work and the art of cooking had at the time. Thus, comparing Catholic theology to the realm of the kitchen made the institution and its representatives appear comical and ridiculous.

In England, the same method was used in political satire during the eighteenth century. When William Verral, chef of the White Hart Inn in Sussex, published *A Complete System of Cookery* (1759), a cookbook of French and French-inspired dishes, he was attacked in the prestigious *Critical Review,* a British journal edited by Tobias Smollett, with contributions by David Hume, Samuel Johnson and Oliver Goldsmith. The anonymous author reviewing Verral's book wrote that it should have been called "a complete system of politics" because all the world knows "with what propriety the metaphors in politics are fetched from the figures and terms used in cookery."[67] He went on to mention "political pancakes" and a statesman who "cooked up a rare *hachis* in politics," and he described a political faction as "an *olio* of different humours." He asked Verral how he could introduce French dishes "at this period, when we ought to distinguish ourselves as Antigallicans in everything." The article was published during the Seven Years' War, and the reviewer read Verral's book as a defense for the enemy with its recipes for French sauces that "will poison the nation." However, he recommended Verral's recipes for macaroons with Parmesan cheese and for pears in the Portuguese fashion, as there was nothing to fear at that point from Portugal and the Italian states.

Earlier in the eighteenth century, the writer and composer Henry Carey anonymously published *A Learned Dissertation on Dumpling* (1726), which was read by some as a political satire. The book "revealed" that pudding was first introduced to Britain by Julius Cesar. The humor is simple and nonsensical. The author insisted that basically everything is a pudding: poetry is a pudding of words, the head of a man is a pudding, the universe itself is a pudding of elements, and war depends on puddings and dumplings, "for what else are Cannon-Balls, but Military Puddings; or Bullets, but Dumplings."[68]

But certain readers saw puddings and dumplings as metaphors for contemporary bribery and corruption, exemplified by the Whig prime minister Robert Walpole. There were actually many similar satires and attacks directed against Walpole and other Whigs, including the Duke of Newcastle, who was a lover of French food and employed French cooks.[69]

In the introduction to the book, Carey wrote that pudding was a result of historical development: it began with flour and water, and other ingredients were added through the generations. Voltaire must have been referring to Carey in a letter he wrote to a friend in the Parlement de Bretagne discussing French institutions such as parliaments and the Estates General: "I am rather of the opinion given by an Englishman who said that all the origins, all the rights, all the establishments resemble a plum-pudding: the first only used flour, the second added eggs, the third sugar, the fourth raisins and thus the plum-pudding was created."[70]

A rather different but no less absurd example from the nineteenth century is found in the work of the young Anton Chekhov, who wrote short comic and satiric sketches in humorous journals before he became famous for his plays and short stories. Among his pieces was a calendar that was printed in the magazine *Budil'nik* (The alarm clock) in 1882.[71] For each day, he gave the menu of a dinner consisting of a mix of edible dishes and silly or ridiculous dishes, often with names in the form of puns. Some of the menus have a commentary added in parenthesis, for example: "This dinner is in the book by Mrs. Olga Molokhovets called the lawyers' dinner."[72] In this dinner, the names of the dishes refer to characteristics—or rather prejudices—associated with members of the legal profession. The first dish is cabbage soup with parrots; the Russian word for "parrot," *popugai*, also means a person who parrots, mechanically repeating what others say. The next dish is tongue with peas; the tongue is, of course, the basic organ of a professional lawyer. The third dish is roast goose, made with a special goose, *gus' lapchatyi*, which more or less means a sneaky one, a sly fox, or a trickster—in other words, not an honest person. The fourth and fifth dishes are drinks: sugar water and *voditsa*. Many recipes for *voditsa* can be found in Molokhovets's *Gift to Young Housewives* in a chapter with "light, homemade" drinks fermented with fruits or berries.[73] There is reason to believe that Chekov's inclusion of these rather light drinks was significant, particularly when contrasted with his description of the journalists' dinner, which basically consisted of an increasing number of glasses of vodka.

7

Pedagogical and Didactic Approaches

In a cookbook, the recipe names, index, chapters, headings, running titles, and so on have a practical aim: to provide easy access to the recipe for a desired dish. There are, however, books with a more serious and profound pedagogical or didactic approach that make a point of teaching cookery to beginners through a gradual learning process. In 1881, one author even boasted that her book was "a complete instructor, so that a child can understand it and learn the art of cooking."[1]

This approach, however, is by and large not followed by theoretical discussions or reflections around pedagogical ideas and processes. Most authors, not to mention publishers, may be afraid of scaring away beginners who are interested in practical instruction, but they are not prepared to enter into a broader dicussion of the basic principles of education. Fundamental educational questions are therefore discussed outside the cookbook genre, for example, the question: What is a beginner?

TEACHING THE BEGINNER

The discussion about oral and written instruction raised in chapter 3 is picked up here by the philosopher Michael Oakeshott, who occasionally used cooks and cooking to illustrate his ideas. He wrote in his essay "Political Education" that political *ideology* is a result of political *activity,* not the other way around. One of the examples he gave to prove his point is that nobody can learn how to cook using a cookbook as his or her sole guide. To interpret and understand a ccokbook demands a certain knowledge about cooking.[2]

Oakeshott is probably right in this observation, and his argument is reinforced by the way most cookbooks are written. Recipes leave out much basic information,

Фиг. 19

Надо имѣть нѣсколько *толстыхъ иголокъ* для зашиванія фарши-
рованной птицы и рыбы, а также нѣсколько шпиговокъ для шпигованія
мяса и дичи.

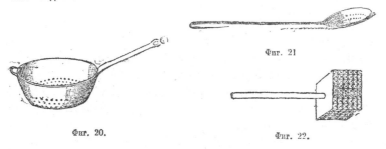

Фиг. 21

Фиг. 20.

Фиг. 22.

Нѣсколько формъ большихъ и малыхъ (фиг. 25, 26, и 27) для
заливанія мясныхъ и рыбныхъ галантировъ, а также для кремовъ и желе.

Фиг. 23.

Мороженица (фиг. 28) послѣдней американской системы. При

FIGURE 16. Illustration of cooking utensils from the Russian cookbook *Polnyi podarok molodym khoziaikam* (Complete gift to young housewives), by K. K. Morokhovtsev, published in Moscow in 1901.

for example, about kitchen equipment of various kinds—such as stoves, mortars, pots, pans, and spits (figure 16). Instructions to fry and boil are given without any mention of what sort of vessel should be used. Older books did not always include measures of heat and time. Today, recipes still presuppose a certain familiarity with culinary language and terms. In other words, even a beginner is expected to have some fundamental idea of what cooking is about. But when that is acknowl-edged, it is possible to make a book in which the recipes are structured to guide the reader in a gradual process of learning the art of cooking.

This process is most visible in manuals written for pupils in home economics courses and cooking schools, where the books are designed to accompany and support the teacher's instructions and demonstrations, and where the education is planned for a certain period (e.g., a school term or year). But the didactic approach was not invented by modern schoolbook authors. As Bruno Laurioux pointed out, pedagogical ambition can be found in some medieval manuscripts that include a progression of recipes with increasing degrees of difficulty.[3] The opening sentence of the fourteenth-century Latin text *Liber de coquina* states that the author intends to begin with the easier preparations.[4]

This method for teaching cookery is part of a general pedagogical strategy. In the eighteenth century, the cookbook author Martha Bradley wrote: "In all Studies it is the regular Practice to begin with the plainest and easiest Things, and from there to arise to such as are more difficult." She then explained that she would follow this rule and start with roasting and boiling before moving on to "the most elegant and difficult Made Dishes." A German cookbook went one step further, stating that a collection of culinary recipes has no value if there is no "thread," no system, no plan that brings clarity and understanding to all the concepts and to the whole field of the art of cooking.[5]

Historians tend to consider the French cook known as La Varenne to have been the first person to systematically try to realize this ideal of clarity and understanding. In his cookbook *Le cuisinier françois* (1651), he distinguished between the basic sauces and preparations and the more elaborate ones, and he also gave cross references, so the book appeared to be "a coherent totality codifying the art of cookery."[6] It is important to note that La Varenne gave information about processes that were used for many different dishes. On the first page of his book, he instructed readers how to make *bouillon* for all pot dishes, such as *potages*. He started another chapter with these words: "Before I discourse about the ways to dress meat, I give you advice about how to garnish your plates with flowers." And he gave general introductions for making pies with various contents.[7] By using this method, La Varenne was able to avoid repeating information. Repetition is a recurrent problem in cookbooks, and another old method to avoid this was used by Scappi, who wrote after his recipe for quince pie: "This preparation is valid also for all sorts of peaches and raw apples."[8] Variants were also introduced with headings such as "another way," "the same," or the Latin word *item*.

However, there were authors in the nineteenth century who defended repetition for pedagogical reasons. The English gourmet William Kitchiner wrote in his classic *Apicius Redivivus, or The Cook's Oracle* that he was so eager to be understood that he intentionally repeated instructions in different parts of his book, stating that he would rather "be censured for repetition than for obscurity." A successful Norwegian writer, Marie Blom, wrote that she had used repetition in her book on purpose because one could not expect readers to remember everything, particularly not the beginners that her book was meant for.[9] It is difficult to say whether authors gave such explanations to defend their principles or as excuses to counter possible criticism.

TYPOGRAPHICAL VARIATION

One way to reinforce a pedagogical system is by using typography. In cookbooks, as in other forms of didactic literature, marginalia sum up important points, different fonts indicate difference in content, and italics and bold type emphasize certain fundamental culinary terms. One very important typographical development over the past two centuries has been to gather the ingredients in a list separate from the description of the preparation. A vertical column with ingredients listed one after another appears in a German manuscript from around 1770,[10] but this was not typical for printed books at the time. The system seems to have evolved gradually, and it began with cake recipes. In 1755, Cajsa Warg, a Swedish housekeeper, introduced what might be called an embryo of the future system in her *Hjelpreda i hushållningen för unga fruentimber* (Household assistance for young housewives). In certain cake recipes, she listed all the ingredients before going on to describe the baking process. In one recipe, she even dropped the ubiquitous "take" and just wrote a list, although there was no typographical distinction between the ingredients and the description.[11] The same method was used in the cake chapters in Elizabeth Raffald's cookbooks from the 1770s onward, and in this case, the list was a logical consequence of what Raffald emphasized in the introduction to the chapter: "Be sure that you get the things ready before you begin." The recipe for seed cake begins this way: "TAKE a pound of flour well dried, a pound of butter, a pound of loaf sugar beat and sifted, eight eggs, two ounces of caraway seeds, one nutmeg grated, and its weight of a cinnamon; first beat your butter to a cream, then put in your sugar . . ."[12] Even though the list of ingredients is not separated from the rest of the text, it is easy to see where the list stops and the description begins.

In the first edition of his cookbook, published in 1817, William Kitchiner occasionally listed ingredients first, for example, in this recipe for "plumb" pudding:

Suet, chopped fine, six ounces; malaga raisins, stoned, six ounces; currants, nicely washed and picked, eight ounces; bread-crumbs, three ounces; flour, three ounces; eggs, three; the rind of half a lemon; sixth of a nutmeg; small blade of mace; same quantity of cinnamon, pounded as fine as possible; half a tea-spoonful of salt; half a pint of milk, or rather less; sugar, four ounces: to which may be added, candied lemon, one ounce; citron, one ounce.

Beat the eggs and spice well together; mix the milk with them by degrees, then the rest of the ingredients; dip a fine close linen cloth into boiling water, and put it in a hair-sieve; flour it a little, and tie it up close; put it into a sauce-pan containing six quarts of boiling water: keep a kettle of boiling water along-side of it, to fill up your pot as it wastes; be sure to keep it boiling six hours at least.[13]

In the 1822 edition of the cookbook and later editions that were revised by Kitchiner until his death in 1827, the list of ingredients was printed as a vertical column, as is common today. Kitchiner had included a few such columns in recipes for sauces and relishes in the first edition. This means that the system had already been introduced in England when Eliza Acton referred to certain "novel features" in her 1845 book, *Modern Cookery*. One of these was "the summary appended to the receipts, of the different ingredients which they contain."[14] In other words, the ingredients were listed at the bottom of the recipe. In Russia, Elena Molokhovets used the same method in her classic cookbook from 1861, but she listed the ingredients more systematically in two columns. In his 1822 book, *Geist der Kochkunst* (The spirit of cooking), the German gastronomic writer Karl von Rumohr presented some of the recipes in two parts, first giving *Quantitäten* (quantities of ingredients) and then *Verfahren* (preparation).[15] But judging from an 1866 cookbook by Maria Schandri, such presentations were rare in Germany in the first half of the nineteenth century. Schandri opened her recipes for sweet dishes with a list of ingredients and remarked in the introduction that this practical method was, as far as she was aware, not found in any other cookbook.[16]

Some authors, including the Frenchman Jules Gouffé, in his 1867 cookbook, presented columns with lists of ingredients embedded within the recipe text where they chronologically were meant to be used. But ingredients often have to be prepared in advance, so this system is less useful than a list separated from the instructions. The system with ingredients in separate columns took a long time to become firmly established and, with few exceptions, did not take off seriously before the last decades of the nineteenth century. Among the books that most eagerly promoted the new setup were manuals for school classes in home economics and cooking schools, where the pedagogical element was fundamental.

The famous Victorian cookbook author Isabella Beeton took the use of typography one step further. She divided the information in each recipe into separate parts with the headings "Ingredients," "Mode," "Time," "Average cost," "Sufficient" (that is, how many people the recipe would serve), and "Seasonable" (what times of the year it was appropriate for). She also gave an explanation for the system, calling it "entirely original and most intelligible." In the linguist Ruth Carroll's opinion, it is with Beeton "that we really see the transition from the recipes of the past to the recipes of today."[17] But even if the book appears to be very well organized, which makes it easy to consult the recipes, the fundamental part of the recipe, the preparation itself—what Beeton calls "mode"—does not function in a particularly pedagogical way. As Elizabeth David demonstrated by comparing the recipes for sole cooked in cream in books by the two authors, Beeton was less successful with her brief instructions than Acton, who provided detailed explanations of every step.[18]

Beeton's arrangement did not gain many immediate followers, but later, in the twentieth century, the step-by-step system was introduced in several books.[19] Steps were either numbered or emphasized by the use of text boxes and separate headings. Carroll explained that the new arrangement derived from a model proposed in a study from 1992, and gave examples of how it functioned.[20]

EXACT MEASURES

In a recipe for an inexperienced beginner, it is important to include not only the preparation steps but also the exact amount of each ingredient, the right strength of heat, and the necessary cooking time. An experienced cook, however, does not rely on such indications, as he or she will improvise during the cooking process, as the eighteenth-century author Menon explained: "Someone competent is in a position to judge for himself, and if he does not want to follow the suggested method, because not everyone has the same taste, he may increase or reduce [the quantity of the ingredients]."[21] There are certainly cookbook readers who interpret recipes in their own creative fashion. This can be compared to the reader-oriented reception aestheticism of the German Konstanz school, where the reader of a literary work is expected to fill in the lacunas in the text and create his own sense and meaning of it. Roland Barthes's famous line about *la mort de l'auteur*—"The birth of the reader must be paid with the death of the author"[22]—is in principle just as valid for cookbooks as it is for other forms of literature.

Some professional cooks didn't see any need for precise instruction. Marx Rumpolt, private cook to the prince-elector in Mainz, wrote in his 1581 cookbook that weighing was unnecessary and that it was not possible to carry around a pair of scales all the time. In his opinion, it was easy to judge if there is too little or too much of something. In *La cuisine du marché* Paul Bocuse referred to a cookbook by the chef Fernand Point, who did not give any weights or proportions. This was going a little too far, according to Bocuse, who called the quantities in his own book "approximatives."[23] But a beginner will probably stick to the words of the author and not do any experimentation. It is of course necessary to emphasize that even the most detailed explanations do not guarantee a perfect result. A culinary recipe is not comparable to instructions for how to use an iPad or install a computer program. But exactitude is a valuable first step in a pedagogical process.

In the introduction to his recipe collection, published in the early nineteenth century, William Kitchiner stated in the introduction that he aimed to give the quantities of ingredients in number, weight, and measure with a precision never before attempted in a cooking book. He contrasted this practice with that of earlier books, which used vague expressions like "a handful of this," "a pinch of that," "a shake of pepper," "a squeeze of lemon," or "a dash of vinegar."[24]

Such expressions had been common through the centuries and continued to be used even after Kitchiner's time—and to be fair, not always with bad results. The question of precision has to be related to which function a recipe is meant to have and which readers it is intended for. This is important to keep in mind when we go back to the oldest manuscripts and the first printed cookbooks, which contain very few, if any, measures. This text from the English *Forme of Cury* is typical of medieval recipes: "Malaches. Take blode of swine, floure, & larde idysed, salt & mele; do hit togedre. Bake hyt in a trappe wyt wyte gres."[25] Recipes like this were without doubt meant for professional cooks, who knew how to calculate the right amount of food for a certain number of guests and how to regulate the fire. These cooks may have been without theoretical knowledge, but they had developed technical skills based on oral tradition and long experience. This was part of a culture that cooks had in common with other craftsmen. In his study of quantification in Western society in the late Middle Ages and the early modern era, Alfred Crosby observed: "Recipes for making glass, chalices, organs, and other things included very few numbers: 'a bit more' and 'a medium-sized piece' were precise enough."[26]

In spite of this, a closer look at old cookbooks reveals a long tradition of rather precise descriptions in culinary literature, even if they are sporadically rather than systematically applied. The oldest Danish cookbook, from the fourteenth century, does not give weights or volumes but does indicate instead the ratio of the ingredients: "One should take cloves, nutmeg, pepper and ginger, the same amount of each, and of cinnamon as much as of all of the others together."[27] In the same century, a Venetian text gave exact measures. The recipes in this book are listed alphabetically—also a striking exception to the rule of the time—and the first, Amidono d'Amido (amidono of starch), starts with these words: "If you want to make *amiduni* for 12 persons, take two pounds of almonds and one of flour, and a half of sugar and a half of clean pine kernels and half of a quart of cloves." The author was so conscious of the quantities that he added a note after the description about how they could be varied according to the number of guests.[28]

Attitudes toward the use of exact measures seem to have varied depending on national habits. When discussing weighing, the German cook Marx Rumpolt wrote, "the Italians weigh everything" (Die Welschen nemmen alles nach dem Gewicht).[29] He may have been familiar with two earlier Italian cookbooks, *Banchetti* (1549), by Christofaro Messisbugo, and *Opera* (1570), by Bartolomeo Scappi. Messisbugo and Scappi often gave exact measurements, particularly for spices.[30] It is in fact a characteristic feature in early cookbooks that precise measures were used most frequently when spices and sugar were among the ingredients. This is evident in many confectionery books. The first printed book in this genre in Spain is from 1592, and one of the recipes calls for one pound of anise, six pounds of sugar, and three pints of water.[31] In other words, precision was more often found in recipes that were not culinary in a strict sense but were produced by professionals other than cooks.[32]

The precision in such recipes may also have to do with the fact that spices and sugar were more expensive than other ingredients, but price was not the only factor. Sugar and spices were sold by apothecaries and prescribed by physicians in remedies for diseases, and prescriptions were often printed along with culinary and confectionary recipes in old cookbooks. Physicians and apothecaries did not only think of taste but also of medical effect, and they wrote recipes with accurate quantities of each ingredient. In an English book on preservation and distilling from 1671, a recipe with all quantities given in pints, pounds, drams, and ounces is attributed to a "Mr. Philips, Apothecary."[33] A system of accurate measures for medicines was firmly established in England after the publication in 1618 of the official *Pharmacopoeia Londinensis, or The London Dispensatory*,[34] which laid out instructions and regulations for apothecaries, but this does not mean that exact measures were absent earlier. In the English cookbooks attributed to Thomas Dawson from the 1580s and 1590s, there is a recipe for a medicinal drink for sick people that begins: "Take Rennish wine a quart, or Spanish wine a pint, rose water a pint and a half, Sinamon brused a pound and a halfe . . ."[35] Through the centuries, the use of precision increased generally, but the differences in the level of precision between books were still rather significant, and the old expressions mentioned by Kitchiner were still in use.

References to the price of products were also common: "six Pennyworth of the coarse lean Part of the Beef," "a shilling dissolved yeast," "one fourth of a five-kopek French roll," "eight maravedis of spices."[36] Size was given by referring to the dimensions of coins—"as broad as a shilling," "the thickness of two silver rubles"[37]—or to the dull edge of a knife (*messerrückendick*).[38] But most popular in all languages was the use of fingers, hands, and feet. A book published in 1604 in Liège uses all of these human appendages to indicate size: "the half of a little finger," "the size of a hand," "broad as half of a foot."[39] Another method was to refer to common objects, such as a hen's egg or a walnut.

During the eighteenth century, more and more authors defined cooking as a branch of science or a form of chemistry.[40] In Sweden, Cajsa Warg took up the scientific challenge and applied it in her 1755 cookbook. At around this time, the Swedish scientists Andreas Celsius and Carl Linnaeus were gaining international fame. Their mentalities and ambitions were shared by the Stockholm elite, the milieu in which Warg lived, as she was not only a housekeeper but also the sister of the housewife she worked for. In the preface to her cookbook, she wrote that the most important aspect of cooking was "the science, how things ought to be measured, divided, and mixed, and to obtain this I have given weight, measure, and time for the preparations."[41]

One of the first authors in Britain to express the new scientific attitude was William Kitchiner, who explained in detail by which means and apparatuses exact measures might be realized: "The measure, the liquid graduated measure of the apothecaries, as it appeared more accurate and convenient than any other: the pint being divided into sixteen ounces, the ounce into eight drachms; a middling-sized teaspoon will contain about a drachm."[42] Such precise measurements required readers to be prepared and well equipped to follow them. In her enormous *Book of Household Management* (1861), Isabella Beeton emphasized: "Among the most essential requirements of the kitchen are scales and weighing machines for family use."[43] She seemed to take for granted that everyone within the social group she was addressing had the standard pint container, tablespoons, and teaspoons. In the United States, where a decimal system had been proposed in the 1790s without success, the measuring cup became the norm. From the 1880s, manufactured cups were on the market, as described by the cooking-school teacher Fannie Farmer: "Tin measuring-cups, divided in quarters or thirds, holding one half-pint."[44] Raymond Sokolov traced this tradition back to Miss Beecher's *Domestic Receipt Book* (1846), in which the author—a prominent domestic-science teacher—described how the cup could be used as an alternative to weighing.[45]

In Russia, Elena Molokhovets was well aware of the usefulness of precision, but it was apparently not generally accepted in her country. In the preface to her 1861 book, which appeared in reprints as late as 1901, she wrote that exact measures were considered strange and even comical, particularly by the lower classes, among them the cooks, who were still mostly illiterate.[46] Molokhovets also took into consideration how many people a dish was supposed to serve; in her book, the recipes are for six portions. Many authors seemed to forget to give this information, even when they indicated quantities for ingredients, but as time passed, it became more common to clarify the number of servings in the preface or in the recipes themselves. In certain books today, different quantities are given for daily meals and for more formal dinners with many people present. In *La comida de la familia* (The family meal), the Catalan chef Ferran Adrià offers recipes for home meals that serve two or six people and "professional" meals that serve twenty or seventy-five guests.[47]

Molokhovets still used the old system of weights and measures. The metric system was known at the time she first published her cookbook, but it became mandatory in Russia only in 1918. It had been invented in France after the Revolution and was gradually introduced in European countries during the nineteenth century.[48] But official introduction of the new system did not lead to an immediate change in cookbooks; only gradually did grams and liters replace pounds and pints. There were certain difficulties that had to be smoothed out during the transition period, partly because one pound was equal to 453.59 grams. One example of what this resulted in is shown in a cookbook from 1898, where measures for sugar included 96, 188, and 314 grams. But after a while, the recipes were revised, so measures became 100, 200 and 300 grams. The metric system certainly made it easier to indicate size. Traugott Hammerl was able to modify an old expression, "not too thick" (nicht zu dick), with the addition of "barely 1½ cm."[49]

PRECISION OF COOKING TIME AND TEMPERATURE

Exact cooking times were also generally absent in early cookbooks. In the Roman cookbook attributed to Apicius, references to time do not go beyond simple expressions such as *cum coctus fuerit*, "when it has been finished," without any indication of how long that might be.

For several hundred years, cookbooks simply instructed readers to boil, fry, stew, and roast and did not mention the time, or they used expressions such as "when the soup is ready" or "when the dish is cooked." Sometimes, the expressions were a bit more specific: "until it becomes thick," "until it be a fine pulp," "until it becomes red brown."[50] But as early as the fifteenth century, Martino, who used expressions like "when it seems cooked," gave a much more precise description in one of the recipes: "To know when it is cooked, take notice of when the upper crust raises, then it is good and may be lifted from the fire."[51] In the eighteenth century, Hannah Glasse also used this kind of observation when she wrote that a brawn from calves' feet (she called it a "sham braun") shall boil "till a straw will run through it."[52]

Some authors compared cooking times to the time it took to complete well-known tasks, for example, the time it takes to make a hardboiled egg.[53] Some of these comparisons relied on a common cultural heritage in Christian Europe. In a 1555 confectionery recipe, the astrologer Nostradamus mentioned "the time it takes to say Ave Maria."[54] In a recipe for tea, written in the mid-seventeenth century, Kenelm Digby warned against letting the tea stay in water too long: "The water is to remain upon it, no longer that whiles you can say the *Miserere* Psalm very leisurely."[55] Most common among these religious references was the Lord's Prayer: "Boil the time of a paternoster," or "six paternoster."[56] Martino also referred to the paternoster in several of his recipes, but Platina changed this to a recommendation of a "little boiling."[57]

Unfortunately, historians who have studied the history of time and clocks have shown little interest in cooking; consequently, we have very scant information about the use of mechanical clocks in kitchens.[58] The old way of keeping track of time was with bells in church towers, monasteries, and town halls. The bells called monks to prayer, farmers to mass, and townspeople to work, and they signaled the opening of markets and the closing of town gates. They would ring every hour and perhaps also every half hour or even every quarter. Gradually, the towers were equipped with dials and hands that indicated hours and minutes.

In the late Middle Ages, hourglasses became a rather common instrument for measuring time, and they may have been used by those cookbook authors who gave precise cooking time in their recipes. Although it was not a widespread practice, some authors, such as Martino, referred to hours, quarters of hours, and even half-quarters.

Mechanical clocks had been invented sometime before 1300, and in the early fifteenth century, smaller clocks were produced to be used in private houses. They were very expensive, and only in the sixteenth century did clocks become more common in the homes of the aristocracy and the rich bourgeoisie, who probably saw them more as status symbols than as practical devices. But by the beginning of the eighteenth century, things had changed. In Britain, there were over three times as many clocks in 1715 than there had been in 1685. Lorna Weatherill observed that in the wealthy households of the London freemen, clocks "were already recorded in over a half in 1675, but increased until nine out of ten had them in 1715."[59]

Consequently, it became normal for authors to refer to exact times. In England, Elizabeth Raffald used hours and minutes in her 1769 cookbook, but she also noted that knowing the exact time was not sufficient to prepare a good dish, so she combined it with other indicators, such as in this recipe for ox cheek soup: "When the head has simmered a quarter of an hour, put to it six quarts of water, and let it stew till it is reduced to two quarts."[60]

In 1867, the French cook Jules Gouffé declared in his book: "It has been important for me to give the most precise measures in the household recipes. I have not edited a single one of my elementary specifications without having constantly the clock under my eyes and the scales in my hand."[61] As time passed, clocks and watches became part of daily life for more and more people, but it was still necessary for cooks—professionals and amateurs alike—to use their own judgment when preparing a dish. So the Greek gastronome and poet Archestratus was perhaps not so wrong when, more than two thousand years ago, he wrote: "Then put into hot ashes and use your intelligence to work out the time when it will be roasted; don't let it burn up."[62]

While it became progressively easier to give exact measures and times, it was still difficult to give an accurate temperature, something we take for granted today. Gouffé emphasized that the heat should be "even" or "moderate"; Beeton recommended "a brisk fire"; Molokhovets instructed, "first a big fire, then small"; Artusi warned, "not too hot." Such descriptions lasted into the twentieth century and were in principle not any different from much earlier instructions, such as "with low fire" (with esy fyr), which appeared in a fourteenth-century English manuscript, or "very slowly on the coals far from the fire" (pian piano su le bragie, lontan dalla fiamma), from Scappi's sixteenth-century *Opera*.[63]

In some cases, the verbs themselves indicated how high the heat should be, such as "simmer" and "stew," and for most cooking, general instructions worked well enough. Exact temperatures were important for baking, however, and so in the mid-eighteenth century, the Swede Cajsa Warg explained to readers how to use small bits of paper put in the oven to judge the temperature, differentiating between "when the heat is such that a paper . . . becomes a little yellowish" and "when the paper in the stove becomes dark yellow." In Germany a century later, Henriette

Davidis took this to a more systematic level: "If [the paper] is put in the oven and it quickly becomes yellow but not black, the heat is of the first degree and suitable for pastry dough and yeast dough. If the paper slowly becomes yellow, the heat is of the second degree and suitable for most bakery. Even weaker heat, of the third degree, is for things that must dry up."[64] In her recipes, Davidis referred to the three different levels of heat.

At the same time, Hanna Winsnes in Norway made a general introductory comment in her cookbook that the heat used for dark bread would be the standard scale for all baking. In her recipes, she recommended that sandkager (sand cakes) be put in the oven one quarter of an hour after bread has been baked; jødekager (Jew cakes), one hour after bread; and so on.[65] Even if this was not a satisfactory scientific instruction, it no doubt filled a practical function.

When electrical stoves made it possible to set exact temperatures, this information was almost immediately introduced in cookbooks. Molecular gastronomy took this precision a step further, specifying far more exact temperatures than ever before. In a 2002 article about how to prepare a hard-boiled egg, Hervé This wrote: "High quality thermometers now make it possible to cook eggs at temperatures closer to those at which their proteins are denatured: at 62°C (144°F) one of the proteins in the white (*ovotransferrin*) is cooked, but the yolk remains liquid because the proteins that coagulate first in this part of the egg require a temperature of 68°C (154°F)."[66]

APPROACHING NEW MARKETS

How cookbook authors chose to teach their method of cooking depended partly on their background but more on what public they intended to reach. Who were the potential buyers or readers? Three examples from late seventeenth-century England illustrate how different the attitudes and markets were. The professional cook Robert May, who had worked in aristocratic houses, wrote that his book was directed to "all honest well intended men of our profession."[67] The housewife Hannah Woolley stated that her book was intended for "All ingenious persons of the Female Sex."[68] And Mary Tillinghast, who ran a cooking school, said that her book was "Printed for the use of her scholars only."[69] The expressed intention to reach a particular group of readers did not, however, guarantee that different approaches were consciously chosen in the books. That would have implied an understanding of the balance between the two "voices" appearing through the text: one being the voice of the technical authority, the specialist in cooking, and the other being the voice of the pedagogue, the communicator of technical knowledge. A relevant question is whether the voice of the specialist dominated more in books for professional cooks than in books for amateurs. Scholars have only recently begun discussing and researching such questions, and there is no reason to believe that producers of early cookbooks were aware of these kinds of issues. What's more, commercial considerations were often given priority, overriding the solemn words in prefaces.

Several of the books written by or attributed to chief cooks or court administrators in the seventeenth and eighteenth centuries stated—as Robert May's book did—that they were meant for professional cooks, and they often emphasized the need to instruct young and inexperienced cooks.[70] The Austrian court cook Conrad Hagger even considered his 1718 work to be part of a greater program for the education of the young. He referred to the popular encyclopedic work *Cosmographia,* by the polyhistor Sebastian Münster, which discussed how useful and necessary it was to describe all arts, skills, and other memorable things for the young.[71]

But cooks hardly constituted the main market for booksellers, since most of them had neither money nor literacy enough to take advantage of literature. The professional secrets had to be passed on indirectly. In aristocratic courts and mansions since the Renaissance, the chief steward and other officials who were responsible for banquets had to acquire knowledge of new, fashionable dishes and their ingredients and convey the relevant recipes to the cooks. In his 1591 cookbook, the Czech scientist Bavor Rodovský wrote in his opening dedicatory letter, addressed to a noblewoman, that both husband and housewife needed the cookbook he had written if they wanted to make sure that they got the dishes they wanted, explaining that there were more bad, dirty, and amateurish cooks than experienced, clean, and professional ones.[72]

In private families, particularly among the affluent bourgeoisie, the housewife or a trusted housekeeper had responsibility for the household management, and she was in charge of cooks and maids with different duties. As early as 1430, the author of an Italian book wrote that the housewife must know the art of cooking, not because she was supposed to cook but because she needed to command and teach less proficient servants.[73] According to the scholar Suzanne Hull, sixteenth- and seventeenth-century English guidebooks for ladies were not only for aristocratic houses but in fact "appear to be directed primarily to a middle-class audience, to women who perhaps had servants but who were not removed from the mechanics of household affairs."[74] Housewives bought cookbooks, read them, and explained recipes to their cooks, as we saw in chapter 2.

In areas of western and northern Europe where literacy was widespread rather early, many cooks and maids knew how to read in the eighteenth century, and most of them were literate by the nineteenth century. But the Czech Dobromila Rettigová advised housewives and housekeepers to know the details of the work, because even if they didn't cook themselves, they needed to understand the procedures if they wanted to give good orders.[75] In another corner of the continent, the Norwegian Hanna Winsnes wrote that housewives who did not understand the instructions they gave would instruct badly, lose the respect of their servants, and often be deceived.[76]

As literacy increased among women, the market for cookbooks grew, and more middle-class housewives could benefit from the books. Authors and publishers were well aware of this new audience. The 1814 cookbook of the celebrated Paris restaurateur Antoine Beauvilliers was clearly not intended only for his colleagues in restaurants and royal courts or for dedicated amateurs. He wrote that his book would teach a housewife how to cook all known dishes, the fashionable ones as well as the exquisite traditional ones.[77] Some years later, in 1847, the great Carême, who wrote for the *hommes de métier* and the male gourmets of the period, also mentioned how valuable it was for a housewife to read his cookbook (instead of a novel!) and thus be able to instruct her cook about her "goûts sensuels."[78] And in 1895, Pellegrino Artusi—gentleman writer and amateur cook—said that his book was written especially for "the kind ladies and good housewives."[79] In the early twentieth century, when, in some countries, literacy had reached the entire population, the democratization of culinary knowledge increased, and new, very simple, cookbooks were published.

TERMINOLOGY AND LANGUAGE

All this is proof that in the eighteenth and nineteenth centuries, authors and publishers were increasingly interested in reaching members of a new social class: people who had greater resources to spend on food but lacked basic knowledge of elegant cuisine. To communicate with this new audience, authors had to adapt their writing to the fact that many readers not only were beginners in the art of cooking—the issue discussed in the opening paragraphs of this chapter—but also often had no experience with written instructions. It was thus important to find a language that everybody could understand, with simple and comprehensible descriptions. One particular pedagogical problem related to language concerned terms for methods used in the kitchen. The basic words, such as "boil," "fry," and "bake," were simple enough, but new French terms were introduced along with new techniques, like *blanchir, braiser,* and *sauter.* After the publication of the first edition of his cookbook *Le cuisinier françois,* in 1651, the French innovator La Varenne became aware of the need to explain special expressions. In a later edition of the book, he added a clarification after the word *blanchir:* "This means to put for some time in fresh water or bouillon."[80] The word originally meant to make white, or to bleach, so it was necessary to give a more precise explanation to the readers who did not know what this technical term implied in culinary science.[81]

This became even more important with French culinary terms that passed on to other countries. They couldn't be translated properly, as explained in chapter 4. They were therefore kept in their original form in many foreign cookbooks, sometimes with little orthographic adaptations and often with short lists explaining what the terms stood for. One example of this can be found in a German cookbook from 1858: "I have as much as possible used German expressions," the author states, "but this is not always practicable. I permit myself therefore to refer to the list of foreign words in the appendix." Among the explained words in the list, all of them French or based on French, we find "Sauce (Brühe)," "Omelettes (Pfann-kuchen ohne Mehl)," and "Grilliren (auf dem Rost rösten)."[82]

But language is not enough to realize pedagogical ideas. The most knowledgeable authors were able to offer other valuable pedagogical aids. It is evident that authors who had stood by the oven, worked out their own solutions, and then tried them out repeatedly were able to give the most specific advice. Drawing from their own expe-riences, they suggested practical steps. Before baking a cake, for example, the right amount of sugar needs to be crushed, the flour sifted, the lemon zested, the fruits stoned, and so on. They were even able to offer suggestions if something went wrong. Very early—already in the fifteenth century—we find advice on how to remedy acci-dents during cooking, such as a dish that is too salty or has a burnt taste.[83]

The best authors understood that it was necessary to state the reasons for each step in the culinary process, to explain *why* things ought to be done this or that way. In a Spanish cookbook from 1607 that included several dishes containing sugar, the author recommended low heat, explaining that this was because sweets can easily burn.[84] Cajsa Warg wrote in 1755 that when the *fricadeller* are finished, they ought to be placed on a linen cloth because the cloth will absorb the water.[85] In 1653, the author of *Le pastissier françois* (The French pastry cook) explained why a dough should be made differently in winter than in summer: "It ought to be fat-ter in the winter to be easier to handle, while in summer less butter is necessary."[86] In 1851, Alexis Soyer recommended in a commentary to Printanière Soup to cut vegetables in pieces of the same size, "for if some pieces should be small and others large, the smaller pieces would be quite in purée, whilst the larger ones would still be quite hard."[87] But explanations of this kind were not always correct. Many authors just repeated old traditional "truths." Hervé This collected twenty-five thousand culinary dictums, mainly from French cookbooks, and after testing them, he found many good recommendations, but also a lot of really bad ones.[88]

In *The Craftsman,* the first volume of an ambitious trilogy on material culture, the sociologist Richard Sennett stated that in the workshop, "The spoken word seems more effective than written instruction." He showed how this principle is practiced by writers of fiction in the dictum "show, don't tell!" Is it possible to realize this maxim in written recipes? Sennett analyzed two recipes for Poulet à la d'Albufera, a boned and stuffed chicken—a difficult dish to make, particularly the boning part, which must be done with a sharp knife. Sennett referred to two recipes for the chicken, one by the chef Richard Olney and the other by the TV cook Julia Child, and made clear that it is not enough to give a correct description; the writer must identify with the inexperienced reader. He found that "Child's recipe reads quite differently than Olney's precise direction because her story is structured

FIGURE 17. Illustration accompanying a recipe for *fricadeller* (meatballs) in
Charles-Emil Hagdahl's *Kok-konsten som vetenskap och konst*. In the text,
Hagdahl explained how to form the meat mixture into balls, or quenelles, with
the help of two spoons that have been warmed in hot water.

around empathy for the cook; she focuses on the human protagonist rather than on
the bird." Sennett argued that a writer who has acquired a skilled technique in his
or her work and wants to provide guidance to others must return emotionally to the
point just before the technique was acquired: "So for a moment Child will imagine
holding the knife awkwardly. . . . This return to vulnerability is the sign of sympathy
the instructor gives."[89] This is of course a challenge very few authors live up to.

THE VALUE OF ILLUSTRATIONS

Sennett commented on the drawings in Child's book and compared them to the
close-ups she pioneered in her TV shows. The drawings "focus on the hardest procedure the hand will have to work with."[90] That illustrations can assist written
instruction is evident in a number of cookbooks. The Swedish gentleman gourmet
Charles-Emil Hagdahl often combines the description with a drawing (figure 17).

There were eighteenth-century authors who gave theoretical reasons for including illustrations in their books. Some, for example, wrote that the images could be
useful to illiterate cooks. As mentioned in chapter 2, Conrad Hagger's book had
pedagogical copper engravings of pie forms.[91] Martha Bradley wrote that the great
number of copper plates in her book were more than embellishment; by consulting
the illustrations, she pointed out, "even those who cannot read will be able to instruct
themselves."[92] But even literate cooks could benefit from illustrations. In the great
German *Illustriertes Kochbuch*, published in the nineteenth century, the author perfectly understood the difficulty of explaining how to prepare dishes. He wrote that
where necessary, his book included illustrations, "to make the descriptions comprehensible, which is particularly important in understanding the mechanical manipulations, since they are easy to demonstrate, but hard to describe."[93]

Illustrations were included in manuscripts before the invention of printing, and they appear in the earliest printed books. David Shaw, a specialist on early modern book history, wrote that "the sixteenth century saw the development of woodcut and copper-engraved illustrations in a wide range of books, scientific, religious, and popular."[94] But apart from ornamental elements (initials, borders, head and tail pieces, etc.), there were fairly few illustrations in early culinary works. Some Italian and English cookbooks had portraits of the authors, a practice not found in other countries, but these were often the only illustrations. And when illustrations were included in early cookbooks, they normally had no pedagogical function; they might not even be correct, a feature they had in common with illustrations in other books. One often-mentioned example is *Liber chronicarum,* created in 1493, where the same woodcuts were used to illustrate different historical persons or different towns.[95]

Similarly, in one of the most lavishly decorated cookbooks of the sixteenth century, Marx Rumpolt's *Ein new Kochbuch,* more than a fourth of the illustrations are repeats. For example, four different fish—European sturgeon, Danube salmon, carp, and ide—are illustrated with the same woodcut.[96] Some of the illustrations were used on the title pages and frontispieces of books by different German printers and publishers, possibly, as the scholar Gertrud Benker has suggested, in a "regular exchange of woodcuts and engravings" (regelrechten Tausch mit Holzschnitten und Kupfern).[97]

German illustrations were also used in other countries. A Dutch book from 1556 featured on its title page a woodcut of a cook in a kitchen, an image first used by a German printer more than twenty-five years earlier.[98] This means of course that the cook's clothing and the objects seen in the woodcut did not necessarily correspond to what would have been found in a Dutch kitchen at the time the book was published. Illustrations are therefore not always the best sources for historical information, and particularly not those that appeared in early cookbooks. Even if an illustration appears detailed, it is absolutely necessary to know the actual history of the image before drawing conclusions. Illustrations may provide more information about book history than food history.

Ivan Day showed that illustrations of meat-carving methods and table settings are more numerous in early cookbooks of the sixteenth and seventeenth centuries than illustrations of cooking techniques and recipes. The exceptions are designs for pie forms and custards; beginning in the eighteenth century, confectionary was far better illustrated than other dishes.[99] Most illustrations in the nineteenth and twentieth centuries show how a dish should be mounted or placed on a plate; the decorative element was still the most important one.

In some more recently published cookbooks, illustrations accompany step-by-step descriptions of culinary preparations, but this is far from the norm. Today, although textbooks follow this pattern, authors and publishers of commercial cookbooks are less concerned with pedagogy than with presenting a new and different product that will appeal to readers in a market flooded by cookbooks. And in this context, illustrations—which are now mostly high-quality color photos—tend to fill a decorative or aesthetic function rather than a pedagogical one.

A major stumbling block in any discussion of pedagogical intentions and approaches is the regrettable lack of systematic studies of readership in this field. This makes it difficult to establish precisely in what ways and to which readers cookbooks were useful in the kitchen.

8

Paratexts in Cookbooks

The author's name, along with the title, preface, headings, illustrations, and index of a book, make up what French literary theorist Gérard Genette called "paratexts"—the texts surrounding and accompanying the basic text, or "constituent part," which in a cookbook would be the recipes and other culinary instruction.[1] Genette focused mainly on French literature from the nineteenth and twentieth centuries and above all on literary fiction,[2] which means that his conclusions are not necessarily valid for all literature. Many of his observations, however, shed light on the cookbook genre (and on nonfiction in general) and demonstrate how it has an obvious place within the history of literature while simultaneously showing how cookbooks are different from belles-lettres.[3]

TITLES

According to Genette, a title has three functions, the first being to identify the work.[4] In fiction, books tend to have unique titles (e.g., *Hamlet, Faust*), whereas, through the centuries, cookbooks have frequently been titled simply "cookbook": for example, the French *Livre de cuisine* (1530), the German *Kochbuch* (1790), and the American *The Cookbook* (1918). A variation of this is "collection of recipes" or "recipe book." Sometimes, the title will include the number of recipes, as the Spanish *Milochenta recetas de cocina* (One thousand and eighty recipes for cooking) or the American *Five Hundred Ways to Cook California Sea Food*. Occasionally, an epithet is added—such as "complete," "useful," "modern," "noble," "small," or "big"—but this does not help identify the book. Such titles, however, do fill the second function in Genette's list, which is indicating a work's contents (figure 18).

Kucharſtwij:

O rozličných Krmech: Kterak ſe uži tečně s chutij ſtrogiti magij. Pakožto Zwě tzyna/ptácy/Ryby: A giné mnohé Krmě Wſſelikému Kuchaȓy/a neb Hoſpodaȓzy. Knijžka tato potrzebná/y vžitečná.

A Ocet yak ſe dělá také zadu nagdeſſ.

FIGURE 18. Title page of the Czech cookbook *Kucharzstwij* (Art of cooking), printed by Jan Kantor in Prague around 1570. The rest of the title reads, "About various foods, how to prepare them in a useful way and with taste, venison, birds, fish and many different dishes, a necessary and useful book for every cook and householder." Early cookbooks often had a short title followed by a long explanation of the contents, which was used as a form of publicity. Photograph from the ethnographical journal *Český lid* (Czech nation), no. 16 (1907): p. 169.

This is true of most cookbook titles, and in particular those constructed with the words "cookery," "cook," and "cookmaid." The epithets used in cookbook titles can be rather general, praising the quality of the book: "good," "accomplished," "perfect," "practical," "universal," "ideal," "tasteful." The cook or housekeeper the book is directed at is generally described as "sensible," "experienced," or "wise," while the housewife is referred to as "prudent" or "frugal." But there are also epithets that are used to indicate that a cookbook is of a particular type. They may refer to the expected market: "royal," "court," "bourgeois," "city," "town," "country," "cottage," "popular," "family." Others go the opposite direction, claiming that they are "for all." Some directly indicate economical cookery: for example, the Italian *La cuoca risparmiatrice* (The thrifty cook) and the Danish *Billig mad* (Cheap food). Health is given priority in titles such as the Dutch *Gezonde voeding* (Healthy food) and the American *Health through Diet*. A few titles refer to special kinds of cuisine: "classic," "old," "traditional." Many titles refer to geographical areas, cities, regions, or countries: *Wiener Kochbuch* (Vienna cookbook), *The French Cook, Russkaia povarnia* (Russian cooking), *La cocina vasca* (Basque cuisine).

Cookbooks are didactic works, and quite a few titles invoke this by using terms such as "guide," "manual," "ABC," "companion," "monitor," "school," and "instruction": *The Cook's Guide, ABC der Küche* (The ABCs of the kitchen). These kinds of titles correspond to titles of works in other practical genres from the early days of printing and even before; they may actually have been modeled on them. The Spanish *Arte de cozina* has a parallel in *Arte de pintura*, by Velazquez's teacher Francisco Pacheco. *The Art of Cookery* and *Kochbuch* have parallels in *The Art of Navigation* and *Illuminierbuch*. The link to the mechanical arts is easy to see in a title such as *De re culinaria*, which corresponds to *De re metallica, De re militari*, and *De re nautica*.

Certain early cookbooks have titles with words that we find in other practical as well as moral and religious works, such as *Brevière du gastronome*. Other keywords allude to well-established genres: "dictionary," "encyclopedia," "calendar." The popularity of the almanac is proved by the titles of cookbooks published in many European languages over a long period, including *Kok-Almanach* (Dutch, 1774), *The Cookery Almanac* (American, 1842), *Al'manakh gastronomov* (Russian, 1852), *Küchen-Almanach* (German, 1853), *Almanak do cozinheiro* (Portuguese, 1858), and *Kjøkkenalmanakk* (Norwegian, 1936). Other key words are "secrets," "treasure," "delight," "jewel," *fleur*, and *Schatzkammer*, which are often combined with "cuisine" or "cookery": *Fleur de cuisine, The Cook's Delight*. But there are also more imaginative titles, such as *Ocios de dispéptico y ensueños de famélico* (Leisures of the dyspeptic and dreams of the famished), *Les dons de Comus* (The gifts from Comus), *Der elegante Gaumen* (The elegant palate), and *Poesia Nascosta* (Hidden poetry), to say nothing of *Out of the Blue Grass*, a title many will associate with music and not recipes for fried chicken.[5] Such titles belong to the group Paul Lehmann identified in his study of medieval book titles as metaphorical (*metaphorische*).[6]

The length of cookbook titles varies, but there are a few with long, ornamented titles, which were particularly popular in Germany during the Baroque period. The best example of this is a big recipe book published in Nürnberg in 1691: *Der aus dem Parnasso ehmals entlauffenen vortrefflichen Köchin, Welche bey denen Göttinnen Ceres, Diana und Pomona viel Jahre gedienet, Hinterlassene und bisshero, Bey unterschiedlichen der Löbl.Koch-Kunst beflissenen Frauen zu Nürnberg, zerstreuet und in grosser Geheim gehalten gewesene Gemerck-Zettul* (Notes by the excellent cook who had run away from the Parnassus, having for many years served the goddesses Ceres, Diana and Pomona, until now kept in great secret and spread among different ladies of Nuremburg eagerly engaged in the praiseworthy art of cookery).[7]

These metaphorical titles were probably intended to seduce the public, the third function in Genette's list. In *Titulus,* an entertaining survey of historical book titles, Werner Bergengruen pointed out that books with such titles are expected to spark attention and curiosity.[8] This would also be true for *How to Cook a Wolf,* by M. F. K. Fisher, a collection of essays and recipes from 1942, where the wolf is the metaphor for hard times during war. Another curious title is *How to Bake Pi* (2015), where "pi" is not a misspelling of "pie" but rather indicates the number π, a mathematical constant that is often rounded off to 3.14 but is in reality an irrational number. The subtitle explains what the basic intention of the book is: *Cakes, Custard, and Category Theory: Easy Recipes for Understanding Complex Maths.* But even if mathematics is the book's first priority, every chapter opens with a recipe and gives many tips about how to make the dishes.[9] A final example in this category is *Eine Bombe unter unsere Kochbücher!* (A bomb under our cookbooks!), published in 1906 by an author who promised to simplify cooking.

Giving a cookbook a title that was in a different language than the recipes may also have been an attempt to gain attention. Such cookbooks are rare, but there are some examples in the manuscript era of vernacular books with Latin titles, for example, the English *Diversa cibaria* and the Danish *Libellus de arte coquinaria.* Unfortunately, we don't know who created these titles, so it is difficult to know what their purpose was. We know more about the few such books published in the seventeenth century. When John Evelyn gave his salad book the Latin title *Acetaria* (with the subtitle *A Discourse of Sallets*), it was probably because he wanted to prioritize the botanical information and academic references and play down the recipes, which, in his eyes, did not have the same prestige. A German book by Hans Schuppe, a court cook, was called *Traiteur à la mode* but had the German subtitle *Kochbuch.* In this case, the French title was obviously chosen to tempt the German aristocracy, which was strongly influenced by French culture and fashion after the Thirty Years' War. The aristocratic Polish *Compendium ferculorum,* by Stanislaw Czerniecki (referred to in chapter 2), certainly appealed to an elite audience with its Latin title. In England, the title *Archimagirus anglo-gallicus* was no doubt chosen to create curiosity, but the work was probably a hoax; the recipes

were compiled from earlier English books, but hardly by the royal physician Theodore Turquet, who was credited as the author but died three years before the book
was published. There are two interesting examples from the early nineteenth century. William Kitchiner was eyeing contemporary gourmets when he called his
book *Apicius redivivus,* but from the third edition, the subtitle, *The Cook's Oracle,*
was used as the book's main title. Alexander Hunter's *Culina famulatrix medicinae,*
with the subtitle *Or Receipts in Modern Cookery,* was a recipe book that included
medical observations mixed with merry quotations, and it was also republished
later with the subtitle as the main title.

Two prominent authors quoted by Genette—Gotthold Ephraim Lessing and
Umberto Eco—categorically stated that a title, metaphorical or not, should not
reveal what the reader would find in the books. Lessing wrote in one of his shorter
reflections: "A title must not be a menu. The less it betrays of the contents, the better it is." Eco, in his postscript to *The Name of the Rose,* discussed and explained the
title of his book and concluded: "A title must confuse the ideas, not regiment
them."[10]

But Genette, Lessing, and Eco were discussing belles-lettres. When their statements are applied to the titles of cookbooks and handbooks in general, confusion
is not the ideal. On the contrary, it seems absolutely necessary for the title of a
cookbook to indicate what the book is about. But this is not as important today as
it was in the centuries before mass media advertisements and commercials. Ada
Boni had great success in Italy in the 1930s with a cookbook called *Il talismano
della felicità* (The talisman of happiness). The title does not include a word about
food, but according to the historian Piero Camporesi, it has a clear ideological aim:
to suggest that perfect happiness in the family will be reached through "culinary
magic" (la magia culinaria), which the book claims it can help the reader obtain.[11]

There is also another way to seduce the public: using alliteration and rhythm.
Some cookbook titles that take this approach are *Thousand Tested Treats, Dyets
Dry Dinner, Koch und Kellerei* (Cook and wine cellar), and *Goede recepten voor
schlechte tijden* (Good recipes for bad times). Bergengruen claimed that in some
titles, the importance does not reside in the message but in how it sounds.[12]

A successful cookbook may be printed over and over with the same title, but
the title may be changed if the author or the publisher finds it useful for commercial reasons. Pierre de Lune's French cookbook was first called *Le cuisinier* (The
cook), then *Le nouveau cuisinier* (The new cook), and finally *Le nouveau et parfait
cuisinier* (The new and perfect cook).[13]

Sophie Wilhelmine Scheibler's German cookbook was first published in 1815 as
Allgemeines deutsches Kochbuch für bürgerliche Haushaltungen (General German
cookbook for bourgeois households), but by 1853, the last three words had been
changed to *für alle Stände* (for all classes).[14] A Danish book was called *Husholdning
paa landet* (Household management in the country) in 1941, but with increased

urbanization, the title was changed to *Husholdning, land og by* (Household management, country and city) when it was republished in 1953.[15]

Titles may also be changed to adapt to new political realities and constitutional systems. André Viard's cookbook came out as *Le cuisinier imperial* in 1806, when Napoleon was emperor, became *Le cuisinier royal* during the following monarchy, *Le cuisinier national* during the Second Republic, *Le cuisinier imperial* under Napoleon III, and finally *Le cuisinier national* after the establishment of the Third Republic. In Germany, Marie Ewald's *Kochbuch,* published in 1846 in Königsberg, followed the territorial ambitions of Prussia. The book became *Kochbuch für preussische Hausfrauen* (Cookbook for Prussian housewives) in 1859, then *Allgemeine Kochbuch für deutsche Hausfrauen* (General cookbook for German housewives) in 1861, and *Das Reichskochbuch* (Cookbook of the Reich) in 1890 after the establishment of the German Empire.

DEDICATORY EPISTLES

Several early cookbooks followed the established tradition in publishing of opening the work with a dedicatory epistle, a text written by the author (or in the name of the author) and directed to a person of authority. In the case of cookbooks, the dedicatees were often the author's current or former employers. They might be princes or aristocrats, the patrons of many early cookbook authors. Marx Rumpolt, private cook to the prince-elector of Mainz, dedicated *Ein new Kochbuch* to a former employer, Anna, daughter of the Danish king and wife of the prince-elector of Saxony. The English cook Robert May dedicated *The Accomplisht Cook* to several aristocrats who had employed him during his long career. Sometimes, the dedicatee was an author's professional superior. Bartolomeo Scappi, the private cook to the pope, directed his epistle to a *scalco,* or chief steward, in the Vatican household, a person who had helped him progress in the culinary arts.

In the centuries before authors could expect to receive some sort of pecuniary remuneration for their work, settled by a contract with the publisher, the dedicatory epistle was a way to secure financial support. According to Genette, it was in fact one of a writer's sources of income.[16]

Many dedicatory letters were filled to the brim with flattery, and they were normally written in an established rhetorical style. The dedicatees were often credited as being responsible for the success that the author had obtained and was "humbly" acknowledging. The French cookbook author La Varenne wrote his *épître dédicatoire* to the Marquis of Uxelles, in whose service he had been for ten years, and described his book and his accomplishments as a result of this employment.[17]

But there were also dedicatory letters that were not exclusively laudatory; these gave information about the work and explained the author's reasons for writing it, elements which were later generally printed in a preface. This was the type of dedication John Murrell wrote to Martha Hayes, daughter of a London lord mayor. He explained that many earlier books "have instructed rather to marre then [mar than] make good Meate" but that his "gives each Meat his right for the manner of dressing."[18]

Before the eighteenth century, several authors defended the cookbook genre and their interest in food in the dedicatory letters. The first to do so was Platina, who discussed and explained the concept of *voluptas* (pleasure) in his dedication to Cardinal Roverella. In the dedication to his cookbook, the Czech scientist Bavor Rodovský disagreed with those who found cookbooks unnecessary and argued that they represented an important tradition and that, in addition, they helped people appreciate food as God's gift. Later, a similar defensive approach was taken by the Neapolitan Antonio Latini, who insisted that his book was frugal, and by the Englishman John Evelyn, who wrote that he saw his work as part of natural science.[19]

A few dedicatory letters stand out. One of them appeared in an anonymous French cookbook printed in 1740, *Le cuisinier gascon*. The dedicatee was the Prince de Dombes, grandson of King Louis XIV, but this may have been a gimmick, as the book is thought to have been written by the prince himself. Beatrice Fink pointed out the playfulness of the text ("ton badin, voire ludique"), and it is enough to read the first lines to understand what she meant: "A dedicatory letter would be a very bad dish for Your Highness and at the same time for me a badly chosen application of my talents." No cook would speak like that to his master.[20]

Another humorous dedication was written by Pellegrino Artusi in *La scienza in cucina*, which he published at his own expense because no publisher wanted it. He dedicated the book to his two cats with these words: "For you, who were in my kitchen when I tried out the dishes and rubbed your upright tails against my legs, yearning to be the first ones to give me your opinion."[21] But by this time, the tradition of dedicatory epistles was long gone. One of the few significant examples of this type of dedication from the past two centuries was written by the illustrious French chef Carême for his masterwork about French cuisine in the nineteenth century, which he dedicated to the Baroness Betty de Rothschild, who was a former employer, and to the author Lady Sidney Morgan, who had praised his culinary art in her writings.[22]

PREFACES

Prefaces express, as demonstrated in chapter 2, the reasons and motivations authors have for writing a cookbook. The preface is also a place to indicate the intended market, explain the choice of technical terms, or note the use of more exact measures (described in chapter 7). The following chapters will examine social, moral, religious, medical, and aesthetic values that have been conveyed in the prefaces of cookbooks for Jews and vegetarians, in national and nationalist cookbooks, and in cookbooks published during wars and hard times. This chapter will address a few other aspects of the preface genre.

Words such as "preface," "prologue," and "foreword" refer to something that comes *before* the main text. Genette discussed a long list of types of introductory texts, but the most interesting part for a study of cookbooks is what he said about didactic works, where two or more such texts may appear together. In such cases, a preface assumes a function that is simultaneously more formal (*protocolaire*) and more circumstantial than other introductory texts, while an introduction is more closely tied to the subject of the text.[23] This is a typical pattern found in a great many cookbooks in many languages.

As for the form of the preface, Genette observed that it might contrast with the form of the main text; it may be written as a *discours* rather than in a narrative or dramatic mode.[24] This is evident in cookbooks where the preface has a discursive prose form that is distinct from the more formulaic language of the recipes. The style of the preface is generally more elaborated than the rest of the text, but there are great variations between different authors. There are prefaces with very simple sentences, often intended for young and inexperienced people, pupils, and apprentices. But there are also prefaces larded with Latin expressions and references to learned works, even if this is more common in dedicatory letters. One very highbrow preface introduces a three-volume French work from 1742. It is in fact an essay, fifty-three pages long, with quotations from Seneca, Tertullian, Galen, Voltaire, and Saint- Évremont.[25]

But prefaces are not always written in prose. In early German cookbooks, there are prefaces written completely or partly in rhymed verse.[26]

In a cookbook, the preface aims to explain to the reader what the book is about. In the early years of printing, this information was often given in a long title that filled most of the first page; further details were given in a table of contents. But these did not give an author enough space to explain which principles the book was based on, which readers it intended to satisfy, how it was organized, and which subjects were treated and which were left out. The preface explained how the menus were to be set up, how illustrations were to be interpreted, what types of kitchenware were necessary to prepare the recipes, how food should be purchased, and so on. The more technical information was often given in the introduction, which was more systematically organized, but the difference between preface and introduction is not entirely consistent in many books.

Prefaces were above all a form of marketing, regardless of the intentions they expressed. Quite early on, the people responsible for marketing had to take the growth in cookbook production into consideration because there was no point in putting a new title or a new edition onto the market if the need for cookbooks had already been met. Before they launched arguments for the value of their work, many authors took the state of the market as their starting point and admitted that the public might feel that there were enough cookbooks already. As early as 1692, Maria Sophia Schellhammer reminded her readers of the words by the wise Solomon, who said that "of making many books there is no end," and expressed her view that "during the last ten or twenty years such a multitude of works were published that they would have served better in the kitchen as firewood under the pots than as instructions."[27] In 1759, a French author acknowledged the situation in these words: "What! people may say, another work about cooking?"[28] And in 1785, the same preoccupation was put forward in an Austrian book: "Another cookbook? the public will exclaim."[29] In other words, authors and publishers were aware of the competition and had to demonstrate that their books were better than others. This took the form of a combination of apology and attack.

Normally, when authors within a certain field—academic or technical—criticize earlier books, it is part of the progress in that field or at least a positive exchange of ideas and views. Cookbook authors also criticized older works, but many of them used a defamatory language that seems a bit over the top—more insulting than insightful. In 1758, one English author concluded her criticism of earlier works with these words: "Many of them to us are impracticable, others whimsical, others unpalatable, unless to depraved Persons."[30] In 1674, a French author condemned one of the most successful cookbooks of the seventeenth century as "absurd and disgusting."[31] In mid-nineteenth-century London, the English-born and French-educated Charles-Elmé Francatelli attacked a number of cookbook authors by naming the titles of their works and listing what he considered were their gravest errors.[32] But in general, the criticism in cookbook prefaces was not as often about the culinary preparation of the dishes as it was about the use of ingredients that were considered too expensive or too exclusive, and even more about the presentation, which was accused of being too long and complicated for the intended readers, who were not supposed to understand a sophisticated language. In other words, the culprit was the writer rather than the cook.

The language question is an old concern in the history of didactic texts. The German philologist Gerhard Eis, who studied the practical handbooks and other forms of nonfiction texts from the medieval period, stated that while these books did not demand aesthetics, the statements had to be clear, unequivocal, and exact.[33] Scientific writing was expected to be clean, logical, and classical. In the seventeenth century, Francis Bacon criticized language that was abstract and not based on experience, the language that belonged to the *idola fori*—the prejudices of the marketplace. His own aim was to write as plainly and perspicuously as possible, "for nakedness of the mind is still, as nakedness of the body once was, the companion of innocence and simplicity."[34]

Later prefaces in cookbooks sound like echoes of Bacon. The ideal was writing that was plain and easy, clear, and understandable. A Portuguese cookbook author pointed out that he wrote in a simple language because he was not a literary man.[35] There almost seems to have been a competition among cookbook writers to determine who was the best at escaping the "high" style and writing so simply that all—even the most "ignorant"—could understand the text without resorting to "laborious reflection."[36] Susanna Egerin, a German author, wrote that it was not necessary in a cookbook to use "high words" that women were not expected to understand.[37] Literary language and eloquence were referred to with something close to contempt. Another author emphasized that she would not trouble the brains of her readers with multitudes of words for little or no purpose or with vain expressions of things that are altogether unknown to the learned as well as the ignorant.[38] Cajsa Warg used a culinary metaphor to describe her feelings about language: "The same way that I always found dishes with too much spices unsavory I would also consider it unfortunate to sprinkle flowers of eloquence on descriptions which ought to be judged valuable solely on the basis of their clarity and truth."[39] The Italian court cook Bartolomeo Stefani made it clear that his small book came not from the academy but from the kitchen; he wanted to satisfy the palate rather than flatter the ear. He stated that the book did not propose rules for good language but for good cooking, although by using a pun ("ben dire" / "ben condire") to state this, he (or the person who wrote the preface) revealed a fascination for words and language after all.[40]

Cookbook authors also seem to have been fascinated by culinary history. The prefaces have surprisingly many sketches of the cuisine and cookery of the past, with references to the Bible (Abraham's veal dish and Esau's lentil soup), to the great names of antiquity (Apicius, Lucullus, Elagabalus, and Horace), and often to the gradual but nevertheless decisive progress of culinary art. Urbain Dubois, one of the great cooks of the nineteenth century, observed that there was a sort of culinary awakening or at least a very pronounced tendency toward perfection in France as well as abroad.[41] And many authors agreed that the progress was not only in taste but also in health. Health is often linked to hygiene, which was considered important by cooks in the early modern period, but which became one of the most important subjects in the prefaces of nineteenth-century bourgeois cookbooks aimed at modern housewives (but not in the books about *grande cuisine*). At this time—when cookbooks reached a broader market—household economy also became an important issue, as demonstrated by many of the titles.

One particular aspect of prefaces in general that has been observed and discussed by literary critics is summarized in a German cookbook dictionary from 1878: "Most of the prefaces consist of excuses and justification by the author because he dares to present his work to the public."[42] What is expressed in this cookbook preface is in fact a description of one of the topics (*topoi*) in rhetorics, what the literary historian Ernst Robert Curtius called "affected modesty" (affekti- erte Bescheidenheit).[43] The roots of this method are found in judicial oratory in antiquity; the purpose was to bring the listener into a positive state of mind (*cap- tatio benevolentiae*). This is in fact true for all orators (and writers): they want a favorable public, and they try to create it by appearing modest. But they have to draw attention to this modesty themselves, and this is why it is called affected; it is not genuine. Several cookbook authors took this approach, pointing out that they did not consider themselves better or more qualified individuals than others. Even the great Austrian court cook Conrad Hagger contributed with a typical expres- sion: "as much as my poor intellect [*geringer Verstand*] has permitted."[44]

According to Curtius, the modesty topos is often followed by information about why the author dares to present his or her work to the public. Many authors claimed that they had done so only because they were requested or even ordered to by a friend, a patron, or someone in a superior position. Curtius took his examples from classical literature, but there are plenty of these statements in cookbooks, like this one, from the Dane Louise Nimb's major work: "Only repeated requests and urgently pronounced wishes have moved me to take this step."[45]

But these pleas of modesty in no way meant that the authors themselves believed what they were saying. It was part of a larger strategy, as Genette explained; the best way for an author to neutralize critics was by pointing out his or her own weaknesses first and thereby beating the critics to the punch.[46]

The modesty topos was often followed by statements going in the opposite direction; most of the authors contradicted their false humility when they empha- sized the great value of their long experience. They boasted of having worked as cooks in the palaces of princes and aristocracy, in clubs, restaurants, and inns, or as housekeepers and chief stewards for the rich bourgeoisie, in institutions, or in schools. These are statements of capacity rather than incapacity. And they made the contradiction even more evident when they used the plural "we," which turned out to be much more of a *pluralis majestatis* than the intended *pluralis modestatis*.

This was often followed by another topos: stressing that the book was novel and original, presenting something totally new and different. Among the many decla- rations in cookbooks is Conrad Hagger's statement in his 1718 work: "Up to our time such a rare and precious cookbook has never been made and brought to light."[47] Another example from almost two hundred years later is from Angel Muro, who wrote that "until today no book planned like this one has ever been published in Spain or—I think—abroad."[48] Such boasting was, however, not always based on truth. The English author of *The Queen's Royal Cookery* (1713), T. Hall, declared in his preface: "It is not stuff'd with superfluous Trifles, as most of its Nature are; or with old and antiquated Receipts; but with Things wholly new and useful, which are daily the Practice of every Nobleman's and Gentleman's Kitchen."[49] But Gilly Lehmann pointed out that he took forty of the recipes from Sir Kenelm Digby, and she called his book "the most old-fashioned of all the court-cooks' books."[50]

Several authors seem to have been aware of or afraid of negative reactions from the public. In 1769, Elizabeth Raffald wrote: "When I reflect upon the number of books already in print, and with what contempt they are read, I cannot but be apprehensive that this may meet the same fate from some, who will censure before they either see it or try its value."[51]

"Envy" is a word that often appears in prefaces, even in books by great cooks. Conrad Hagger wrote that anyone "not troubled by envy and resentment" would accept that he had written a great book. Robert May stated that he wrote his cookbook to pass on his experience to other cooks but added that he was afraid that he "may be envied by some [cooks] that only value their private Interests over Posterity and the publick good." La Varenne said that he did not wish to shock or offend anyone with the publication of his book but explained that malevolent and envious people would not accept that.[52]

There are examples of offended undertones, but there are also more amusing and ironic statements, such as one that appeared in a 1698 German book, which gives us reason to believe that the text reveals the type of criticism that was most frequent at the time. The author wrote he would try not to be accused by Brother Envy (Bruder Neidhard) and Blaming John (Tadel-Hans) of ignoring them, so he recommended that they help themselves to all the misprints and incorrect "Distinctiones, Commata, Puncta" and enjoy them as a rare delicacy for breakfast.[53]

In a few cases, authors used prefaces to attack publishers they had conflicts with. Hannah Woolley, who had been presented as the author of *The Gentlewoman's Companion,* published in 1673, repudiated this in a book the next year and explained that she had been asked by her publisher to rewrite an earlier work, which she had done, but claimed that the publisher had not followed her instructions and had not paid her properly.[54] Maren E. Bang, author of the first printed cookbook in Norway, attacked a publisher in the preface of a later book and accused him of printing a new edition of her first book without permission.[55] The Czech Dobromila Rettigová explained in a preface how a publisher, without informing her, had printed an earlier version of her manuscript under the name of another author. She had only discovered this when she was accused of plagiarizing the counterfit work.[56]

Genette concluded his discussion of the preface by noting that many prefaces, paradoxically, expressed a kind of reservation or embarrassment about the obligation—often put forward by the publisher—to provide a preface. He quoted an ironic statement by Marivaux, who wondered whether a book without a preface was really a book: "Un livre imprimé, relié sans préface, est-il un livre?"[57] Direct or indirect polemics against the use of a preface can also be found in cookbooks. In *The Compleat Housewife*, for example, the author, E. Smith, wrote: "It being grown as unfashionable for a book now to appear to People without a Preface, as for a Lady to appear at a Ball without a Hoop-Petticoat, I shall conform."[58] Margaret Dods included this commentary in her preface: "Those who hate prefaces, may, if they please, stop here."[59]

In some cases, both the preface and the introduction were written by someone other than the person who was responsible for the recipes. Printers and publishers often wrote prefaces when they felt that the cooks who had delivered the recipes did not have a satisfactory level of literacy. But there are also prefaces written by celebrities and by people with a certain reputation for knowledge of a particular subject. In the nineteenth century—when nutritional science was introduced in bourgeois cookbooks—chemists and medical doctors wrote prefaces or introductions for recipe collections made by housewives.

BLURBS

One form of paratext that is common today in many genres is the "blurb," an expression coined by the American humorist Gelett Burgess and defined as a promotional description. They are generally found on the jackets of books, but texts with the same purpose in prose or rhyme have been used through the centuries, except they have been printed within books rather than on book jackets. There are many of them in *Don Quijote;* Cervantes managed to include them in his satirical concept by stating that he preferred to present his work without a preface and "the customary sonnets, epigrams and tributes which they usually place at the beginning of books."[60] Most books that include such texts, however, clearly use them as part of the marketing, and this also goes for certain cookbooks.

In Antonio Latini's cookbook from 1692, there are several sonnets and short verses praising the author as an ennobled *scalco,* and there are playful anagrams in Latin on his name Antonius Latinus, for example, "An in Lautis notus" (known for his merits).[61] In Vincenzo Corrado's *Il cuoco galante* (1786), four letters directed to Corrado, complementing his work, were written by so-called "illustri personaggi," among them a cardinal and a knight.[62] Even Pellegrino Artusi included laudatory letters from a countess and other notabilities.[63] It seems that such texts were most common in the culinary literature of Italy, although they are also found in English and French cookbooks. In the mid-seventeenth century, Robert May included a few in his book, and William Rabisha presented a long poem in "Commendation of the Author."[64] Audiger's *La maison reglée* included a sonnet, an epigram, and two madrigals.[65]

Another type of paratext is the list of books advertised by the publisher, usually put at the end of the work. Rarer are personal advertisements from the author, but Hannah Woolley, who included medical information in her recipe collections, gave her address, "if any Person desire to speak to me," and explained that said "Persons may have of me several Remedies for Several Distempers, at reasonable Rates."[66] Extra information about authors and publishers, which is particularly valuable to literary and book historians, is also found in the official privileges—an early form of copyright—printed at the beginning or end of a book.

9

The Recipe Form

"Recipe" is a relatively new word in English for a cooking instruction. It comes from the Latin word *recipe,* a verb in imperative singular, meaning "take." *Recipe* was used in medieval dietetic and culinary manuscripts, such as in the fourteenth-century *Liber de coquina,* where one of the recipes, De Leguminibus (Legumes), opens this way: "Recipe cicera et pone . . ." (Take chickpeas and put . . .).[1] "Recipe" is regularly used in English culinary literature beginning in the eighteenth century, but the older term "receipt" endured long into the nineteenth century, even in cookbooks by prominent authors, such as Judith Montefiore and Eliza Acton.[2]

The word "receipt"[3] is known from cookbooks in most European languages, with small orthographic differences (*recette, Rezept,* etc.),[4] but it took some time before it was established as the authoritative term. The term did not originally refer to a written or printed text but rather to a method of preparation.[5] The same is true for the word used in ancient Greek, *skevasía.*[6] In ancient Rome, Plinius used the word *compositio* for a medical prescription, and Platina copied this usage in his Latin cookbook.[7] But it is probably indicative of the increasing popularity of the term "receipt" that the word *compositio* was rendered into "composition et recepte" in the French translation of Platina's book (1505) and "recept composition" in the German translation (1542). The 1487 Italian translation was slightly different: "compositione laquale ricevuta." However, it is worth noting that the sixteenth-century printed Italian cookbooks by Messisbugo and Scappi referred to culinary recipes as *compositioni.* In the nineteenth and twentieth centuries, a few writers chose other terms, for example, *formule* and *procédé* in French and *formula* in Italian.[8]

Historically, "receipt" was used in several professions outside the medical and culinary ones—as was indicated in chapter 3. The first occurrence of the word in

English—*receyt*, in Chaucer's *Canterbury Tales* (c. 1386)—actually represented an alchemical formula.[9] The form of nonculinary recipes often showed a close similarity to the average culinary recipe. In the medieval household manuscript *Le menagier de Paris*, a recipe for ink begins with these words: "To make three pints of ink, take . . ." (Pour faire iii. pintes d'encre, prenez . . .).[10] In a German book about manuscript decoration from 1578, there is a description of how to make liver color (*Leberfarb*): "Take grated red chalk and grate a smaller amount of burnt grape seeds, mix it with parsley color and you will have a good brown liver color."[11]

As Bruno Laurioux has pointed out, the term seems to have entered the culinary field through confectionary, which is where it first appeared. Products made from sugar—which was considered to have a medical value—were long made by apothecaries instead of cooks.[12] This is confirmed by what has been observed about measurements, which were much more precise in confectionary recipes than in culinary ones (see chapter 7). But it is evident that the word "receipt" was used rather early for culinary preparations. In his *Boke of Nurture*, from around 1460, John Russell warned satirically in the chapter "Fried Metes" that cooks had "receytes" for a great variety of "newe conceytes" (culinary delicacies), an excess of which would bring one's life to an end.[13]

As mentioned in the preface, the study of cookbooks (and recipes) has often been limited to a search for new information for scholars investigating different aspects of food history. There are, however, studies in several countries that have examined culinary texts from linguisitic and literary angles. Unfortunately, there is little systematic bibliographical documentation of this research; among the exceptions are Laurioux's books on medieval manuscripts and Anna Wolańska-Köller's detailed accounts of German research.[14] This chapter will refer to some of the most quoted works on the recipe form.

RECIPE STRUCTURE

As briefly mentioned in chapter 3, many early recipes are just an enumeration of ingredients with a few indications of cooking methods, and the use of headings is irregular. But during the nineteenth and early twentieth centuries, a recipe structure was established that is still common in most cookbooks today. This structure consists of three main parts: a heading (the name or description of the dish), a list of ingredients (often presented vertically, in one or two columns), and instructions (a text in prose with a description of how to prepare the dish). Before the ingredients, there may be an introduction with general remarks about the recipe or background information, but this is more of an individual choice. The ingredients are normally given in a sequence corresponding to when they will be used, but they may also be divided into different groups. Michel Guérard distinguished between "main ingredients," "seasoning ingredients," "ingredients for the liaison," and so on. Ferran Adrià divided ingredients into groups such as "from the market," "from the pantry," "from the fridge," and "from the freezer."[15] The instructions are usually printed in one block or divided into several paragraphs separated by blank lines and headed by a number or a title. Paul Bocuse called this third part "éléments" and divided it into "préparation" and "cuisson (cooking)."[16]

In spite of the changes that occurred throughout the era of documented written recipes, from the beginning there has been a very stable pattern in the main body of the recipe text: the culinary instruction has been in the form of a step-by-step procedure, describing the preparation as it is executed in the kitchen. Chronological order is followed in almost all recipes, as in the recipe How to Make Blacke Puddinges from *A Booke of Cookerie* (1597): "Take Oatmeale and steepe it in sodden Milke, then take Hogges suet & good hearbes and chop them small, then put in Fennel seed, pepper and Salte."[17]

The chronological order may be broken when there is a reference to a process that has to be done before the actual preparation, as when Eliza Acton instructed her readers: "Have ready boiled . . . potatoes." The author may list an ingredient that has to be prepared separately. In some cases, these ingredients are just referred to; for example, the author of *The Compleat Cook* (1671) called for a "strong broth" without giving any indication of how to prepare it. Other authors are aware of the problem this may pose for readers. Elizabeth Raffald proposed in a recipe to use forcemeat, and in an added note after the main description, she gave directions on how to make it.[18] But although this recipe follows the main text, it is work that has to be done *before* preparing the main dish.

Additional information of various kinds after the description proper is rather common. Most typical are suggestions for how to garnish the dish or how to serve it: "Send it up with wine sauce in a boat"; "You may lay sassages round your dish if you please"; "Serve with Apple sauce"; "Always serve plenty of French bread with *moules marinières*"; "Serve with lemon juice"; "You can color it and make it green with crushed herbs"; "& sugar & cinnamon."[19]

Another type of addition is an explanation of how variations of the dish may be made. These often refer to the practices of other cooks: "Some, instead of the pudding in the belly [of the hare], roast a piece of bacon"; "Some cooks stew the horseradish in vinegar for ten minutes."[20] Certain books give dietetic advice about which people the dish is healthy or suitable for. There are German recipes, for example, for women in confinement, people after bloodletting, and soldiers at war.[21] Some authors add personal comments and observations. The American Amelia Simmons concluded her recipe for roast beef with these words: "Rare done is the healthiest and the taste of this age."[22]

Particular to books before the seventeenth century was a proud finishing statement about the quality of the dish: "It will be excellent"; "It will be tasty and good";

"It is a good sauce."[23] Here we detect a certain formulaic character, which is typical of other final phrases (*explicits*) as well, such as "and serve": "and serve it to the Table"; "e da' mangiare"; "und gib sie hin"; "puis seruez"; "daj na misu."[24] As Ruth Carroll observed, the same is found—albeit in a less fixed form—in medical recipes (which often include phrases like "you shall be whole" or "for this is proven"), and it corresponds to similar formulaic endings in other completely different genres, such as fairy tales: "And they lived happily ever after."[25]

The chronological, step-by-step instruction form is probably the reason behind the paratactic sentence structure that is characteristic of most recipes. Main clauses follow each other, separated by typographic marks (such as commas, colons, semicolons, full stops, slash marks, hyphens, and ampersands), the conjunction "and," or temporal adverbs (e.g., "then," "next"). In some cases, recipes start with the adverb "first": "First wash and scoure it clean, then perboyle it"; "First make your paste . . . then make . . ."[26]

The use of subordinate clauses does not necessarily change the chronological procedure. When the text goes, "Put the rest of your gravy into the sauce pan, and when it boils, thicken it up with yolks of three or four eggs," there is no difference in function between "when it boils" and, for example, a main clause such as "bring it to a boil." But a conditional clause may be used to indicate a possible failure or difficulty: "If the hen does not give enough fat, add a little butter."[27]

More complex sentences occur above all when authors go outside of the chronological pattern, making digressions, telling anecdotes, and giving background descriptions. This is typical in Platina's recipes but also in more modern books. In his recipe for *sopa de puchero,* written in the 1890s, Angel Muro gave a step-by-step description of the preparation, but when he came to the point where he instructed the reader to make a dry crust, he put in a subordinate clause about culinary terms before continuing the description: "which in cooking is called *gratin*."[28] Sometimes, authors break up the instructions for one recipe with a cross-reference to another recipe. Margaret Dods started a recipe this way: "Dress a cow's head as directed for ox-cheek-soup, page 154, and, when boiled till very tender, cut the meat into small pieces, shaped as directed, No. 460."[29] But the basic structure of the recipe is still a point-by-point procedure.

PARTS OF SPEECH IN RECIPES

The vocabulary in recipes is dominated by nouns and verbs, describing—to put it a bit roughly—the "what" and the "how" of a dish, but other parts of speech serve to modify or give greater precision.

The nouns (often with adjectives or determiners added) can be divided into the following four groups:[30]

1. Necessary technology, such as heating equipment ("fire," "oven," "cooker," "hotplate"), roasting instruments ("spit," "gridiron," "grill"), and vessels ("pan," "pot," "casserole," "tin"). The vessels are often qualified with adjectives indicating dimension ("big," "small," "deep," "wide") or describing quality ("clean," "dry," "warm") or with participles specifying the necessary preparation ("buttered," "floured"). Some forms of kitchenware are not directly named but rather implied by certain verbs: "cut" indicates the use of a knife, "whip" involves a whisk, "mix" necessitates a spoon, and so on.

2. Ingredients, such as basic foodstuffs ("veal," "salmon," "kidney," "carrot," "fennel"), the parts of food in question ("filet," "rib," "head," "leaves"), and ingredients made outside the house and bought in shops ("wine," "vinegar," "sugar," "flour"). These nouns are qualified with the use of adjectives ("good," "best," "small," "big," "young," "fresh"), epithets made from participles of verbs describing processes that need to be carried out before the actual preparation ("sliced," "sifted," "sodden," "shredded," "grated," "beaten"), and determiners ("one," "3/4 teaspoon," "two pounds"). In early cookbooks, the preparation of the ingredients was described in the recipe instructions (e.g., "take and slice your onions"), or in separate recipes (e.g., "how to clean sugar"). Later recipes anticipated that the ingredients would be prepared before the cook began to use them, referring to, for example, "finely chopped echalottes" and "a pound of chocolate finely grated, and a pound and a half of the best sugar finely sifted."[31] And finally, these specifications were moved to the ingredients list and not repeated in the main text. In a 1985 cookbook by Claudia Roden, for example, we find in the ingredient list: "One large onion finely chopped, 2–3 tablespoons caster sugar, 3/4 teaspoon ground allspice."[32]

3. Intermediate and final products: "mixture," "broth," "sauce," "dish."

4. Forms: "rolls," "buns," "cubes," "patties," "slices," "loaves," "sheets," "squares," "diamonds," "lozenges."

In older cookbooks, when nouns are objects of transitive verbs, they often appear with determiners: "Take a Carp"; "Take two Crabs"; "Put halfe your broth"; "Simmer your bread."[33] But in more modern recipes, where the ingredients are already specified in a separate list, the determiners are normally dropped in the main text. In a recipe for mock bisque from her 1896 cookbook, Fannie Farmer gave the quantities in the ingredients list ("1 quart milk, 1 slice onion, 4 tablespoons flour") and dropped determiners in the recipe: "Scald milk with onion, remove onion, and thicken milk with flour."[34]

Rather early on, in cases where the meaning was clear—for example, when the ingredients had been mentioned once—pronouns were sometimes substituted for the nouns. In a sixteenth century recipe, "To dresse a hare," the hare is referred to as "her," the ingredients for sauce as "these," the apples and onions as "them," and the whole dish as "it."[35] But the objects were dropped completely in Farmer's book: "Add butter, sugar, and salt to scalded milk; when lukewarm, add dissolved yeast cake and three cups flour. Cover and let rise."[36] In normal prose, the reader would probably expect, "When this mixture is lukewarm," and, "Cover it and let it rise," but the deletion of objects in recipes is a tendency that has strengthened over the past few centuries.

This is called "null objects" or "zero anaphors as direct objects." In his study of English recipes, Christopher Culy found that this is an exceptional feature of the English language, used only in telegraphese and note taking for personal use. Based on a selection of recipes from different centuries, Culy demonstrated that the use of pronouns declined and the use of zero anaphors strongly increased over the past century, going from 2–3.4 percent in books before the mid-nineteenth century to 37–52 percent in contemporary books.[37] Even if the selection of works in the study is in no way representative (due to the limited availability of material, according to Culy), the increase is so large that it must be considered significant.

Such elliptic phrases are also observed in other languages and in other genres. A study of Russian cookbooks from 1988, for example, compared recipes to biographies in encyclopedias, another form of reference books, and found similar features.[38]

Verbs are used in recipes to describe necessary actions, such as the preparation of ingredients ("clean," "cut," "slice") and ways of cooking ("boil," "fry," "stew"). Adverbs are used as modifiers to give greater precision to verbs—for example, "Mix them well," "Let them stew slowly," "Boil them thoroughly," "Gently turning the spit," and "Heat it gradually." Much attention has been given to the verbs in recipes because they are often used in a particular grammatical mood. In English and some other languages, most sentences in recipes start with a verb in imperative singular or plural: "take" in English, *nimm* in German, *prenez* in French.[39] This particular grammatical form may suggest that the recipe is an order or a command and that recipe collections are consequently examples of normative texts, like statutes, laws, regulations, and commandments. But the imperative is not as narrow or limited in its function as this. One of the early representatives of the linguistic theory of "speech acts," J. L. Austin, stated: "An 'imperative' may be an order, a permission, a demand, a request, an entreaty, a suggestion, a recommendation, a warning, . . . or may express a condition or concession or a definition."[40] What needs to be understood is that the imperative form in a recipe should be conceived of as a convention that is applied in a special context. We know that recipes are generally more open to interpretation and variation than most normative texts. That is why exact measurements have been considered less important in culinary recipes than in medical prescriptions, for example.

An interesting approach to this situation is found in a commentary by the semiotician Algirdas Greimas. In an analysis of a recipe for *soupe au pistou,* he wrote that "the cookery recipe, although formulated at the superficial level with imperatives, cannot be considered as a prescription." There is nothing of *devoir-faire* (obligation) in the text but rather of *savoir-faire* (know-how). He considered the recipe a *discours* similar to musical scores or architectural plans, all of which are "manifestations of competence that are actualized before being put into practice." The recipe can also be considered a contract: "If you carry out the whole of the instructions correctly, you will obtain a *soupe au pistou.*"[41] If we reverse the clauses in Greimas's contract, we get: If you want to make a *soupe au pistou,* follow these instructions. This formula will immediately ring a bell to readers familiar with the so-called hypothetical recipe openings in medieval handbooks.[42]

Although the imperative is—or has been—the most common grammatical form in recipes in certain languages, it is far from the only form. There are also participles, infinitives, subjunctives, passive constructions, modal verbs, impersonal constructions, and even sentences with the ingredient as subject ("the milk boils")—and there are cases where several of these forms appear in the same recipe.[43] This may be due to the lack of professional editing that was typical for personal manuscripts, such as the one by Sabina Welserin (see chapter 3), but this also occurs in badly edited printed books.

The impersonal construction using the pronoun *man* ("one") followed by a verb is frequent in Germanic languages.[44] The verb is mostly in the indicative, but the subjunctive is used in a few cases. Modal verbs may or may not be added, such as in a late medieval Danish recipe: "Man skal takae" (One shall take).[45]

But even though different forms may be found in cookbooks from the same period, the relative importance of forms has changed over the centuries. According to several studies, statistics based on representative selections of German recipes document that the imperative form was dominant until the eighteenth century. Then follows an increasingly important use of the passive and the impersonal *man* construction, and these two forms became dominant in the nineteenth and early twentieth centuries.[46] Inge Wiedemann explained that this change was sparked by a growing bourgeois self-confidence that made it difficult for cookbook authors to "duzen" their readers—that is, use the informal second-person singular (*du*). Karin Becker observed a similar change from imperative to impersonal form in the later editions of the *regimina sanitatis,* which were directed to a more aristocratic audience, "un public courtois."[47]

After World War II, the infinitive became the dominant form in German.[48] This increased use of the infinitive calls for special attention, particularly because it entered recipe terminology in other European languages. In a Swiss cookbook—written in German—from 1923, the author gave the reason for her use of the infinitive. She wrote in the preface that she made an effort to write in a terse style that made things easier to understand: "Instead of the traditional [form] one takes [*man nimmt*] I have used the infinitive, which has become common in French cookbooks."[49] But how common was this form in France at the time? It is possible to find infinitives in older French cookbooks, but they are generally used with a modal word, for example, "Il faut prendre" (One must take). In the second half of the nineteenth century, Urban Dubois used the infinitive in *Cuisine de tous les pays* (1872), but in his later works, he used the imperative plural, which was the common form in other French books at the time. In *Dictionnaire universel de cuisine* (1889–91), Joseph Favre used the infinitive in all his recipes, and Auguste Escoffier followed the same practice in *Le guide culinaire* (1903), but other authors continued to use the imperative, for example, Édouard Nignon in his *Éloges de la cuisine française* (1933). According to Nicola Hödl, the real break with the imperative and the definitive introduction of the infinitive in France happened between the 1970s and the 1990s.[50]

To understand why cookbook authors started to favor the infinitive over the imperative, it is important to point out that this is not a trend that was unique to recipes. Many languages use the infinitive form as a request. In French books, it is common to refer to a page by using the infinitive: "Voir page 72." In Spanish everyday speech, the infinitive may be used instead of the imperative in expressions like "Venir chicos!" (Come, boys!). In a study of contemporary recipes in Russia, where the infinitive has been common since the oldest printed books, Sigrid Robaschik explained that the infinitive form used as a request (common in military, sports, school instruction, and theater direction) generally conveys a relatively strict, categorical order (*Befehl*), but in the case of recipes, the request is clearly weakened. It is more of a recommendation, an indirect request without the words *nado* and *nuzhno,* implying obligation.[51]

But *why* is this form used in recipes? It is possible to consider it as the final stage in a long process that started with the direct request using the imperative singular, then the imperative plural, and finally increasingly formal and courteous forms of requests or recommendations. By using the infinitive, one does not need to choose between a formal and a nonformal way of addressing people. Trude Ehlert saw the use of the infinitive as a way of emphasizing the culinary action itself and putting the sender and receiver more in the background. She found that one possible reason for this development was the "increasing demand for autonomy by the individual" and the gradual democratization of social relations, which meant that giving and receiving orders no longer felt natural.[52]

In her study of German grammar, Elvira Glaser observed that the infinitive has historically been quite common in oral use when giving orders and speaking to children, and in written language in official instructions. "The use of the infinitive in recipes appears to be connected with these functions," she observed, "but the exact link is still to be established."[53]

In languages that do not use the infinitive in recipes, the progression of verb forms has been completely different. An interesting study was published in Sweden, where the imperative dominated in the seventeenth century but was replaced in the eighteenth century by passive constructions and the impersonal *man* construction.[54] This corresponded to the more formal character of the language of the period and to the introduction of polite forms of personal pronouns in conversations, the second-person plural and third-person singular. But this stage was not followed by an infinitive, as it was in Germany. On the contrary, the imperative second-person singular was reintroduced in Swedish recipes in the 1960s, at a time when the way people addressed each other had already changed to a more informal character with the use of second-person singular.[55]

In Czech, where the imperative second-person singular was common starting with the first printed books in the sixteenth century, passive constructions appeared frequently in books of the nineteenth century, but from the 1920s, when the Czech-speaking areas that had been part of Austria became the independant republic Czechoslovakia, a new form appeared, the first-person plural.[56]

Pronouns are—as described above—first of all used as objects, replacing full designations of ingredients and utensils. Personal pronouns are often used in the second person (singular or plural), as if the author is talking directly to a listener. In languages where the verb is declined according to person, the pronoun itself may be left out. The use of the second-person singular is particularly prominent in German and Scandinavian cookbooks for children. But the use of the second person may also have a social connotation. The difference can easily be seen in two separate books by Charles-Elmé Francatelli. In both books, Francatelli used the imperative, but in *The Modern Cook* (1846), which was aimed at an upper-class audience, he gave instructions in a more polite voice: "When about to prepare for the reception of company, it is advisable to begin . . ."; "The turkey may be stuffed either with veal stuffing or *quenelle* of fowl." For his other book, *Plain Cookery for the Working Classes* (1847), he used a more direct and slightly patronizing voice: "When it happens that you have a dinner consisting of bacon and cabbages, you invariably throw away the liquor in which they have been boiled, or, at the best, give it to the pigs, if you possess any; this is wrong"; "I hope that at some odd times you may afford yourselves an old hen or cock; and when this occurs, this is the way I recommend that it be cooked."[57]

In the last of these recipes, Francatelli used the pronoun in first-person singular. This is not common in recipes. There is a traditional convention in nonfiction to limit the use of this form to the preface and other paratexts, and this rule is also generally followed in cookbooks. However, there are exceptions, beginning with the oldest manuscripts and the very first printed cookbooks, such as the manuscript *Tractatus,* from the fourteenth century, and *Küchenmeisterei,* published in the fifteenth century.[58] In the sixteenth century, the Italian Bartolomeo Scappi frequently expressed his personal opinion with comments like, "Ma io non lo lodo" (But I don't praise it).[59] Such remarks—made with "I" or "we"—appear occasionally in later books, such as cookbooks by La Varenne, Antonius Magirus, and Elizabeth David, but they are more often found in editorial commentaries than in the recipes themselves.

The use of the first-person singular or plural may have been a rhetorical way of establishing a credible teaching situation—authoritative but also open for individual variation—between master and pupil, while the lack of the first person may indicate authority through objectivity and neutrality, expressing a knowledge considered above doubt and not open for discussion—authoritarian rather than authoritative.

A systematic use of the first-person singular is most evident in cookbooks written in a prose different from the standard recipe form—for example, epistolary or dialogue cookbooks (discussed in chapter 10). But some of the most extreme examples of what have been called "talking recipes" are found in recent African American cookbooks. In a study of this literature, Andrew Warnes pointed out an oral quality that he compared to contemporary trends within poetry and novels by African American writers.[60] One of the examples he gave was from Sheila Ferguson's recipe for brains from her book *Soul Food* (1989): "Now listen, folks, I have got to admit that I have never put a single brain into my mouth. . . . But this is the most typical dish from the deeeep deep South and lots of people like it."[61]

Recipes using the third person—not counting the impersonal *man* construction—occur occasionally, but it is not a common form in recipes where instruction is the basic aim. The third person (he, she, they) is more frequent in narratives, for example, in fiction or in general descriptions of various practices in a society, as demonstrated later in this chapter.

THE RECIPE AS TEXT-TYPE

Modern readers of cookbooks will easily recognize the culinary recipe as a special type of text, not only because of its subject (food preparation) and its graphic form (standardized since the late nineteenth century, with a separate ingredients list) but also because of characteristic features of the language.

Linguists have studied the recipe, trying to define the text type to which it belongs. Different authors with rather diverging theoretical basis and scope have applied several terms in various languages. The recipe is considered a form of technical language (*Fachsprache* in German, *fackspråk* in Swedish). Some linguists have named the particular text type the culinary recipe belongs to a *technolect,* or a language typical of a certain technical field, and more particularly a *minilect,* which is defined by a more stereotypical structure than technolects in general.[62]

Within the category of technical language, the recipe has also been defined as a *Funktiolekt,* in which the contents and language of the text are formed by the special function they are supposed to have.[63] The function of the recipe has been determined by some German linguists as instruction, and the texts have therefore been called *Anweisungstexte* (instruction texts). Thomas Gloning preferred to call recipes *Beschreibungstexte* (description texts), because their basic text function is, in his opinion, to describe how something is made—a dish, for example. This description may be used for different purposes, such as instruction or as aiding memory.[64]

One particular problem with many of the studies and papers on the linguistics of the recipe is that they are based on limited empirical material. Some studies concentrate on only one language and then draw general conclusions without taking into consideration the great variations between grammatical forms in, for example, English, German, and Swedish recipes. Other studies cover only a certain historical period. When Neal Norrick defined recipes as texts about edible products with pictures and a bipartite structure, he ignored the historical tradition. But even when the scope is wider—as it is in Manfred Görlach's study—it is still not broad enough to understand the recipe as a text type that is representative of fields outside the medical and the culinary fields, as Ruth Carroll has demonstrated.[65] She followed Douglas Biber in defining a text type "by linguistic characteristics only."

The point-by-point enumeration of procedures and ingredients in recipes invites a discussion of whether it is possible to consider them lists. In *The Domestication of the Savage Mind* (1977), the sociologist Jack Goody took up this challenge. Goody began exploring administrative lists in texts from Mesopotamia that were almost four thousand years old and found that lists were "characteristic of the early uses of writing." He emphasized that recipes list "not only what ingredients are required but what actions have to be carried out."[66]

Goody's analysis started with medical recipes; his discussion of culinary recipes is more superficial, as it is based on rather limited and arbitrary material. The publication of original texts and research within the field of food history during recent years has provided much richer material than Goody had access to when he wrote his book in the 1970s. The interdisciplinary French project POLIMA (2015–19), which is studying the power of lists in the Middle Ages, may therefore come up with new ideas.[67] The project résumé states that the list is a form of writing common to a great many medieval textual productions, and it makes clear that texts do not necessarily have to appear like lists at first sight: "Any text constructed in paratactic form can be included in the corpus."

As demonstrated above, the paratactic form is typical for culinary recipes. Several late medieval recipes illustrate this. Consider, for example, the following, which appears in a fifteenth-century English manuscript: "Take egg yolks, hardboiled, and saffron, and bread, ground, with cow milk, boil. Add egg white, cut small, and rinds of pork, carved. Mix it a little with raw egg yolks."[68] In this and other recipes from that time, the ingredients and preparation methods are not listed separately, but the recipes can still be considered lists, particularly if they are listed vertically:

Take egg yolks, hardboiled
and saffron
and bread, ground
with cow milk
boil.
Add egg white, cut small
and rinds of pork, carved.
Mix it a little
with raw egg yolks.

A study of recipes from this perspective may complement information about how knowledge is formatted and passed on in material form (point 2 of POLIMA's research objectives). But it would probably be difficult to compare recipes to tables and catalogs with an intention of classification. Recipes can hardly be put into the category Umberto Eco called practical lists. In his book *Vertigine della lista* (2009), Eco distinguished between poetical lists, which have an artistic aim, and practical lists, such as shopping lists, menus, library catalogs, museum inventories, and receipts for purchased objects. Eco established three characteristics of a practical list. First, the function of the list is purely referential; it itemizes and catalogs the items on it. Second, the list is finite; it enumerates all relevant objects but nothing more. Third, the list is unalterable.[69] It is easy to see that a recipe does not fit these characteristics because its function is not to catalog ingredients but to demonstrate how they can be used in the production of a certain dish. In the short recipe from the fifteenth-century manuscript above, the verbs "boil" and "mix" are not ingredients but rather instructions on how the ingredients are to be treated. But even a modern list of ingredients is not a list after Eco's definition because it is alterable; the ingredients and amounts suggested may be changed. And it is not even finite, because ingredients may be dropped or added.

Recipes have often been characterized as monotonous and stereotyped texts, echoing Alexander Pope's lines "Some dryly plain, without Invention's Aid / Write dull Receits how Poems may be made." Gillian Riley called them "the neat, bland, tidy and impersonal voice of a home economist," and Piero Camporesi described them as "arid, scientific, unalterable. . . . Rigidly imperative as a formula."[70] Riley and Camporesi made these generalizations to emphasize the richness in style of Bartolomeo Scappi and Pellegrino Artusi, respectively, but such interesting writers are not limited to a few exceptions. First of all, it is worth noting what Gerhard Eis said about the medieval *Artes-literatur:* even if cookbook authors lay no claim to an aesthetic assessment, many of them put considerable effort into stylistic aspects of the language (*sprachliche Darstellung*).[71] And closer to our time, there are actually quite a few cookbook writers who break with the recipe stereotype, as the example above from the African American writer Sheila Ferguson demonstrates. There are, in fact, recipes written in verse, as dialogues, in scientific prose, and as travelogues.

RECIPES IN VERSE

Didactic works in verse go back to Hesiod's *Works and Days,* written around 700 BCE, and are found in the Middle Ages and the early modern period. Several versions of *Regimen sanitatis* were circulated in verse starting in the thirteenth century, many of them written in a Latin close to the vernacular Italian. In England, there were John Russel's treatise on household duties, *The Boke of Nurture* (ca. 1460), and Thomas Tusser's *A Hundred Good Points of Husbandry* (1557). According to the German scholar Bernhard Dietrich Haage, the bound form is used in practical literature as a mnemonic aid, but it might also have been used to give material an aesthetic value.[72]

Several early cookbooks open with a verse, either written by the author to serve as a preface or written by someone else as a recommendation for the book, but there are also examples of rhymed recipes from the fifteenth century in German and English manuscripts.[73] According to the historian Hans Wiswe, however, one of the German recipes is "a humorous Intermezzo in a book that is otherwise so matter-of-fact."[74] This can be explained by what Haage said about versification of practical literature for the upper levels of society: "It is mainly for fun" (Aus reinen Spieltrieb).[75]

There is a long tradition in European literature of verses about food, often with a comic or playful element, and the humor is quite obvious in the collections of rhymed recipes ("poetic cookbooks") from the eighteenth century onward. The first of these books was the French *Festin joyeux,* printed in 1738. One of the recipes is for *perdreaux aux écrévisses* (partridges with crawfish) and it starts like this:

> First you cook everything well,
> And mix with a light ragoût,
> Add sweetbreads and truffles too,
> And let cockscombs and champignons swell.[76]

Typical for the recipes in this book is that they can be sung, as they were written to well-known tunes from light and popular music genres. Referring to himself as a cook, the alleged author made excuses for the bad rhymes in his verses, which he said were certainly not as Scarron would have written them. By referring to the seventeenth-century burlesque poet Paul Scarron, the suspicion is strengthened that the verses belong to the century before the book was printed, and it has been suggested that the real author was the aristocrat Louis de Béchameil, although this has not been confirmed.[77]

In the nineteenth and twentieth centuries, French, German, Spanish, American, Danish, and Norwegian books of recipes in verse were published. A Norwegian book from 1833 versified the recipes of the first printed cookbook in Norway, published only two years earlier, and the verses were written to melodies used for national anthems, drinking songs, and hymns.[78] By using tunes for hymns in these merry songs, the author, a church warden and rebellious publicist, did the opposite of men such as Martin Luther and William Booth, who wrote religious hymns to popular, secular melodies.

Were these recipes intended to be used to help in the kitchen? Some of them did in fact emphasize that that was the basic idea. The Danish *Kogebog for musikalske husmødre* (Cookbook for musical housewives) professed in verse in the preface:

> The housewife now can cook her meat
> While singing from a music sheet.[79]

But in spite of the declared intentions, these books were probably made more to amuse readers than to instruct them. Most of the verses were rather amateurish, with clumsy rhymes and hobbling rhythms, and could not hope for a glorious after-life in the history of literature. There are, however, recipe poems that were written by authors with acknowledged literary qualities. They followed the same chronological progression as the ordinary recipes, giving step-by-step instructions, but they added aspects and elements that were generally absent in cookbooks. Here follow five examples in five languages and from different literary contexts.

The first was by a representative of Polish romanticism, Adam Mickiewicz, who in his epic poem *Pan Tadeusz* actually used a 1682 cookbook to describe an old Polish dinner. But he also gave, as part of his description of old national traditions, the "recipe" for *bigos,* a dish still popular in Poland. He admitted that words and rhymes—he used thirteen syllable lines with caesura and rhymed couplets—were not sufficient to transmit a real appreciation of "the most wonderful flavor, the smell and the color."[80] He listed the ingredients of the dish—good vegetables, chopped sauerkraut, morsels of meat—and explained that they should all be simmered in a pot. But he did not follow the traditional recipe form; his recipe is a narrative told in the third person and without the particular verbal forms indicating a request.

Other writers, however, chose the imperative. The French dramatist Edmond Rostand included in his most famous play, *Cyrano de Bergerac,* a scene where the protagonist's friend, the *rôtisseur* and *pâtissier* Ragueneau, proudly declares that he has versified a recipe: "J'ai mis une recette en vers." The recipe is for *tartelettes amandines* and is written in a light, elegant poetic form that plays with the rhymes and rhythm, making it very difficult to translate.[81]

While Rostand kept the imperatives in the second-person plural, which was typical of most French culinary recipes at that time, the Argentine-born Spaniard Ventura de la Vega—who wrote many occasional poems—chose the first-person singular when he described his method of making garlic soup, *sopa de ajo*. The Voltaire-admirer-turned-Catholic paid tribute to the soup as a dish for Lent, but he also declared it the basis of the Castilian diet. The personal tone in the poem creates an atmosphere similar to the one in Pablo Neruda's *Odas elementales* (which is about tomatoes, potatoes, and other foodstuffs), combining the solemn and the ordinary: In a casserole, boil salt, pepper, and small bits of bread in olive oil, and in this swelling mixture, "I will hide two well-peeled cloves of Spanish garlic."[82] Instead of Neruda's free verse, Vega chose the bound form, and the Spanish composer José María Cásares later composed music for it. The text and the notes were printed in Angel Muro's original cookbook, *El practicón* (1894).

Another original and much praised cookbook, *Modern Cookery,* by Eliza Acton, included a recipe in rhymed verse in the 1855 edition. In a note, Acton wrote that this was the first time the poem was printed, after it had been circulated among the friends of the author, the poetic reverend Sidney Smith.[83] But in contrast to the serious, almost religious tone in Vega's verse, Smith's poem is filled with the light-hearted humor he was famous for. The ingredients for his salad dressing are enumerated with the common imperatives, but they are not always used in the traditional manner: "Let onion atoms lurk within the bowl," he instructed readers in one line, and in another, he told them to add "a magic soupçon of anchovy sauce." He even resorted to alliteration: "Of mordant mustard add a simple spoon." And then he expressed his enthusiasm for the result: "Oh, green and glorious! Oh, herbacious treat!"

A final example, which also raises theoretical questions, is a poem the German romantic poet Eduard Mörike wrote about *Frankfurter Brenten,* a type of small cookies. The first surprise is perhaps his use of the imperative second-person singular, a dated and very uncommon form in the mid-nineteenth century:[84]

> Start with almonds, I suggest,
> Take three pounds, or four at best.[85]

This poem, which is included in Mörike's collected works, was originally published in a German journal for ladies, *Frauen-Zeitung für Hauswesen, weibliche Arbeiten und Moden,* in 1852, and Horst Steinmetz used it as an example of how context may decide the reception of a text.[86] The readers of Mörike's complete works may have considered the recipe as a poem on a par with the other poems in the book, which describe feelings and phenomena of the human universe. The ladies who read

"Frankfurter Brenten" in the journal may have looked at the text as a practical instruction—a recipe—even if they observed and appreciated the form as an amusing variation and perhaps made no practical use of the recipe in the kitchen. Yet a closer reading of Mörike's text reveals that it has elements not expected in recipes. Consider, for example, these lines:

> Now put all this while it is hot
> Onto a plate (but poets need
> A rhyme here now, and therefore feed
> The finished stuff into a pot).[87]

With this ironic remark, which breaks up the sequence of instructive steps, the poet seems to make fun of his own role; it is a kind of *Verfremdung,* or alienation, that creates a distance between Mörike as a poet and as a cooking teacher.

These rhymed recipes seem to have been written with very different intentions: to inform, to instruct, to entertain, or to create art. This is of course also true for recipe poems in unbound form by Günter Grass and others.[88] But there is a noticeable difference in intention when recipes appear in prose works other than culinary works.

RECIPES IN FICTION AND NONFICTION PROSE

Recipes can be found in books on ethnology, anthropology, sociology, geography, and many other scientific works; in travel writing; and in practical books, where they fill a variety of functions. They can even be found in bookkeeping accounts; Bruno Laurioux has referred to such material in the Archivio di Stato di Roma and has shown how much information these sources can give the food historian, among them descriptions of culinary preparation that resemble real recipes.[89]

Recipes in very rudimentary form are also occasionally found in dictionaries. Take, for example, the soup borscht, which is described in a Russian dictionary as a "liquid dish, a sort of soup of beets, cabbage, and various spices."[90] There are, however, philological works that contain descriptions that more closely resemble recipes. In the kingdom of Denmark and Norway during the seventeenth and eighteenth centuries, scholars and senior civil servants with an academic education were asked by the authorities in Copenhagen to collect words and phrases in local dialects. Most of the words were defined simply with the corresponding word in Danish, the official language in the two countries, but some words represented objects or phenomena not found in official dictionaries. One such example was recorded by a vicar on the coast of northern Norway: "*Kalv-dantz*—the feet and the head of the calf is boiled, then the meat is taken from the bones, then chopped small, and boiled in milk with some barley grits, then put on a dish. When it is cold, it is sliced and put on a plate."[91] This step-by-step description is good enough to cook from, but the form is a sort of report or narrative rather than a recipe.

The same form is documented in descriptions based on research in natural and social sciences. In a Renaissance study of different fish species and what distinguishes them, the prominent French physician and naturalist Guillaume de Rondelet wrote about *chien de mer* (a type of shark). After his scientific observations, he noted that the liver was considered a delicacy by some, who kept it salted and ate it cooked in wine or roasted. He then continued with this passage: "It is very good boiled with hyssop, bay leaves and similar herbs, and with cinnamon, nutmeg and cloves added."[92] There is no imperative used here but another grammatical form, the third-person indicative ("on le garde salé, il est très bon"). Even if it would be possible to use the text in the kitchen, it is not a classical recipe but rather a description given the same way as other general information in the book.

There are prose works with recipes written with a special intention. Elizabeth Romer's *The Tuscan Year* (1984) is an example. Romer wanted to record for posterity old cooking processes in a rural community. In the introduction, she admitted that the book was not a regular cookbook, and she often starts out by describing dishes in the third-person singular indicative, explaining, for example, how a local woman, Silvana, makes *crostini* with hard boiled eggs at Easter: "She chops them very finely with her mezzaluna on her big old chopping board." Then, when the description is finished, she gives a recipe, opening with the second-person indicative: "To make *Crostini con Uova* you need three large eggs, two tablespoons of vegetables preserved in wine vinegar . . ." This corresponds to the ingredients list. The instructions follow in the second-person imperative: "Shell the eggs and chop them finely. Next chop the preserved vegetables finely . . . " This is not too different from the three stages in Sabina Welserin's recipe for *sultzfisch* (referred to in chapter 3), but while Welserin wanted to record recipes for her family, Romer's intention was to record traditional recipes for the next generation of Tuscans and Italians.[93]

Recipes in works of fiction are written within different prose genres. A number of twentieth-century novels, including spy stories and love stories, contain long and detailed recipes, for example, *Es muss nicht immer Kaviar sein* (*It Can't Always Be Caviar*), by the Austrian Johannes Mario Simmel. The book has entire menus with starters, main dishes, and desserts, including real recipes, written with the traditional *man nehme* construction. These menus and recipes are printed with a special typeface on separate pages, but the cooking is well integrated in the narrative. In *Como agua para chocolate* (*Like Water for Chocolate*), by the Mexican author Laura Esquivel, the cooking is even more integrated into the narrative; the recipes are woven into the story with evident dramaturgical function. Each chapter has the name of a month and the name of a recipe. First comes a list of ingredients, followed by the recipe, which starts with a traditional formula: "Se toman los huevos" (One takes the eggs). But then something else happens in the kitchen, and the story goes on independently of the cooking until attention suddenly turns back to the preparation of the dish, but now not necessarily in the recipe form but rather as a part of the story, told in the third-person present indicative.[94]

A similar combination of a story and a culinary preparation, albeit on a very different level, is found in the Swedish children's book *Totte bakar* (*Thomas Bakes a Cake*), by Gunilla Wolde. The book is told in simple sentences, as are the other books in Wolde's series about Totte, which follow the boy as he plays, builds, goes to the doctor, and so on. But since this story is about a cake, it is possible to follow the steps, mix the given measures of egg, sugar, butter, and flour into a dough, and bake it in the oven.

Most of these recipes are intended to be tried out, and many of them are absolutely worth making, but in other cases, one has to take care. In the preface to *Deadeye Dick,* Kurt Vonnegut calls the recipes in the book "musical interludes for the salivary gland." He refers to the titles of particular cookbooks he has read but admits that he has "tinkered with the originals, however, so no one should use this novel for a cookbook."[95]

HUMOROUS RECIPES—PARODY AND SATIRE

Recipes from the late Middle Ages and Renaissance often seem strange or even funny to modern eyes because of special ingredients or combinations of ingredients that were common in certain areas in earlier periods but are quite unheard of today. But in the history of cookbooks, there are also recipes that were intended to be humorous and bring entertainment to the reader and perhaps also to the eater. Such recipes in verse have already been mentioned above.

Barbara Ketcham Wheaton has suggested that humorous recipes may be divided into three different categories.[96] The first one is for "recipes intended to be read as jokes," and she gives as an example the witty German recipe mentioned by Wiswe and referred to earlier in the chapter. A more modern example is a recipe for "clear soup" from Fred. H. Curtiss's *The Comic Cookery Book,* first published in 1890: "Take two pints of water, wash them thoroughly on both sides, pour into a dish or something and stir round the kitchen until tired. Dilute with ice water, cook until it comes to a boil. Have the boil lanced and serve."[97]

The second category is for "genuine recipes which are intended to produce food which will trick or amuse the reader." She mentions pies with birds flying out at carving time and disguised dishes, such as "bacon" that is made from curdled milk. Such dishes will be further described in chapters 13 and 17.

Wheaton's third category is for "recipes intended to parody fashions in food preparation." She gives no example, but it is evident that formulaic texts invite parody. This is not true only of recipes; an important part of popular culture in Europe is made up of parodies of religious and legal texts, such as sermons, liturgy, funerals, and trials, for example, "Sermon Joyeux de M. Saint Hareng" and "Funeral

Procession of Madame Geneva."[98] Typical for such parodies is that the originals were well known by the public, and so was the standard recipe form. As Manfred Görlach observed: "How much the pattern of cooking recipes has become general knowledge is illustrated by playful misuses."[99] He quoted a poem by Alexander Scott to demonstrate what he meant, but this poem has nothing to do with food. The culinary terms in the poem ("take," "sieve," "spice") are used as metaphors. A famous example of this kind is "Mutter Goethes Rezept zu Neujahr" (Mother Goethe's New Year recipe), allegedly written by the author's mother around 1800. This is a poem giving moral advice that begins with the *man* formula: "One takes twelve months, polishes them quite clean of bitterness, meanness, pedantry, and angst, and divides each month into 30 or 31 parts, so it will last as provisions for a year." Recipes in this category have also been published in culinary recipe collections. "How to Cook a Husband," for example, was printed in various American cookbooks: "Make a clear, steady fire of love, neatness and cheerfulness. Set him as near this as seems to agree with him. If he putters and fizzes do not be anxious; some husbands do this till they are quite done."[100] Another very different example of playful misuse of recipes is the experiment made by the American author Harry Mathews, who rewrote Keat's poem "La belle Dame sans merci," using vocabulary from a cauliflower recipe by Julia Child, and vice versa.[101]

Some of the most extreme and uncommon printed recipes are found in an English cookbook from 1664, *The Court and Kitchen of Elizabeth, Commonly Called Joan Cromwell, the Wife of the Late Usurper,* a satire of the alleged bad taste, eating habits, and culinary pleasures of the Lord Protector Oliver Cromwell and even more so of his wife. The publication is part of a popular literature, written in verse and in prose, that circulated orally as well as in print during the Cromwell era. The cookbook is a rude attack, starting with a long introduction and then moving directly on to the recipes themselves. One recipe, How to Bake a Venison-Pasty, starts like this: "This is called the King of dainties, which Oliver stole by retail (as he did a more real Regality) many years before, and shared this sovereign delicacy among his accomplices. But now, more than bold Robin Hood, he was lord and avowed master of game, and therefore that his fellow deer stealers may know how to dress their prey à la mode Cromwellian, take this prescription, for to other persons it will be of no use."[102] After this introduction follows the recipe itself, but a closer study of the text shows that it is taken from William Rabisha's *The Whole Body of Cookery Dissected,* published in 1661, in other words, after Cromwell's death and the Restoration. Of the 102 so-called Cromwellian recipes in the book, at least 39 are from Rabisha and 23 are from *The Accomplish't Cook* (1660), by the Royalist Catholic Robert May. But one recipe has no known parallel in other cookbooks, and it is a good example of the satiric spirit of the book. It describes how to cover a pig in clay and cook it in the embers for twenty-four hours. Part of the recipe refers to the *cuirassier,* the heavy cavalry in the English Civil War: "Arm him [the pig] like a cuirassier or one of Cromwell's Ironsides hair, skin and all (his entrails drawn and belly sewed up again) with this prepared clay."[103]

As this chapter demonstrates, a recipe may be anything from a simple list of ingredients to a narrative with allusions and fantasies. Recipes take their form according to which function they are meant to have. In a discussion of English medieval recipes, Carrie Griffin emphasized that recipes are not always utilitarian, but "may have functioned as fiction, a narrative with lists of delicacies and combinations that may or may not have been realistically possible."[104] And the same can be said about more recent texts. The collection of recipes—the cookbook—is consequently also a highly varied literary product, one that is not easy to define from a "genre" point of view.

10

The Cookbook Genre

In this study, the word "genre" has been used to indicate certain types of texts—for example, the recipe or the cookbook—but it has not been specifically defined. Within the field of literary criticism, the concept of genre has been the subject of discussion and controversy for a long time, and several theories have been launched to find a more valuable approach than the classical distinctions between drama, epic, and lyric. There have also been attempts within the field of nonfiction to find a relevant use for a genre concept in the definitions and delimitations of different texts. The aim of this chapter is to determine the place cookbooks have in the literary landscape and what relationship they have to the broader literature about food and drink.

THE RECIPE COLLECTION

In the preface, the cookbook was described as a collection of recipes, which is probably the way most people look at it. In his discussion of the cookbook genre in the medieval manuscript era, Bruno Laurioux starts by saying that everybody today would recognize a cookbook, and he thinks that this was probably the case in the Late Middle Ages as well. He gives a precise definition of a cookbook as "a group, organized or not, of recipes for the preparation of food for human consumption."[1]

The simplest form of cookbook is a pure collection of culinary recipes, a form that may be compared to other recipe collections—for example, medical—and considered a "genre" as such.[2] The recipe collection may further be grouped with collections of aphorisms, adages, proverbs, and sayings, such as almanacs and calendars,[3] and even to anthologies of poems—by one or more persons—on a common topic.[4] Michael Hoey used the term "text colonies" to describe such texts, and he added dictionaries, telephone books, shopping lists, and hymn books. He defined this type of text as "a discourse whose component parts do not derive their meaning from the sequence in which they are placed."[5]

But this kind of cookbook—the pure recipe collection, one that does not include any other text-types—is far from the only one or even the dominant one. First of all, as discussed in chapter 7, the recipes in some early cookbooks were arranged in order of difficulty based on a pedagogical idea of a gradual learning process. By the Late Middle Ages, culinary manuscripts were being expanded by the addition of nonculinary recipes (for confectionary and spiced drinks, for example) and texts that were not in a recipe form (such as rules for carving and menus for the different seasons according to the religious calendar). The intention was to teach readers not only how to prepare the food but also how to complete all the other tasks needed to arrange a meal, particularly a festive one. Some manuscripts had an even wider scope, and they included medical advice and general household hints. But as long as culinary recipes make up a substantial part of a book, there is still reason to classify it as a cookbook. However, there were early books in which culinary recipes constituted only a minor part. Laurioux has studied the more than one hundred existing medieval manuscripts containing culinary recipes. In addition to the relatively "pure" culinary works, which contain mostly recipes for foods (*recettes alimentaires*), he listed three other genres of books that included recipes: *manuels d'hôtel*, about court administration, carving, table decoration, and so on; *cuisine medicale*, where the boundary between culinary and medical is often vague; and *livres mixtes*, such as encyclopedias with household and moral advice.[6]

A study of books including culinary recipes produced during the first centuries of printing, from 1470 until 1700, shows that more than half of the total 164 works included other content: 28 had medical material, 22 had general household information, 14 had recipes for confectionary and preservation of foodstuffs, and a few works had information about a mixture of various subjects, such as carving, gardening, and menus. Seventy-one books were pure recipe collections, and two-thirds of them were published in the seventeenth century, when the production of confectionary books and household encyclopedias also increased.[7]

The enormous increase in cookbook production since 1700, with brief interruptions during periods of war, has been accompanied by a differentiation of the genre, with more books on special subjects. At the same time, general cookbooks have continued to include more than just recipes for cooking. In addition, there are cookbooks where the recipes are organized alphabetically, like dictionaries, and cookbooks where the recipes are put into frameworks favored by totally different genres, such as dialogues and letters.

FIGURE 19. Frontispiece of *Stockholmisch Koch-Gesprächs Vortrab, zwischen einer flamischen und niedersächsischen Köchin* (Stockholm culinary conversation, between a Flemish and a Low Saxon cook), by Ditlevus Maius, royal master cook, printed in Stockholm in 1644. The engraving is by Fredrik Herman Höjer. Kungliga Biblioteket, Stockholm, F1 1700 3543.

COOKBOOKS IN DIALOGUE AND EPISTOLARY FORM

A literary form chosen in certain cookbooks is the dialogue, a genre with roots in antiquity that became very popular in the Renaissance among prominent authors such as Desiderius Erasmus, Thomas More, and Baldassare Castiglione. The dialogue was first and foremost a pedagogical text, and Torquato Tasso, who himself wrote a household book in this form, claimed that while the reasoning in comedy and tragedy was done through acts, the act in a dialogue melted into the reasoning—the dialogue imitated the reasoning.[8]

The first dialogues with recipes were published in the early modern period. The most fascinating example is *Stockholmisch Koch-Gesprächs Vortrab* (Stockholm culinary conversation), printed in Sweden in 1644 (figure 19). It was written in High German but sprinkled with words in Dutch, Low German, and the popular dialect of Stockholm. The conversation is between two cookmaids and concerns the differences between various foodstuffs and how to handle and prepare them. Martha, the wise and knowledgeable one, instructs and corrects Magdalena, who has worked in a simple rural household and reveals many weaknesses during the conversation. She is surprised when she learns that vinegar can be brewed:

Magdalena: What do you mean? Is it possible to brew vinegar?

Marta: Yes, didn't you know that?[9]

Magdalena contributes, among other things, a recipe for black pudding, and the language becomes more technical when the recipe starts. The conversation between the two maids—typographically arranged as in a dramatic text—is rather vivid, but this is not the case in most other such books. These types of dialogues seldom represent real discourses; instead, the questions are phrased to elicit the correct answers.[10]

Some of these dialogues are closer to catechisms, a format popularized by Martin Luther, who transformed old systematic theological material into questions and answers. This new catechism form was a great success, and the idea was copied by other Christian denominations, other religions, and even political movements (*Republikanischer Katechismus*, 1848). Producers of new machines used the new form; one example is *A Catechism for the Steam Engine*.[11] Around 1800, the first catechisms on cooking were published in Germany, Sweden, and Denmark.[12] Later, several books introduced the question-and-answer method without using the word "catechism" in the title.

A few culinary writers adopted a genre that had been popular since the eighteenth century: the epistolary novel. The letter was used in antiquity as a literary form—in fact, it was the first form in prose to use the first-person singular—and it continued to be used as a didactic genre in the Middle Ages. Letter writing increased rapidly among literate Europeans when the postal services were effectively organized in the seventeenth century. The distinguished Madame de Sévigné embellished her letters so that they became a form of literature that was interesting for an audience much wider than the original addressees. Novels such as *Pamela*, by Samuel Richardson, who also published a letter-writing manual; *La nouvelle Heloïse*, by Jean-Jacques Rousseau; and *Die Leiden des jungen Werthers*, by Wolfgang von Goethe got a very wide readership, and this inspired Alexis Soyer, a French cook in London, to use the letter form in his cookbooks to establish a closer communication with the reader. A recipe for hare soup in his cookbook for working-class people starts this way:

MY DEAR ELOISE,—Since the alteration in our circumstances I have learnt to practise the most rigid economy, which you will remark in this receipt. When I buy a hare, as I sometimes do, for two shillings, skinning it myself, and selling the skin for fourpence, I save all the blood in a pie-dish, take out the heart and liver, removing the gall; I then cut the hare into two, across the back, close to the last ribs, and cut this part into pieces, using it for soup, and the hindpart I keep for roasting the following day.[13]

The real recipe follows this introduction, and Soyer continues to use the first-person: "I then proceed as for giblet soup." But in most of the recipes, he resorts to traditional, technical descriptions (using the imperative). The same is true of an 1850 German book, in which the household tasks are explained in letter form, allegedly letters from an experienced lady to a young friend. The general instructions follow the model of the epistolary novel, but the recipes are printed as appendices in a traditional form.[14] This recipe form is probably what the author was referring to as the "dry prose" she wanted to blend with poetry, which was one of her personal comments in the letters. But according to Gert Ueding, a German scholar, this poetry is nothing more than kitschy clichés borrowed from the sentimental prose found in contemporary family novels.[15] Soyer probably did better, as he stuck to the description of specific tasks and acts in a simple prose without breaking the bond established by the personal letter form (figure 20).

CLASSIFICATION OF COOKBOOKS

Dialogues and letters are just two examples of the great diversity in recipe form and organization, but they illustrate how difficult it is to classify cookbooks, a problem that has materialized in different cataloging systems in libraries and bibliographies.

One of the oldest bibliographies with a separate section for cookbooks is Andrew Maunsell's catalog of English printed books, from 1595.[16] In the chapter "Mathematicke, Phisicke," there is a subsection called "Of Cookery (which is phisicke of the kitchen)." In other words, Maunsell considered cookbooks a branch of books about medicine (which was called "physick" at the time). This should come as no surprise, as we have already seen that many of the medieval manuscripts included both medical and culinary material. One of the oldest European recipe collections, the fourteenth-century Danish *Libellus de arte coquinaria,* was attributed early on to the physician Henrik Harpestreng, probably because it was bound in with his medical books, an herbal, and a book about gems.[17] Bruno Laurioux has demonstrated that in medieval manuscripts with mixed contents, culinary recipes are most often found in a medical context; three-quarters of the culinary manuscripts included one or more medical texts.[18]

In her work about three medieval German cookbook manuscripts, Doris Aichholzer argues that such manuscripts should be classified under the label "medicine," citing scholars who have emphasized the importance of the medical aspects in much of this literature.[19] She also refers to the twelfth-century theologian Hugh

FIGURE 20. Title page from the 1861 edition of *The Modern Housewife*, by Alexis Soyer. Soyer used the epistolary form in the books he wrote for the middle classes and working classes. Nasjonalbiblioteket, Oslo, N 1721.

of Saint Victor, who in his classification of crafts into seven *artes mechanicae*, listed cooking under medicine, although he realized that such classification was problematic. Hugh in fact saw that food also had to do with two other arts, *agricultura* (agriculture) and *venatio* (hunting), and a later theoretician actually renamed this category *spisinde kunst*, "art of eating."[20]

However, starting in the fifteenth century, cooking was often listed under agriculture. In a study of the *artes* literature in the Middle Ages and early modern period, Bernhard Dietrich Haage and Wolfgang Wegner disagree with Aichholzer and argue that cookbooks should be classified under agriculture and household, in company with books on various agricultural activities and gardening, books on distillation, herbal books, and household books, the so-called *Hausväterliteratur.* One of their arguments refers to the old link between cookbooks and the household books, which has roots in antiquity.[21] These household books are often called "economic literature," referring to *oikonomia,* the rules for the house, the farm, and the estate (*oikos* in Greek). Encyclopedic household books, very popular in the Renaissance and the Baroque,[22] were often written by prominent personalities from the aristocracy or the liberal professions. The most extensive of these works covered a variety of subjects relevant to the running of an estate or a big farm, with chapters on outdoor work such as agriculture, gardening, viticulture, hunting, and fishing and on indoor activities such as baking, brewing, cooking, and medical assistance for the people living on the estate. In keeping with their antique models, these books gave recipes for the preservation and conservation of foodstuffs, particularly for fruit, the basis of many sorts of confectionary, which were made more accessible by the increasing import of sugar to Europe in the sixteenth century. Some of these books, such as *Oeconomia oder Hausbuch,* by the German theologian Johannes Coler, also had chapters with culinary recipes.[23] It is indicative of an increasing interest in cookery that the great Austrian study by the baron Wolf Helmhard von Hohberg, *Georgica curiosa,* which was originally published without recipes, had a complete cookbook added (probably by the publisher) in an edition printed after the death of the author.[24]

An Austrian historian, Otto Brunner, has explained this broad economic literature as an expression of a total concept of life on a farm, the autarky of the *ganzes Haus,* where everything consumed is also produced.[25] This interpretation has been criticized as a romantic and idealized vision of medieval and early modern rural life. But the question is not simply whether Brunner correctly interpreted the social situation; it is also whether he fully understood how the book industry worked and operated at that time. Even if publishers had an eye to the needs of big estates, they also wanted to sell old and new texts to a broader readership, even if such texts consisted of "Dishes for show and alchemical tricks."[26] In a mid-seventeenth-century book called *Oeconomia nova paa danske,* the Danish publisher combined cooking and household administration with instructions for how to make inks, dyes, beer, and confectionary, how to catch fish, and how to prepare an herb garden.[27] Several of the texts had been translated from rather old foreign books—among them Alessio Piemontese's *Secreti,* published in Venice in 1555— and not necessarily of any practical use a century later.[28]

The fact that many household books included recipes strongly influenced early classification systems. Robert Clavell, in the catalogs he compiled after the Great Fire of London in 1666, grouped husbandry, horsemanship, and gardening with cookery, preserving, and candying.[29] From this time, cookbooks were listed under economy (in the sense of "household") in most cases. When A. A. Schleiermacher created his cataloging system for use in German scientific libraries in 1847, he created a category called *Ökonomische Wissenschaften* (economic sciences) and a subcategory called *Haus- und Landwirtschaft* (domestic and agricultural economy), and under this heading he listed *Anleitung zur Kochkunst* (directions for cooking).[30] In 1876, in the first edition of his decimal system—which was introduced in libraries all over the world and is still in use—the American Melvil Dewey listed cookbooks under "641 Cookery," a subgroup of "640 Domestic economy."[31] The entire 600 group was originally called "Useful arts," a clear allusion to *artes mechanicae,* but it was later changed to "Technology (applied sciences)."

What the Dewey classification clearly implies is that cookbooks do not belong to the category of literature, which has its own number. This category includes drama, poetry, and fiction as well as essays, speeches, letters, humor, and satire. There is a subdivision called "Professional, technical, expository literature," which mainly consists of works on legal matters, natural history, engineering, and so on. Cookbooks are not included, as they are not considered to have literary value but are only interesting as a form of assistance to a technical activity, cooking. This is probably the most practical way of cataloging these books, but it emphasizes the difference between cookbooks and literature.

As mentioned in the preface, the term "literature" was gradually narrowed during the nineteenth and twentieth centuries to mean fiction. This is why the study of medieval literature tended to ignore nonfiction books from this point onward. A Dutch medievalist called nonfiction works "ascetic and didactic rubbish."[32] One of the first people to reverse this trend was the German philologist Gerhard Eis. In the 1950s, he coined the term *Fachliteratur*—*Fach* meaning "subject," "matter," "discipline," or "line of work." This literature, which often contains recipes for practical use, was later termed pragmatic: utilitarian prose, *littérature utilitaire,* *Gebrauchsliteratur.*[33] Cookbooks—being books with instructions—have also been grouped within "didactic literature."[34] A study of different practical how-to books for women applied the term "technical writing" to books on cooking, gardening, midwifery, estate management, and so forth.[35]

In *Theory of Literature* (1949), which became a classic in its field, the authors René Wellek and Austin Warren strongly argued for using the term "literature" for texts characterized by fictionality, invention, and imagination. They were, however, careful to emphasize that this classification is not an evaluation; it has nothing to do with quality, and it does not mean that nonfiction is an inferior form of literature. This point has become even more important as interest in popular culture in general and in light fiction in particular (*Trivialliteratur, littérature populaire, letteratura di consumo*) has increased.

Wellek and Warren suggested looking at the particular use of language in literature: "The main distinctions to be drawn are between the literary, the everyday, and the scientific uses of language."[36] But since the 1940s, new research into various literary aspects of nonfiction has made it much more difficult to accept a distinction based on language, because many nonfiction writers use literary devices tradition- ally applied in fiction.[37] Scholars have analyzed a wide range of texts, from essays and scientific publications to government decrees, computer manuals, and shop- ping lists—in other words, texts from all sorts of "text cultures"—and they point out that it is impossible to work with these texts from a static, abstract genre concept.[38]

In this context, cookbooks are interesting as examples of a text culture with certain characteristics, but it is still difficult to define cookbooks because so many texts combine recipes and other information about food, especially those pub- lished from the nineteenth century onward. A special form of bibliography intro- duced in the 1880s tried to solve this dilemma by grouping all books about food together. Carl Georg used the inventory of Theodor Drexel's collection to prepare a catalog of "literature about food and drink."[39] Then, in 1890, Georges Vicaire published what is still an important reference work, *Bibliographie gastronomique.* He called the listed books "ouvrages gastronomiques" (gastronomic works), and among them were not only cookbooks but also works about agriculture, wine, cof- fee, carving, nutrition, digestion, table manners, domestic economy, and food his- tory and even popular plays and songs with subjects touching on food and drink.[40] In his preface to a later reprint, André L. Simon described the books as "dealing with the fascinating subject of gastronomy in all its different aspects."[41]

To group books by a common subject or theme has a practical function for col- lectors, but these books can hardly be called a genre from a literary point of view. The genre concept has, however, been used more recently in a more narrow defini- tion of "gastronomic literature," which refers to a special group of texts, first pub- lished in France in the early nineteenth century.

COOKBOOKS VERSUS GASTRONOMIC LITERATURE

In 1801, Joseph Berchoux, a minor poet, published *La gastronomie,* a long poem about the history of cuisine and the arrangement of dinners, with advice on serv- ice, manners, and conversation, all larded with allusions to and quotations from classical authors and references to seventeenth- and eighteenth-century cook- books.[42] The poem has never been considered an example of great art—it was typical of the popular heroic-comic or burlesque tradition—but it became a great success and was reprinted several times. The word *gastronomie,* based on the Greek *gastronomía,* found in a text from around 200 CE, was either picked up or reinvented by Berchoux.[43] It soon became a household word among the French elite and surfaced in a vast number of books, the best known of which were by Grimod de la Reynière and Brillat-Savarin.[44]

The writings of these two founding fathers of gastronomy and their followers in France and England have been discussed by many scholars.[45] Two of them, Stephen

Mennell and Denise Gigante, wrote books that had chapters titled "Gastronomy as a Literary Genre." But both of them are also willing to accept certain cookbooks into this exclusive group of gastronomic literature. Other writers have gone further and considered cookbooks to be the most superior examples of gastronomic literature. Jean-François Revel, without doubt, views the cookbooks written by great cooks as the most important. In his description of *littérature gastronomique,* he divides the works he discusses into three categories, roughly by the audience they are written for. The first category, which he calls learned gastronomy, contains cookbooks by professionals, for professionals; this group is represented by Antonin Carême, Jules Gouffé, Urbain Dubois, and others. The second category contains cookbooks for families and the general public, most of them by women, for women, and he mentions English writers such as Eliza Acton and Isabella Beeton. Finally, the third category contains essays by gourmets, journalists, and commentators—including Grimod and Brillat-Savarin—written not for the producers but for the consumers of food, the enlightened gastronomes.[46]

Phillippe Gillet, a sociologist, is unyielding in his support for cookbooks and his disdain for what he calls "the official gastronomic literature," which he finds doughy, confused, and complacent. He is provoked by the fact that this literature is esteemed more highly than recipe collections, which to him constitute "the real gastronomic literature." Cookbooks, he says, are often read and appreciated as gourmandise in themselves because they fuel the readers' dreams more than they help them manage a kitchen.[47]

But this is exactly the opposite of what the two founding fathers themselves thought of cookbooks, particularly Grimod, who is exceptionally negative in his description. Many years after the publication of his *Almanach des gourmands* (figure 21), he explained his "éloquence gourmande" in a letter to his old friend, the Marquis de Cussy. He wrote that the reason for the success of his journal was that the readers appreciated a style that was different from the one used by cooks, with their formulas and recipes ending with "dressez et servez chaud," which he called their Gloria Patri. According to Grimod, readers had for the first time discovered a style of writing that would later be called *littérature gourmande.*[48]

Grimod and Brillat-Savarin stated very firmly that they had no intention of becoming cookbook authors. In the 1807 edition of the *Almanach,* Grimod emphasized that his journal was not a cookbook: "Our duty is to stimulate the appetite of our readers, to satisfy it is the responsibility of the artists [i.e., the cooks]."[49] Brillat-Savarin wrote on one occasion that he had planned to illustrate his ideas by giving a recipe but ultimately decided to refrain from doing so, explaining: "We thought it would be unfair to the various collections published later, including the one by Beauvilliers."[50] In other words, he would not compete with Beauvilliers and others who published cookbooks during the years he was preparing his own book. Grimod and Brillat-Savarin had a few recipes in their books, but it seems as if they

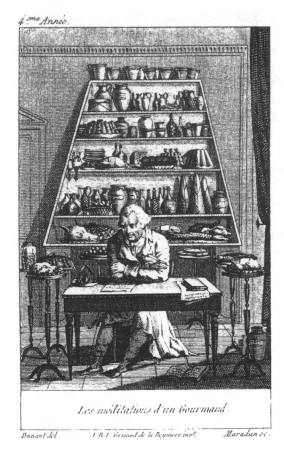

ALMANACH

DES GOURMANDS,

SERVANT DE GUIDE DANS LES MOYENS
DE FAIRE EXCELLENTE CHÈRE.

PAR UN VIEIL AMATEUR.

QUATRIÈME ANNÉE,

Contenant un grand nombre d'Articles de
morale Gourmande et de Considérations
alimentaires ; beaucoup de Recettes
Gourmandes inédites et curieuses ; la
Description de plusieurs espèces de ragoûts , tant exotiques qu'indigènes ;
la Petite Revue Gourmande , ou troisième Promenade d'un Gourmand dans
Paris , les Découvertes Gourmandes et
Friandes de l'année 1805 ; la Nécrologie
Gourmande de 1805 , etc.

Nil actum reputans si quid superesset agendum.
Lucan.

DE L'IMPRIMERIE DE CELLOT.

A PARIS,
Chez MARADAN, Libraire, rue des Grands-
Augustins , n°. 9.

M. D C C C. V I,

FIGURE 21. Frontispiece and title page of *Almanach des gourmands* (Paris, 1806), by A. B. L. Grimod de la Reynière.

wanted to downplay their importance. Grimod introduced one recipe with the words: "The recipe, or rather the description."[51] Brillat-Savarin explained that the recipes in his books were not his own, and in one case, he did not call a recipe by that name at all but rather titled it "Préparation," and he added his own "notes théoriques pour les préparations."[52]

The attitudes these utterances reveal can be explained only by social status. Even if the two gastronomic writers acknowledged the qualities and capacities of the cook as an artist (meaning a craftsman), he was still a servant—if not simply a commodity (implied by references to "your" or "my" cook). Brillat-Savarin speci-fied that the cook is just one of many contributors to the preparation of food; cooks are joined by farmers, winemakers, fishermen, and hunters.[53] What was needed, he contended, was someone who could coordinate these contributions, a gastronome with "rational knowledge" of everything that has to do with food. In this way, Brillat-Savarin gave legitimacy to the social position acquired by the new gastronome.

When Brillat-Savarin admitted that he would like—if he had enough time—to make a collection of gastronomic poetry through the centuries, he explained that it was because he wanted to demonstrate the intimate alliance that had always existed between eloquence and eating, "L'art de bien dire et l'art de bien manger."[54] He said nothing about cooking. This sums up the gastronome's point of view: the literary aspect of food is connected to the art of eating, not to the art of cooking. The cook is to the gastronome what philosophy was said to be to theology in the Middle Ages: *ancilla*—a maid-servant. And here, we are literally talking about servants.

One of the writers from outside the French- and English-speaking world who commented on the value of cookbooks was the German art critic Karl von Rumohr. He published his *Geist der Kochkunst* (Spirit of cooking) in 1822, after Grimod had published his works but before Brillat-Savarin had written *Physiologie du goût*. He is generally considered a gastronomic writer, but he had a different attitude and style than his French counterparts. There is less playfulness in his writing; he was a classicist, serious and a little dry, which perhaps can be explained by the Biedermeier culture he was part of. But Rumohr has the following to say about culinary literature: "I do not consider the increasing number of cookbooks and recipe collections as scholarly works. . . . They are the result of either banal, unreflected experience or quite simply of compilations, and they are consequently without any scientific understanding."[55]

Another art critic, Elizabeth Robins Pennell, who became a prominent author of gastronomic essays and a collector of books on food, published a bibliography of cookbooks in 1903. In the introduction, she gives her reason for recording only books printed before 1800:

> In the nineteenth century there are, on the one hand, the cookery books prosaic as primers, that, with their business-like, practical, direct methods, were more useful in the kitchen than entertaining in the library; on the other hand, the books about cookery, so literary in flavor that they were not adapted to the kitchen at all. The new writers, of whom Grimod de la Reynière was the first great master, brought about such a revolution in not only the style, but the very attitude of writers on cookery, that I prefer to consider their work by itself.[56]

The poet W. H. Auden also made this kind of distinction in his preface for *The Art of Eating*, a collection of essays by M. F. K. Fisher. Auden opened with these words: "Though it contains a number of recipes, *The Art of Eating* is a book for the library rather than the kitchen shelf. If it were simply a manual of culinary technique, I could not discuss it because, much as I enjoy reading recipes, they remain for me mysterious magical spells, like most people who cannot cook."[57] Even if "mysterious magical spells" may from one point of view be considered positive, he used words such as "simply," "manual," and "technique" in his description of cookbooks (by which he means recipe collections)—in other words, his evaluation is in line with Pennell's characterization of cookbooks as "prosaic," "businesslike," and "practical."

What, then, did the cookbook writers of the nineteenth century think about gastronomic writing? There are not many testimonies indicating how professional cooks judged the new form of writing, but two representatives had a certain knowledge of this literature when they commented on it. The first was the French cook Louis-Eustache Ude, who worked for aristocrats in England, and who wrote in the preface to his cookbook: "Many writers have exercised their pen upon the subject, and yet know little about it." As examples of this phenomenon, he mentioned Grimod's *Almanach des gourmands* and Berchoux's *La gastronomie,* calling the latter "a poem on the subject of cookery, without teaching it." He added that while both works were excellent to read after dinner, they didn't give any advice on how to prepare a dinner properly. Ude clearly expressed the professional pride of a craftsman.[58]

The second was the great French celebrity chef of the early nineteenth century, Carême, who recognized certain positive aspects in Grimod's work but didn't find that the man had contributed in the least to the rapid advances in modern cuisine in the early nineteenth century. He gave credit for this progress to "the brilliance of our contemporary cooks," not to the author of *Almanach des gourmands.*[59]

What all this demonstrates is that various opinions exist not only among the authors themselves but also among the contemporary scholars who have studied them. The question is whether there are common literary features in these gastronomic writings that justify the use of the term "genre."

DEFINING GASTRONOMIC LITERATURE

Stephen Mennell has suggested that gastronomic literature be defined by its four characteristic themes, or components:

1. correct practice: menus, service, sequence of courses;
2. diet: what constitutes the proper form of cookery for good health;
3. history: myths, biography, anecdotes about cooks, and cooking;
4. nostalgia: the evocation of memorable and notable meals and menus.[60]

Whereas Mennell, a sociologist, sought to identify the different kinds of content and themes within gastronomic literature, the literary scholar Denise Gigante pointed out the wide variety of literary forms: "Gourmand maxims and reflections, gourmand meditations, gourmand geographies and travel narratives, fictional and nonfictional epistolary exchange between epicures, as well as poems, dialogues, satires, and parables on the gastronomical model."[61]

Both of these approaches can be useful guides to gastronomic literature, but it is also possible to view the authors of these works as representatives of established genres who applied these genres in exploring new subjects. Grimod, for example, was a theater critic who used his critical experience to judge the quality of food products and restaurants, assisted by a testing jury, a *jury dégustateur*. In doing so, he introduced a particular new form of gastronomic text, one that is still common today in newspaper columns, journals, and special guidebooks. With his reports and articles about various shops in Paris, bakers, butchers, winemakers, cheese-makers, producers of lemonade, and so on, he brought a new field of the society into journalism, a genre that was experiencing rapid growth at the time.

Brillat-Savarin chose an academic genre, the thesis, with definitions, methods and theories, for his work, and he labeled his form of investigation "physiology," a term that had been used in many medical and scientific books in the years before he published *Physiologie du goût* (Physiology of taste) in 1825.

Many of the later gastronomic writers chose other established genres, such as essays and poems, so it is not the formal features of their works that unite the different authors of gastronomic literature. Rather, it is their basic attitude to what was called the "pleasures of the table." Grimod and Brillat-Savarin gave high priority to the distinction between glutton and gourmand, and they criticized the definitions of "gourmand" in contemporary French dictionaries.[62] They showed an almost missionary zeal in their propaganda for a refinement of the art of eating, championing moderation instead of excess, and they wanted to spread this refinement to the postrevolutionary bourgeoisie. The author of a gastronomic work assumes a middle position, Karin Becker explained in her great work about gastronomy in French literature: "He is an intermediary between the producers, restaurant cooks, and grocers, on one side, and the public, the consumers, and the new bourgeois gourmets, on the other."[63]

This basic attitude is found in many nineteenth-century examples of gastronomic literature, primarily in France, England, and the United States, where such books flourished. Works from these countries are among those most quoted and most often referred to; among the twelve authors in Gigante's anthology, three are French, and nine are written in English. Far less known internationally are books published outside of these areas, many of them directly inspired by Brillat-Savarin. His work not only was translated but also was read in the original French by the sophisticated cultural elite in many countries.[64]

The German writer and psychiatrist Gustav Blumröder, who wrote under the pseudonym Antonius Anthus, was inspired by the new French literature and had high praise for Grimod. His literary form is revealed in the title of his 1838 book, *Vorlesungen über die Esskunst* (Lectures on the art of eating).[65] He is widely read in many disciplines, including medicine, dietetics, ethnography, and history, but his pieces are first and foremost lectures about aesthetics; he compared the art of eating to music, painting, and literature. Consequently, he referred to the "gourmand" as an *Esskünstler*, an artist in the art of eating. His title sounds like an echo of Hegel's *Vorlesungen über die Ästhetik* (*Lectures on Aesthetics*), which had been printed shortly before the publication of Blumröder's work.[66] This is perhaps ironic, as Blumröder once went to a lecture on the science of taste (*Geschmackslehre*) and felt offended when nothing was said about the art of eating.[67] According to Gigante, "Elevating gourmandise to the status of fine arts and establishing its legitimate link to aesthetic taste was a project of Romantic era gastronomy."[68]

In 1851, the German baron Eugen von Vaerst, a military officer, poet, and theater manager, published *Gastrosophie oder die Lehre von den Freuden der Tafel* (Gastrosophy, or the theory of the pleasures of the table). His form was the thesis; in addition to culinary history and a collection of aphorisms, the book contains the author's analysis of different foodstuffs and dishes. He distinguished between three levels in the relationship to food. The gourmand is the lowest category; he is greedy without measure. The gourmet wants everything that is attractive to palate and eyes. The gastrosoph, however, takes into consideration what is healthy and proper when he chooses the very best to eat and drink, selecting not only what has the most excellent taste but also what is the aesthetically finest, "in der schönsten Form."[69]

Health was also important to the Italian physician Giovanni Rajberti, but his book *L'arte di convitare spiegata al popolo* (The art of inviting to dinner explained to the people) is primarily a guide for hosts and guests that gives information about the rules to be followed when arranging or taking part in a formal meal. The physician was a connoisseur; he could distinguish between ordinary wine (*vino da tavola*) and exceptional wines, for example, Bordeaux. He acknowledged the quality of many common Italian dishes, but he wanted to refine them. He abhorred meals consisting of enormous quantities of food, as if the guests were elephants and whales. His ideal is expressed in a quotation from antiquity, "Ne quid nimis" (Nothing in excess). For him, moderation was more than just a maxim for good living; it was the principal element of beauty in all art.[70]

The Russian representative of gastronomic writing in the nineteenth century, Vladimir Sergeyevich Filimonov, also disdained gluttons and promoted refinement. Like Brillat-Savarin, Filimonov was a civil servant (he was the governor of Arkhangelsk). In 1837, he published a poem à la Berchoux, *Obed* (The dinner), with the same historical anecdotes, a survey of Russian food traditions, souvenirs of a memorable banquet, and a body of laws for dinners with numbered articles. The 150 pages are written in a iambic tetrameter, perhaps inspired by *Eugene Onegin*, but without Pushkin's elegant and complicated rhymes. In the poem, he complains about the bad manners and gluttony of Russians, who, he says, eat without refinement or culture, and he attacks in particular a gourmandizing representative of the young generation with a vulgar attitude to fine wine and gastronomic wonders:

Like kvas he drinks the sacred nectar,
Like gherkins truffles are consumed.[71]

Many of Mennell's components of gastronomic literature are found in the works of these writers, but they are also found in some books that are generally considered to be cookbooks. Mennell openly admitted that "there is an ill-defined margin at which the gastronomic essay gradually shades into the cookery book. The more learned sort of cookery book, such as those of Dumas and Ali-Bab, or more recently of Elizabeth David or Jane Grigson, might be considered gastronomic literature as much as cookery books."[72] He later added M. F. K. Fisher to his list. Gigante also included Dumas's cookbook in the cannon of gastronomic literature, and she added William Kitchiner's *The Cook's Oracle*, which, according to her, "initiates the English gastronomical tradition as a philosophical literary genre of writing about food."[73]

Mennell called these cookbook authors "learned," a characteristic appropriate for gastronomic writers. But in that case, why didn't he include the work of Isabella Beeton, who had so much cultural background material in her book? In her *Book of Household Management* (1861), Beeton clearly expressed the feeling that a cookbook was not a literary accomplishment: "I have striven, too, to make my work something more than a Cookery Book, and have, therefore, on the best authority that I could obtain, given an account of the natural history of the animals and vegetables, which we use as food."[74]

The reason for the exclusion of this young editor's wife probably had less to do with her erudition than with her tone, which was far more down-to-earth and matter-of-fact than what was typical of more mondaine writers, who created passages that stay in the mind long after the reading is over. Beeton lacked a certain form of *esprit*, or "saveur de style," to quote Balzac, who, in his 1835 portrait of Brillat-Savarin, compared the gastronome's prose to that of La Bruyère and Le Rochefoucauld.[75] But Beeton also lacked wit, which was a striking quality in much of the gastronomic literature. In his portrait, Balzac noted the humor in Brillat-Savarin's work and commented that what set it apart was "le comique sous la bonhomie" (the comedy beneath the affability). Gigante mentioned as a characteristic feature in this literature "a serious philosophical effort, expressed in a lively tongue-in-cheek manner."[76] Roland Barthes said that Brillat-Savarin treated science seriously and ironically at the same time.[77] Revel, who tended to see the gastronomic genre as a "branche notable de la poésie heroï-comique," mentioned Brillat-Savarin's humor and "clin d'oeil au lecteur" (wink to the reader).[78] This humor is what Pascal Ory, with a more elegant expression, called Brillat-Savarin's "hédonisme textuel," his "plaisir du texte."[79] There is no doubt that this element in Brillat-Savarin's book was fundamental for the later notions of gastronomic literature, which, Gigante wrote, included expressions about "its own satiric, self-mocking style" and "inevitable self-ironizing in tone."[80]

The connection between humor and food is nothing new in literature, but since antiquity, food as a subject belonged to the "lower" genres of comedy, satire, and parody—take the works by Matro and Petronius, for example.[81] It has been common to make fun of gluttony and culinary snobbery ever since, but the question is whether this type of humor has changed with the gastronomic writing of the early nineteenth century, when what we would call a gourmet attitude was defined as something different from gluttony. We can observe a more refined form of playing with words and use of metaphors and figures in works of gastronomic literature. Brillat-Savarin introduced his work with a list of numbered aphorisms, and aphorisms are scattered throughout Grimod's text, very often making a comparison between food and literature: "Pastry is in cooking what rhetorical figures are in a speech, it conveys life and ornament."[82] Grimod brings forth a smile from the reader when, with a merry anthropomorphism, he calls the salmon proud, the sturgeon bold, the turbot majestic, the mackerel cunning, the whiting modest, and the herring humble and gives the pike nicknames like Prince Freshwater and Attila of the Ponds.

This does not mean that all the gastronomic authors were witty, at least not all the time. Grimod was very matter-of-fact and serious in much of what he wrote, and so was Kitchiner, not to mention Filimonov. Blumröder, who believed that laughter and cooking were the two qualities that distinguished man from animal, was full of interesting and important observations and reflections, but he was not overtly funny. Rajberti, however, was witty from the first page, where he discussed the genre of his book and admitted that it could be compared to earlier books about correct behavior, such as Giovanni Della Casa's *Il Galateo* from the Renaissance and Melchiore Gioia's 1802 *Il nuovo Galateo* (The new Galateo). He called Gioia's work "fiacco, stracco, bislacco" (dull, dead, odd) and wrote that its only quality was to put readers to sleep.[83] In the twentieth century, the Spanish author Julio Camba was a representative of real gastronomic wit. He called Italian cuisine simple but lyrical, in need of a mandolin as much as tomatoes. Camba had a predilection for such figures of speech, called *zeugma*. He described Spanish cuisine as full of "garlic and religious scruples" and referred to vegetarianism as a sect of people "with little humor and even less gastric acid."[84]

The light-hearted mondaine and witty tone is a characteristic the essayists shared with the gastronomic cookbook writers named by Mennell and Gigante. But as mentioned earlier, such writers were also found outside of France and the English-speaking world. A group of gentlemen writers and amateur cooks wrote books around the end of the nineteenth century that were influenced by Brillat-Savarin, Dumas, and French cooks but adapted to their own societies in a way that made them national classics: the Swede Charles-Emil Hagdahl wrote *Kok-konsten som vetenskap och konst* (Cooking as science and art) in 1879, the Italian Pellegrino Artusi published *La scienza in cucina e l'arte di mangiar bene* (Science in the kitchen and the art of eating well) in 1891, and the Spaniard Angel Muro wrote *El practicón* (The great practitioner) in 1894.[85] Outside their own countries, the most illustrious among them was Artusi. The immediate seduction of his writing was, according to Alberto Capatti, a result of his anecdotes and witty remarks, in addition to his use of colloquial Italian.[86] Piero Camporesi called Artusi's cookbook "a long *causerie* stuffed with recipes" and a sort of "culinary novel" (romanzo della cucina).[87]

A dissenting judgment from a female rival ought to be added. Ada Boni, a successful cookbook writer after Artusi, called his work "the humorous masterpiece of culinary incompetence."[88] Such confrontations between men and women have been referred to earlier; women often accused men of being spendthrifts and epicures. When it comes to gastronomic rather than culinary writing, many commentators have observed that almost all authors of this literature from the nineteenth and twentieth centuries were men. "Women do not have access to the cult," observed Jean-Paul Aron. "If a woman appears, she is either a parasite or a visitor."[89] According to Becker, the language used to describe the pleasures of the palate was clearly an "androcentric discourse" (androzentrischer Diskurs).[90] There were many arguments made for male dominance; one of the most ridiculous was set forth by the Swiss physician Hans Balzli, who claimed that women had a weaker and less extensive taste than men. He admitted that it was possible to find gourmands among women, as Brillat-Savarin himself had accepted, but he asserted that there were no female gourmets, a fact proved by the language itself, as the word *gourmet* has no grammatical feminine form.[91] Balzli wrote this a generation after Robins Pennell published her excellent essays and only a decade before M. F. K. Fisher started her literary career.

However, there were also women among the cookbook writers with a gastronomic reputation. One of the really entertaining culinary works of the nineteenth century, *The Cook and Housewife's Manual* (1826), was written by a Scottish woman, Christian Isobel Johnstone, who was a novelist in the national romantic tradition. She published the book under the pseudonym Mistress Margaret Dods, whom readers of Walter Scott's novel *St. Ronan's Well* will recognize as the hostess of Cleikum Inn.[92] In Johnstone's long introduction about the "Institution of the Cleikum Club," we meet characters from Scott's novel and from an anonymously published novel by Susan Ferrier, and Johnstone reproduces Scott's style "with scintillating panache."[93] Several of the recipes are kept within the frame story, and some are even named after Scott's characters. In one recipe for soup, we are informed that the members of Cleikum Club disagreed strongly on the question of historically correct ingredients, and one of the characters actually gives a speech about "gastronomic science." Johnstone has exactly the kind of wit typical for gastronomic literature, which she obviously had a certain knowledge of, possibly from Kitchiner's *The Cook's Oracle,* which she mentioned in her preface as one of only two important English books on culinary art from the past twenty years.[94]

Johnstone's recipe collection flirts with narrative fiction. This is a phenomenon more typical of the traditional gastronomic works, described by Becker as possessing "high literary value"; the aesthetic style and learned allusions of these books bring them closer to the belletristic,[95] but as we have seen, there are also cookbooks worth considering in this group.

THE QUESTION OF GENRE

When Mennell said that some cookbooks might as well be considered gastronomic literature, he added, "They seem intended to be read as literature."[96] He was evidently treating the word "literature" as synonymous with belles-lettres, and what he meant was probably that these cookbooks can be read for enjoyment and not used simply to prepare food, or what Pennell and Auden referred to as library versus kitchen. But trying to detect the intention behind a book is a task many literary critics abstain from, and we do not know if the aforementioned cookbook writers gave highest priority to their works being read as belles-lettres or as instruction. Most traditional cookbooks open with a preface stating that the book is intended to give culinary knowledge, often specific to certain market segments and occasionally specific to special dishes.

In addition to providing instructions about the preparation of dishes and the arrangement of the meal, cookbooks may contain information that is irrelevant to both cooking and the meal itself. They may discuss the qualities of foodstuffs, the history of ingredients, or famous banquets of the past. With important exceptions, such as Platina's book, this kind of extra material constitutes only a minor part of a culinary work and is generally limited to the preface, but in gastronomic literature, these are the favored subjects. Gastronomic works may also have instruction as their main aim, but this instruction is not directed toward the cook or housewife responsible for the food. Rather, the instruction—often more suggestive than directly informative—is for the host and the guests around the table, teaching them how to appreciate the different tastes, enjoy the food, and conduct an interesting conversation.

When they are well written, these books bring, in addition to advice, a form of entertainment to the reader, not only through the contents but also through the text itself. A fascinating fact, however, is that many readers find a similar pleasure in ordinary cookbooks with recipes, as Phillip Gillet noted. In his book about lists, Umberto Eco wrote that a practical list (a menu, for example) may be read as if it were a poetical list. The difference is, in reality, only the intention with which the list is read—in other words, the intention with which it was written does not matter.[97]

But intention alone is not enough to define a genre, nor is a special attitude or a common subject. It would be more logical to say that gastronomic works belong to several genres—to essays, journalism, travelogues, poems, and so on. We don't throw Tolstoy's *War and Peace,* the military works of Clausewitz, and the poems of

Rupert Brooke and Wilfred Owen together in a common "war genre." It is consequently difficult to accept the notion of gastronomy as a literary genre. Cookbooks,
on the other hand—technical ones and humorous ones alike—may be considered
a genre from a formal point of view; they have in common recipes as a literary
form in addition to the subject. The definition of the cookbook genre can be modified by adding that works in this category may also contain a certain amount of
other material relating to food and that they may represent other literary forms.
This will put Dumas and Elizabeth David in the same category as Julia Child and
Jamie Oliver. There is a question that may complicate this solution to the genre
problem: How much of this material can be included before the book ceases to be
a cookbook? To answer this, we may consider "convention." For example, Platina's
De honesta voluptate is the world's first printed cookbook. It has a section with
recipes, and various recipes are spread in other chapters, but it also contains medical advice, historical information, etymology, philosophy, reminiscences of good
meals, and cheeky commentaries about friends. The book has been labeled a "bas-
tard," and some scholars have discussed if it is right to call it a cookbook at all. But
the history of its reception makes it clear that readers have considered it a cookbook, even a book with authority in the culinary field.[98] I conclude this chapter
with Platina because much of the discussion has been about the relationship
between culinary and gastronomic literature. When we read Platina's book, we
realize that all books about food must be understood in a historical and intertex-
tual perspective because there are long roots and traditions behind both cook
books and gastronomic works. Cristian Guy said that real gastronomic literature
was born in the nineteenth century,[99] but it is nevertheless true that Platina created
a sort of genre or at least the matrix that eventually gave birth to "the Western
gastronomic discourse."[100]

PART THREE

The Text and Its World

11

Cookbooks for the Rich and the Poor

Two foreigners in Victorian England proved through what they wrote that they had an eye for the connection between food and social class: Friedrich Engels and Alexis Soyer. Engels, a German, was only twenty-two years old when he was sent to Manchester to manage his father's cotton factory. The young man—who had already met Karl Marx and was interested in philosophy and politics—was so indignant when confronted with the living conditions of the workers that he made a study of the English working class, which was published in 1845. Among the facts he presented in the book was that the amount of meat products in the average diet diminished for every step down the social ladder. At the bottom were the Irish, who were nourished by nothing but potatoes.[1]

The French-born Soyer was a success in British high society and became chef at the prestigious Reform Club in London, but he also got involved in charitable work. He elaborated his theories and culinary practice in books aimed at the different social groups in Great Britain. His breakthrough came with *The Gastronomic Regenerator* (1846), four editions of which were printed in the first year of its publication. This was a book for professional cooks employed in the upper classes, and it consisted of two parts: "Kitchen of the Wealthy," for grand dinners and banquets, and "Kitchen at Home," for daily meals. One year later, Soyer established soup kitchens in Ireland, where the failed potato crop had led to a fatal famine. He saw the necessity for simple recipes and published a small booklet, *Charitable Cookery, or The Poor Man's Regenerator* (1848), with recipes for soups, puddings, and stews. It cost a sixpence, and one penny of every book sold went to charity.

Between the very rich and the very poor, we find the majority of the British people of this time, and Soyer provided them with cookbooks corresponding to their needs. He wrote *The Modern Housewife* (1849) for the rapidly growing middle class, which desired fashionable and modern dishes adapted to their economic means and the abilities of their cooks. Finally, Soyer published *A Shilling Cookery for the People* (1854), which was meant for "the artisan, mechanic, and cottager."[2]

Engels's book was published in Leipzig, Soyer's books in London—and around the same time, another work was published in Christiania, the small capital of Norway: Hanna Winsnes's classic, *Lærebog i de forskjellige grene af huusholdningen* (Manual in the different household branches, 1845). But the cookbook was considered too elegant, and she was encouraged to follow Soyer's example. So she published two more books, one for middle-class households and one for lower-income families.[3] In the latter, however, she emphasized that the booklet was meant for people who owned a pig or a sheep, not for the very poor, who lived by potatoes alone—in other words, not those at the bottom level of society, such as those Engels had found in England.[4] The conservative parson's wife observed the same social inequities as the coauthor of *The Communist Manifesto,* but they drew very different conclusions.[5]

CODIFYING SOCIAL DIFFERENCES

The books by Soyer and Winsnes give us an idea of the different social levels in a society. Such stratification goes far back in history; starting very early on, good food was a privilege reserved for people of high rank. In the medieval *Edda,* a collection of poems describing events in the Germanic pantheon, there is a myth explaining the origin of the different estates in Norse society, and food is part of what distinguished the nobleman (who consumed game birds, white bread, and wine), the farmer (boiled veal), and the slave (coarse bread and thin gruel).[6]

The association of different social groups with particular culinary practices was so established by the Late Middle Ages that playwrights had success with farces in which ignorant peasants celebrated "grotesque feasts" by mixing low-class and high-class dishes in the most ridiculous combinations. In an Italian story from around 1600, peasants are warned against coveting dishes reserved for aristocrats: "Chi è uso à le rape non mangi pastici" (He who is used to turnips doesn't eat pastry).[7]

The different diets of the social classes were often elaborated in detailed rules in the residences of the European aristocracy. Take, for example, the protocol in the household of the Reichsgraf Joachim von Oettingen in Bavaria around 1500: the count was served eight dishes at the main meal; the members of his council and young ladies, six; the clergy, the gentry, and the marshals, five; and other employees, four.[8] In the former French principality of Dauphiné, an ordinance from 1336 fixed the dinner menu for the different levels of the household: the Dauphin Humbert II and his wife received two pies each made with poultry; the barons were served only one pie; the lower knights were allotted one half pie made with poultry

FIGURE 22. Illustration for a banquet menu for the burgher in Marx Rumpolt's *Ein new Kochbuch* (Frankfurt am Main, 1587). The woodcut is by Hans Weiditz, the famous Petrarca-Meister, and was originally used in the book *Vom Wirtschaften,* published around 1520. Nasjonalbiblioteket, Oslo, qLib.rar. 1065.

and pork; and so on, down the social ranks, with increasingly smaller pies and less prestigious meat.[9]

This form of methodical culinary system is also documented in one of the great cookbooks from the Renaissance, *Ein new Kochbuch*, by Marx Rumpolt. The book has menus for different categories: the emperor, kings, prince-electors, archdukes, counts, gentry, burghers, and farmers (figure 22). The number of dishes decreases according to a hierarchical pattern, going from 144 dishes for the emperor, to 61 for counts, and down to 19 for burghers and 11 for farmers. The farmers are served beef broth and capon, but this is food for a banquet and not a daily meal, and it is not meant for workers and servants.[10]

In Rumpolt's list, the burgher is second from the bottom, but as the growing bourgeoisie gradually had more money to spend, they did not want to be told by superiors what to eat and how to dress. Members of this newly empowered middle class began to eat foods and wear clothes that had previously been reserved for the nobility, making it difficult to distinguish between people of different rank. This was a problem for the ruling elites, who were eager to maintain the established order and tried to enforce it in various ways. When sumptuary laws were introduced to limit excessive consumption of luxury goods, the rules were set in accordance with the lifestyles of the various social groups. An English law under King

Henry VIII limited the number of dishes in a banquet: nine for cardinals, seven for higher nobility, six for lords, three for gentry.[11] A Danish law from 1683 prescribed that the number of courses served at weddings was limited to four for artisans and eight for burghers, but there were no restrictions for aristocrats.[12] One important aim of the sumptuary laws was to reduce the import of luxury items to protect manufacture of national products. Consequently, in Sweden, a law established limits on how much foreign wine could be served to burghers and mandated that servants be served only Swedish beer.[13] In Leipzig, restrictions were put on marzipan (which was made with imported almonds and sugar). Gifts to godchildren were not to exceed one piece of marzipan costing two units of the local money, and it was forbidden for artisans and servants to buy gifts of marzipan.[14]

Respect for the social hierarchy is also seen in household books for country estates, such as *Le théâtre de l'agriculture* (1600), by Olivier de Serres. When he received guests, Serres made sure to serve them according to their rank. The upper crust, *les personnes honorables,* got fruit preserves (*confitures*) produced with sugar. The visitors belonging to the middle class got a simpler and cheaper variety sweetened with grape must, while lower-class guests got unsweetened jam, if anything at all. Serres also made a clear distinction within his own household: he and his family were served fresh white bread and good wine, while the servants got coarse bread and *piquette,* a drink of inferior quality.[15]

Servants were served special food, but such food was rarely described in cookbooks. There is, however, a sixteenth-century Czech culinary work that includes a chapter about *kaše* (porridge), after a series of chapters describing expensive dishes, with a note by the editor that he will present simpler porridges for the servants.[16]

Closer to our times, there are a few examples of servants' food in books from the north of Europe. In the 1840s, the popular Russian cookbook author Ekaterina Avdeeva suggested sheep's head, noodles, pan cakes, and cabbage as suitable foods for servants. According to Joyce Toomre, Avdeeva recommended that the cabbage dishes utilize "the weak ill-formed heads and the tough outer leaves of the firmer heads."[17] The point was to serve simple and cheap products, often of inferior quality. The cultural historian Catriona Kelly has observed that even in the last years of the tsarist regime, "most domestic manuals still carried sections of suitable servant food, consisting of cheap, monotonous, and starchy dishes such as kasha, broths with pearl barley and noodles, rice and kasha pies, and kisel' or apple pie to follow."[18]

In her 1861 classic Russian cookbook, Elena Molokhovets gave a simple recipe for kvas, "for the servants and the preparation of cabbage soups, borscht, etc."[19] In later editions of the book, she included two recipes for kvas probably not meant for servants, as they are called "excellent" and are made with much more expensive ingredients.[20] Her chapter of menus gives a good idea of the differences between the family, who are served six courses with sturgeon and turkey, and the servants, who receive simple one- or two-course dinners with potatoes and cabbage.[21] After the revolution,

Molokhovets was attacked as a monster by the Soviet poet Arseny Tarkovsky, who based his cruel lines on a passage from the cookbook in which Molokhovets proposed giving the remains left from making juice to the servants in the kitchen.[22]

In Norway, Hanna Winsnes published recipes for dishes that she specially recommended be served to servants. They were based on food of inferior quality, such as salted halibut instead of fresh or smoked, sausages and dumplings made with simple ingredients, and sheep's blood, because the taste of this blood was considered too strong for the palates of the elite.[23]

The difference in food between social groups was accompanied by a gradual segregation of meal times. The old social structure on farms and estates, where everybody ate together, broke up during the eighteenth and nineteenth centuries, but the first signs of this development came much earlier. Already in the sixteenth century, noble Romans were excluding their servants from the master's table in the dining rooms.[24] Historian C. Anne Wilson noted that in early England, when the higher aristocracy began to retire to dine in separate chambers rather than in the hall with the extended household, this habit "passed rapidly down the social scale to reach even the meanest gentry by the mid to late seventeenth century."[25] In the final years of the eighteenth century, the German author of a book about etiquette condemned the new relationship between the father of the house and the employees: "The servants are no longer seen as part of the family but as hirelings."[26]

FROM ROYAL COOKBOOKS TO POPULAR COOKBOOKS

Cookbooks may reflect social differences in society and general attitudes to food, but they cannot be read as reliable sources of the culinary habits of different social groups. They are not descriptive works giving details of culinary practice; rather, they describe the culinary preparation of dishes that may appeal to readers. Cookbooks planned for different markets have different recipes, because cookbooks are first and foremost commercial products.

Titles and prefaces often announced whom the dishes described were meant for. The first printed cookbook in England, *Boke of Cokery* (1500), opens with the information that it is for a prince's household.[27] A similar ambition is emphasized in the first Spanish cookbook, *Libro de cozina* (1525), which states that it is for the houses of kings and "great men" (grandes señores).[28] An early Italian cookbook, *Banchetti* (1549), claims to be for great princes: "ogni gran Prencipe."[29] But it is worth remembering that these texts were written long before they were printed; the books were based on manuscripts from court circles. The new publishers quickly discovered that they had to aim for a larger audience.

The growth of the new bourgeoisie in early modern Europe demanded new strategies in the book trade and new cookbook titles with information about the contents and the intended market. In France, books with titles containing words such as *royal* and *cour* (court) had been published earlier in the seventeenth century, but in 1691, a book was published with a title typical of the transition to a new era: *Le cuisinier royal et bourgeois*. The author, François Massialot, pointed out that the dishes would suit many bourgeois families. But it is important to make clear that this was not food for everybody. Massialot emphasized that he was not writing for the "lowest bourgeois" (le dernier bourgeois).[30]

In England, a similar step down the social ladder can be seen in the publishing history of the court cook Patrick Lamb's *Royal Cookery,* first printed in 1710. The book was initially presented as an example of "the Grandeur of the English Court and Nation," but it did not meet with commercial success. Six years later, the publisher released a new and expanded edition, still in the name of Lamb, who had died in 1709. The preface explained that while the first edition had been for "the Kitchen of Princes and Great Men," this one had cheaper dishes and could be used by private gentlemen. Most of the new recipes were taken from the translation of Massialot's book, *The Court and Country Cook* (1702).[31] We have every reason to believe that this revised edition was produced by one of the publishers, Abel Roper, who was a professional writer and also had a nose for new and broader markets, although still within the circle of "gentlemen."

Early cookbooks for courts and mansions took for granted a large staff of kitchen employees with different functions. Starting in the eighteenth century, many cookbooks were intended for middle-class households with fewer servants, where the kitchen was managed by a female cook with cook-maids to assist her. The transition from male to female cooks is documented in the title of the great French bestseller *La cuisinière bourgeoise* (1746). The author, Menon, who had written many works for the elite and their professional male cooks, now advised female cooks how to prepare simple, good, and new dishes. But like Massialot, he was eager to mark his distance from what he called "le bas peuple," an expression used before the French Revolution to designate the lowest social groups.

The distinction between middle and lower classes was still important in the nineteenth century, when German cookbooks used epithets such as *feine, elegante, vornehme* (noble), and *herrschaftliche* (stately) in their titles. But this was also the era of simpler and smaller cookbooks, such as those by Soyer and Winsnes. Soyer's rival, Charles Elmé Francatelli, author of the five-hundred-page *The Modern Cook,* published *Plain Cookery for the Working Classes*.[32] Selections of Isabella Beeton's recipes, published after her death, were given Soyer-inspired titles: *Shilling Cookery Book, Penny Cookery Book,* and *Sixpenny Cookery Book.* The Belgian star cook Philippe-Édouard Cauderlier's bestselling *L'économie culinaire* was published in an abridged version with the title *La cuisinière*.[33] In Prague, Magdalena Dobromila Rettigová had great success with her *Domácý kuchařka* (Domestic cookery), but it was followed by a simpler version for country housewives.[34] Even in tsarist Russia, there was a demand for alternatives to the great cookbooks. The tenth edition of Molokhovets's classic was printed in 1883, and at this point, Molokhovets also published an abridged version which had only around 150 pages (of the original 700).[35] The gentlemen writers and amateur cooks Hagdahl, Artusi, and Muro did not follow this tradition. The former banker Artusi bluntly stated that he was writing only for the well-off, "alle classi agiate."[36]

LANGUAGE AND TYPEFACE

The titles or prefaces of cookbooks often expressed what their intended market was, but there were many other details that pointed to readers of a special social group. Reading in itself was a skill not shared by everybody. In the infancy of printing, the market for books in general and for cookbooks in particular was limited to the literate elite, such as aristocrats, clergy, administrative officials, and the educated urban population—people who read Latin and the vernacular and were interested in new information and new phenomena.[37]

Much of the early printed literature was written in Latin, even material that was first made known to the public in the vernacular, such as the sermon. Gabriele Barletta and Olivier Maillard, popular preachers in the late fifteenth century, used Italian and French, respectively, when they preached, but their sermons were later printed in Latin, "making it clear that the audience envisaged was very different from the original listeners."[38] This can be compared to the way Platina translated Martino's Italian into a Latin that better suited his learned friends. All the same, Latin was rarely used in cookbooks, one of the genres where the vernacular dominated very early. Apart from Platina's many Latin editions, almost all printed cookbooks were written in the vernacular.[39] But even if cookbooks were printed in the vernacular, it took a long time before a majority of the population was able to read them. There were great differences in literacy among Europeans. Some artisans had more experience with reading and writing than others. Generally, the craftsmen in the towns boasted a higher level of literacy than farmers and peasants; in the countryside, hired farm workers were the most illiterate. Women were generally less literate than men. In the latter part of the seventeenth century, only 2 percent of women in the diocese of Durham knew how to sign church documents.[40] In Europe at this time, England was somewhere in the middle as far as literacy went, because there were great variations in literacy rates in different geographical areas, and these lasted a long time. As late as 1850, when illiteracy was reduced to 30 percent in England and 10 percent in Sweden, the numbers for southern and eastern Europe were dramatically different: 75 percent in Italy and Spain and 90 percent in Russia.[41] And these numbers are only the average. Russian statistics reveal that in 1897, illiteracy was still 75 percent in the countryside and remained especially high among women.[42] One consequence of this was that the market for cookbooks varied greatly from country to country.

Certain physical features of books, such as format and typeface, also had social significance. Cookbooks in the big folio format, common in academic works, were nearly nonexistent. The more practical quartos and octavos were the normal format for cookbooks and most other books. In the sixteenth and seventeenth centuries, combined recipe collections (with recipes for food, confectionary, medicine, and cosmetics), particularly favored by women of the elite, were often printed in duodecimo or sextodecimo formats, which were conventionally used for prayer books and popular tales.

In the choice of typeface, cookbooks followed the common style for all other books. Gothic was replaced by roman type in the sixteenth and seventeenth centuries, except in northern Europe, where this development did not take place until the nineteenth and twentieth centuries.[43] But if we take a closer look at these transitions, we find interesting differences. The shift from gothic to roman type in France and England was first made in cookbooks intended for the upper classes; books for a more popular market kept the old typeface longer. The same development took place in Norway, where sophisticated cookbooks were printed in roman type around 1900, while cheap and simple cookbooks stuck to gothic, as did popular romantic stories and devotional books meant for a wider market. There are several examples of the same author publishing books for different market segments in different type.[44] However, the new roman type was considered more difficult to read and more socially exclusive by the less literate, who were accustomed to the old type. In the case of a cookbook for Swedish speakers in Finland, *Tant Hildas kokbok* (Aunt Hilda's cookbook), readers protested when the book was first published in 1878 in roman type (called Latin by most people at the time). Two years later, a new edition was published in gothic, and the reason given in the preface was: "Since this book is primarily intended for cooks and servants and many of them complain about their inability to read Latin, this new edition has been given a less pretentious attire."[45]

A QUESTION OF PRICE

The first printed books were so expensive that few people had the money to purchase them, but books gradually became more accessible. In the sixteenth century, a Bible cost more than the monthly salary of a worker. In 1711, however, the price corresponded to the average earnings for one and a half days. Most cookbooks cost less than a Bible, and there were rather few cookbooks before 1800 with expensive paper, illustrations, and binding. But cookbooks were still out of reach for the poorest classes of society for a long time. This was unfortunately also true for recipe collections intended for the most destitute social groups.

One such book was written by Jacques Dubois, a Parisian doctor, in 1546.[46] He promised to give his readers "health rules for the poor, easy to follow," and explained the nutritional value of different foodstuffs. He gave simple recipes for soups and porridges made with bread, onion, roots, vegetables, and offal. Yet this book, small and modest as it was, was probably not bought by the poor because they could not read and had no money. From 1500 to 1800, it is estimated that between one third and one tenth of the population in Europe lived below the poverty line. About half of the inhabitants in larger cities were poor or marginalized, but the majority of the poor lived in the countryside, simply because urban Europe was so limited. In 1500, less than 5 percent of the population lived in towns with more than ten thousand inhabitants. We have reason to believe that Dubois's book and other books like it were bought by charitable doctors, priests, and various civil servants or landowners who wanted to help the most marginalized groups.

Between the seventeenth and the nineteenth centuries, cheap books were distributed in France by peddlers, who traveled to most of the country. The books were labeled *la bibliothèque bleue*—the blue library—because they were bound with cheap blue paper. The genres on offer were popular stories, almanacs, and handbooks of various kinds, among them certain cookbooks. But even these books cost a day's salary for a worker.[47]

Early in the nineteenth century, the preface of a Swedish collection of simple recipes read: "These recipes are not intended for the poor class, they will not have money to buy it and no interest or time to read it."[48] Many cookbook authors complained in their prefaces about how expensive some cookbooks were, and they emphasized their efforts to make their own books simple and keep the prices low.[49] But the real poor still had little chance of acquiring such books. The publishers and authors were conscious of the difference in purchasing power and therefore tried to present books in different price categories. The cheapest of Alexis Soyer's books cost six pence, which was about 2 percent of the price of his most expensive book.

But the price of cookbooks was only one part of the financial barrier; the other was the price of food. The most expensive books would generally also have the most expensive ingredients. Menon, who in his *La cuisinière bourgeoise* pointed out the difference between the ordinary bourgeois and the "bas peuple," commented on this difference in detail. He wrote a long list of what the bourgeois liked. His examples of the beef cuts favored by the upper-middle class were entrecôte, leg, sirloin, brisket, and shank, and he contrasted this with "la basse boucherie" (the lower meats), that he would not go into at all.[50]

The Norwegian Henriette Schønberg Erken clearly demonstrated class differences in two books she published in the same year, 1914. *Billig mad* (Cheap food) includes recipes for very simple meat and fish dishes and all sorts of soups and stews made with cabbage, peas, beans, potatoes, and roots. *Stor kokebok* (Complete cookbook), which cost twenty to thirty times as much, depending on the quality of the binding, has all sorts of international dishes and a rich variety of greens and vegetables, such as asparagus, artichokes, eggplant, and endive, which were very exclusive ingredients at that time in Norway.[51]

Joyce Toomre pointed out a similar pattern in her study of Alexis Soyer's books. She found 106 different ingredients in the upper-class *Gastronomic Regenerator*, 90 in the middle-class *Modern Housewife*, and 76 in the popular *Shilling Cookery*. There are more meat and fish dishes in the first and more vegetable dishes in the last, and *Shilling Cookery* uses cheap coloring and flavoring agents "as substitutes for the more costly and complex glazes and gravies of the wealthy." Soyer even gave different names to dishes according to class: "Potage à la Crécy" in *The Gastronomic Regenerator* becomes "Crécy Soup, or Purée of Carrots" in *The Modern Housewife* and "Red Carrot Soup" in *Shilling Cookery*.[52]

That certain vegetables were looked down on is evident in cookbooks from seventeenth-century France. In one of them, the author wrote that *rave*, used in casseroles by peasants in Limousin, are so coarse and vulgar that he regretted spending time and paper describing them.[53] In another book, the author wrote negatively about carrots, Jerusalem artichokes, and "many other miseries that only Arabs and the like are willing to endure."[54]

Emilia Pardo Bazán's *La cocina española antigua* (1913) has recipes for different potato dishes. One is made with pork fat, while another, called *guiso pobre de patatas* (poor potato dish), is made with olive oil.[55] The reason for the name may have been that olive oil was cheaper than pork fat, but it is also true that historically, oil did not have a high standing in Spain. Oil was used during Lent and on fasting days, when animal products were forbidden, and in earlier centuries it was associated with Jews and Muslims, whose religion did not allow the use of pork.[56]

Offal is more ambiguous. There are recipes for several types of offal in very old cookbooks—for example, in *Apicius* and in the books by Martino and Platina. Menon, in his list of what the bourgeois like, mentions brain, tongue, kidney, and tail. Sweetbreads are among the most prestigious offal. Erken's upper-class cookbook has eight elegant recipes for them; in the book with cheap dishes there is a note about sweetbreads being an expensive product, and no recipes are given. Kidneys are still popular in English pies, and they hold a special place among many French gourmets, who praise the particular taste of urine, just as the protagonist in James Joyce's *Ulysses* did. Tripe is often considered a rather simple and popular ingredient, but one that can be lifted to higher status if identified as a component of a national or a mythical dish. Scottish haggis was lauded by Robert Burns in a poem and by Christian Isobel Johnstone in her cookbook.[57] It is not too different from the *nyanya* in Russia, described by Gogol in *Dead Souls* and by Nikolai Osipov in his cookbook.[58] In northern Europe around 1900, some cookbooks emphasized what a cheap and nourishing food offal was,[59] and during the twentieth century, there was no lack of recipes for such products. Consumption dropped, however, in many European countries in the same period, and even more in the United States, where dishes made from offal were hidden behind the euphemism "variety meats."

GAME AND SUBSTITUTES

Game is among the most high-ranking of all meat. Walther Ryff, author of several medical and recipe books, attacked the rich epicures who ate deer, hare, pigeons, pheasants, and peacock while the poor had to be content with turnips, oats, chestnuts, and cabbage.[60] In *La cuisinière bourgeoise,* Menon wrote that dark game—such as red deer, roe deer, and wild boar—was rarely used by the bourgeois and gave only a few general comments on this meat, but his book with court dishes, *Les soupers de la cour,* includes eight full pages of detailed recipes.[61] This attitude to game has to do with the old aristocratic privileges of hunting, laid down in laws and regulations that the privileged groups long sought to defend.[62]

This admiration for game and birds resulted in a general preference for poultry: chicken, duck, and goose. In a French cookbook from 1815, poultry was called the "heart of a meal."[63] Fowl and poultry had such a high status that imitations were made from veal (as well as beef and pork), as documented in many cookbooks: *tordi finti* (mock thrushes) in Italy, *kalfkylling* (veal chicken) in Sweden, *benløse fugler* (legless birds) in Norway, *kälberne Vögerl* (veal birds) in Austria, and *špaňhelské ptáčky* (Spanish birds) in Bohemia.[64] This tradition goes far back. The fourteenth-century *Le menagier de Paris* has recipes for partridge made from chicken and wild boar made from pork. An English manuscript from the fifteenth century has a recipe for "alosed beef," which is beef prepared as birds. In Robert May's aristocratic cookbook from 1660, there is a recipe called "To bake Beef, red-Deer fashion in Pies or Pastries," and the author proudly states that "a very good judgment shall not know it from red Deer."[65] Samuel Pepys seems to have had a more negative experience with mock venison; he writes in his diary about a "venison" pasty that was "palpable beef, which was not handsome."[66] Lots of similar recipes can be found, and one of the most popular was mock turtle soup, which first appeared in a cookbook published in England in 1758[67] and was later immortalized in cookbooks printed all over Europe and in Lewis Carroll's *Alice in Wonderland.*

Sugar was another product that was often substituted for because it was expensive, as the different types of fruit preserves mentioned by Serres at the beginning of the chapter demonstrated. Several authors suggested using honey instead of sugar. In one of his recipes, Marx Rumpolt instructed the readers to use sugar, honey, or sweet wine, depending on how much money they wanted to spend, because these products had very different prices.[68] Christofaro di Messisbugo had another solution. He wrote that a gentleman of middle rank ("gentil'huomo mezzano") could simply reduce the amount of sugar to half or even a third of what the recipe called for.[69]

HORSE AND WORSE

There have been several propaganda campaigns over the years to substitute beef and other meats with horseflesh. The most consistent ones took place in nineteenth-century France, where young scientists, veterinarians, physicians, and sociologists took a closer look at statistics. They saw that the consumption of meat among lower-class Parisians was dramatically down, but at the same time, there was a surplus of horsemeat, which was mainly fed to dogs. The French historian Madeleine Ferrières wrote that they considered both the social and the economic aspects, "des bonnes intentions sociales et du calcul économique."[70] They were up against old prejudices and religious traditions. In the Middle Ages, the church banned the consumption of horseflesh. In 732, when the missionary Bonifacius wrote to Pope Gregor III that the Germans ate horseflesh, the pope told him to suppress the habit.[71] It is therefore surprising that Marx Rumpolt included a recipe for wild horse prepared with pepper or garlic in his 1581 cookbook (figure 23). He recommended salting the meat because it was sweet, which indicates that he may have tasted it.[72] It has been pointed out that Rumpolt's recipe was for wild horse,[73] but Pope Gregor III's letter to Bonifacius explicitly stated that both wild and domestic horses were included in the ban. Although this recipe is an exception, it is generally believed that horseflesh was eaten in Europe despite the ban, particularly in times of hunger and famine. Modern consumption of horseflesh began in the nineteenth century, and France still has special horseflesh shops today, albeit in decreasing numbers.

Horseflesh never made a successful entry into cookbooks. According to a study, horseflesh is not mentioned in German books published during World War I, when the meat was very popular and sought after in Germany.[74] The few times that horseflesh is included in cookbooks, the recipes are for sausages and dried meat, as in a book from Tatarstan, or there are no specific recipes but rather a recommendation to prepare it like beef.[75] One exception is a short Norwegian book written by Erken in 1905 that clearly shows that horseflesh had a low social status. This book is explicitly presented as a resource for lower-class families, and it gives the price of horseflesh as forty-five to fifty-five Norwegian øre, compared to eighty for meat from other animals. Erken gave recipes for horsemeat roast, sauerbraten, stew, steak, and meatballs.[76]

In France, horse, donkey, and mule meat play an important role in two cookbooks published during the siege of Paris by the Prussians, which lasted from 1870 to 1871: *La cuisine pendant la siège* (Cooking during the siege) and *La cuisinière assiégée* (The besieged [female] cook).[77] The books give recipes for dishes made from the meat of these animals as well as from the offal. *La cuisinière assiégée* is a

FIGURE 23. Illustration accompanying the only known recipe for meat from wild horse, in Marx Rumpolt's *Ein new Kochbuch* (Frankfurt am Main, 1587). Nasjonalbiblioteket, Oslo, qLib.rar. 1065.

rare exception in the cookbook genre as it also has recipes for dogs and cats. Particularly interesting is a comment that the cat, "did not need a siege to deserve its reputation; it has for a long time been a substitute for rabbit."[78] This attitude is also expressed in a Spanish proverb about how to fool a customer: "Vender gato por lievre"—to sell a cat as a hare. And there is actually a recipe for roast cat in the first Spanish cookbook and the first Catalan cookbook, both published in the early sixteenth century.[79]

During the Siege of Paris, people got so hungry that they ate anything edible. *La cuisinière assiégée* has a short description of how to boil rats to make them safe to eat, but there are no proper recipes. On November 27, 1870, Victor Hugo noted in his diary: "They say it [rat] is good." On December 30, he wrote: "Yesterday I ate rat." He made no remark about the taste.[80] In other notes, Hugo mentioned the culinary use of animals from the city's zoo in the Jardin des Plantes. The zoo sent the distinguished author bear and antelope meat.[81] Such delicacies were special alternatives for the privileged and were allegedly served in a few restaurants during the siege. A menu from Christmas Day in 1870, the ninety-ninth day of the siege, shows elephant bouillon, roast camel, bear cutlets, kangaroo stew, leg of wolf, and terrine of antelope.[82] The two siege cookbooks do not give any recipes for the exotic animals, although they are mentioned in the poetic preface to *La cuisinière assiégée:* "We never expected that the camels, these intelligent vessels of the desert, the antelopes, these gracious animals from the oasis, and the elephants, these living mountains from African forests, who have received us in the Zoo, would come visit us at the tables."[83] What kind of cookbook was this? No author is given. Was it a work of gallows humor for the less hungry? Some historians consider the book to be a work of fantasy with no basis in the actual situation. The desperate masses in Paris hardly needed this information and were probably strangers to this kind of culinary exotism.

Today, cookbooks are not explicitly aimed at different social groups—rich or poor—but the choice of ingredients in some books—oysters, lobster, and truffles, for example—may indicate that they're destined for a more affluent segment of the population than the average family. Books with cheap or quickly prepared dishes are often presented—at least in wealthier parts of the world—as cookbooks for everyday use. There is also a tendency to glorify dishes that in the past were considered "vulgar" or "poor," due to a romantic nostalgia for a simplicity that probably was not as cherished by those who ate these dishes daily. The late medieval myth of Cockaigne, the land of plenty, describes abundance but also excellence— for example, there are flying plates of carved roasted goose. This may express popular desires better than the frugal meals idealized in Renaissance utopias by members of the intellectual elite. The Cockaigne myth not only was part of an innocent fantasy but also was linked to social unrest and protest and an ambition to turn the world upside down, as was enacted in carnivals.[84] The current fascination for "peasant food" in Europe is a reversal of this phenomenon. Now, a privileged elite, fed up with delicacies from Cockaigne, are, thanks to creative chefs and good authors, being introduced to new and surprising dishes, both in select restaurants and at home.

12

Health and Medicine in Cookbooks

Many cookbooks today are promoted more as a path to better health than as an invitation to culinary pleasure. This approach is nothing new, as a few historical examples will show. An English culinary manuscript from the fourteenth century describes the art of cookery as the best medicine: "Coquina que est optima medicina."[1] The first printed cookbook in Germany, from the end of the fifteenth century, states that a good cook with well-prepared, natural food is the best doctor.[2] And in the first modern French cookbook, *Le cuisinier françois* (1651), the publisher argues in the preface that it is better to spend money on delicious dishes to maintain life and health than to waste fortunes on medicines and other remedies.[3]

Even if such statements are the exception rather than the rule and more a form of marketing than medical theory, they express convictions and ideas that were quite widespread. In several books, the rhetorical assertions were followed by dietetic advice in the recipes themselves. Platina signaled his aim in the work's title, *De honesta voluptate et valetudine* (On right pleasure and good health), and he added medical commentaries to the culinary material he had taken from the cook Martino. A recipe for soup, for example, ends with a sprinkling of spices in Martino's version, but Platina adds that it is nourishing, fattening, and helps protect against liver and heart ailments.[4]

From the Renaissance to the twentieth century, we find recipes for dishes adapted to sick people. One of the six parts of Bartolomeo Scappi's 1570 cookbook is dedicated to dishes for *convalescenti,* two hundred recipes in all, and the author says they are based on his experience providing nourishing food to the higher clergy when they fell ill. Most of the dishes consist of eggs, fish, chicken, or veal, but others are just infusions—boiled water with herbs and spices.[5]

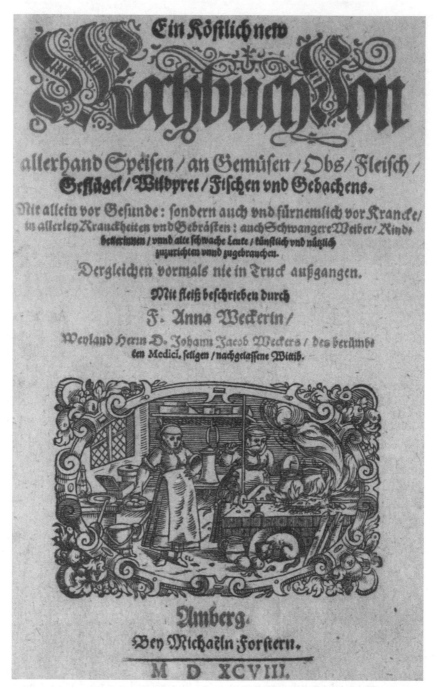

FIGURE 24. Title page of *Ein köstlich new Kochbuch* (An exquisite new cookbook) (Amberg, 1598), the first printed cookbook attributed to a woman, the German Anna Wecker. The design was clearly modeled on the title page of Marx Rumpolt's *Ein new Kochbuch* (see figure 1). Bayerische Staatsbibliothek, Munich, Res/Oecon. 2174 b, Titelblatt.

The German author Anna Wecker—the first woman to have her name on the title page of a printed cookbook—went a step further than Scappi and claimed that her entire book was not only for healthy people but also, and particularly, for the sick, old, and weak, as well as for pregnant women and women recovering from childbirth (figure 24). She was the widow of the famous doctor Johann Jacob Wecker, and she explained that she had helped her husband, who would rather have remedies from the kitchen than from the apothecary. As in Scappi's book, many of the recipes are for soups made with the herbs and spices that were common during this period.[6]

Several books suggest substitutes for certain ingredients if a dish is to be served to a sick person. In the first printed Dutch cookbook, there is a recipe for a capon casserole. It is followed by a chicken recipe that begins with the words: "If you want to make a stew for sick people."[7] However, no real medical arguments were made as to why the special ingredients should be used. Chicken and veal were considered to be more easily digestible than beef and pork, and spices were valued more for their curative effects than for their taste.

Dietary advice was often given without any medical basis. The cook Marx Rumpolt, for example, claimed that a certain dish made of eggs was good for both sick and healthy people because something that was good for the sick could not harm the healthy.[8] But there were also more serious authors who tried to apply medical ideas to practical cookery. These medical and dietetic ideas had been dominant since the Middle Ages, and they had their roots in antiquity.

GALEN AND THE HUMORAL THEORIES

Knowledge of medicine from the Hippocratic school in Greece was organized and systematized by Galen of Pergamon, who lived in Rome in the second century CE and was physician for the emperor Marcus Aurelius. Hippocratic medicine was based on the four elements—air, water, earth, and fire—which were believed to be the basis of all living things, as Platina noted at the beginning of his cookbook.[9] It was thought that the elements decided the quality of every natural thing, whether it was dry or humid, cold or hot. Humans were believed to have four humors—the Greek word is *chymos,* meaning "juice." Galen developed a system based on the idea that whichever humor was dominant in a human being decided his character and temperament, which was either sanguine, choleric, phlegmatic, or melancholic. That this Galenic theory was widely acknowledged during the Middle Ages is demonstrated in *The Canterbury Tales,* where the physician is introduced with these words:

> He knew the case of everich maladye,
> Were it of hoot or cold, or moiste, or drye,
> And where engendred, and of what humour,
> He was verrey parfit practisour.[10]

The ideal was for the four humors to be in harmony—in a "good mix," or *euc-rasis*. If they weren't, the person would be ill, suffering from *discrasis*, "wrong mixture," and this needed to be treated. According to Galen, there were three possible treatments: medication, surgery, and diet. Behind these therapies, there were different professions. Apothecaries produced various medical mixtures, often on orders from physicians. Surgeons, who among other things were responsible for bloodletting, were trained in guilds, like other craftsmen, and had a lower status than physicians, who attended university and had theoretical knowledge. Physicians were responsible for dietetics, which was a much wider concept than it is today, with food as only one of several elements. Like the other therapies, diet was meant to restore balance in the body. Since everything in the world was defined according to whether it was cold or hot and humid or dry, this was also valid for food, so an important task for physicians was establishing the various qualities of different fish, animals, and plants. This knowledge was important to cooks, as it enabled them to give relevant food not only to patients but also to healthy people, because foods had both preventive and curative effects.

Cooks were supposed to participate in the therapy of sick people. Not only were cooks often considered the best doctors, they also often worked together with physicians. As mentioned in chapter 2, the late medieval manuscript cookbook *Forme of Cury* (Method of cookery) was allegedly compiled by the cooks in King Richard II's kitchen and sanctioned by his doctors.[11] In the early sixteenth century, the physician Andrew Boorde wrote that a good cook was half doctor and that cooks and doctors ought to cooperate in preparing food for sick people.[12] And in the fifteenth-century German cookbook *Küchenmeisterei*, there is a line that reads, "If you know your nature, you will understand what is good for you, and you prepare your food based on that knowledge."[13]

Relevant theories and information about foodstuffs and their qualities were published in dietetic works during the Middle Ages. These works explained how different types of meat varied, because meat from different animals, fat and lean meat, meat from old and young animals, and meat from male and female animals did not have the same qualities. Galen was one of the first to write such works, but his original Greek texts disappeared from Europe after the fall of the Roman Empire in the West. During the following centuries, these and other dietetic texts were translated into Syriac, Persian, and Arabic with additions and commentaries. Most famous are the editions and compilations of medical treatises by the Persian Ibn Sina (Latinized as Avicenna) and the Andalucian Arab Ibn Rushd (Latinized as Averroes), which were translated into Latin and aquired a status of canon. These two, along with Hippocrates and Galen, were called "the four princes of medicine,"[14] but when the Greek originals came back to the West from Constantinople in the fifteenth century, the attitude toward Avicenna and Averroes changed. The

German botanist and reformer Otto Brunfels, who protested against the Catholic Church because it had moved away from the original source, the Bible, attacked contemporary medicine along the same lines, saying that it had "wandered away from the correct ancient fountains, Hippocrates and Galen, and fallen into the stinking puddles of the Arabs, Avicenna, Serapion and their like."[15] François Rabelais, whose story about Gargantua is larded with references to humoral theories in descriptions of food, was skeptical about the Arabic compilers, so he published his own Latin translations of Galen and Hippocrates directly from the Greek originals. It is possible to detect these shifting attitudes in the works of Andrew Boorde, who aspired to adapt the old dietetic ideas to England. He showed respect for the great names, but he did dare to criticize Avicenna, for example, about his views of mutton.[16] But authors continued to refer to Galen directly and indirectly for centuries. In 1607, a Spanish cookbook author mentioned him in a recipe for suckling pig, which he stated ought to be eaten in humid weather, according to Galen. His recipe for lentil soup ends with the words: "This is a good soup, but melancholic, according to Galen chapter 5."[17]

MEDICINE AND RECIPES

The basic idea when using food as a therapy was to restore the body's balance, or in other words, to "correct" an imbalance. Such corrections were sometimes mentioned at the beginning of a recipe. In the twelfth century, Hildegard von Bingen wrote in her *Physica* that domestic lettuce was very cold and thus should be eaten with garlic, vinegar, or dill, the dill being defined as hot and dry.[18] Boorde demonstrated the same idea in *Dyetary* (1542): "All maner of flesshe the whiche is inclined to hymydyte, shulde be rostyd. And all flesshe the whiche is inclined to dryness shulde be sodde or boyled."[19]

Fruit was considered humid, so it was recommended to eat apples baked or fried rather than raw. Vegetables were dry and should therefore be boiled. But not all ingredients were so simply defined. Boiled meat, for instance, was humid on the outside but dry inside, and the opposite was true of grilled meat. Putting meat inside a dough or a sheet of lard helped preserve the humidity, and this thinking led to the invention of new dishes.

Among the dietary works written during the Middle Ages were both theoretical and practical texts. One of the most widespread traditions was the one called *regimen sanitatis*—"rule of health."[20] The health rules treated various human activities and necessities, the "six non-natural things": sleep, rest, exercise, digestion, sexual intercourse, and—most extensively—food and drink.[21]

In certain cases, the commentaries and prescriptions in these texts are given a form very similar to a recipe, and some of the works contain so many "recipes" that

Melitta Weiss-Amer, a Canadian scholar, has called them "quasi cookbooks" with dietetic overtones.[22] She noted that recipes for almond milk and blancmange could be found in medical works thirty years before they appeared in normal cookbooks. Even if there is no proof of cause and effect, it is interesting to see the link between medical advice and culinary recipes.[23] One example is the preparation of lamprey, which was coveted in the Middle Ages and highly regarded by gourmets. It was considered very cold and humid. One of the *regimen sanitatis* books recommends putting the fish alive in excellent wine until it dies and then preparing a *galentina* with the very best spices. The author then adds his own recommendation: "Parboil it twice in wine and water and then cook it to perfection."[24]

This description can be compared to the recipe for lamprey in the German manuscript cookbook by Meister Hans, compiled in the fifteenth century. In Hans's recipe, the lamprey is put in good wine until it dies, then the blood and phlegm are washed away and the fish is cut into pieces, boiled in wine, and finally fried and sprinkled with good spices.[25] It is not difficult to see the parallel with the medical advice.

In some scientific works published in the sixteenth century, there are small statements reminiscent of recipes, where foods are defined and characterized. Much of this preparation advice can be traced back to the *Tacuinum sanitatis,* an eleventh-century health handbook by Ibn-Butlan, an Arab physician.[26] One such health book from the Renaissance was written by the Bolognese physician Baldassare Pisanelli, who was well versed in philosophy and botany. The book has a systematic description of 138 foodstuffs, and because he was trying to reach a broader market than medical experts, Pisanelli wrote in Italian instead of in Latin. In the schematic layout, each foodstuff has one page that reviews the item's nature and quality, effect on health and digestion, the best season for consumption, and a suggested remedy for correcting imbalances, which Pisanelli called a *rimedio.* His preparation for lamprey is similar to the earlier quoted recipes: "The fish is drowned in malmsey wine, the mouth is shut with nutmeg, other openings with clove; it is cooked in a pan with hazel nuts, bread, oil, spices, and malmsey wine."[27]

A special but absolutely pedagogical system of the old dietetic rules was launched in an Austrian medical book that became extremely popular around 1700. The author was Eleonora Maria Rosalia, Duchess of Troppau and Jägerndorff, who added an appendix to the second edition, a cookbook in which Hippocrates and Galen were listed as authorities on a healthy lifestyle.[28] The pedagogical innovation introduced in the work is the index, which links diseases to recipes for curative dishes. If you look up *Katarr* (inflammation), for example, you are referred to recipe 38, Oat Soup. As is so common in this genre, the recipes were not created by the author but were taken from other books, a French pastry book and an Austrian book with medical and culinary recipes in two separate parts but without cross-references.[29]

CONFECTIONARY, COSMETICS, AND ASTROLOGY

Numerous books combined culinary and medical recipes in the sixteenth and sev-enteenth centuries, but in most cases, medical recipes were—as mentioned above—combined with confectionary. Over the course of the sixteenth century, sugar became an increasingly accessible commodity; sugar imports to Europe went up 1,500 percent during that century, and the number of sweet dishes in cookbooks increased correspondingly. The titles of such books are revealing. Take, for example, the Catalan manuscript *Llibre de drogues i confitures* (Book of medi-cines and preserves) and the German *Confect-Büchlin und Hauss-Apoteck* (Con-fectionary book and house apothecary), or the subtitle of an English book pub-lished in 1608: *The Art of Preserving, Conserving, and Candying . . . Also Divers Soveraigne Medicines and Salves for Sundry Diseases.*[30]

Sugar had for a long time been considered a medical remedy, and the first printed book of confectionary in Spain, published in 1592, states that sugar strengthens the human body.[31] The medical doctor Nostradamus wrote that the sweet product chased away melancholy and helped cholerics contain themselves.[32] The apothecary and prolific medical author Walther Ryff specifically commented that physicians appreciated sugar more than honey because it was medically more precious, stronger, less stimulating, and did not spoil food.[33] Platina's comment on the quality of sugar followed Galenic ideas. He noted that it was warm and humid and nourished the stomach.[34]

In England, booklets about medicines and confectionary were sometimes printed separately and sometimes bound together for sale but with separate pagi-nation. These combined volumes often included a third part: a collection of culi-nary recipes. But it seems that these recipes did not have the same prestige. The medical recipes, in some cases attributed to royal or aristocratic ladies, such as Queen Henrietta Maria or Elizabeth Countess of Kent, were set first, followed by the confectionary section, and cookery came last.[35]

There were also combination books that included cosmetic information, such as how to color hair, whiten teeth, and make skin smooth. Two men produced such books during the Renaissance, Nostradamus in France and Hugh Plat in England. In 1555, Nostradamus published a little book with a long title that promised readers instruction on how to "embelir la face" and "faire confitures de plusieurs sortes"—in other words, the book had recipes for cosmetics and confectionary. Hugh Plat, who was knighted for his skill as an author, wrote a modest but beautiful book that was printed in at least twenty editions: *Delights for Ladies* (1602). According to the subti-tle, the aim of the book was "To Adorne Their Persons, Tables, Closets and Distilla-tories; With Beauties, Banquets, Perfums & Waters."

Nostradamus, whose French name was Michel de Nostredame, is today best known as an astrologer who made many predictions about the future. That doctors were astrologers is not surprising in light of Hippocratic and Galenic ideas. The physician in *The Canterbury Tales* was "grounded in astronomye" (which was the basis for astrology). Medicine and dietetics were understood as part of a complex interaction between human beings and their surroundings, not only the close, terrestrial surroundings but also the whole universe. When Nicholas Culpeper settled in Spitalfields, London, in the early seventeenth century, he presented himself as an astrologer and physician. His magnum opus, known today as *Complete Herbal*, gave descriptions of hundreds of plants. In the epistle to the reader, Culpeper wrote: "The whole world, and every thing in it, was formed of a composition of contrary elements. . . . He that would know the reason of the operation of the Herbs, must look up as high as the Stars, astrologically. I always found the disease vary according to the various motions of the Stars."[36]

Since cooks were supposed to follow the instructions given by doctors, they needed to have the same knowledge. Twenty centuries before Culpeper, a *mageiros* (cook) in a Greek comedy said that he had to know "the heavenly bodies and the setting and rising of the stars and when the sun rises for the longest and the shortest day and in what part of the Zodiac it is. For almost all our cooked dishes and foods take on different delights in different circumstances according to the movement of the whole universe."[37]

Many books containing recipes for remedies were presented as having important news for a broader public. They claimed to offer readers information that had previously been the exclusive knowledge of physicians at the courts of kings and nobles—the closets and cabinets of aristocratic manors and royal palaces were now opened to the general public. Their titles demonstrate this: *The Ladies Cabinet Opened, The Queen's Closet Opened, The Gentlewomen's Cabinet Opened, The Closet of the Eminently Learned Sir Kenelme Digbee Kt. Opened* (all published in the mid-seventeenth century). The "secrets" such books divulged were bits of artisanal lore that members of the guilds were prohibited from giving away, but with the introduction of new printing techniques and a gradually weakening position for the guilds in this period, many saw that they could make a profit by publishing this professional knowledge. In addition to books with recipes for medicines, cosmetics, and confectionary there were works with information about chemistry, mineralogy, and alchemy and practical instructions for the production of dyes and inks. Much of this literature belonged to a tradition known as "books of secrets"—books in which recipes and practical formulas were part of a "popular science," in William Eamon's words.[38] One of the most widespread examples of the genre was simply called *Secreti* in its original Italian edition, printed in 1555. The author, Alessio Piemontese, claimed that there was an altruistic intention behind the publication. A physician had once asked him for a secret to cure a patient, but Alessio refused, and the patient died. This made him change opinion; he would no longer keep the professional secrets to himself.[39]

One important shift that occurred during the sixteenth and seventeenth centuries is that medical information was given in the vernacular and not only in Latin. This helped spread knowledge and information that had earlier been held only by physicians. When Culpeper translated his *Pharmacopoeia Londinensis* into English, in 1649, he must have known that his colleagues would be annoyed, but he believed that people should not suffer illness simply because they could not read Latin.[40] Walther Ryff was conscious of a new and broader public when he wrote his medical and other works, including his 1545 *Neu Kochbuch für die Krancken* (New cookbook for sick people). He explicitly made a point of writing for "der gemeine Mann"—the common man—which in this case was the literate but not learned part of the population: burghers, artisans, and farmers who owned their land and had households with family and servants. Ryff was criticized by academics and called *Plagiator* because he compiled and popularized material from academic books written in Latin. But Ryff also picked up information from apothecaries, surgeons, and even representatives of "popular medicine." At the time, there was a quarrel going on between university-trained physicians and unofficial healers, who were called quacksalvers, charlatans, geomancers, mountebanks, and worse by the academics.[41] Many of them were women, and they were often considered or even condemned as witches and sentenced to punishment.

Reading some of the popular recipes today, it is not easy to understand how they could have been taken seriously. *A Closet for Ladies and Gentlewomen*, an anonymous booklet first published in 1608 and often attributed to Hugh Plat, mainly contains recipes for confectionary, but it ends with a few medical tips, for example: "For a woman that hath too much of the Flowers. Take the foot of an Hare; burn it to powder, and drinke thereof with red Wine and Cinamon first and last nine dayes, and it will helpe her."[42]

However, there were prominent persons who saw the positive side of popular medicine. The Swiss physician Paracelsus, who rebelled against official medicine and was the first to lecture at a university in German instead of Latin (in Basel in 1527), is known for this opinion: "The physician does not learn everything he must know and master at high colleges alone; from time to time he must consult old women, gypsies, magicians, wayfarers and all manner of peasant folk."[43] This is the same attitude that is expressed in the preface to Alessio Piemontese's book about secrets: "By the which diligence and curiositie, I have learned many goodlye secretes, not alonely of men of great knowledge as profound learning, and noble men, but also of poor women, artificers, paysantes, and all sortes of men."[44] Somewhat later, even the English philosopher Thomas Hobbes dared to state that he would rather have the advice or "take physick" from an experienced old woman who had been at many sick people's bedsides than from a learned but inexperienced physician.[45]

THE END OF GALEN

We have seen how Galenic ideas permeated cookbooks for centuries; there were links between medical knowledge and culinary recipes. But this was not the whole truth and not always the case. Galen himself made it clear that he had little esteem for cooks because they used the wrong kind of spices and in too large quantities. The American scholar Ken Albala demonstrated that there are great contradictions between Galen's fundamental dietetic ideas and the food culture that developed from the Renaissance onward. Attention to taste often brought cuisine in direct opposition to medical advice, and it was something many physicians criticized.[46]

It is also evident that there was an increasing skepticism about Galenic medicine, or its more extreme representatives at any rate, before it finally fell out of favor. Around 1600, Galen's theories were depicted in satirical form by two of the greatest writers of the time, Shakespeare and Cervantes. The satires were based on the way doctors were supposed to advise nobles about diet. In his cookbook, Scappi always defers to doctors when giving recipes for the sick: "Secondo la commissione de Phisico."[47] A fourteenth-century report from the Duke of Burgundy describes how doctors act in a real situation: "When the Duke is at table, these Doctors are behind the bench, and they see what dishes and foods are served to the Prince and they advise him which foods in their opinion are the most beneficial to him."[48]

This positive description does not exactly correspond to the satiric versions. In a passage from *Don Quijote*, Cervantes placed the newly appointed governor Sancho Panza at the dinner table looking forward to enjoying all the wonderful dishes, but the physician standing at his side refuses almost everything by referring to the great Hippocrates and using expressions from Galenic theories.[49] Shakespeare gave his critique in *The Taming of the Shrew*, where there is a conversation between Katharina and her servant Grumio. Katharina is refused everything she likes: tripe is too choleric, mustard too hot.[50] These examples are from a time Albala refers to as the third period of dietetic works in the Renaissance: "The breakdown of Orthodoxy (1570–1650)."[51]

In the eighteenth century, European cookbooks concentrated more on cookery and left medical recipes and advice to specialized works, such as *The Poor Man's Medicine Chest* (1791) and *Gesundheits-Katechismus* (1794), and scientific works. But the medieval ideas lived on in some cookbooks, even those by acclaimed authors. In one of Menon's books, the recipes are introduced with general considerations about the qualities of different animals, for example: "Meat from a newborn lamb is very humid and phlegmatic."[52] In the preface to his 1742 cookbook, François Marin stresses that a good cook has to know the qualities of everything he uses in order to correct and perfect the foodstuffs that nature gives us totally raw and unprepared.[53] But as David Gentilcore has observed, the lighter and more natural French cuisine in the late seventeenth and the eighteenth centuries was obviously influenced by new medical works and ideas from that time.[54]

Even if the old theories, particularly the notion of "hot" and "cold" foods, lived on in the collective consciousness and were expressed in certain cookbooks well into the nineteenth century, more serious medical research started in the seventeenth century, when William Harvey discovered how blood circulates. Medicine gradually left the realm of speculative philosophy and entered an age of modern science. In the late eighteenth century, chemical elements were discovered in nutrients, oxygen, and certain acids. In the middle of the nineteenth century, the German chemist Justus von Liebig studied and analyzed the biological processes that transform food to energy, and he classified nutrients into four categories: fats, carbohydrates, proteins, and salt. On this basis, he made a system showing what relationship there ought to be between the nutrients in a human diet. It was very important to Liebig that the nutrition value in food not be undermined or weakened during cooking.

The revised editions of Eliza Acton's *Modern Cookery for Private Families,* originally published in 1845, give us an idea of how quickly such ideas spread to cookbooks. Acton read the English translation of Liebig's book about the chemistry of food, and in the preface of the revised editions of her book, she referred to the German baron and said that if his rules were closely followed, they would lead to progress in the art of cooking.[55] She changed her recipes in accordance with Liebig's theories—for example, she instructed readers to put meat directly into boiling water or to fry it on very high heat. The idea was that these methods would seal the meat so the juice was kept inside, though it was later proved that neither technique accomplished this.[56]

A German cookbook that tried to implement the new scientific ideas was a "chemical cookbook" published in 1857 by the German physician Hermann Klencke.[57] The book was translated into Swedish and Norwegian and influenced Scandinavian nutrition debate.

By the end of the nineteenth century, it was relatively common to see the new concepts presented in cookbooks, often in prefaces by doctors or chemists. New genres, such as school cookbooks and textbooks for education in home economics, based their cooking instruction directly on the current nutritional theories. This became even more important when nutritional science developed further, with the identification of vitamins in the early twentieth century. Vitamins became central in studies launched by nutrition specialists in the 1920s and 1930s. The League of Nations introduced a project on diet, and an expert committee appointed in 1935 proposed a new classification system that divided foodstuffs into two categories: "protective food," which was necessary to prevent deficiency diseases, and "energy-bearing food," which consisted of fat and carbohydrates, which create energy. This concept was introduced into new cookbooks of that period.

In recent decades, new theories of diet have been launched advocating the avoidance of particular foods, such as fats or carbohydrates. Books about Atkins, vegan, Paleo, Ornish and other diets, with the relevant recipes included, have flooded the market. They promote different ideas, often contradicting guidelines laid down by official health institutions. Some diets focus mainly on weight loss, while others reflect ideological views or emphasize general health and recommend variation. One difficulty with devising standard diets is that they tend to mask the fact that people respond differently to specific foods for a variety of reasons, for example, as a result of their genes. Therefore, an individualized approach to the best diet may be better than general recommendations. In many ways, this was what the Galenic physicians aspired to do, but their knowledge of the body and how it functioned cannot be compared to what dieticians know today.

13

Recipes for Fat Days and Lean Days

There are cookbooks in many countries that have been organized according to religious calendars, giving rules for what can and cannot be eaten during specific periods of the year. The practice of abstaining from certain foodstuffs, and in extreme cases from all food, for a period of time is something found in many religions and cultures. In Christian Europe, these rules basically concerned the banning of meat during fasting days prescribed by the church. The first printed cookbook in German, *Küchenmeisterei,* published at the end of the fifteenth century, reflects this in the arrangement of the text: the first chapter gives recipes for *Fastenspeys* (fasting food), and the second has dishes with meat. In other words, the book opens with food that deviated from the daily diet: fish, seafood, and vegetables.[1] Although not all books followed this sequence, most early manuscripts and printed works had separate sections for meat and fish.

THE RELIGIOUS CALENDAR

In the first known accounts of Jesus—the Gospels—he is said to have fasted for forty days in the desert, but Jesus and his disciples did not fast the way the Pharisees and the disciples of John the Baptist did. There are examples of early Christians fasting in connection with prayer, but the custom did not play the same role in the New Testament as it did in contemporary Judaism. The Torah gave specific dietary prescriptions, which were expanded in commentaries from learned rabbis.

Early Christian hermits and monks abstained from meat, and the practice gradually gained prominence within the Church, even if the apostle Paul had warned against forbidding certain foods by saying that "every creature of God is good, and nothing is to be rejected, if it is received with thanksgiving."[2] The monastic rules elaborated by Benedict of Nursia forbid the consumption of quadrupeds and, during fasting periods, of all meat.[3] Exempted from this ban were very weak people ("preter omnino debiles ægrotos"), because meat was considered the most nourishing food. But according to Galenic medicine, meat excited the sexual appetites of healthy people, a view supported by the great medieval theologian Thomas Aquinas,[4] and the faithful were to abstain from sex as well as from certain foods during fasting periods.

For most of the population, abstaining from meat was not a big sacrifice because they could seldom afford to eat it in their daily lives. In an 1866 book about peasants in Bavaria, Felix Dahm noted: "Characteristic of the diet of southern Bavaria is the almost universal dominance of grain-, milk- and fat-based dishes with some vegetables added, while meat is limited to the five greatest holidays of the year: Shrovetide, Easter, Whitsuntide, *Kirmes* and Christmas; for the peasant meat and festival is one and the same."[5] For centuries, many people in the European countryside lived on a diet of grains, roots, pulses, and vegetables, at best with the addition of a little fat, the only thing that gave some extra taste to the otherwise bland food. But even this was forbidden during periods of fasting.

Fish was one important alternative to animal products. According to Galenic medicine, it was cold and moist and consequently less exciting than meat. But fish was not readily available to the lower classes. In certain areas, fish was more expensive than meat—particularly during Lent, when the demand was great. A report from Catholic Munich in 1792 shows that a trout cost more than a duck; certain fish were six times as expensive as beef, and salmon cost twice as much as exclusive game.[6] The poor people who did eat fish were generally those who lived near the coast, and they ate only the cheapest fish, because sought-after specimens were sold to bring in cash. In some areas, such as northern Scandinavia, ordinary people had more access to lakes, rivers, and the ocean, but in the rest of Europe, such waters were generally regulated according to privileges held by the aristocracy and the church (described in chapter 11), and fish was consequently not a food for the peasantry and other common people.

In addition to meat, other animal products, such as eggs, milk, butter, and cheese, were banned on some of the most important fasting days up to the early modern period. There are traces of this in the medieval texts. In Meister Hans's fifteenth-century German manuscript, a recipe with eggs ends with these words: "On fasting days, grate bread instead of eggs."[7] These restrictions were problematic in the northern part of Europe, where there was no olive cultivation and thus no olive oil. Today, with easy access to all sorts of vegetable oils and margarines, it is hard to understand the problems people were confronted with in a food culture where animal fats were necessary for cooking. But these difficulties made dispensations more and more common during the late Middle Ages. In Germany, the special permissions to use butter during Lent were called *Butter-Briefe*. In France, the Tour de Beurre (butter tower) of the Rouen cathedral was probably paid for with the money from permissions to use butter in that city. Normandy—where Rouen is situated—and Brittany were the big butter-producing regions of the country, and a text from the fifteenth century explained that people in Brittany exported butter and ate it during Lent because they had no oil. Butter production was so big that butter was called "the fat for the poor."[8]

By the end of the Middle Ages, bans on these products were gradually lifted in Catholic Europe, but an interesting trace of the old rules can be found in *Neues Hamburger Kochbuch*, published in Protestant Hamburg in the nineteenth century. A long and detailed recipe for Easter bread (*Pasch-Semmel, Osterbrot*) includes this comment: "For the Catholic rite these breads are also baked at Easter, but the milk is replaced by half wine and half water, there are no eggs, and fine oil instead of butter."[9]

The first printed Russian cookbooks are from the end of the eighteenth century, and they had separate chapters for dishes that could be eaten during Lent. There was even a special book of these recipes, *Postnaia povarikha* (Fasting dishes), published in 1793.[10] This is due to the fact that the Orthodox Church continued to uphold restrictions on egg and milk products for the most important fasting days. On some days, the church also continued to ban fish, a constraint that had disappeared early on in Western Europe. A good illustration of the Orthodox practice is given in a cookbook with old Russian dishes, published first in the 1790s and then reprinted in 1816. The author explains that there are two kinds of fast dishes, "proper" (*sobstvennyi*) and "half fast" (*polupost*), the latter of which can include fish, egg, milk, cream, and butter.[11] He therefore gives three different versions of the two classical soups *shchi* and *borscht*.

Although the first edition of Elena Molokhovets's nineteenth-century classic *Podarok molodym khoziaikam* (A gift to young housewives) did not include a separate chapter for fasting dishes, there was practical advice in the recipes on how to exchange ingredients during Lent by using fish instead of meat, oil instead of butter, and so on. In later editions, Molokhovets introduced a separate chapter with fasting dishes, and other authors did the same (figure 25).

REPLACING BANNED INGREDIENTS

The simple solution during Lent and fasting days was to eat vegetables (and fish, if permitted) and not think about what was missing. But people with sophisticated tastes and gourmet appetites wanted to eat dishes that reminded them of what they had to avoid, so many cookbooks had recipes for substitutes for different dishes and important ingredients.

One challenge was finding replacements for butter, which was a key ingredient in many dishes. Martino instructed readers how to make substitutes for butter and

РЫБНЫЙ И ПОСТНЫЙ СТОЛЪ.

Г Л А В А XIV.

FIGURE 25. First page of the chapter with fasting dishes in K. K. Morokhovtsev's cookbook *Polnyi podarok molodym khoziaikam* (Complete gift to young housewives), published in 1901.

ricotta cheese in his cookbook and made clear that they were meant for use during Lent. In his version, Platina described these products as "artificial" (*fictus*).[12] Both products were made with almonds, which were often used in fasting dishes. In his fifteenth-century cookbook, Meister Hans gave a recipe for an egg substitute based on almonds: the yolk was colored with saffron and packed in a layer of white almond paste.[13] Traditional bird's eggs were sometimes replaced with roe—in other words, fish eggs. Fat from pike could be used instead of animal fat. Salmon could be made into a mock ham, and stockfish and rice could be used to make ersatz suet.[14]

The late fourteenth-century French manuscript *Le menagier de Paris* gives a Lenten recipe for flan, which is typically made with eggs, cream, and sugar. The revised recipe recommends using milt from carp or pike. It also suggests adding saffron, probably to give the dish the yellow color the egg yolk would have contributed. The fasting dishes were meant to look like the normal versions of the dishes, and in this case, even the linguistic similarity of ingredients was appreciated: the French word for "milt" is *laitance,* while "milk" is *lait.*[15]

Another example of a meat dish that was modified into a fasting dish by using fish but making it look like meat can be found in a German manuscript from the 1440s. There is a detailed recipe that involves carving two pieces of wood into molds in the form of half partridges. Spicy minced fish meat was then packed into the hollowed molds. Then the two halves were pressed together so that the contents took the shape of a partridge, and this was then roasted.[16]

Cookbooks had innumerable recipes for these kinds of substitutions. But they also had recipes for food that we hardly would put in the fish category today. The most astounding example is perhaps the beaver. It is a mammal, a rodent, that lives partly in water, with scales on its tail and webbed hind feet. Beaver tail was considered a delicacy. In England, there is an early record of beaver tail as food in a book from the fifteenth century, which gives carving instructions for fish, including "þe tayle of þe bevere."[17] But recipes for beaver tail are mainly found in German and Central European books. Meister Hans's manuscript gave a recipe for fried beaver tail seasoned with spices.[18] *Küchenmeisterei* recommended frying it with ginger or boiling it with black pepper.[19] Rumpolt proposed boiling it first in vinegar and salt and then preparing it in a pepper sauce.[20] A modern and more detailed recipe can be found in the cookbook of the Austrian Katharina Prato, who pointed out that the preparation could also be used for otter. Prato instructed readers to first remove the skin from the tail and then cut the meat into pieces and salt it; after this, it could be steamed with butter, roots, spices, and lemon peel and then boiled in a dark sauce of pea broth and lemon juice. It could also be fried, but in that case it should first be larded with anchovies and then covered with butter, marinade, cream, lemon juice, and capers, if wanted.[21]

Ocean mammals, such as dolphins, porpoises, and whales, were classified as fish. Recipes for snails, turtles, and frogs were also placed among the fasting foods in many cookbooks. In France, where common people without access to rivers and lakes, which were reserved for the aristocracy, caught frogs in the marshes and swamps, this little animal was known as "the lark of fasting days."[22] But the frog seems to have been considered amphibious in more than one sense of the word. A sixteenth-century French treatise about fish reported that in eastern France, the hind part of the frog was eaten as fish on fasting days, while the front part was consumed as meat on fat days.[23]

Even fish-eating seabirds were included among fasting foods. Menon included recipes for scoter in the 1789 edition of his cookbook *La science du maître d'hôtel cuisinier* between whiting and sole—in other words, between two types of fish— and he explicitly described the seaduck as fasting food.[24] This may, however, have been a disputed practice; Grimod wrote that *gelinottes d'eau*, a type of grouse, were said to be suitable for lean days but that this was something Jansenism, a pious Catholic movement, contested.[25] However, a hundred years later, in Italy, Artusi explained that coot could be called a "bird fish" because the Church gave permission to eat it during Lent.[26]

Much has been said and written about the captious and hair-splitting disputes among medieval scholastics, and at first sight the classifications of fasting foods seem to confirm the stereotype. But there was a logic behind this classification, and it was based on Galenic medicine. All of these animals had natural qualities that corresponded to those fish had: they were moist and humid, and they could be eaten without any danger of exciting the sexual appetite.

SPECIAL DAYS AND PERIODS

The number of fasting days has varied through the centuries, but at times almost half of the days of the year were included. Of the weekdays, Friday—the day of the crucifixion—was the most important fast day. But depending on the place and the century, fasting was observed on other days as well: Wednesday to remember the day Judas received thirty silver coins to betray Jesus, and Saturday to honor Virgin Mary. But these days were less demanding from a culinary point of view, as the church distinguished between strict and milder abstinence.

Some old cookbooks have separate chapters for Saturday dishes. A Spanish book from 1607, written by the cook at a college in Salamanca, has, in addition to the main sections for meat and fish dishes, a small section with nineteen dishes for "la comida de sabados."[27] These recipes are based on offal and the other less prestigious parts of the animal. The editor of a modern facsimile edition of the book, published in 1999, explained that such meals seem to reflect the rules (*constituciones*) that were observed in public and religious colleges, hospitals, and other institutions.[28] But is it possible that this practice for Saturdays was the result of a bull? According to Voltaire, the pope sent a papal bull to Spain during the reign of the Catholic Monarchs, Queen Isabella I of Castile and King Ferdinand II of Aragon, that allegedly gave Spaniards permission to eat *grossura* on Saturdays. Voltaire explained *grossura* as different dishes made from liver, kidney, sweetbreads, head, and feet.[29] A Czech cookbook from 1542 has three parts, one with meat dishes, one with lenten fare (called Friday dishes), and a third one with Saturday dishes, *krmie sobotnij.* The last part contains a lot of fish dishes, but above all *kaše,* various sorts of porridge, or *pap,* based on fruit, berries, nuts, peas, mushrooms, and prepared with cream, cheese, and eggs.[30] This organization was dropped in a later edition, which was expanded and revised by a nobleman scholar.[31]

Some English cookbooks from the late sixteenth and the early seventeenth centuries have menus for meat days and fish days; in one of them, these are specified as "Fish-dayes, Fastingdayes and Ember-weekes, or Lent."[32] Ember-weeks consisted of three ember days—Wednesday, Friday, and Saturday—and they occurred four times a year, during Advent and Lent, after Whitsuntide, and in September, and they had stricter rules. The official Latin term was *quator anni tempora* (the four times of the year).[33]

The most important fasting period was Lent, which began on Ash Wednesday and ended on Easter Eve. It was meant to represent the forty days Jesus fasted in the desert, and its name in Romance languages is therefore derived from the Latin word for "fortieth," *quadragesima* (e.g., *carême* in French and *cuaresma* in Spanish). In Slavic and Germanic languages, it is called "great" and "long." The Greek term combines the words for "great" and "fortieth."[34]

The French book *Le cuisinier françois* (1651) gives a good idea of the differences between the fasting periods. Some dishes are meant for the regular fasting days during the year, others are particularly for Lent, and there is a special chapter for dishes suitable for Good Friday, which are based entirely on vegetables and roots.[35]

The days just before Lent were celebrated with extra-rich foods. In Russia, the period was called butter week, and Molokhovets wrote that Russians considered *blinis* to be a necessary part of the meals, while Catholics served *Krapfen* and Lutherans ate German buns.[36] During these days, there were popular festivals and processions, collectively known as carnival. In paintings and literature, the allegorical battle between carnival and Lent was often recreated with drama and humor, but there is no trace of this in cookbooks, which simply give recipes for the different occasions.

THE REFORMATION AND FASTING TRADITIONS

Around 1500, the established fasting traditions in Western Europe met with increasingly strong criticism from people who wanted reforms, and many of the reformers eventually left the Catholic Church and created new Protestant communities, where fasting was never a fundamental issue, even if certain discussions about food continued to be important.[37] In Zurich, followers of Ulrich Zwingli broke the dietary rules during Lent in 1522 and were put in prison. In a sermon—later published under the title *Von Erkiesen und Freyhait der Speisen* (Choice and purity of food)—Zwingli attacked fasting and claimed that there was nothing in the Bible that justified the practice; he argued that fasting was just an old tradition perpetuated into the sixteenth century.[38] Jean Calvin and Martin Luther felt that there were certain benefits to fasting, but they emphasized that it was not a path to salvation. Luther criticized Catholic preachers, who made people believe it was a greater sin to eat butter than to tell lies in court. He said that the Gospel made it clear that all food could be eaten, and he attacked the papal sale of dispensations. In his opinion, Rome mocked the fasting rules when it gave pilgrims from abroad oil that the clergy would not even grease their shoes with and then later granted freedom to eat butter to those who could afford to pay for it.[39]

Several reformers criticized fasting as hypocritical because it was an "epicurean fasting." The Church Father Jerome had already warned against this hypocrisy, and Calvin took it a step further and called fasting absurd. He said that at no other time of the year was there such an abundance and variation of dishes as during fasting periods and that Catholics mocked God when they praised fasting but ate the most exquisite fish dishes. In their opinion, Calvin wrote, the highest form of worship was to abstain from meat, and they believed that eating a little bit of bacon as the greatest lack of piousness, one punishable by death.[40] Calvin knew that a little bit of meat was all poor people could afford. The element of social criticism is also evident in the writings of the Catholic reformer Desiderius Erasmus. In one of Erasmus's colloquies, a participant said that to demand of the poor to abstain from meat when they lived far away from rivers and lakes was to decree hunger or famine. Erasmus was sharp in his criticism of the way many Catholics made a great effort in preparing exclusive Lenten dishes: "The rich, forbidden to eat meat, turn to dainties instead."[41] Several cookbooks give reason to believe that Calvin and Erasmus were right. In his 1570 cookbook, the papal cook Scappi gives a lunch menu for a fasting day. The whole meal is based on sturgeon, and he offers seventeen different preparations for the fish, a veritable demonstration not only of culinary art but also of luxury and pleasure.[42] The idea that fasting could be used to satisfy gluttony rather than to curb or prevent it was taken up by Walter Benjamin. In one of his *Denkbilder* (mental images) from the 1920s, "Falerner und Stockfisch" (Falerner wine and dried cod), he wrote, "Fasting is the initiation to many secrets, not least the secret of eating. And if hunger is the best cook, fasting is the king among the best."[43]

COOKBOOKS AND THE REFORMATION

One result of the Reformation was that different cookbooks were published in different parts of Europe, depending on whether the regions were Catholic or Protestant. The first Scandinavian cookbooks were printed more than a hundred years after the Reformation and consequently did not include recipes for fasting dishes. The only exception was the abridged Swedish translation of *Le cuisinier françois,* which kept some of the original lean dishes and Good Friday dishes.[44] The first printed cookbook in Scandinavia, published in Copenhagen in 1616, also had some traces of fasting dishes.[45] The recipe "sausage to make from minced fish" is a typical example of a meat substitute that could be used during periods of fasting, but there is nothing explicitly said about fasting in the recipe.

In Germany, the difference between the Protestant north and the Catholic south is clear in cookbooks from the two regions. Separate sections for meat dishes and lean dishes disappeared from cookbooks published in the north of the country after the Reformation. Marcus Loofft's influential work from 1758, published in the northern German cities of Lübeck and Altona, does not mention fasting dishes at all. In the southern areas, such as Bavaria, books with special fasting dishes were published as late as the nineteenth century and even into the twentieth. The same is true for the Habsburg Empire, where the system was kept in German, Czech, and Hungarian books. Katharina Prato's book *Die süddeutsche Küche,* published in Graz in the second half of the nineteenth century, has an index with "Fish and other fasting dishes," where frogs, beaver, otter, and snails are joined by wild duck and heron. Dobromila Rettigová's classic nineteenth-century Czech cookbook contains recipes for fried frog and frog fricassee with parsley in the fish chapter.[46]

In mixed areas, both religious groups had to be taken care of. In Nuremberg, for example, an important cookbook from 1691 had an significant number of fasting dishes.[47] The city was dominated by Protestants, but it had a large Catholic minority, and the publisher probably also wanted to sell the book in other, more Catholic parts of Bavaria. The Protestant northern part of the Netherlands broke away from Spain and created a separate political entity, while the south continued to be ruled by Spain and later by Catholic Austria. But many Catholics lived in the north, and several cookbooks published in Leiden and Amsterdam made it clear on the title page that they had dishes for Catholics to make during fasting periods and on fish days. One book was even "written by a Catholic," albeit anonymously.[48]

In England, where the political power struggle between the king and the pope led to an Anglican state church and restrictions on the life and rights of Catholics, cookbooks reveal no clear allegiance. Some English cookbooks gave different menus at the beginning of the books, but there were no separate chapters for fasting dishes. In a few books, however, it is possible to see remnants of a fasting practice. In his 1660 cookbook, *The Accomplisht Cook,* the Catholic Robert May included only one menu with fasting dishes, and it seems to be presented as a historical curiosity with the words: "A bill of Fare formerly used in Fasting days, and in Lent."[49] But some eighteenth-century authors showed more interest in Lent, perhaps because the Catholic question has become less problematic. Hannah Glasse included a special chapter with Lenten dishes in *The Art of Cookery* (1747), but she noted that the dishes could also be used at other times; in other words, the religious aspect does not seem to have been so important to her. In the nineteenth century, Eliza Acton and Isabella Beeton gave no recipes for Lent in their cookbooks, but Beeton wrote a few lines giving historical background and medical opinions on fasting. A couple of small books with exclusively Lenten dishes were published in the late nineteenth and the early twentieth centuries, but they dropped the references to Lent in later editions.[50]

In southern European Catholic countries, detailed recipes for fasting dishes were kept in cookbooks longer. In the early twentieth century, Spanish cookbooks with recipes for Lent were published and approved by church authorities.[51] But there were also many cookbooks published in these countries that did not follow the system of separate sections for fat dishes and lean dishes. In his 1891 cookbook, the Italian Pellegrino Artusi gave a few menus for Lent, and there is a soup chapter, "Minestre di magro" (lean soups), with a frog soup and a frog risotto. He also remarked that on fasting days, *baccala* (dried and salted cod) competed at the fish market with fresh cod, which was more expensive but not always that fresh.[52] Angel Muro's popular *El practicón* (thirty-four editions were printed between 1894 and 1928) is totally without reference to fasting.

In eighteenth-century France, there were complaints from religious circles about the paucity of Catholic cookbooks compared with the increasing number of secular cookbooks.[53] This was during the Enlightenment, when scholars were having serious scientific and theological discussions on piety and the value of Lenten food.[54] However, there was also a general secularization taking hold in France, and anticlericalism was strong long before the French Revolution. One of the most severe critics of Catholicism was the philosopher Voltaire, who followed in the footsteps of Calvin and Erasmus with his attacks on hypocrisy and social injustice. In the entry for *carême* (Lent) in his *Dictionnaire philosophique*, he wrote: "Why does the Roman Catholic Church during Lent consider eating animals a crime, but to be served soles and salmons as a good deed? The rich papist who has fish for 500 francs on the table, is saved, but the poor who close to death eats salt meat for 4 sous, is damned."[55]

Voltaire's dilemma was not discussed by Antonin Carême. *L'art de la cuisine française au XIXeme siècle,* Carême's posthumous masterpiece of more than a thousand pages about French cuisine in the nineteenth century, has many recipes for *maigre* (lean) dishes and sauces. He was also well aware of the challenges a cook was confronted with during Lent. He wrote, "It is in the preparation of cuisine for fasting times that the science of the cook can show itself in new and dazzling dishes."[56] In the introduction, he mentioned a cook in a Catholic monastery who would put veal broth in the sauces during Lent to make them richer, something that was obviously against ecclesiastical rules. Carême's *maigre* sauces, however, have no animal ingredients, only fish and vegetables. Anything else would ruin the reputation of a cook who had worked for church dignitaries.

In the entry for *maigre* in his *Grand dictionnaire de cuisine*, Alexandre Dumas repudiated the idea that meat was not healthy and that lean dishes were preferable. He also commented on the earlier ban of eggs and milk during Lent and mentioned that the archbishop of Paris at the time had authorized those products. This, he wrote, came as a relief to poor people, who did not have the means to purchase fish, which was very expensive during Lent, and therefore had to eat meat, which put them in danger of incurring the wrath of God.[57]

14

Vegetarian Cookbooks

THE PYTHAGOREAN DIET

The production of vegetarian cookbooks has flourished at several points during the past two hundred years, often in parallel with the development of certain ideological movements and alternative lifestyles. But vegetarianism itself goes back thousands of years. In Europe, the tradition is generally acknowledged to have started with Pythagoras, the Greek philosopher who lived in the sixth century BCE and is best known today for his mathematical theorem of the right-angled triangle. In the religious society he founded, one of the many strict rules for an honorable lifestyle demanded absolute abstinence from meat; this may have been a consequence of the belief in reincarnation that certain authors of antiquity claimed Pythagoras subscribed to. Some of these authors were vegetarians themselves, such as the prolific Plutarch, who in his essay on eating flesh tried to imagine what Pythagoras must have felt: "How could his eyes endure the spectacle of the flayed and dismembered limb? How could his sense of smell endure the horrid effluvium? How, I ask, was his taste not sickened by contact with festering wounds, with the pollution of corrupted blood and juices?"[1]

Plutarch's severe words were often reproduced later, for example, in the intellectual preface to *Les dons de Comus,* one of François Marin's eighteenth-century French cookbooks. The author of the preface takes Plutarch's views seriously and discusses them with reference to current anthropological and zoological knowledge before he continues his arguments for culinary refinement.[2]

Il cuoco galante (The gallant cook), another eighteenth-century cookbook, brings up Pythagoras as well, but without mentioning Plutarch's horror story. The author was an intellectual Italian, Vincenzo Corrado. Orphaned at a young age, he worked as a page at a princely court, entered a monastery, and was then sent by the superior to study science, philosophy, and foreign languages. He became a specialist in agricultural affairs and husbandry, was appointed supervisor of kitchen and banquet arrangements at several courts, and dedicated himself to the art of cooking. One of the chapters in *Il cuoco galante,* later printed as a separate book, treated the Pythagorean diet. As an introduction to a description of different vegetable products and recipes for their preparation, Corrado wrote: "The Pythagorean diet consists of herbs, roots, flowers, fruits, seeds, and everything that grows on the earth to feed us. It is called Pythagorean because Pythagoras, according to tradition, only used these products from the earth." He added that there was no doubt that "this diet is the most natural for humans and the use of meat is harmful."[3] Corrado was influenced by Jean-Jacques Rousseau, who recommended eating lots of fruit and vegetables, but even if he was convinced of vegetarianism himself, it does not come through in the rest of his cookbook, which gives many recipes for all sorts of meat.

Some of the earliest cookbooks had recipes based on fruit and vegetable products. Platina, who was praised by Leonardo da Vinci for his vegetable dishes, used the expression *cena holitoria* for a vegetarian meal, in other words, a "garden meal," which is more descriptive than ideological. Books based exclusively on vegetarian products had a breakthrough in the seventeenth century, when botany developed into a serious natural science and orchards and vegetable gardens popped up all over Europe, often with the aim of satisfying the desires of royalty and the aristocracy for new and exclusive tastes. But most of these cookbooks were practical and did not advocate vegetarianism. There was, however, one author who combined practical recipes, medical arguments, and vegetarian propaganda: Thomas Tryon.

THE PIONEER THOMAS TRYON

Thomas Tryon wrote a great number of books and booklets on humanitarian issues and—not surprisingly—a work on Pythagoras. He was a great inspiration for Benjamin Franklin, who ate a mostly vegetarian diet.[4] An important issue for Tryon was to stop people from practicing "the depraved custom of killing and eating their Fellow Creatures," as he phrases it in the introduction to a "bill of fare" of seventy-five dishes made without meat or fish, printed in 1691 as an appendix to *Wisdom's Dictates,* a book with rules for a healthy life. Far better for the health than meat, in Tryon's opinion, were fruit and vegetables, oil, cheese, milk, and grains. One of the entries in the list reads: "Asparagus, boiled and eaten with Bread, Butter and Salt, is a most delicious Food, they afford a clean nourishment, and are friendly to the Stomach, opens Obstructions, loosens the Belly, and powerfully purges by Urine."[5]

The recipes in most of Tryon's books are more complete and detailed, but they are often intertwined with his opinions; this is the case in *The Good Housewife Made a Doctor*. Some of the recipes in this household book were picked out and collected in a little booklet, *A Pocket-Companion*. These recipes have been revised and are more practical and simpler. Take, for example, "Of Puddings": "The best way of making them is this: Take Milk and Water, Wheat-flower, and Eggs, of each a convenient quantity, and put a little Salt in; beat them well together, put this Batter into your Bag, boil it in good store of Water, your Potlid off, and over a quick, clear fire, when boil'd sufficient, take it off, butter it, and eat. Bak'd Puddings are not so good."[6]

Tryon's arguments against eating meat were numerous and various. He went back to vegetarianism in Genesis, where God offers man all herbs and fruits on the face of the earth. He referred to medical ideas from antiquity and the Middle Ages about the qualities of meat. He gave hygienic reasons for avoiding eating meat: animals have diseases, butchers are unclean, and so on.

Tryon also found something barbaric and even unaesthetic in a table set with meat from dead animals. In this, the seventeenth-century autodidact had the same opinion as his contemporary John Ray, a Cambridge-educated botanist and member of the Royal Society. Ray combined the aesthetic with the dietetic in his arguments against the consumption of meat. How much more innocent, sweet, and healthful is a table covered with plants than one heavy with all "the reeking Flesh of butcher'd and slaughter'd Animals," he wrote. He also stated that eating meat was not part of man's destiny, an opinion that many other vegetarians had pronounced before him: "Certainly Man by Nature was never made to be a Carnivorous Creature; nor is he arm'd at all for Prey and Rapin, with gag'd and pointed Teeth and crooked Claws, sharpned to rend and tear."[7] This statement was quoted with approval by another member of the Royal Society, John Evelyn, in *Acetaria*, a book with recipes for salads. Although he was not a vegetarian, Evelyn eagerly recommended that people eat more vegetables.

In the eighteenth century, several books were published with vegetable recipes, but they did not argue for vegetarian principles. Finally, in the nineteenth century, a recipe collection appeared with the expressed intention of promoting a vegetarian diet. The printer George Nicholson, who wrote books on various subjects, published *The Primeval Diet of Man: Arguments in Favour of Vegetable Food* in 1801. To facilitate the introduction of such a diet, he added recipes to the second edition of the book for the preparation of "one hundred perfectly palatable and nutritious substances, which may easily be procured at an expense much below the price of the limbs of our fellow animals."[8]

At this time, an organized form of vegetarianism started to develop. An early collective experiment was undertaken in 1809 in Manchester when members of the Bible Christian Church chose to abstain from meat and alcohol. This initiative was quickly followed by the publication of cookbooks for those following the new diet. In 1812, the first in a series of small recipe booklets appeared, and it was printed as a cookbook in 1821 with the title *Vegetarian Cookery.* The British Vegetarian Society was founded in 1847, and *A Few Recipes of Vegetarian Diet* was published in London the same year. The old name "Pythagorean diet" disappeared.

Vegetarianism was only one of many nineteenth-century movements that were demanding reforms of British society and more justice for all. There were also groups fighting for the abolition of the slave trade, expanded suffrage, temperance, the emancipation of women, new pedagogical ideas, and the protection of animals. Many of the people promoting these ideas based their arguments on statements in the Bible. Joseph Brotherton was one of the leaders of the Manchester Bible Christian Church, and his wife, Martha, had edited *Vegetarian Cookery.* He was also a well-known reformer who criticized child labor and spoke against capital punishment in the House of Commons. But other groups and individuals were also aggressive in attacking the establishment. One of these was the poet Shelley, who wrote the famous lines:

> . . . no longer now
> He slays the lamb that looks into his face,
> And horribly devours his mangled flesh . . .[9]

BACK TO NATURE

One important ideal from the last part of the eighteenth century can be summarized in the expression "return to nature." Nature was seen as the ideal for an original way of life, and there was talk of vegetarian food being the "natural diet."[10] The first vegetarian recipe collection that referred to nature was *Nature's Own Book,* by Asenath Nicholson, who, together with her husband, had established the Temperance Boarding House in New York in 1832. Part of the book is a general introduction to healthy and vegetarian cookery, and there are twenty-seven recipes. One of them is for pies, and there is a footnote saying that pies are normally prohibited because of the butter in the crust, but she gives an alternative: "Apple pies may be made simple, palatable, and healthy, by sifting coarse flour, and taking hot, mealy potatoes, and rubbing them in as you would butter; then take pearlash, and sour milk, or water, and wet it, rolling the crust if you please in fine flour; if you wish to give it a whiteness, prepare your apple without butter or spice, with sweetening, and a little oil of orange."[11]

Nicholson had a special knowledge of how to use products such as corn and rice. She was very accurate in her instructions on how to boil rice, for example, "twelve minutes only," a far more precise direction than what was common at that time. She had learned to cook rice this way when she was traveling in Ireland helping the suffering poor—like the cook Alexis Soyer had done. She noticed that the middle-class ladies who were cooking food for the poor were destroying the rice by boiling it too hard.[12] By following her method, the rice would be "whole, dry and tender; with the additional benefit of being much better for the stomach, than when reduced to a pulp in water."[13]

Nicholson makes no secret of how she had been inspired by the reformer Sylvester Graham, whose rules for the Temperance Boarding House in New York were included in the book. In the nineteenth century, many boarding houses were established that adhered to Graham's ideas and rules, which included cold showers, hard mattresses, and physical activity. Graham, who had converted to vegetarianism after being exposed to it by immigrants from Manchester Bible Christian Church, argued that the consumption of meat, alcohol, and strong spices excessively stimulated the nervous system and made the body weak and vulnerable to diseases. But he is remembered for his opposition to white bread made from sifted flour. He believed that food should remain as it was in nature, as created by God, and should not be tampered with, such as by removing the bran from the grain to make white flour. He defended the use of wholewheat flours by referencing a line from the Bible used in wedding ceremonies: "What God hath joined, let no man put asunder."

VEGETARIANISM AS IDEOLOGY

In Germany, there were few examples of books about vegetarianism before the 1860s. The inspiration came from Great Britain and the United States, and several of Graham's works were translated into German. One of the German pioneers of vegetarianism was Eduard Baltzer, who wrote the preface to *Vegetarianisches Kochbuch* (1869) and is often presented as the author of the recipes as well. He was a pastor in a free church and an advocate for democracy. In 1867, he founded the first vegetarian society in Germany, the name of which was a reflection of nature and the natural as ideal: Verein für natürliche Lebensweise (Association for a Natural Lifestyle). During the following years, there was much talk of a *Lebensreform*, the introduction of a new and more natural way of life. Another prominent German reformer, Gustav von Struve, considered vegetarianism to be part of a new worldview.[14] But this "new" lifestyle was in fact something to return to; the ideas of reform were combined with a wistful nostalgia for what was conceived of as a much more desirable past, a lost golden age. This nostalgia increased in the second half of the nineteenth century, as the food industry modernized. New machines were developed to make food production more efficient; new processes, such as pasteurization and canning, were introduced; and foodstuffs began to be adulterated with chemical additives. This pushed many people to seek out fresh and unprocessed products, preferably cultivated in their own gardens.

Cookbooks that advocated putting ideas about "natural" diets into practice appeared rather slowly in Germany, but they reached a point of explosive growth in the 1890s. Baltzer's *Vegetarianisches Kochbuch* was printed in many editions. Another short book from 1871 was continually revised until 1896, when it was expanded into a big illustrated vegetarian cookbook with more than eight hundred recipes, *Illustriertes vegetarisches Kochbuch*.[15] On the beautiful cover of this book, we find the names of two men. It is only on the interior title page that we are informed that a woman, Bertha Wachsmann, was also part of the team. She was probably responsible for creating the recipes, a typical example of the gender division of labor. Eva Barlösius, a German scholar, has observed that many vegetarian cookbooks are organized in two parts: an introduction about the principles of vegetarianism, often written by a male theoretician, and a recipe section written by the author's wife or one of his female followers.[16] One example is Ottilie Ebmeyer's more than five-hundred-page book, published in 1878, where the preface is by Dr. W. Dock, a spa physician.[17] It is difficult to document whether women also contributed to other cookbooks during the 1870s and 1880s that were published under the names of male naturopathists. At any rate, Barlösius was correct that the male "prophets" of vegetarianism floated at high intellectual altitudes with their philosophical, religious, medical, and historical reflections, while women with experience in the kitchen were expected to convert their ideas into practical cookery. Women constituted only 20 percent of the members of German vegetarian associations. In other parts of Europe, influences from England, the United States, and Germany were important for the development of vegetarian movements.[18]

THE KELLOGG HERITAGE

Sylvester Graham has had a great historical impact because many people adopted his ideas. One of them was Ellen White, one of the founders of the Seventh-day Adventist Church. The members of this movement were vegetarians from the beginning and also abstained from alcohol, tobacco, coffee, and tea. They became well known in the United States and the world, in particular because of their sanitarium in Battle Creek, Michigan, which was a model for later health spas in America. White appointed the doctor John Harvey Kellogg, who had already published books about vegetarianism, to run the sanitarium.

A problem vegetarians faced when they were promoting their diet was that not all vegetarian dishes were tasty enough to tempt people to abstain from meat. Many objected to the blandness of vegetarian cuisine in the West—as opposed to the rich and tasty vegetarian cuisine in India, for example. Western vegetarian food had too few spices and other seasonings, a fact pointed out by Mohandas Gandhi during his first visit to Europe.[19] This was, however, in accordance with many of the early theoretical works about vegetarianism. Abstinence from meat was only one aspect of a vegetarian diet; it was also important that the food not be refined or complicated, as its aim was not to increase the appetite. This was an attitude that went all the way

FIGURE 26. Cover of the 1904 edition of *Science in the Kitchen,* by Ella
Eaton Kellogg.

back to antiquity. The puritan Sylvester Graham praised the sweetness and richness
of the wholewheat bread of his childhood, baked by his mother, but he opposed the
use of seasonings such as pepper, cinnamon, ginger, and mustard and recommended modest use of eggs and dairy products.

This puritanism was practiced at the Battle Creek Sanitarium. In her cookbook
Science in the Kitchen (1893), Kellogg's wife, Ella, wrote: "The cultivation of a taste
for spices is a degradation of the sense of taste" (figure 26). She continued, stating

that "the step from gormandizing to intoxication is much shorter than most people imagine." She did allow that variation was important but wrote that it was not necessary to prepare every dish "in the most elaborate manner."[20] In spite of such statements, it is obvious that the staff at Battle Creek was focused on inventing more tempting products that were also wholesome, and two of the most famous are cornflakes and peanut butter. Peanut butter was a very successful substitute for other fats, since Seventh-day Adventists and other vegetarians considered vegetable fats in general, and especially the fat of nuts, preferable to animal fats in any form.

Ella Eaton Kellogg was probably responsible for more products than she has been credited for. She was the one at work in the kitchen, experimenting with new tastes. There were recipes for meat in the first edition of her monumental cookbook, but she dropped the pattern of a traditional cookbook over the course of the 1890s, replacing the meat chapter with a chapter on nuts in later editions. A quick glance through the fourth edition is therefore surprising, as it is filled with such words as "roast," "steak," "fricassee," "cutlets," "fillet," "ragoo"—which are normally used for meat dishes. The recipes, however, contain neither meat nor fish. They all use vegetarian substitutes made from special products developed at Battle Creek: protose, nuttose, and nuttolene. As Ella Kellogg explained it, "Protose, or vegetable meat, forms a most excellent substitute for the various flesh foods, resembling them in taste and appearance, and being composed of the same food elements."[21] It is a bit strange that she considered it valuable that the substitute tasted and looked like real meat.

These products were distributed in cans, just like ordinary canned meat, and were meant to be used like corned beef: cut in slices or mixed into various dishes. Some of the dishes have simple names, such as Protose Steak or Nuttolene Cutlets. But Kellogg also reintroduced the old term "mock," a word that had been used in classical recipes such as mock turtle soup, which was based on veal instead of turtle meat. In Kellogg's book, there are recipes for Mock Turkey, Mock Chicken Salad, and even a Mock Hamburger Steak, made this way: "Mash fine one-half pound of protose, and one-eighth pound of nuttolene. Add one large or two small eggs, and one-half granose biscuit, ground fine. Season with grated onion, sage and salt to taste. Form into small patties and bake on an oiled tin in the oven, or broil over coals. Serve with hot tomato sauce." Granose is one of several grain products developed by John Harvey Kellogg particularly for diets for the sick. Granose, granola, granuto, and avenola got their names from the Latin words for "grain" (*granum*) and "oats" (*avena*).

Mock fish dishes could also be made with these products. The book has a recipe for Protose Fish, for example: "Roll sliced protose in salted beaten egg, then in granose flakes, and bake in a moderate oven until the protose is heated through. Serve hot with tomato jelly." Coffee substitutes could be made from different grains, browned beans, and molasses, the basis for the so-called Caramel Coffee.[22]

THE BATTLE FOR RAW FOOD

The modern vegetarian movement started in the early 1800s, but it was only in the last decades of that century that the real breakthrough took place. The rapid expansion of vegetarianism can be documented by two quotations from vegetarian cookbooks. In 1866, John Smith, in the preface to his *Vegetable Cookery*, wrote, "Cookery books exist in abundance; but they relate almost exclusively to the preparation of dishes from animal food." In 1903, the preface to the fifteenth edition of *Vegetarianisches Kochbuch* proudly stated, "The vegetarian cookbook literature is rapidly multiplying."[23]

The thirty-seven years between these two books saw more organization, more cookbooks, new alternative products, and novel and more far-reaching ideas. One of these ideas led to the battle for raw food, which was very strong around 1900. In the search for the best possible "natural" diet, as opposed to an industrial diet, the belief emerged that *any* preparation involving heat, such as boiling or frying, reduced the nutritional value of foodstuffs. This was a sharp break with what cookbooks held to be the generally accepted view of correct cooking. In 1896, the American Fannie Farmer, author of *The Boston Cooking-School Cook Book*, wrote that vegetables ought to be "cooked until soft," and the same attitude is found in Europe, particularly in the northern part of the continent.[24] But Sylvester Graham had already suggested that man ought to eat raw food, as Adam and Eve had done before they were driven out of Eden. In his book *Vital Food* (1892), the English philanthropist and vegetarian Arnold Hills recommended a raw diet because, in his opinion, raw fruits and vegetables had certain vital qualities.[25] In the 1890s, the Swiss physician Maximilian Bircher-Benner—the inventor of the cereal dish muesli—claimed that his experience and experiments with patients proved that a raw diet was best. He wrote several books about his own recovery from jaundice by eating raw food, and these books were later translated into other European languages. Typical of the limited roles women had in the vegetarian movement, two of his sisters published cookbooks that put Bircher-Benner's principles into practice.[26]

A vegetarian who gradually adopted a raw diet as her basic principle was the eccentric Russian Natalia Nordman, who was the daughter of a Swedish admiral and the common-law partner of the artist Ilya Repin. However, her 1911 cookbook, *Povarennaia kniga dlia golodaiushchikh* (Cookbook for the hungry), was not the first vegetarian cookbook published in Russian. Alongside and perhaps influenced by Lev Tolstoy's works on the subject, certain vegetarian recipe collections had been published, and in the 1901 edition of Molokhovets's classic cookbook, dishes suitable for vegetarians were marked with a star. Molokhovets also had a chapter called "The Vegetarian Table," with fifty-seven recipes and commentaries about which foodstuffs vegetarians abstained from.[27]

Another vegetarian cookbook had been published two years before Nordman's, and Nordman picked up some of the recipes from it. The title of this book was *Ja nikogo ne em* (I eat nobody), and the author was given as Vegetarianka, the pseudonym of O. K. Zelenkova. Her preface is preceded by a scholarly introduction by a medical doctor, A. P. Zelenkov, who may have been her husband or a relative.[28]

According to the food historian Darra Goldstein, Nordman started by following a traditional vegetarian diet but gradually became a strict vegan.[29] She was also eager to convert all her guests, among them prominent writers, such as Vladimir Mayakovsky and Maxim Gorky. She served only vegetarian dishes, but contrary to how most vegetarians entertained at the time, she used spices in her food and served wine, which she believed gave extra power to the body. It is evident from guests' descriptions of her meals that the food was delicious. But as Nordman became more extreme, she suggested the use of food waste, such as potato peels and apple skins, and she used grass and hay as ingredients. A recipe for hay soup calls for hay, onion, bay leaves, and whole pepper. But her book also contains more conventional dishes, such as chestnut purée with Jerusalem artichokes and stewed green peppers with tomatoes, onion, and olive oil.

Today, vegetarian cookbooks are found everywhere and in many variations, but vegetarianism is still a minority movement, and one that is often—just as in the past—linked to alternative movements that promote organic food and criticize industrial food production.

15

Jewish Cookbooks

"The laws do not only concern the religion and social life of the Jews," states the preface in a Jewish cookbook published in Germany in the 1930s, "but have shaped all facets of life in the Jewish home."[1] An important part of Jewish religious laws consists of diet prescriptions. Best known among these laws is the pork taboo, which, according to archeologists, goes back to ancient Israel. There have been many discussions about the background and origin of this taboo, and hygienic, ecological, and symbolic explanations have been proposed. The Jews themselves have discussed this proscription. Take, for example, *Kochbuch für die jüdische Küche* (Cookbook for the Jewish kitchen), written by teachers in two German domestic science schools and published in 1926 by the League of Jewish Women (Jüdischer Frauenbund). The book concludes that nobody knows the reason for the distinction between animals that Jews are forbidden to eat and animals that they are permitted to eat. It states that no attempt to find the reason has led to a satisfying result. The preface refers to Moses Maimonides, one of the learned Jews from the Middle Ages, who tried to explain biblical laws with rational arguments. He reasoned that eating unclean animals was forbidden because they were bad for your health, particularly the pig, which lived in dirty conditions and ate disgusting food. But the main point made in the 1926 cookbook is that there is no need to know the reason for the dietary laws; they are an obligation purely because they are mandated by God.[2]

God's commandments are described in the Torah. Through the five books, however, there is a development in the dietary rules. The first order from God was that man could eat all fruits and vegetables growing on the earth—in other words, a vegetarian diet. But after the flood, God said to Noah: "Every moving thing that is alive shall be food for you; I give all to you, as I gave the green plant. Only you shall not eat flesh with its life, that is, its blood."[3] The third step in the development of the kosher diet was the elaboration of a detailed legal system—*kashrut*—in the two final books of the Torah. Here, the basic dietary rules are laid down. Mammals can be eaten if they chew their cud (ruminate) and have cloven hooves; consequently, camel, hare, and pig are among the forbidden animals. Fish can be eaten if they have fins and scales; thus, shellfish are not kosher. Apart from a special type of locust, all insects are forbidden. It is therefore not only for hygienic reasons that Marie Kauders instructed readers of her book, the first ever cookbook written for Jews in Bohemia: "Cleansing of vegetables and pulses, as well as of fruits, is of greatest importance, because they often contain worms and small insects or their eggs."[4]

COOKBOOKS WITH A DOUBLE FUNCTION

The function of Jewish cookbooks was not only to give recipes for tasty and healthy dishes but also to provide practical instructions for how to follow religious dietary prescriptions. The oldest printed Jewish cookbook was written by a cook at the court of the Grand Duke of Baden and published in 1815. No known copy of the book exists, but its long title gives an indication of its contents: *Kochbuch f. Israeliten, oder praktische Anweisung, wie man nach den jüdischen Religionsgründen alle Gattungen der feinsten Speisen kauscher bereitet* (Cookbook for Jews, or practical instruction in how to prepare all sorts of fine food in a kosher way after the Jewish religion).[5] About twelve thousand Jews lived in Baden at that time, and they were gradually being granted more civil rights, which gave them the possibility to have a more comfortable lifestyle and a chance to prepare fancy dishes.

The next known book, by Rahel Aschmann,[6] was published in 1835 in Saxony, which was another region where reforms improved living conditions for Jews in the nineteenth century. But at the time, very few Jews lived in this kingdom, and so the book was probably sold in other German states and possibly at the important market fair in Leipzig, where it was printed. According to the title page, Aschmann had many years of culinary experience, but nothing else is known about her. Leafing through the book, it is easy to see that there is a big difference between this and other German cookbooks of the period. There are no recipes for pork or crayfish. It is quite clear that the dishes are kosher, but there is no discussion of the characteristics of the Jewish diet. The book obviously takes for granted that the readers are familiar with the dietary rules—this is, which products are forbidden to eat and which products are permitted to eat at the same meal. There is no specific mention of this last point in the Torah, but rules about it are given in commentaries by learned rabbis.[7] A pronouncement in the Torah, "You shall not boil a kid in its mother's milk,"[8] has been interpreted as a ban against eating milk products and meat at the same meal. In the kitchen, this means that ingredients may need to be replaced depending on what else was on the menu. There is an example of this in a recipe for celery soup in Aschmann's book. The recipe starts like this: "A small piece of butter is heated in a casserole, a spoon of flour is added and when it is yellow, add a celery root cut in small dices, let it stew a quarter of an hour and then pour as much hot water as is necessary to get a soup. As soon as the celery is tender, add some spoonfuls of cream, white sugar and mace."[9] So far, it is a recipe with dairy products but without any trace of meat. Following the recipe, however, is an *Anmerkung*—a commentary—in which Aschmann notes that if the soup is to be served in a meal also consisting of meat dishes, goose fat should take the place of the butter and two egg yolks should be used instead of the cream. This way, the dairy products are eliminated, and the meal is kosher.

Apart from the two restrictions mentioned above, there are also rules concerning the preparation of food for the Sabbath, since no work is permitted from sunset on Friday until sunset on Saturday. This has led to one of the most characteristic Jewish dishes, cholent (or *hamin*), a casserole prepared before sunset on Friday and simmered over low heat all night, so it is ready for the Sabbath meal the next day. Recipes for special Sabbath dishes like this are found in Jewish cookbooks, but some books also give advice on how to prepare the whole Sabbath meal. One book even includes specific Bible passages to pronounce at the different stages of the preparation, and they are written in Hebrew, a feature that immediately distinguishes the book from other cookbooks.[10]

REFORM AND ORTHODOXY

Most Jewish cookbooks in the nineteenth century were in German, although they were printed not only in German cities but also in Prague, Budapest, and Brno. The most popular—Rebekka Wolf's *Kochbuch für Israelitische Frauen* (Cookbook for Jewish women)—was translated into Dutch and Polish. It was published in fourteen editions, the last one in 1933, the year Hitler came to power. The first edition was printed in 1853, and Wolf emphasized in her preface that the book was for young girls who had not learned the religious diet rules in their homes.[11] The book would provide them with an introduction to religiously correct household management.

Wolf wrote that religious practice was being neglected in many Jewish homes, which is probably significant for this period. In England at about the same time, the non-Jewish author Eliza Acton included some Jewish recipes in the 1855 edition of her cookbook. She gave substitutes for milk and butter but added in a commentary, "We are credibly informed that the restrictions of which we have spoken are not at the present day very rigidly observed by the main body of Jews in this country, though they are so by those who are denominated strict."[12] It is quite clear that not all Jews followed the dietary rules.

Judaism has a long history, and many schools and movements have developed within the religion with different conceptions of tradition. In the nineteenth century, when the first Jewish cookbooks were published, many Jews were consciously or unconsciously dropping a systematic *kashrut* practice. This had to do partly with demography; in parts of Europe, Jews moved from the countryside to the cities, as other groups did. Although they often settled together in the same neighborhoods, they lost the old community of the shtetl, something Franz Kafka, who was from one such village, commented on in *Brief an den Vater* (*Letter to His Father*).[13] In Prague, the old Jewish graveyard gives witness to the fact that the city was a center for learned rabbis and one of the biggest Jewish urban societies in Europe in the seventeenth and eighteenth centuries. There was a tendency within the community to move away from traditional Jewish life at that time. When Kafka was growing up, there was a Jewish cooking school in Prague, and one of the teachers, Maria Kanders, wrote several books about Jewish cooking. In one of them, she addresses herself especially to young women who are preparing themselves for matrimony and a "religious household management." These women "must not let themselves be misguided by modern education, which sometimes causes a failed enlightenment [*Aufklärung*] in religious questions."[14] The enlightenment the author refers to is in all probability the changes in religious practice advocated by Reform Judaism (later also known as Liberal or Progressive Judaism). Influenced by the ideas and the philosophy of the Age of Enlightenment, a reformed version of Judaism, Haskalah, was founded in the late eighteenth century with the aim of bringing the religion more into harmony with Western values and modern thinking without renouncing the Jewish community. Unlike Orthodox Jews, Reform Jews interpreted the Torah through the eyes of modern textual criticism, just as many Christian theologians were doing with the Bible at that time. They accepted certain eternal truths in the Torah but also believed that many of the laws and habits described belonged to a bygone era and should be adapted to every new generation. Some Reform Jews probably saw the changes as a way of keeping Jews in the religious community, which many were leaving. There were Jews who married non-Jews, Jews who converted to Christianity, and Jews who became less orthodox as a result of a general secularization of society.

These developments may explain the emergence of cookbooks with kosher food in the nineteenth century, not only on the continent but also in Britain. When the first cookbook for English Jews—*The Jewish Manual*—was published, in 1846, around thirty-five thousand Jews lived in England; more than a third of them were settled in London, and most of these in the East End.[15] Those who succeeded economically moved west, and some of them even bought country houses and adopted an aristocratic lifestyle. In the process, some Jews lost contact with their religious community, but many of them wanted to maintain their Jewish identity. In 1842, the West London Synagogue of British Jews was inaugurated. Behind this initiative were Jewish men who were among the London elite. They introduced several of the reforms that were already being practiced in Germany. Among these were modifications to religious services, which were often criticized for elements of disorder and lack of proper decorum. The aim of the Anglo-Jewish elite was to integrate into British society without having to renounce their faith. "Anglicization and acceptance" were their dominant concerns.[16] Even if they were legally close to full emancipation and formal equality with other British citizens, they were still victims of prejudice. And that this was based not only on religion but also on race was proved by the racist caricatures of the politician Benjamin Disraeli, a former Jew who had converted to Anglicanism but enjoyed the savoir vivre on display at dinners offered by Rothschilds and Montefiores.[17]

MONTEFIORE AND ENGLAND

The struggle for acceptance within the British elite may have been one of the motivating forces behind *The Jewish Manual*. The author—"a lady," according to the title page—was Judith Montefiore, who was married to the prominent financier Moses Montefiore. Judith and Moses Montefiore had not always been strict in their adherence to *kashrut*. It was not so easy to keep kosher in England when they were guests of non-Jews or had to eat at hotels and inns while traveling. After a visit to Palestine in 1827, however, Moses adopted a stricter attitude toward Jewish dietary laws.[18] He had initially supported the idea of certain liturgical reforms, but he became one of the most conservative Jews of his time, confronting several leading reformers.[19] In other words, he put more value on upholding the dietary rules than on fighting for civil rights, a struggle that was so important to many other Jews. He was also wealthy enough to have his own slaughterer (*shohet*) accompany him on trips. He even built his own synagogue at his estate in Ramsgate, on the coast of the English Channel, where he also erected a mausoleum for his wife.

Judith Montefiore had a double aim with her book. She opened her preface by stating that although there were numerous cookbooks, there were "none which afford the slightest insight to the Cookery of the Hebrew Kitchen." In her opinion, these cookbooks were completely valueless to the Jewish housekeeper, not only because they had no typical Jewish dishes but also because they had ingredients and combinations of ingredients prohibited by Jewish dietary laws. Her cookbook, she wrote, would therefore include English and French dishes as well as the best recipes "hitherto bequeathed only by memory or manuscript, from one generation to another of the Jewish nation."[20]

But in addition to providing instruction for young Jewish housewives, she wanted to enrich British cuisine in general. She believed that her original dishes might be acceptable to ladies "who are not of the Hebrew persuasion" and her rare and exquisite compositions delicious enough to merit "the unqualified approbation of the most fastidious epicures."[21] This seems to be a typical attitude among Jewish cookbook writers in several countries. Rebekka Wolf pointed out that her book was not only for those who wanted to maintain a kosher household but also for anybody who wanted to prepare nourishing, healthy home cooking (*Hausmannskost*) in an economical way.[22] A cookbook published in Copenhagen in 1915 was "written for a Jewish household, but may also be used in all others." The author was convinced that if a family tried the recipes, "it will not be the last time the old, Jewish dishes are served."[23] These examples indicate that there was no intention of isolation behind the books; on the contrary, the authors wanted Jewish food traditions to be recognized as valuable not only from a religious point of view but also from a culinary one. For Judith Montefiore, this was part of a greater scheme. She wanted, according to the scholar Sandra Sherman, to convince non-Jews in Britain that Jews, while preserving a distinct religious tradition, conformed "to standards of British taste." This makes *The Jewish Manual* in many ways a political book.[24]

One important element of Montefiore's culinary strategy was finding kosher substitutes for English ingredients. There were two particular challenges that stood out in British traditional cooking: sauces were often made with butter and cream, and many dishes called for bacon and lard. Serving sauces containing butter and cream with meat dishes is not kosher, so Montefiore often made sauces with eggs instead, but she did not talk about *kashrut*. She gave a recipe for a celery sauce made with three egg yolks, but she ended the recipe with the words: "Cream, instead of eggs, is used in English kitchens." She added an egg yolk to a mushroom sauce but remarked that "English cooks add cream to this sauce." She also gave a recipe for something she called "egg sauce," a white sauce for white meat. Her comment had nothing to do with *kashrut* but with quality: "This sauce will be found excellent, if not superior, in many cases where English cooks use melted butter."[25]

Montefiore was more specific when she discussed the sauces velouté and béchamel. They were so frequently mentioned in English cookery, she wrote, that she would give recipes for them, "although they are not appropriate for the Jewish kitchen."[26] But after the recipes, she gave "an excellent substitute for these sauces" for Jewish kitchens. In other words, she first gave two recipes for sauces that were not kosher and then showed how they could be made kosher.

Lard was replaced in Montefiore's book with suet, but again, she gave no excuse for this choice; in her opinion, suet was a better alternative from a culinary point of view. After giving an explanation of how to prepare it, she wrote that it was a very useful product "and will be found, if adopted in English kitchens, to answer the purpose of lard and is far more delicate and wholesome."[27]

One ingredient Montefiore referred to often and used in many dishes was "chorissa," which she defined in the cookbook's short glossary as "a sausage peculiar to the Jewish kitchen, of delicate and piquante flavour" and praised as the "most refined and savoury of all sausages."[28] She noted that it was made from beef, but she gave no recipe; readers would have to buy the sausage from Jewish butchers. This kind of sausage has its root in Iberian cuisine, and it is an example of how Sephardic Jews from Spain and Portugal brought with them to Britain traditions they had adapted to *kashrut*. The original Spanish *chorizo* and Portuguese *chouriço* are based on pork.

After *The Jewish Manual,* more Jewish cookbooks were published in English, and some of them stated that they were built on Orthodox principles. If we look at the early twentieth-century cookbook *The Little Book of Jewish Cookery,*[29] we can clearly see the differences from Montefiore's work. There is first of all a social difference. While Montefiore addressed herself to the wealthy and hoped to raise the reputation of Jewish cookery among the British elite, *The Little Book* is addressed to families without housekeepers or servants. There is information about how much a dish will cost, a typical feature at that time in cookbooks for a broader (or more working-class) market. There is also a cultural difference, since *The Little Book* contains mostly Ashkenazi dishes. Montefiore's book offers a rich variety of Sephardic dishes—Moses belonged to a Sephardic family from Italy—in addition to specialties from her own family, which had Dutch Ashkenazi roots. Finally, *The Little Book* differs by placing a stronger emphasis on Orthodox diet rules and how they should be followed, which was probably a reflection of the influx of Jews from Eastern Europe, where there had been no strong Reform movement.

Many of the Jews who had the ambition of integrating into British society had been critical of the use of Jewish dress and other visible marks of their religion. As the poet and Reform Russian Jew Judah Leib Gordon phrased it, one should be "a person outside of the home and a Jew in one's home."[30] But starting in the 1880s, a great many Eastern European Jews arrived in London; many of them were poor, and others were small textile merchants. Of the almost 145,000 Jews in London around 1900, 120,000 lived in the East End, and they were very visible, a fact criticized by *The Jewish Chronicle,* a weekly newspaper representing the old elite. The journal pointed out that Jews in Whitechapel drew attention by "their peculiarities of dress, of language, of manner," attention that would keep alive and strengthen "the vulgar prejudices of which they were the objects."[31]

COOKBOOKS IN YIDDISH

Most Eastern European Jews had grown up with Yiddish as their mother tongue, a language built on medieval German but with elements of Hebrew and Aramaic as well as Slavic and Romance languages. Most German Jews dropped Yiddish in the eighteenth century and spoke German, as recommended by Moses Mendelsohn, an Enlightenment leader who considered Yiddish jargon and thought that adopting German would facilitate integration. But in Central and Eastern Europe, Jews continued to use Yiddish, or more correctly, Yiddish dialects. A serious effort to standardize grammar and vocabulary did not come until the 1930s, but the first Yiddish novels, periodicals, and cookbooks entered the market in the middle of the nineteenth century.

Handwritten cookbooks in Yiddish were without doubt circulating in the nine-teenth century, and perhaps even earlier. A few have survived from the Czech area, but the first printed book was published in Vienna and Pest in 1854. There is unfor-tunately no known copy of this book, but we know from the title that its aim was to give advice about *kashrut,* including how to prepare the meat correctly.[32]

The next Yiddish book was published in 1896 in Vilnius, which was then part of the Russian Empire; a second edition was published in 1898 in New York.[33] Accord-ing to its title page and preface, the book was written for young housewives and for cooks. The author wrote that housewives—not only inexperienced young women but also housewives with many years of experience—have felt the need for instruc-tion in kitchen work. The title page promised that the book would offer readers recipes for all kinds of food as well as "special Jewish dishes, for Sabbath, the Fes-tivals and Pesach." There are both cheap dishes and dishes fit for the kitchens of the wealthy. The book has 651 recipes that originally appeared in earlier cookbooks in many languages. As demonstrated by Barbara Kirshenblatt-Gimblett, an Ameri-can scholar, most of them come from Rebekka Wolf's book.[34] The author, Oyzer Bloshteyn (also known as Auser Blaustein), was a prolific writer, who had pub-lished novels, witty sketches, a Russian grammar for Jews, and several translations.

The New York edition initiated the publication of a great number of Yiddish cookbooks in the United States, a response to demographic changes in the coun-try. Between 1870 and 1914, about two million Jews arrived in the United States, most of them from Eastern European villages and urban neighborhoods where Yiddish was spoken, even if it was not accepted by the authorities, who demanded the use of the official languages. These immigrants left their mark on New York: in 1914, daily newspapers in Yiddish were printed in half a million copies. Many Yid-dish cookbooks, both general family cookbooks and specialized cookbooks for vegetarians, were also published there. But in Cincinnati and Minneapolis, com-panies within the food industry published books with recipes to be made with their own products. There were producers of flour for matzo and a special oil clas-sified as "pareve," a term from *kashrut* indicating a product made without meat or milk and consequently suitable for meat and dairy dishes. These commercial books were normally printed with both English and Yiddish text. In the 1930s, the number of Yiddish-speaking Americans peaked, but two daily Yiddish newspa-pers continued until the 1970s—when Isaac *Bashevis* Singer was awarded the Nobel Prize in Literature for his books in Yiddish.[35]

NONKOSHER JEWISH COOKBOOKS
IN THE UNITED STATES

The first Jewish cookbook in the United States was not in Yiddish but in English. *Jewish Cookery Book,* published in 1871, was written by Esther Levy, who had probably emigrated from England but had become well established and integrated in her new country.[36] The book has German and English dishes, like sauerkraut and Yorkshire pudding, and some American specialties, such as hominy fritters, okra soup, and succotash. But there are also Jewish dishes, some of them for special occasions: grimslechs and matzo fritters for Pesach, a special pudding for Purim, and a soup for Tisha B'Av. One of the dishes is boiled rice with sausage, probably a veal sausage that Levy gives a recipe for, but it has the curious name "wosht." This must be derived from the German word for sausage, *Wurst,* and is a philological (but not culinary) parallel to Montefiore's *chorissa.*

Levy emphasized religious obligations and gave thorough and detailed instructions about how to clean foodstuffs before cooking. She was eager to instill the kosher rules in young girls preparing for matrimony and a life as housewives. She did not seem completely satisfied with culinary preparations common among certain Jews: "Some have, from ignorance, been led to believe that a repast, to be sumptuous, must unavoidably admit of forbidden food."[37] This can only be interpreted as a thinly veiled criticism of Reform Jews, who had a strong position in the United States in the last part of the nineteenth century, something clearly demonstrated in the cookbooks following Levy's. The scholar Barbara Kirshenblatt-Gimblett notes, "Most [Jewish] cookbooks published in America before World War I were not kosher."[38] In *Aunt Babette's Cook Book* (1889), nothing in the preface points to Jewish practice.[39] A closer look reveals that there are recipes for lobster, crab, shrimp, oysters, a ham sandwich, beans cooked with salt pork, and different rabbit dishes. But this is not all: Aunt Babette uses butter when cooking rabbit—in other words, she mixes meat with a dairy product. According to the Orthodox view, this is nonkosher: *treyf* in Yiddish (*trefah* in Hebrew). But this was not the way Aunt Babette saw it. Her real name was Bertha Kramer, and she was a wealthy Jewish housewife in Chicago. She claimed that "nothing is Trefa that is healthy and clean," a typical Reform point of view.[40] The Bloch company, which published the book, represented the moderate wing of the Reform movement, and the publisher's sister was married to the leading rabbi within the movement. Kramer does not permit everything, however; she makes it clear that the "lard" called for in one of the recipes is cottonseed lard, which is made from cottonseed oil and not from pork. The only part of the book that indicates a Jewish audience is the description of Seder, the Pesach meal.[41]

Kramer's book was a success, and *The Settlement Cook Book* (1901) was an even greater one, with 1.5 to 2 million copies printed.[42] *The Settlement Cook Book* represents a genre that became very important in the United States: fundraiser cookbooks published to bring in money for charity. The book was edited by a woman from the German-Jewish elite with Reform views. There were many such nonkosher books in this period, but when more Orthodox immigrants started to arrive around 1900, new books that observed the dietary laws appeared on the market. At the same time, many Reform Jews adopted a more positive attitude to the old culi-nary traditions.

EUROPE IN PEACE AND WAR

While Jewish cookbooks flourished in the United States, relatively few Jewish cookbooks were published in Europe. In the Netherlands, where the Jewish popu-lation passed one hundred thousand before the end of the nineteenth century, a couple of books with kosher recipes were printed during the fifty years before the German invasion in 1940, notably one by Sara Vos, printed in seven editions between 1894 and 1926.[43] In 1932, the year after the establishment of the Union for Liberal-Religious Jews in the Netherlands,[44] a book was published in Amsterdam with the title *Geillustreerd ritueel kookboek* (Illustrated ritual cookbook) contain-ing recipes approved by the Chief Rabbi of Holland.[45]

In Italy, the Jewish population was less than fifty thousand in 1938, the year of Mussolini's *Manifesto della Razza* and the introduction of anti-Semitic racial laws. To judge from a 1931 cookbook with the beautiful title *Poesia nascosta* (Hidden poetry) and the subtitle *Seicento ricette di cucina ebraica in Italia* (Six hundred recipes from the Jewish cuisine in Italy),"[46] there had been a tendency among Jews in Italy not to observe *kashrut*. The Padua section of the Association of Jewish Ital-ian Women had collected traditional recipes from all over Italy, and the book gave menus for all the religious festivals. In the preface, Lucia Levi writes about the positive nostalgic memories many have of old Jewish dishes, but she states that the rules are "known and practiced by only a few families."

In Germany, many new editions of old Jewish books were published until 1933, when Hitler and the Nazi regime started a program of systematic discrimination, prosecution, and extermination of Jews. Only one Jewish cookbook was published during the Nazi years, first in 1935 and then in 1937: the revised version of *Kochbuch für die jüdische Küche,* originally printed in 1926 by the League of Jewish Women.

In the 1920s, it was obvious that not all Jews in Germany followed religious dietary rules. During the Weimar years, many Jews belonged to modern avant-garde artistic circles that were critical of authorities and traditions. The 1926 cook-book acknowledged that many Jews had long felt that the dietary laws were strange and even disgraceful, and it claimed that during the previous generation, many Jews dropped or even opposed them. The book argued that the Jewish religion had been stigmatized as a "kitchen religion."[47] The League of Jewish Women wanted to reverse this development and therefore provided detailed information in the cook-book explaining *kashrut* and discussing the positive aspects of the rules.

In the revised editions of 1935 and 1937, such information was even more impor-tant in the struggle for Jewish identity. These editions were published by Philo Verlag, a German-Jewish company printing books to oppose the anti-Semitic movement during the Weimar years. After Hitler's seizure of power in 1933, the publishers chose a lower profile and released books intended to strengthen knowledge about Jewish traditions. The 1935 and 1937 editions gave accurate descriptions of how to prepare for Sabbath and Pesach, but they also gave recipes for many special Jewish dishes (*Jüdische Spezialgerichte*) and even explained the origin of the dishes and their symbolic meanings.[48]

One of the important tasks for the League of Jewish Women in those years was to help German Jews who wanted to immigrate to the British Mandate of Palestine. This work was a consequence of the Haavara Agreement, which was signed by representatives of the Zionist movement and the Nazi government in August 1933. The agreement allowed Jews leaving for Palestine to bring more of their assets with them than Jews leaving for other destinations. The Nazis saw this as a means of getting the Jews out of Europe, and more than fifty thousand Jews moved to Palestine between 1933 and 1939.[49] Some of them may have brought the League of Jewish Women's cookbook, which had a special chapter of *Palästina-Rezepte,* or Palestinian recipes, which had been created at the Hadassah Medical Organization in Jerusalem and at the women's agricultural college in Nahalal. The recipes showed how to cook and prepare local products, such as tomatoes, red peppers, and above all eggplant. It also gives helpful hints, such as a warning about how difficult it is to store foodstuffs because of the climate.

In 1936, the first Jewish cookbook in Palestine, *Wie kocht man in Erez-Israel?* (How to cook in Palestine?), was published in Tel Aviv. The author, Erna Meyer, was a specialist on kitchen machines and gave information on the use of primus stoves. The book was originally written in German and was intended for Central European Jews, but it had parallel texts in English and Hebrew.

A Jewish cookbook of a very different kind was written in the early 1940s in Theresienstadt, the German name of the Czech town Terezin, where the Nazis built a prison camp that they showed to Red Cross visitors. That didn't mean the conditions were particularly good, however, and many prisoners perished of hunger and malnourishment. Those who managed best were strong women who tried to overcome their hunger by talking about dishes they had grown up with and had cooked hundreds or thousands of times. As the scholar Janet Theophano put it, "food, memories of it, missing it, craving it, dreaming of it, in short the obsession with food colours all the Theresienstadt memoirs."[50] Recipes were scratched down on whatever small scraps of paper were available and bound into a "book" by the art historian Mina Pachter, who died from starvation at Theresienstadt in 1944. The book survived and reached her daughter, who later helped to edit an English translation of it.[51] The recipes were written in German and Czech "in an informal style that is reminiscent of a diary or a conversation," observed Kathleen German, who has discussed the recipes as markers of identity, reminders of relationships, and connection to community through ritual.[52]

Jewish cookbooks from the late twentieth century and the beginning of the twenty-first are—apart from the fact that the recipes follow kosher rules—not very different from other cookbooks. They are typical of the general development within the cookbook genre: they are professionally edited, elegantly produced, and show an increasing interest in history, culture, roots, and identity.[53]

One interesting question may be raised: Do all these Jewish cookbooks published through the centuries and in different countries represent a particular Jewish cuisine? The Jewish cookbook writer Claudia Roden, who was raised in Egypt and went on to become a TV cook in Britain, pointed out that Jews have been marked by the cuisine in all the countries they have lived in and "never developed a cuisine of their own except for a few traditional holiday favourites." Instead, she writes, "it is the limitations necessary for the observance of the laws of Kashrut" that have "stamped the food with Jewishness."[54]

16

Cookbooks and Aspects
of Nationalism

To what degree have recipes and cookbooks been considered expressions of national identity and consciousness? "National dish" and "national cuisine" are popular concepts today, but what is the history behind them? There are without any doubt dishes in certain nations or regions that have a documented history—the language of the names of some dishes, for example, indicate their geographical origins: sauerkraut, paella, pizza, bouillabaisse, borscht, and haggis. Many dishes have names that refer to countries and regions, but as demonstrated in chapter 6, many of these names are a result of chance or misunderstanding and do not represent a long tradition or a particular tradition in the area. There are also, as several food historians have pointed out, examples of "cultural constructions" of dishes, an expression introduced by scholars from various fields since the 1980s in a critical evaluation of "national traditions." Perhaps it is possible to talk about an "imagined culinary community" in the way Benedict Anderson described an "imagined political community."[1] And finally, there is a long history of stereotypes, particularly in the characterization of dishes from areas other than one's own. In a recipe for *maccheroni col pangrattato,* Pellegrino Artusi quoted Alexandre Dumas, who said that the English live on nothing but roast beef and pudding; the Dutch on oven-baked meat, potatoes, and cheese; the Germans on sauerkraut and bacon; the Spanish on chickpeas, chocolate, and rancid lard; and the Italians on *maccheroni.*[2]

NATIONAL DISHES

One problem with the term "national" is that it can be interpreted in at least two different ways, exemplified by the definitions of the word in the *Oxford English*

Dictionary. The first meaning is "Of or belonging to a (or the) nation; affecting, or shared by, the nation as a whole." The second is "Peculiar to the people of a particular country, characteristic or distinctive of a nation."[3] But there is of course a great difference between those dishes that *belong to* or are *shared by* a nation (but may also belong to and be shared by other nations) and those that are *peculiar, characteristic,* and *distinctive* of a nation.

This chapter will not go into the broader and deeper discussions of national identity and national tradition that fill volumes of modern works, nor will it give a general analysis of food history according to such ideas. The focus is on how the terms "national" and "regional" are to be understood in cookbooks that use or allude to them.

Early on, cookbooks documented an awareness of different culinary traditions. Take, for example, the well-traveled court cook Marx Rumpolt's cookbook from 1581. In a recipe for stuffed sheep's stomach, he noted that it was possible to add Parmesan cheese, a method many Germans, according to him, had learned when traveling in Italy. But he added a commentary expressing a general judgment: "Every country has its own uses, ways of doing things, and its own characteristics [*Eigenschaft*]."[4]

Rumpolt's remark can be seen as typical of the situation in the late Renaissance: "By the sixteenth century the various European peoples were increasingly conscious of national identities and differences."[5] "Difference" was an important word in this process. Anthony D. Smith, a prominent historian of nationalism, has pointed out that "members [of a particular group] dress and eat in similar ways and speak the same language; in all these respects they differ from non-members, who dress, eat and speak in different ways."[6] Alberto Capatti and Massimo Montanari, two Italian food historians, explained that identity, which has to do with belonging, "is also (and perhaps above all) defined as *difference,* that is, difference in relation to others."[7] This corresponds to the *Oxford English Dictionary*'s second definition of "national."

The awareness of differences between cultures is also documented by what happened as culinary recipes were diffused. When traditions crossed frontiers and entered new areas, they were absorbed by other cultures in an exchange of ideas about how to select, combine, and prepare different ingredients. There are numerous examples of consciousness of such differences in the culinary field. In chapter 4, we saw that an early seventeenth-century Italian cookbook was revised when it was published in Brussels: the original recipes were adapted to local conditions, mainly by substituting ingredients that were more easily available in Flanders. A similar adaptation was made to a late eighteenth-century English cookbook when it was published in Denmark: not only was it translated, but many Danish ingredients, particularly vegetables, were added to the recipes.[8]

These examples illustrate differences in available products, but many changes also had to do with differences of taste. A Swedish classic from the nineteenth century claimed that many of the foreign dishes that had been introduced into the country's cookbooks "do not appeal to Swedish taste."[9] In the United States, the author of *American Cookery* (1796) rejected garlic in cooking, even if it was "used by the French."[10] Sometimes the commentaries had a polemical tone, as when Pellegrino Artusi criticized the English method of boiling vegetables without spices by stating that the people of southern Europe desired more exciting flavors.[11] Whatever the reason, that the need for such adaptations was broadly acknowledged is proved by the many book titles referring to adapting foreign cuisine to English homes and American kitchens.[12]

But there is still a long way to go from an acknowledgement of culinary differences to a consciousness of national identity through national dishes and national cuisine. This type of identity had a real breakthrough only with the nationalism of the nineteenth century. In the final years of the eighteenth century, Goethe described the French pot-au-feu as a "landsittliche Kochvorbereitung," which can be translated as "national dish."[13] In 1810, a Danish scientist mentioned "Our national dish of sheep's milk and apple pudding," and in 1850, the *Illustrated London News* defined plum pudding as a "national symbol."[14]

One of the first cookbook authors to discuss the concept was Christian Isobel Johnstone, a Scottish novelist. Her cookbook—published under the pseudonym Margaret Dods—has a chapter titled "Scotch National Dishes" and another called "Miscellaneous National Dishes." She stated, "It has been remarked, that every country is celebrated for some culinary preparation, and that all national dishes are good." Continuing, she wrote, "The Spanish *olio,* the Italian *macaroni,* the French *ragoût,* the Turkish *pillau,* and, though last not least, in our good love, the *Scotch haggis,* differing essentially as they do, are, nevertheless, all equally good after their kind." Johnstone had such a good knowledge of cooking that she was able to draw comparisons and point out differences between mulligatawny and a similar Scottish dish. She consequently put one mulligatawny dish in the chapter with national dishes and another one in the general chapter about soups. She did not use the expression "national cuisine," but she indicated a similar idea with the chapter title "French Cookery."[15] Elisa Acton used a similar term in her 1845 cookbook, which has a chapter called "Foreign and Jewish Cookery." But Acton did not use the term "national dish"; she referred instead to "foreign receipts." For example, she called *stufato* a "Neapolitan receipt." Her recipe for mulligatawny was not singled out as foreign but was placed in the soup chapter, and she admitted that it was "the sort of receipt commonly used in England."[16] In France, the question of nationality came up in a book published in 1868 that included recipes from many countries. The author presented "popular and national dishes" and on one occasion referred to "a national dish from the cuisine of Genoa."[17] But there are few such references, and the author did not discuss what the term "national" implied.

REGIONAL COOKBOOKS

Much of what can be said about national dishes and national cuisine can also be applied to regional and local dishes and cuisines. Today, the terms "regional dish" and "regional cuisine" are often used as part of a broader strategy, such as the commercial promotion of certain culinary products from small, local producers.

In Europe, the first strong interest in regional culture was the result of new ideas about simplicity and a return to nature, which emerged at the end of the eighteenth century and the beginning of the nineteenth. In the Romantic era, these ideas were linked to a fascination for the past, a nostalgia for a preindustrial and pre-urban culture with traditional family values and village loyalties. With regard to French cuisine, scholar Julia Csergo wrote that local dishes based on locally available products and traditional preparation methods "were instruments in the construction of ideas about the national, the regional, and the local during the nineteenth century's political, economic, and cultural changes."[18] German author Hanna Dose sees regional cookbooks as typical for times of social unrest and upheaval. The industrial revolution challenged the new nuclear family, which gave the "housewife" a different position in society and pitted her against a growing food industry that alienated her from the art of cooking. In such periods, regional cookbooks most importantly had an identification function.[19]

In discussing the differences and similarities between regional and national cuisines, the French author Jean-François Revel claimed that it made no sense to talk about national cuisine because the real contradiction was between regional and international cuisine. Regional cuisine consists of a certain set of recipes that are attached to a region and its products. When it comes to international cuisine, however, recipes are not as important as a set of cooking principles that can be used to create different dishes depending on the situation. Revel claimed that international cuisine, such as the French *grande cuisine,* is able to pick up dishes from different countries and areas, refine them, and improve them. The motivation is curiosity, he asserted, which is the opposite of the driving force behind regional cuisine, which refuses to take into consideration any taste range other than its own.[20]

Revel may have been right in his observation that international cuisine is innovative, even if it has periodically been fossilized, provoking the emergence of "new" cuisines, something that can be seen in several cookbooks. Revel's characterization of regional cuisines as static, however, seems to ignore examples of how popular cuisines have integrated new products, such as potatoes, corn, and tomatoes. Regional cookbooks mirror foreign influence just as much as local tradition. A French scholar, Florent Quellier, therefore took a critical look at the promotion of local and regional cuisines over the course of the past decades: "Far from being the result of a lost culinary paradise, our regional cuisines today, so strongly influenced by American plants, are recent." Therefore, he calls the very concept of "regional cuisine" deceptive, claiming that it is both mythical (*mythifié*) and mystifying (*mystificatrice*).[21] The historian Piero Camporesi, who analyzed the various factors behind culinary change in Italy, wrote that the very notion of "regional cuisine" has become vague and dubious, and he characterized dishes claimed to be typical, indigenous, and homestyle as dietary kitsch.[22]

REGIONAL AND NATIONAL COOKBOOK TITLES

Many cookbooks with titles that refer to regional cooking are not what they claim. *Le cuisinier gascon* (1740), *Il cuoco piemontese* (1766), and *La cuisinière genevoise* (1817), for example, are not collections of traditional recipes from Gascogne, Piedmont, and Geneva, respectively. Several books with regional titles combined local dishes with dishes from other areas or countries. In France, *Le cuisinier méridional d'après la méthode provençale et languedocienne* (The southern cook based on the method in Provence and Languedoc) was a general cookbook, although it did have a far greater proportion of recipes for dishes from the south of France than other cookbooks in the eighteenth or nineteenth centuries.[23] The 1691 *Vollständiges Nürnberger Kochbuch* (The Complete Nuremberg cookbook), based on recipes from the bourgeoisie in the commercially important Bavarian city, did not forget *Knödel* and other regional specialties, but most of the recipes were from other nations, particularly France. A study of regional German cookbooks published before the 1930s showed that the books did not express an intention of collecting traditional recipes but rather simply gave a description of what was eaten in an area without questioning where the dishes originally came from. The idea was that cherished dishes acquired a local identity, or *Heimatrecht*.[24] This argument was directly put forward in a nineteenth-century book called *Die Süddeutsche Küche* (The south German cuisine), in which the author admitted that she included many foreign dishes but explained that they had long ago been integrated into the culinary practice of southern German-speaking areas (including parts of Austria).[25]

Using the name of a region or a city in a cookbook's title certainly made it especially interesting to people in that area, but it was important for the book to appeal to a larger audience as well. *Mecklenburgisches Kochbuch,* for instance, had dishes that the author claimed were generally served in Mecklenburg, but she assured readers that they would also be useful in other areas along the North Sea and Baltic Sea.[26] The author of *Pfälzer Kochbuch* even added a note about the title, explaining that although the dishes were German, the title was justified because Pfalz, the Palatinate, was the pearl of the old German Empire.[27] In some cases, the regional titles were intentionally fraudulent. In Germany, for example, Bertha Schneider wrote a book in the nineteenth century that was published with dozens of different titles referring to various regions and cities—*Breslauer Kochbuch, Dresdner Kochbuch, Wiesbadener Kochbuch,* and so on—although all of them had the same recipes.[28]

One of the first books with a national title was *Le cuisinier françois* (The French cook), published in 1651 (figure 27). There were recipes in the book based on innovations in French cuisine, but the title was hardly meant to express a belief that the dishes were typical of the French nation; rather, they belonged to the elegant cuisine of the elite. To grasp the full meaning of the title, it is necessary to note that in the years preceding the cookbook's publication, books such as *Le philosophe françois* (1643) and *Le courier françois* (1649) had been printed in Paris. We have reason to believe that the titles expressed a new national consciousness and confidence. In the grand siècle, France had become a cultural role model in Europe. The preface of *Le pastissier françois* (1653), a collection of pie and pastry recipes, emphasized that books with the word "French" in the title had become very popular among foreigners. This fact is demonstrated by the many translations of such books. Also interesting is the preface of *Le jardinier françois* (1651), in which the author explained his choice of title. He wrote that other books about gardening had only described the conditions within a certain area with a certain climate. As an example, he mentioned Michel de Serres, who "has composed his work in Languedoc, which is a region [*païs*] very different from Paris and the surrounding area."[29]

In general, however, national titles were uncommon before the late eighteenth century, and most of the early examples are from England and Denmark. More of these books emerged in the nineteenth century because many new nations were established or were struggling to become independent during this period. The foundation of the new German Empire in 1871 led to a stronger emphasis on common German values and ideas and therefore also to the publication of cookbooks with titles such as *Deutsches National-Kochbuch, Das neue Kochbuch für das deutsche Haus,* and *Neues deutsches Kochbuch.* In the 1890s, several German cookbooks had the title *Reichskochbuch.*[30] The idea behind *Deutsches National-Kochbuch* seems to have been that a collection of various regional dishes would serve to strengthen national identity,[31] but there were also books with ideas that were not far from the extreme nationalism promoted by Heinrich von Treitschke and others.[32]

Cookbooks with national titles published in the century of nationalism did not always include dishes with roots in national traditions. Cookbooks printed in Belgium and Norway are good examples of this. When Belgium became an independent state, in 1831, it was dominated by the French-speaking elite, and French was the only official language. In the north of Belgium, however, people spoke Dutch dialects, but there was no written language based on these dialects, so if these northern Belgians wanted to publish something, they had to use the official language of the Netherlands. It is no surprise, then, that the cookbooks printed in Dutch for the Belgian public after Belgian independence did not include traditional dishes from the Flemish countryside; instead, they were reprints of books originally published in the Netherlands but with *Hollandsche* and *Nederlandse* in the titles changed to *Belgische* or *Vlaamsche.*[33]

FIGURE 27. Title page of the 1656 edition of *Le cuisinier françois* (The French cook), by La Varenne, published in Amsterdam. The cookbook was printed in almost fifty editions, some of them pirated copies printed outside France. Kungliga Biblioteket, Stockholm, Elz. 2292.

A similar situation occurred in Norway. Norway was a part of Denmark from the end of the Middle Ages until 1814 and in a political union with Sweden until 1905. The nineteenth century was a period when traditional Norwegian fairy tales, legends and folk songs were recorded in books with titles in which the word "Norwegian" featured prominently. This was copied in many cookbooks despite the fact that these books had little to do with popular Norwegian diet, and they were printed in Danish, which was the official written language of Norway but comparatively different from Norway's spoken dialects.[34]

The use of "Norwegian" and "Belgian" in cookbook titles can be understood as part of the development of national book industries in these two countries. There is, in other words, no doubt that the publication of these books expressed a new national attitude, a national struggle, but it was not based on culinary traditions. The same phenomenon is obvious in the cookbooks published in other nations struggling for political and cultural independence in the nineteenth century.

COOKBOOKS AND THE STRUGGLE FOR INDEPENDENCE

History and tradition were important for supporters of national independence movements, and the publication of cookbooks in national languages is therefore significant. The first cookbook in Icelandic was published in 1800, in Greek in 1828, in Finnish in 1834, in Romanian in 1841, and in Slovak in 1871. But a study of these new cookbooks shows that they were not inventories of popular diet. The recipes were either from the dominant culture of the earlier rulers or from modern, industrialized countries in Western Europe, some of which had long cookbook traditions.[35]

The early cookbooks in Finland and Iceland are examples of how the use of a national language did not stop authors and publishers from taking recipes from the cultures of their former rulers. The first Finnish cookbook, a booklet of simple recipes for hard times, published in 1834, had originally been written in Swedish and published in Sweden.[36] Finland had been part of Sweden from the late Middle Ages to 1809, and the Swedish-Finnish elite dominated economically, politically, and culturally even after independence. The Finnish language was not given equal status with Swedish until the late nineteenth century. Two more cookbooks were published in 1849 and 1869, both of which were translations from Swedish but clearly demonstrated the development of a Finnish culinary language. The book from 1849 used Swedish words with Finnish morphology—for example, *pakkelse* instead of Swedish *bakelse* (cake)—while the later book introduced new Finnish culinary terms.[37]

The first Icelandic books had recipes from Norway and Denmark.[38] The island had been colonized mainly by Norwegian settlers before the year 1000, but it was ruled by the Danes from the late Middle Ages until the end of World War II. That the early cookbooks were based on foreign dishes is surprising considering that an article written in Icelandic in the late eighteenth century gave detailed information about traditional Icelandic dishes.[39] Even if the description in the article was not in recipe form, it could have served as a source. The language in the first Icelandic cookbook was marked by many foreign loanwords, most of them from Danish. It was only with the puristic language policy implemented in Iceland during the nineteenth century that these words were replaced by new Icelandic words that were invented or constructed from Old Norse expressions.

The first Greek cookbook, published in 1828, was a translation of an Italian cookbook,[40] and the second, published in 1860, was a translation of a French cookbook.[41] The French influence was also strong in later Greek cookbooks printed in the nineteenth century, even though the authors were Greek chefs and the dishes were given Greek names and prepared with ingredients in the Greek colors, white and blue.[42] Greece, in other words, looked to the West for inspiration and turned its back to Turkey, where the first printed cookbook was published in 1844.[43] After the establishment of the Greek state, development in the country was led by Greeks of the diaspora, who opted for assimilation with the West, imitating Western habits and customs and adapting them to urban life in the rapidly growing capital of Athens.[44]

The first cookbooks in Romanian and Slovak were not translations, although they were strongly influenced by French and German models. The first Romanian cookbook, published in 1841, was written by two prominent personalities from the country's cultural elite.[45] Their nationalist ideas, however, did not result in the inclusion of classic and well-known Romanian dishes. They even left out most of the traditional soups and sauces and used more Mediterranean ingredients. They also adapted the language: they introduced the words *supă* (from the French *soupe*) and *sos* (from the French *sauce*).[46]

Language was important in the first Slovak cookbook, as demonstrated by its title: *Prvá kuchárska kniha v slovenskej reči* (First cookbook in the Slovak language).[47] It was published in 1870, a time when the Slovaks were struggling to establish a national identity, independent not only from the Hungarian government but also from the Czechs, who had established a written language centuries earlier. The author was part of a movement that was focused on building a new standard Slovak language based on regional dialects, and he did his part by creating a culinary terminology.[48] Many of the new words he used were based on German, and in some cases he added German words in parentheses, possibly because he thought his readers would have knowledge of German and German cookbooks and thus would better understand the meaning of the new expressions.[49]

The explanation for the absence or scarcity of traditional local dishes in these new books was partly social. Even if the authors were nationalistic and patriotic and wanted to promote their culture, most of them belonged to the elite and thus had little sense of simple, popular diets. Apart from the goal of political independence, there were two important aspects of the nationalism of these areas. One was language: there was a desire to create literary languages that could be used in all possible areas and fields. The other was a modernizing project: the nationalists in these regions wanted to bring the economy, industry, culture, education, and health of their countries up to the same levels as they had seen during their visits to the more "advanced" countries of Western Europe.

AMERICAN COOKBOOKS AND NATIONAL IDENTITY

In 1776, many years before the aforementioned European nations started to fight for independence, a new independent country had been created in North America: the United States. After the Declaration of Independence and the American Revolutionary War, a growing national consciousness was observed among the inhabitants of the nascent state. This new patriotism was strengthened by new national symbols; before the turn of the century, the United States had a flag, the Great Seal, and a national bird, the bald eagle. The first cookbook written by an American is also from this period: *American Cookery,* by Amelia Simmons, was published in 1796. The subtitle claimed that the book was "adapted to this country." There are recipes for Independence Cake and Federal Pan Cake, but more important is the use of indigenous foodstuffs, such as corn, squash, and Jerusalem artichoke.[50]

The language of the book has many interesting features. For example, it introduced several Americanisms that had not yet been referred to in American dictionaries. One of them was "slapjack" (a corn pancake), a word probably based on a misreading of the English "flapjack"; at the time, the *f* and the long *s* (ſ) were very similar in print. The book was also the first to use two words borrowed from Dutch: "cookey," from the Dutch *koekje,* used for what English cookbooks called "little cakes," and "slaw" from the Dutch *sla,* meaning "salad."[51]

The author—of whom we know nothing more than we can read in the book—presented herself on the title page as "An American Orphan." Why did she give this peculiar biographical information? Some scholars have interpreted it as a national metaphor. The author had to support herself without any help from a parent, just as the United States needed to survive without England. If this interpretation is correct, the book is an even stronger proof of national attitudes.

It should be mentioned that not all the recipes in Simmons's book are American. She included traditional English recipes, many of them taken verbatim from English books. But the American recipes in Simmons's book were noticed by both readers and publishers; in the following years, new editions of old English books were printed with the addition of American recipes, many of them taken directly from *American Cookery.* The title of her book also heralded a period when the American angle was emphasized. In the years leading up to the Civil War, more than twenty cookbooks used the word "American" in their titles: for example, *The American Housewife, American Domestic Cookery, American Receipt Book,* and *Modern American Cookery.*

The United States was a society dominated by immigrants from many European countries, and one of the characteristics of cookbook publishing, like other fields of publishing, was the high number of books in languages other than English (figure 28). The first French cookbook in the United States was published in 1840, the first Spanish in 1845, and the first German (Pennsylvania Dutch) in 1848, and they were followed by cookbooks in Italian, Yiddish, and Scandinavian languages, mirroring the country's different immigrant groups.[52] Some of the books were printed in two languages—for example, Yiddish and English, or French and English.

Most cookbooks in foreign languages catered to large immigrant groups who wanted to preserve their culinary heritage, but there were also foreign-language cookbooks with a very different intention. A particular genre consisted of works with recipes written in two parallel columns, one in American English and the other in Danish, Swedish, or Finnish. They were meant to help American house-wives communicate with their Scandinavian servants—of which there were a large number in the United States around 1900. The housewife would point out the dish she wanted prepared (the dishes in these books were American, not Scandina-vian), and the servant would then use the cookbook as a manual for cooking in addition to as a textbook for the English language.[53]

NATIONALISM, AUTARKY, AND XENOPHOBIA

In years of crisis, governments encouraged citizens to use fewer imported goods and more national products instead. This was a characteristic feature of the eco-nomic policy in several European countries in the 1920s and '30s. The Great War had shown governments the dangers of depending on imports, and "autarky," the ideal of self-sufficiency, became the slogan of the era. But such ideas were not new and not based only on rational economic thinking; there was a long tradition of nationalist notions, rooted in eighteenth-century philosophy (e.g., Herder and Rousseau), about the value of products from a nation's own land. In 1806, the author of a German economic-technical encyclopedia wrote that people would be happier and healthier if they ate food from their own "land and soil" (Grund und Boden).[54] The health and nutritional aspect of national foods was important to Ekaterina Avdeeva, who, in her cookbook, wrote about Russian food, the native dishes handed down from fathers to children through the centuries, which are "justified in terms of the location and climate of life."[55] The Norwegian author and cultural celebrity Hulda Garborg, who included traditional Norwegian dairy dishes in her cookbook, argued that it was important for a nation to build its food culture in the same way as everything else: on home ground. Her model for a

MARCHAND DE MOUTARDE

Tout le mon - de me - re-gard - e mais per-son - ne n'achète rien

achetez de la mou-tar-de çe-la vous fer - a du bi-en

FIGURE 28. Illustration and song from Célestine Eustis's *Cooking in Old Créole Days* (New York, 1903), a regional cookbook with recipes from the southern United States, most of them in English, some in French. The chef is singing: "Everybody looks at me, but no one buys anything. Buy mustard, it is good for you!"

national culinary strategy was that of the French Brie region, where people preferred the cheese they had developed.[56] But there was no chauvinism in these
approaches. Neither Avdeeva nor Garborg repudiated foreign dishes; Avdeeva
made a point of mentioning this in her preface, and Garborg included French and
Italian dishes in her book.

In other cases, however, these nationalistic ideas about food became elements
of extreme ideologies, in which racism played an important part. This was what
happened in Nazi Germany with the slogan *Blut und Boden* (blood and soil),
where "blood" referred to the Nordic race, the most pure "Aryan" race. This attitude was often repeated in cookbooks, for example: "The foreign spices are determined for the tropics, where they are grown. The German housewife has to do her
best to ban them from her kitchen and rather use German herbs. They grow on
German soil and are by nature determined for us humans of Nordic race."[57] But
boycotting foreign products was not enough; defending the race included boycotting Jewish shops. The Jews—even those completely integrated into German society and culture—were considered "foreign" in Nazi ideology.[58]

As a consequence of such attitudes, traditional fare from different German
regions, particularly rural areas, was praised as "national." A collection of such
dishes was published in 1936 under the title *Kochtopf der Heimat* (Kettle of the
homeland). The dishes, which are from all the German "tribes," were, according to
the author, typical of the German palate and represented an appreciation of German nature, a love of the fatherland, and a respect for traditional heritage.[59]

A superlative status was given to the *Eintopf*, a one-pot dish that was used to
create a feeling of national community.[60] In Hitler's Germany, the dish was recommended because it was economical: it had a shorter cooking time than other stews,
and thereby less fuel was consumed in preparing it. At least eight special *Eintopf*
cookbooks were published in 1933 alone.[61] But the stew was also given an ideological superstructure, and it was consumed on the so-called *Eintopf* Sundays, when
the regime arranged enormous public lunches with *Eintopf* on the table and the
leaders of the Third Reich present. In a speech, Goebbels compared National
Socialism to good German popular fare, a one-pot stew.[62]

Inspired by Germany, Spain introduced the Día del plato único (Day of the
Single Plate), which was established by law in parts of Spain held by Franco's forces
during the Spanish Civil War. This was intended to support the rationing of foodstuffs and the ideology of autarky. Until long after World War II, hotels and restaurants were obligated by law to put a one-plate dish on the menu at least once a
week. Just like Germany's *Eintopf*, the *plato único* was a propaganda effort used to
foster the idea of national solidarity, but the truth was that the poorest parts of the
population ate *platos únicos* daily out of pure necessity.[63]

Just as the Germans had used regional dishes to present a national cuisine,
Spain nationalized regional dishes such as the Andalucian *gazpacho*, the Valencian

paella, and the Madrid *cocido.* In "Cocidito madrileño," a popular song from the 1950s, the Spanish singer Pepe Blanco played up antiforeign sentiments with these lyrics:

> Don't talk to me
> About the banquets in Rome
> Or the menu of the Hotel Plaza in New York
> Or pheasant or foie gras.
>
> . . .
>
> Because my food and my pleasure
> Is the charm and the salt
> That a woman's love
> Sprinkles on a *cocidito madrileño.*

Autarky was also important in Italy, and it was linked to the official policy during the fascist period. In *La cucina autarchica,* written by a professor of home economics, there are references to Mussolini and to the slogan "L'Italia ha il dovere di essere forte" (Italia has a duty to be strong). But the author noted, "A people cannot be strong and dominate while depending on food from others." She therefore encouraged readers to consume less white bread, which was based on imported wheat.[64]

This dependence on wheat was the reason for the futurist Filippo Tommaso Marinetti's attack on the *pastasciutta* (pasta dishes). Marinetti was the main author of *La cucina futurista,* with manifestos and recipes published in 1932, and he regarded rice to be superior to pasta.[65] This has been considered rather bizarre and a bit comical by many, but his reasoning was first and foremost economical. Italy produced more rice than anywhere else in Europe, and it was therefore an inexpensive product. But many cooks and other Italians criticized Marinetti because they considered pasta the national dish and pointed out that it was part of a tradition. Such arguments did not matter much to Marinetti; futurism was the opposite of *passatismo* (idolization of the past). Furthermore, he believed that pasta made Italians lazy, heavy, and even neutralist; it was not a food for *combattenti* (fighters). Just like so many other fascists, he adhered to a vitalist philosophy that praised speed, energy, violence, and war. In Mussolini's words: "Only war can bring human energy to a maximum."[66]

Marinetti's attitude to foreign countries and their cultures was a form of xenophobia, which he expressed as a fight against *esterofilia* (love of foreign things). He made clear in his cookbook that this term was a futurist invention. He felt sorry for having to use it, but wrote that in spite of the imperial power of fascism, there were still many Italians who were tempted by foreign things and thereby were guilty of *antitalianità* (anti-Italianness). He attacked people who admired or accepted foreign art, culture, industry, products, and even words on menus. In his opinion, this was snobbery. As an example, he mentioned the admiration for American cocktail parties, which "may suit the American race, but is destructive for our race." He was promoting not only a dish but also a culture when he wrote that Italians, rather than boasting "I have had four cocktails," ought to say "I have eaten a minestrone."[67]

PURIFICATION OF LANGUAGE

Foreign culinary terms have been discussed in various contexts in this book, particularly French terminology. Some authors avoided foreign words or tried to replace them for pedagogical reasons. When cookbooks were printed in new languages, as new nations were in the processes of establishing their own technical terminology, it was important to use local terms. But even within the large language communities of German and Italian, a new attitude to foreign words emerged during the unification processes of those two countries in the nineteenth century.

In Italy, the influence of French culinary language was very strong. In the eighteenth century, the playwright Scipione Maffei made fun of the Italian fascination for French taste in his comedies, and he specifically mentioned the terms *ragù, farsì, gattò, cottolette, crocande, fricandò, canàr,* and *bigne.*[68] Even in the nineteenth century, new French words entered the culinary field: *consommé, croquettes, mayonnaise, purée,* and *vol-au-vent* were among them.[69] The most influential and successful cookbook in Italy in the late nineteenth and early twentieth centuries, Pellegrino Artusi's *La scienza in cucina,* gradually changed this paradigm and created an Italian culinary language. But the language problem in Italy was not limited to the adoption of too many French words. At the time of the political unification of the country, most Italians spoke dialects, which were often understood only in specific regions, while a tiny 2.5 percent of the population spoke literary Italian.[70] Artusi commented on this in one of his recipes, remarking that the names of dishes were so different from province to province that Italy was almost like a second Babel. Then he admitted his own project: "After the unification of my fatherland it seemed to me a logical consequence to think of the unity of the spoken language, something few care about and many oppose."[71] The historian Piero Camporesi claimed that Artusi had done more for national unification than *I promessi sposi* (*The Betrothed*), Alessandro Manzoni's great historical novel, which became an important part of the national struggle.[72] Alberto Capatti gave a detailed analysis of how the revisions of Artusi's cookbook, from the first edition in 1891 to the fifteenth in 1911, developed in two ways: new recipes were added and others were improved, but there was also an increasing amount of attention paid to the question of nationality in terms of both taste (*un gusto nazionale*) and the use of the national language (*italianizzazione della lingua*). In other words, Artusi had two objectives: a gastronomic one and a linguistic one.[73]

After German unification, the new government launched a policy of Germanization in many fields. In the 1870s, Konrad Duden started to work with German orthography, and he published the first of his *Duden* dictionaries in 1880. Beginning in 1885, the Allgemeine Deutsche Sprachverein (Public German Language Society) published dictionaries to facilitate Germanization. In 1888, the first German culinary dictionary was published, and it was printed in at least seven editions. The book opened with a warning in rhymed verse, where the "French poison" was condemned and exemplified by forty-five German verbs that were based on French terms, including *blanchiren, marinieren,* and *panieren.*[74] However, these types of French expressions lasted into the twentieth century, probably because there was no official body to give binding orders to stop their use, as the case was in the postal and railway services, where the vocabulary quickly became completely German.

A new campaign for the German language came during World War I, and it was symbolized by a rather peculiar book title: *Erstes rein deutsches Koch-Lehrbuch unter Vermeidung sämtlicher Fremdwörter* (First pure German cookbook avoiding all foreign words).[75] During the Weimar years, cosmopolitan winds were blowing, but strong anti-Semitic and racist attitudes were dominant in many nationalist circles and in the Allgemeine Deutsche Sprachverein, which claimed that a clear and honest language was a part of the German essence (*Wesen*)—a play on the words *deutsch* (German) and *deutlich* (clear).[76]

When Hitler came to power in 1933, many National Socialists demanded German words to talk about their German dishes. In *Die Küche,* the official journal of the German cooks' guild, there was early on a conscious campaign against foreign language. In an article that appeared in the journal in 1933, a cook appealed to his colleagues to replace French words with German ones.[77] This seems reasonable enough, and the same linguistic changes were carried out in many countries, but in Nazi Germany, it was put into a racist context: "The mother tongue [*Die Muttersprache*] bound the German people together, the same way as the blood."[78]

Some historians have claimed that Hitler was no radical linguistic purist,[79] but he was reported to have attacked culinary language in one of his table talks, in which he called cooks the "Kings of the Cooking-Pots" and described them as "ridiculous idiots, mesmerising the people and intoxicating themselves with a mass of meaningless phrases and obscure names."[80]

WARTIME COOKBOOKS

Nationalist attitudes tend to be strengthened and uncomfortably aggressive in times of international conflict. During World War I, Americans renamed popular dishes of German origin: sauerkraut became "liberty cabbage," hamburgers were called "liberty sandwiches," and frankfurters were dubbed "liberty sausages." This was part of a broad anti-German campaign that was followed by official restrictions on the large German immigrant population, which was suspected of harboring sympathies for the enemy, the German Empire.

Cookbooks published during armed conflicts often contain a combination of patriotic zeal and practical advice. War cookbooks have flourished in periods of conflict; the earliest examples are from the 1860s. A Danish cookbook published in 1864, during the Second Schleswig War with Prussia, started with a list of what the soldiers received from the army every day (beef, oatmeal, and salt) and gave simple recipes for "our brave soldiers."[81] In 1863, during the American Civil War, the *Confederate Receipt Book* was published in Richmond, Virginia—the confederate capital—with recipes and "useful and economical directions and suggestions in cookery, housewifery, &c., and for the camp." There were recipes for Apple Pie without Apples, Artificial Oysters, and Indian Sagamite, a mixture of hominy and sugar browned over the fire, which the book claimed not only appeases hunger "but allays thirst, and is therefore useful to soldiers on a scout."

The basic purpose of such books was to give advice about how to manage when foodstuffs and fuel were in short supply.[82] During times of hardship, simple vegetables were grown in gardens and edible plants were gathered in the woods. In Germany, the tough winter of 1916–17 was called the Turnip Winter because bad weather led to a particularly poor potato crop, which meant that Germans had to subsist on turnips, rutabaga, and kohlrabi. Special cookbooks, such as the *Kohlrüben-Kriegskochbuch* (Kohlrabi war cookbook),[83] were written to encourage the use of these vegetables. During World War II, many cookbooks had a similar aim. The Italian book *Cucina in tempo di guerra* (Cookery in times of war), for example, had recipes for dishes made with vegetables instead of meat.[84]

Appealing to frugality, as these books did, aligned with the plans and wishes of the authorities. Whether it was the intention of the authors or not, the books inevitably became tools for official propaganda. Several books did clearly express this as an aim. In Germany during World War I, the Vaterländischer Frauenverein (Women's Fatherland Association) published a cookbook emphasizing that securing families against malnutrition was best accomplished by adapting to the demands from the military high command.[85] An American cookbook recommended following "Mr. Hoover's rules for patriotic economy."[86] Herbert Hoover, the director of the US Food Administration from 1917–18, made clear that if the Americans did not economize with foodstuffs, they stood a great chance of losing the war. In another cookbook, the author ends the preface with these words: "I hope that the following recipes will prove helpful in carrying out Mr. Hoover's instructions."[87]

During World War II, submission was even more important in Europe's dictatorships, where the obligation was to follow the leaders. The author of an Italian cookbook published in 1942 wrote that Il Duce (Mussolini) had stated that it was necessary for the Italian family to subordinate their needs to those of the country.[88]

Many German cookbooks used National Socialist terminology and even included the Nazi salute (Heil Hitler).[89] In a cookbook she published in 1943, Reich's Women's Führerin (*Reichsfrauenführerin*) Gertrud Scholtz-Klink listed service, duty, and sacrifice as feminine ideals.[90] A 1940 cookbook noted that the sacrifice was "for a higher goal, a goal that was worth it."[91]

Some wartime cookbooks are written in technical language and refer matter-of-factly to the goverment guidelines. But there are also cookbooks that employ a bombastic military rhetoric, using words such as "enemy," "battle," and "victory." German books from World War I emphasized that both men and women were obligated to fight for the Fatherland: men fought the visible enemy on the battle-field, while women fought the invisible enemy—food shortage—at home by efficiently using scarce resources. In this scenario, waste equaled high treason.[92] In spite of their weaknesses, women were considered combatants.[93] These calls to women were often phrased in verse:

> Dear housewife, stand your ground,
> And help to save the Fatherland.[94]

The situation was similar in the United States during World War I. American cookbooks described women as "soldiers of the kitchen" and praised "the army of American housewives." The word "treason" was not uttered, but someone who failed to show loyalty in small things was said to have aided the enemy. A school manual struck nationalist cords when it encouraged American schoolchildren to "prove your Americanism by eating less."[95]

In 1938, the Spanish dictator Francisco Franco proudly declared: "Spain is a privileged country that can support itself." But he also said: "If the fatherland demands it, every Spanish citizen ought to be satisfied with a tomato a day."[96] In a speech to housewives, the German Nazi Party leader Hermann Göring said that a person who could not abstain from a few eggs or a pound of butter was not worthy of being called a German. In Germany, the ladle was "the woman's weapon."[97] In Italy, food was "ammunition."[98]

"Patriotic" was a word that appeared frequently in wartime cookbooks. In *The Allied Book of Recipes,* published in Dublin in 1914, there is a recipe for Patriotic Pound Cake. Patriotic cakes are also found in the 1918 American cookbook *Liberty Recipes,* and the book also uses slogans such as "Peel potatoes thin and help our Sammies to Berlin," and "Be a Cheese Patriot; join the ranks and cheese the Kaiser."[99] The American cookbooks published during World War I seem to use a more cheerful or cheeky language than the German ones. This may have to do with the difference in living conditions in the two countries during the war. The United States was far from the heat of the battle, while Germany was behind the blockade, with Germans living on ever-smaller rations. But there were also differences in rhetorical traditions. In any case, Gabriel Hanotaux, a French intellectual, was actually responsible for one of the crudest examples of patriotic fanaticism and stereotyping of the enemy. *Allied Cookery,* a cookbook of recipes from several of the Allied nations, was first published in 1916 in New York and London.[100] Its French translation was published in 1918. Hanotaux, a historian with a seat in the French Academy, wrote the preface. He stated that the allies, while fighting for civilization, had to also fight for the art of cooking, the basic principle of all civilized life. He claimed that the "Huns" didn't know anything about the art of eating: "These heavy German bellies, this heavy German food, these heavy German body colors are responsible for the heavy German culture and the terrible bestiality in their warfare. As the body, so the soul! Turn away all these dreadful menus that seem to have been written by monsters directly on human skin."[101]

There are later examples of culinary war rhetoric and culinary hate propaganda, although not all of it is recorded in cookbooks. One rather innocent but also puerile example is from 2003, when France refused to support the United States' invasion of Iraq. Congressional cafeterias in Washington, DC, responded by changing "French fries" to "freedom fries" on their menus.

In spite of such examples, the cookbook industry does not seem to be particularly belligerent. In this era of globalization, there are an increasing number both of cookbooks introducing various national cuisines (Thai, Creole, Japanese, Mexican, etc.) and of cookbooks with local or regional (indigenous) recipes. Such trends are unfortunately not accompanied by reflections and discussions of the concepts "national" and "regional." However, it remains to be seen if the more recent nationalist trends in Europe and the United States will find expression in recipes or cookbooks.

17

Decoration, Illusion, and Entertainment

THE MEAL AS AN EVENT

The meal is an event with its own dramaturgy, according to Margaret Visser; it is a play that "organises actions and words into component parts such as acts, scenes, speeches, dialogues, entrances, and exits, all in the sequences designed for them."[1]

This play is a form of communication. Every meal can be interpreted as a form of nonverbal communication. The hosts of a meal reveal—consciously or unconsciously—how they see themselves or how they want to be seen. The meal is a system of signs. The spectacular banquets held at princely courts from the Middle Ages onward, recorded in menus and recipes reproduced in culinary literature, were intended to demonstrate the power and greatness of the prince. The banquets belonged to a category of practical arts known as *theatrica,* which included many activities, from jousting tournaments to theatrical comedies.[2] But with the establishment of an absolute monarchy in France, all royal acts and performances, the morning *levée* and the evening meal included, became part of a total strategy put in place to support military, diplomatic, and economic measures.[3]

The manipulations and mechanisms behind the exalted position of the Sun King, Louis XIV, can best be described by the title and vocabulary in a modern study, *The Fabrication of Louis XIV,* which uses expressions such as "selling" and "packaging" to emphasize the propaganda efforts.[4] Versailles was more than a palace; according to the sociologist Norbert Elias, it constituted the highest level or symbol (*Spitzenphänomen*) of a hierarchically structured and divided society.[5] Many of the elements of the banquet culture at Versailles were picked up and adopted by princes and aristocrats all over Europe, and although new social groups introduced new ideas and ideals, the fascination with the impressive and conspicuous persisted. Cookbooks helped the elite realize their extravagant banquets.

In the elegant cookbook by Antonio Latini, chief steward at the Neapolitan court in the late seventeenth century, there is a drawing on a large foldout plate showing a table heaped with tempting dishes and decorated with flowers, figurines, pyramids, and birds standing on their feet in full plumage. In the long chapter about pheasants, Latini recommended boiling the meat, stuffing it with tasty ingredients, and then putting tail, head, and wings back on, painted with gold and silver. Latini noted that it could be served cold, and added that it would look fantastic, particularly if the birds were standing erect in various bizarre positions on the table. He described this and other dishes as "una suntuosa vista" and "una bella vista."[6] There is no doubt that Latini's aim with these types of dishes was the same as that formulated in the following century in a cookbook by Martha Bradley from Bath: "To please the Palate is one Design of this Branch of Study, and to please the Eye is another."[7]

Serving entire birds was nothing new when Latini wrote his book; it is a tradition that can be traced back to the Middle Ages. There are several recipes for redressed peacock, for example, in Martino's and Platina's texts and in English manuscripts.[8] Another impressive dish was the head of an animal, such as calf or pig. Molokhovets has a recipe for the head of an old boar, in which the ears are decorated with paper figures and greens: "The head and the ears must be handsome [krasivo]."[9] Even oxen seem to have been used; according to Marin's cookbook from 1742, head of ox was served in great meals, but "par fantaisie."[10]

Such dishes were important as a part of the decoration of the table when meals were served à la française, a system that was used in banquets and dinners in many European countries until the mid-nineteenth century. At these meals, each "service" or "course" consisted of a certain number of different dishes; after a while, these were removed, and a new course was served with the same (or a similar) number of dishes. There were generally three or four courses, but in exceptional cases, there were more. The guests helped themselves to the dishes nearby and asked servants when they wanted something out of reach.[11] When they wanted meat from roasts, however, guests absolutely depended on assistance. A carver was on hand to provide the guest with however many slices he desired. This work was a practical necessity, but it also had to be carried out with elegance; the act of carving was no less a part of the embellishment of the dinner than the food on the table.

THE ART OF CARVING

Tableside carving was certainly practiced in the courts of great powers in antiquity, but there are few references to it in the literature of the period. In one of his satires, Juvenal wrote that he was no snob and needed no carver from the school of

FIGURE 29. A page demonstrating carving techniques from *Universal-Lexikon der Kochkunst* (General encyclopedia of cooking), published in Leipzig in 1878. Cookbooks from many countries included illustrated carving instructions. Nasjonalbiblioteket, Oslo, N 1738.

Trypherus, where they cut up hares, boars, and birds from Scythia and wild goats from Gaetulia.[12] But the first written instructions for carving are found in Catalan manuscripts from the fourteenth and fifteenth centuries and in the first printed cookbooks from that region, published in the 1520s.[13] The first printed manual in English was the *Boke of Kervynge*,[14] which was based on a manuscript from around 1440, but the most important texts of this genre were from Italy and Germany: for example, the classic work by Vincenzo Cervio, *Il trinciante* (The carver), which was added as an appendix to the later editions of Scappi's cookbook.[15] Cervio attacked unprofessional carvers and explained how carving should be done properly, directly over the plate, a method Italians called *trinciare in aria* (carving in the air). The techniques for carving various forms of meat were explained in detail in such manuals, and drawings demonstrating the procedures step by step were published in books all over Europe (figure 29). Most of them were reproductions from *Li tre trattati,* a book by Mattia Giegher, printed in 1639 in Padua.[16]

Latini wrote that the carver had to be young because old people might tremble when holding the knife. From the late Middle Ages onward, young sons of aristocrats, employed as pages at the courts, performed this art at table. A German book from 1700 recommended using a nobleman as carver because it was a very high position, but it noted that other qualified persons could take the job if they had an upright and well-proportioned body, gentle hands, and a fearless mind.[17] The authors of carving manuals made an important point of how the carver ought to behave: decently, decorously, and modestly. Carvers were warned against many bad habits, such as exaggerating their movements, adopting affected positions, and using the knife as clowns and charlatans did. The fact that these warnings were so numerous and so specific seems to indicate that these habits must have been quite common.[18] A possible explanation is that the more entertaining carvers knew their actions would be appreciated by most of the guests, who expected more than nutrition from a feast.

SPECTACULAR DISHES

The intention behind some banquet dishes was, as Latini noted, both to impress—by giving diners a "sumptous view"—and to entertain—by arranging the animals in "bizarre positions." Martino proposed putting cotton in the mouth of the roast peacock and setting fire to it. This fascination with flames—still popular in today's flambéed dishes—can also be observed in old German cookbooks, which instruct cooks to sprinkle the heads of calf and swine with ginger and spirits and then light them.[19]

The colors of foods were extremely important, and from the very first cookbooks up to the point that chemical food dyes were introduced, cookbooks gave advice about how to produce different colors: for example, green from parsley, yellow from egg yolk, brown from cinnamon, blue from cornflower, and red from beetroot juice.[20] Dishes of different colors might be very decorative on a table, but colors were also combined in specially designed dishes: a fish in three parts painted golden, silver, and blue; a lamb roasted whole and painted green on one side and yellow on the other; a baked almond and sugar "chessboard" with squares alternating in green, white, and yellow.[21] White dishes, made with ingredients such as whipped cream, egg whites, and sugar and given the name "snow," were popular in cookbooks from the fourteenth to the twentieth centuries.[22] Cooks were probably expected to use colors the same way other decorators did with walls and tables when a banquet was prepared.

Some cooks wanted above all to surprise guests. Great fantasy was demonstrated in new and unexpected dishes. The front part of a cock was sewn together with the hind part of a pig.[23] There were pies with living birds or a living hare inside; living crayfish were painted red and placed among the boiled ones.[24] When a fried piglet was cut open, out came live eels. Birds were served inside of bottles with narrow necks.[25] All of these tricks were explicitly explained as part of the amusement, diversion, pleasure, and delight that was expected by guests.[26]

The idea of culinary illusion existed in antiquity. Examples can be found in the Roman cookbook attributed to Apicius; in Petronius's satire about the arriviste Trimalchio in *Satyricon;* and in a poem by Philoxenus: "Meat that is not meat and fish that is not fish has the best taste."[27] The French word for these spectacular dishes, which were generally served between the different services in great banquets during the Middle Ages, is *entremets,* and they were often accompanied by dramatic and musical pieces. In an old Italian manuscript, they are called *mirabilia gule,* which can be translated as "gastronomic wonders," but the most frequent Italian term is *trionfi,* an expression that was picked up by the Englishman Robert May. In a Polish book, they are called *sekret kuchmistrzowski* (the cook's secret). The German word is *Schauessen* (food for show). In medieval English manuscripts and in the first printed English cookbook, published in 1500, they are called *subtleties,*[28] and they are served at the end of each course. In 1615, Gervase Markham gave a list of dishes that the housewife ought to send to the dinner table "for show only."[29] This indicates that not all the dishes were meant to be eaten. Many of these showy dishes involved big constructions that made use of material that was not edible. In the seventeenth century, a German author distinguished between *Schawessen,* which was impressive to look at but could also be eaten, and *Schawgerichte* (dishes for show), which consisted of wood, wax, cloth, and other materials that could not be consumed.[30]

Early on, the most extreme examples of these dishes for show met criticism. In *The Canterbury Tales,* the parson, a poor and learned man, attacks people who put luxury and pleasure above respect for the Lord, and he mentions "excesse of diverse metes and drinkes; and namely, swiche manere bake metes and dish-metes, brenninge of wilde fyr, and peynted and castelled with papir, and semblable wast; so that it is abusion for to thinke."[31]

In a sixteenth-century book about foodstuffs, *De re cibaria,* the author, a French royal physician, described some of the figurines put on tables as obscene, and according to him, they originated in Portugal, Spain, and Italy.[32] His book was published after Messisbugo's Italian cookbook from 1549, wherein the Italian described a banquet at which figurines made from *pasta di sosameli,* a honey-based substance, were displayed for the guests: there were eight men and seven women with dark skin, nude, with golden laurel wreaths around their heads and "flowers covering the parts that normally are hidden," as the author prudishly phrases it.[33]

Closer to our time, assessments of such decorative dishes have been less moral than aesthetic. In his classic study, *Herfsttij der middeleeuwen* (The autumn of the Middle Ages), Dutch historian Johan Huizinga wrote that this dramatization of the court fêtes was the culmination of the taste for unbridled luxury and barbarous manifestations of arrogant pomp. In his opinion, the *entremets*—pies with musicians inside, full-rigged vessels, castles, monkeys, whales, giants, and dwarfs—were ugly and insipid performances.[34] One might expect that he would have seen in such decorations a "play element," the key word in his later work *Homo ludens.* But in this book, Huizinga repeated his criticism of medieval art. Even if the period was full of play (*Spiel*), he stated, the original expressions were transformed into pure jokes (*Scherze*) and pompous plays of chivalry (*Ritterspiele*) and lost their creativity.[35]

The American food historian Barbara Ketcham Wheaton was not as critical as Huizinga. She compared medieval banquets to illuminated manuscripts from the same period. She equated ordinary dishes on the table to a page of written text, generally plain and only moderately embellished. *Entremets,* however, were like framed illustrations, which put "the significance vividly before the reader, who, in the fourteenth century, may well have given more attention to the picture than to the written word."[36] In Wheaton's opinion, this idea is supported by the fact that the same artists who were called on to produce paintings and manuscripts also worked on feasts.

But this metaphorical approach is hardly a convincing explanation for the broad popularity of *entremets.* It may be more useful to apply Peter Burke's observation of upper-class participation in popular culture at that time. Burke pointed out that the "amphibious" elite had access to "higher" or "greater" classical culture but also took part in popular traditions, like festivals such as carnival: "Clowns were popular at courts as well as taverns, and often the same clowns."[37]

Huizinga criticized court banquets in the late Middle Ages and contrasted their vulgarity with the new and more refined ideas of Renaissance humanism. But in the centuries following the end of the Middle Ages, there was no less interest in the extraordinary. Playwrights, for example, developed a whole range of techniques that were not so different from *entremets* in that they were intended to entertain. William Bouwsma specifically mentioned "the imitation of reality to produce wonder" and "the use of suspension to manipulate and finally relieve anxiety." He called this "clowning and magic—fun for both the masses and the classes."[38]

SUGAR AND MARZIPAN

The fascination with spectacular decorations continued, even if the baroque and rococo periods were giving way to new artistic fashions. Sugar was a favored culinary building material before 1500, and it was sometimes mixed with tragacanth—a transparent gum without taste or smell—to make it easier to handle. Another popular product was marzipan, made with sugar, almonds, and rosewater. Like sugar, marzipan was recommended for its health benefits, but as Walther Ryff pointed out in his 1544 *Confect-Büchlin und Hauss-Apothek,* marzipan was considered better suited to creating amusing decorations for banquets than feeding to the sick.

In a German cookbook from 1723, there is a recipe for a pyramid of stacked marzipan rings of decreasing size, a form that is still used in Denmark and Norway for cakes served on special occasions.[39] But this is nothing compared to the fantasy displayed in other cookbooks of the eighteenth century, when many cookbook authors expressed their enthusiasm for marzipan, the product that made it possible to realize a "gourmand architecture" and build the most incredible rarities, such as castles, pillars, boats, carts, and any animal on earth. The Austrian cook Conrad Hagger wrote enthusiastically about all the different "pictures, pyramids, figures" that could be created with marzipan; he listed forty-one ideas, and gave instructions for how to color the paste with different plants.[40]

But many marzipan products were of less magnificent dimensions. In the seventeenth century, a German cookbook author gave a recipe for "ham" and "sausage" made with red and white marzipan to depict meat and fat, respectively.[41] German and Danish cookbooks published in the following centuries added various figures: fish, apples, egg, potatoes, strawberries, carrots, mushrooms, and asparagus—all made from painted marzipan.[42] But even more comical was a tradition started by the Austrian Katharina Prato: the so-called false sandwiches. This idea was adopted in Scandinavian countries, where it ended in caricature with sandwiches of ham, salmon, roast beef, cheese, sausage, and so on, all sculpted from marzipan and colored with industrially produced dyes.[43] This comic side of marzipan was widely acknowledged. The writer Thomas Mann, who was born in the German marzipan capital of Lübeck, where stars and flowers and all sorts of small figurines were produced, admitted that if someone wanted to make fun of him, they would associate him with the "comical" marzipan and called him a "Lübeck marzipan baker."[44]

Far more impressive sugar works were produced, however, and they can be admired in beautifully illustrated manuals published in France, Italy, and England in the eighteenth and nineteenth centuries.[45] But not everybody was impressed by such displays. In Germany, the exaggerated bakery products inspired the name of a style of architecture with a lot of ornaments and embellishments: *Zuckerbäckerstil* (confectioner style). Many of the decorative confections had an architectural element, something Goethe, with his keen eye for details, explained in *Wilhelm Meister's Apprenticeship*. In the novel, Lothario's aunt remarks that while she had previously considered the master builder and the confectioner to have been students of the same school, she now saw both the confectioner and the servant who laid the table (*Tafeldecker*) as coming from the academy of architects.

Grimod, the prolific French gourmet writer, systematically used architectural metaphors when discussing the dishes in a meal, and he compared potages, hors d'oeuvres, rôtis, and entremets to vestibules, entresols, salons, and mansards, while the sauces corresponded to the furniture, the ornaments of a building. Grimod also praised the Paris decorator M. Dutfoy for his architectural wonders.[46] In 1803 and 1804, Grimod wrote about Dutfoy's culinary works as if they were architectural masterpieces, and he made a connection between his food and temples, using imagery such as an enormous dome, an elegant cupola, a vast peristyle, galleries as far the eye could see, columns, cornices, capitals, gables, and other ornaments.[47]

The man best known for such forms of edible architecture is Antonin Carême, who not only was a gifted cook and confectioner but also put his ideas in print. His cookbooks, published during the end of Napoleon's empire and the beginning of Louis XVIII's reign, have illustrations of temples, fortresses, towers, pavilions, fountains, and even idyllic ruins, which was a popular motive in Romantic art.[48]

FIGURE 30. Typical nineteenth-century illustration of a decorative dish, from M. Schulze's *Kogebog* (Cookbook), published in 1895.

According to the scholar Ivan Day, who has analyzed and described the development of the art of confectionary and pastry, the designs in two of Carême's books, *Le pâtissier royal parisien* and *Le pâtissier pittoresque,* inspired a new style of so-called decorative cuisine that went on to dominate upper-class buffets and tables until the onset of the World War I.[49]

Big constructions of marzipan, sugar, and other materials that were put on tables as centerpieces were called *pièces montées* in French, and it is an expression readers of *Madame Bovary* will recognize, as it is how Flaubert referred to the pompous wedding cake in the novel. He described all the cake's ridiculous details, which were in fact very popular clichés at the time. It is also interesting that the cake was purchased from a *pâtissier* from Yvetot because it was increasingly common that such elaborate works were produced by professional pastry chefs or confectioners.

There were other types of *pièces montées* coming out of the kitchen during the nineteenth century. Some of the most illustrious chefs in France at the time elaborated on Carême's ideas of how to serve meat and fish as sculptured dishes, and the illustrations in the books these chefs published were copied in most European countries and can still be seen in gourmet cookbooks and coffee-table books about the history of cuisine (figure 30).

One reason behind the passion for *pièces montées* was a nostalgia for the traditional French serving style, which had been largely replaced by the new *service à la russe* that was introduced in the nineteenth century. The Russian system was more economical (as it required fewer staff) and more egalitarian for the guests, who were not dependent on servants to fetch them food that was placed at another part of the table. A Russian visitor to Paris in the eighteenth century complained of the difficulties experienced by guests who could not afford to bring their own servants.[50]

Dishes were served one after another in a linear, chronological sequence, which meant that the big steaks and birds were not put on the table; the carving was done before the food was served, in the kitchen or at a sideboard. This reduced the decorative aspect of the dishes. Consequently, table decorations in crystal, silver, and porcelain became increasingly popular, and hosts used specific glasses for different wines and particular cutlery for different dishes to make each setting more impressive. But some of the nineteenth-century chefs considered this display of nonedible decorations to be a fundamental betrayal of their craft and art. They had been taught since their apprenticeships that the characteristic feature of French cuisine was the external appearance, *la physiologie extérieure*. Jules Gouffé suggested a compromise between the old French system and the new Russian one: some of the dishes would be served one by one, particularly dishes that needed to be kept hot, while cold dishes would be placed on the table in all their splendor to please first the eyes and then the palate.[51]

TABLE SYMMETRY

Independently of what sorts of objects adorned the table, there were ideas about how these objects should be arranged. There were practical considerations, but there were also aesthetic ones, and one very common ideal was that of symmetry. This is a basic concept that also exists in many different fields of art. German historian Michael Maurer wrote that the early modern era was characterized by "the spirit of geometry."[52] Geometry was behind the revolutionary use of perspective in Renaissance paintings. In architecture, there was a greater sense for geometric figures, squares, and circles, which dominated surfaces like floors, roofs, and façades. Churches, palaces, fortresses, towns, and gardens were arranged according to an artificially constructed perspective: the birds-eye view. Illustrations of buildings and other construction works, particularly gardens, such as those at Versailles, can be compared to illustrations of table arrangements in cookbooks.

Tables can be square, rectangular, circular, or oval. After Kepler's demonstration of how the planets moved around the sun in elliptical orbits, the oval became very popular. In a German book from 1692, there are illustrations of two different courses served on an oval table, with detailed advice about how the plates and dishes should be arranged.[53] Both have a symmetrical organization, with a main dish in the middle (for example, a *potage*) and one big plate with pies on each side. Around this, four smaller plates are arranged with dishes from the sea, and outside all of this are eight plates with different meat dishes. There is symmetry not only in the arrangement of the dishes but also in what they contain. The basic idea behind filling one of the pies on the big plates with game and the other with fish was to contrast foods from two different environments, the forest and the sea. The small dishes are placed diagonally, opposite one another, and they hold seafood of different types or cooked in different ways: oysters and crayfish, fried fish and boiled fish. The same principle goes for the meat dishes: fricassée and hachée, à la daube and à la mode.

The book was published during the baroque period, and the settings were typical of the ideas and actions that fascinated during this era: *Katalogisierung, Zerlegung, Kombination* (cataloging, dismantling, combination).[54] But this was also the era of rationalism. Corinne Lucas has pointed out that science and mathematics influenced the presentation of meals. The plans for table settings arranged the plates in a mosaic, "a picture where forms and colors draw geometrical motives. More than ever the different tastes are played out against each other."[55]

But even though symmetry corresponded to the main ideas of the baroque, it did not disappear when the period waned. There are illustrations showing symmetrically set tables in the most important nineteenth-century cookbooks, published in England, Russia, and Italy.[56]

In 1821, the gastronomic writer—and art historian—Karl von Rumohr explained that a round table should be laid with a soup tureen in the middle, while a rectangular table should have two tureens filled with different, contrasting soups, one meat and one fish. Other plates are set out around these big tureens, but there must be four, eight, or twelve of them, depending on the size of the table.[57]

This obsession with the even numbers seems to have been common. In his book of menus, published in the second half of the nineteenth century, the *Hofmarschall* to the King of Hanover comes back repeatedly to the concept of symmetry and explains that if the number of dishes is not even and the dishes are not put exactly opposite one another, "the symmetry will be disturbed."[58]

ETIQUETTE AT THE TABLE

The increasing number of different glasses and pieces of cutlery made correct behavior at the table more complicated. Books were—and still are—published with rules for how to attack the knives and forks when confronted with a table laid with cutlery designed for a series of different dishes. Such books also recommended how diners should move their body and hands, what facial expressions they should assume, and what acts they should guard against. Proper behavior was important for maintaining the aesthetics of the meal.

Such advice is generally included in guidebooks of good manners. "Etiquette" is the common word for the set of codes regulating social intercourse. Proper etiquette of course depends on which persons are involved. Looked at from the outside, etiquette often appears artificial, nothing more than imitation and pretense, but it is important to remember that etiquette expresses attitudes that have been developed through history. In a study of ethics and etiquette, Daniela Romagnoli, an Italian scholar, pointed out that a set of rules (a code) for good behavior, even if those rules seem or are superficial, is actually the result of a moral choice.[59]

The rules for good behavior were passed from parents to children, the same way as other forms of basic knowledge. But early on, they were also spread through literature: novels of chivalry, mirrors for princes, edifying stories, and didactic texts in prose and rhyme. The most famous didactic book in this genre is *De civilitate morum puerilium* (*A Handbook on Good Manners for Children*), by Desiderius Erasmus, the great humanist from Rotterdam. His sources were old medieval verses and sayings, which he adapted to the aristocratic ideals of the early sixteenth century. The book, first published in 1530, was printed in many editions and translations, and some of the maxims appeared in household books and cookbooks, side by side with menus and recipes.

A few cookbooks also touched on the difficult question of seating arrangements. There used to be very strict seating rules for royal and aristocratic dinners, as demonstrated in Boccaccio's *Decamerone,* which describes a feast where the king and the Marchioness of Monferrato are seated at one table, while the other guests are placed at tables according to their rank.[60] These rules were observed for official banquets as well, but seating was also important at private dinners. In her classic cookbook published in Victorian England, Isabella Beeton suggested that the host place at his right "the lady to whom he desires to pay most respect, either on account of age, position, or from her being the greatest stranger in the party." The other guests are seated "according to their rank and other circumstances which may be known by the host and hostess."[61] In the late nineteenth century, the Swedish gentleman author Charles Emil Hagdahl gave rules in his cookbook for where the host, hostess, and the most honored guests should be placed. Hagdahl instructed readers to serve the honored guests first, but he added that since it was, after all, a period of growing democratic sentiment, the guest who was the last to be served should be given the next dish first.[62] A few years later, a Spanish author emphasized in his cookbook that the host should treat all guests the same, regardless of their social standing.[63] But there was still the challenge of putting the right people together; it would not do, as Grimod pointed out, to put a priest between a poet and a comedian.[64] This of course has less to do with aesthetics and more to do with taste and pleasure, which will be discussed in the next chapter.

VERBAL DECORATION

The decoration of the table and the appropriate behavior of the guests are visible elements in the dramaturgy of the meal. Another very important component is verbal decoration: the use of words. In the refectories of many monasteries, monks ate while listening to religious literature; the motto was *edere et audire*. Conversation at the table (and in a social setting after leaving the table) has a long history—and literary history, with Plato, Plutarch, and Athenaeus in antiquity and Erasmus and Castiglione in the Renaissance. Even if mealtime discussions are often about topics other than food, there are examples from literature of conversations about eating and cooking; Athenaeus's *The Deipnosophistae* is one such work. How often such dialogues actually took place was not recorded, but we can gain some insight into the matter from an interesting booklet by the Englishman Henry Buttes in 1599. His work is an abridged version of Baldassare Pisanelli's 1583 book on the nature of food and drink.[65] Pisanelli presented historical background material under the title "Historie naturali," although most of it was anecdotal and thus of dubious value. In Buttes's book, this section had the title "Story for Table Talk." Buttes was a scholar at Corpus Christi College in Cambridge, and there is reason to conclude that such themes as the pleasure of eating and the history of food might have been discussed by the erudite gentlemen of the university at social occasions around a dinner table.

But words have been used at the table in many other forms, such as toasts and speeches (both serious and humorous), and songs of various kinds, from drinking songs to hymns. An early edition of the Church of Sweden's hymn book has a section called "Måltids-Psalmer" (Meal hymns). A Jewish tradition that was adopted by the Christian Church is saying grace before a meal (and often after as well). Erasmus discussed grace in the chapter about banquets in his book of manners for young boys, and in his gastronomic work, Rumohr recommended the grace proposed by Erasmus's adversary, Martin Luther, in his catechism.[66]

A more special form of verbal decoration, which can be found in several carving books in Germany and Scandinavia, are rhymed verses, originally meant to be improvised during the meal. They were particularly popular in the baroque period. In German, they were called *Leberreime* (liver rhymes) because they belonged to the moment of a meal when liver was served. A person would pierce a piece of liver with his knife—individual forks were not yet common—and offer it to one of the other guests along with a statement referring to the liver, for example: "The liver is cooked in our city." The receiver had to deliver a response that rhymed, for example: "With disgrace and vice never show pity."

Because spontaneous rhyming is no easy task, many *Leberreime* were printed in relevant books. The form was firmly established as two rhymed lines: the first (by the person offering the meat) about the liver, and the second (by the receiver) with the "morality," because it was often—but far from always—a moral statement. Some of the verses were religious, others were frivolous. References to liver could be difficult to come up with, so an alternative was to say what the liver was not:

> Liver, you don't come from a horse,
> Beer is good, but wine gives force.

Many of the verses were rather primitive in form and content, but several professional German writers composed *Leberreime,* among them Georg Greflinger,
who translated Nicolas de Bonnefons's cookbook from French. Greflinger noted
that the tradition was very popular among the Germans. In literary history works,
however, the verses have mostly been ignored or criticized, although a recent shift
in focus to popular culture has led to a new interest in them.[67]

There is no doubt that aesthetics are an important aspect of a meal: the laying of
the table, the communication between guests, the decoration, carving, and serving, and naturally the dishes themselves. In gastronomic writing from the early
nineteenth century onward, the meal was considered to be a work of art and discussed as such, and gastronomy was considered an integral part of the beaux
arts—at least in France.

18

Taste and Pleasure

Most cookbooks give recipes but do not make any comment about how dishes will taste. But there are books where the authors reveal their favorite recipes ("this is a very good dish") or leave to the reader a freedom of choice according to taste ("if you like"), and some prefaces and introductions discuss central concepts relevant to eating and drinking. One such concept, pleasure, was an important word in the title of the first printed cookbook, Platina's *De honesta voluptate et valetudine* (On right pleasure and good health).

PLATINA, PLATO, AND PLEASURE

What does *honesta* mean in this title? It has been translated as "right," "decent," "honest," and "honorable," and all these words support Platina's energetic and almost aggressive argumentation against the idea that his book had anything whatsoever to do with a pleasure achieved through consuming an excess and variety of foods. On the contrary, he stated that he was trying to help those who sought health and moderation. If the Romans had followed his example of moderation and frugality, he wrote, the city would not have had so many cooks, gluttons, dandies, and parasites.[1]

In the book's preface, Platina referred to many authors from antiquity, first among them the philosopher Epicurus. In the Middle Ages, Epicurus was normally considered a godless libertine, and Dante placed him deep down in the sixth circle of Hell (*Inferno*) in his *Comedia* from the early fourteenth century, while Socrates and Plato were kept at the edge of the first circle.[2] But in the early fifteenth century, a rehabilitation of Epicurus started. Platina praised him and made a point of the fact that Cicero and Seneca defended him. He argued that there was nothing wrong with Epicurus's doctrine on pleasure, claiming that the problem lay in the additions his corrupted followers made to it.[3]

Many cookbook authors agreed with Platina's reservations about exaggerated eating and defended their books against accusations of inciting gluttony. The Italian Pellegrino Artusi almost repeated Platina in 1891 when he emphasized that his interest in culinary arts had to do with his love of beautiful and good things, "il bello ed il buono" and in no way meant that he was a greedy glutton (he used the words *ghiottone* and *gran pappatore*).[4] John Evelyn, a member of the Royal Society, made the same claim when he published a book about salads in 1699. In his dedicatory epistle, he wrote that the book may look like a way to gratify "a Sensual Appetite with a Voluptuary Apician Art," but he assured the dedicatee: "I am so far from designing to promote those Supplicia Luxuriae, (as Seneca calls them) by what I have written; that were it in my power, I would recall the World, if not altogether to their Pristine Diet, yet to a much more wholsome and temperate than is now in fashion."[5]

Few cookbook authors were so well read in philosophy as Platina and Evelyn, so it is difficult to compete with these two when it comes to profound reflections on concepts and ideas. One illustrative example of a superficial and uninformed author is Antonio Latini, chief steward at the court in Naples, who wrote that although at first glance his book may make readers believe that he promoted luxury and intemperance, the truth was that the book encouraged frugality, sobriety, and temperence—words completely in accordance with those used by Platina. But Latini was obviously not informed about the rehabilitation of Epicurus, and he consequently saw his own work in the light of an opposition between Plato and Epicurus. He wrote that instead of teaching readers how to eat a lot, he would teach them how to eat well—to *platonizzare* rather than *epicurizzare*.[6]

There was, however, nothing reminiscent of Plato in Latini's extravagant book. As noted in chapter 1, Plato found culinary refinement morally dubious, just as the church did later. The capital sin of gluttony was a question not just of eating too much and too often but also of finding pleasure in food that was too elaborate. In a household and recipe book from the fourteenth century, *Le menagier de Paris*, the author described the seven deadly sins; he wrote that there were five branches of gluttony, and the fifth was an appetite for exquisite dishes.[7]

SIMPLICITY AND ELEGANCE—ART AND NATURE

There has been constant criticism of refined eating and cooking throughout the history of cuisine. One of the key words for an alternative ideal is "simple," a recurrent term in many of the statements made about taste, culinary pleasure, and the art of cooking. But simple food is not only defended with moral, religious, and social arguments as part of a condemnation of pleasure. For the humanist Erasmus, it was a fundamental idea that pleasure did not depend on luxuriously elabo-rated dishes. In the dialogue "Epicureus," Erasmus warned readers against think-ing that a rich man takes greater pleasure from eating partridges, pheasants, and exclusive fish than a pious man does from eating black bread and vegetables and drinking water, simple beer, or diluted wine.[8]

But most cookbook authors, even if they recommend moderation and simplic-ity in general terms, value recipes that introduce variation and subtle flavors. Pla-tina opposed debauchery (*luxus*), but he recommended not only moderation and health but also elegance (*lautitia*). Closer to our time, cookbook authors such as Auguste Escoffier advocated combining the simple with the elegant. "Simplicité de bon goût" (tasteful simplicity) is the expression he chose when he compared the prewar *vie luxueuse* with the simpler life that became a necessity after World War I.[9] In his cookbook, the Swedish gourmet Hagdahl attacked luxury and abundance and recommended a simple and refined lifestyle, which, according to him, brought *real* pleasure.[10]

From the time of Platina to the present, there has been a constant discussion of taste and pleasure in which moral and aesthetic values are confronted. In this con-text, the art of cooking is surprisingly often compared to the fine arts, a conse-quence of the fact that the word and the concept of "taste" (*goût*) had connections to both. In the sixteenth century, in one of his *Convivia*, Erasmus compared the organization of the dishes in a meal with the rules of drama and oration given in Horace's *Ars poetica*.[11] A few decades later, in the introduction to his cookbook, the Italian Bartolomeo Scappi wrote that the cook should follow the practice of a wise architect, who, after he created a *disegno*, built a foundation for his work.[12] *Disegno* originally referred to a drawing or a sketch, often one used to show a planned project such as a building or a painting, and it became a professional term in the mid-1550s, the years Scappi was cook for the pope. The art historian Giorgio Vasari called *disegno* "the father of the three arts—architecture, sculpture, and painting."[13]

In the seventeenth century, much of the discussion of taste in cookbooks seems to have been influenced by a new artistic ideal of classical arrangement and order, *la doctrine classique*. Contemporary cuisine was attacked for its "confusion." In 1674, in the preface of his cookbook, L. S. R., an anonymous author known only by his initials, virulently attacked contemporary cuisine, calling it antiquated and bizarre and describing it as piles and mountains of food (he used the words *entasse-ment, regorgement,* and *montagnes*).[14] This was similar to the criticism of French cuisine set forth in *Le repas ridicule* (The ridiculous meal), a satire written by Nico-las Boileau a few years earlier. Boileau called contemporary cuisine a confusion of piled meats and gave as an example a dish of three rabbits put on top of a hare and surrounded by six chickens.[15]

Boileau published the theoretical basis for the classicism of le Grand Siècle, *L'art poétique,* the same year as L. S. R. published his cookbook, and he warned against the crazy excesses he identified with Italy. He recommended the opposite, which he defined as common sense and restrained passion.[16] He referred to these as "natural," which was similar to "simple." This is the background for his negative attitude to heavy seasoning; in *Le repas ridicule,* he made fun of the host, who proudly declared that he had put nutmeg in every dish and, after stressing that a sauce should be balanced, added that he liked pepper to dominate.[17]

Criticism of liberal or indiscriminate use of strong spices became rather common in France in the seventeenth century, when cooks were using less of imported spices and more of local spices and milder herbs. L. S. R. warned against using too much salt and pepper on pea dishes because it destroyed the natural taste of the peas.[18] As early as 1654, the French author Nicolas de Bonnefons criticized strong spices because they disguised the original tastes of the other ingredients in a dish. He wanted variation in taste, but believed that it should not be achieved by mixing foods; he felt that it was important to distinguish between the true and natural tastes of different foodstuffs.

In the seventeenth century, "natural" was more or less synonymous with "original," but in the eighteenth century, the term was also used to define the opposite of artificial. In his poem *Le temple du goût* (*The Temple of Taste*), Voltaire declared himself to be the son of nature and claimed that he could recognize false and artificial tastes. In an article in his philosophical dictionary, he compared taste in art and cuisine, and "nature" was again an important word. He wrote that just as having bad taste in the physical sense meant that one was pleased only with seasoning that was too strong and exotic, so having bad taste in art meant that one found pleasure only in ornaments and was insensitive to the beauty of nature.[19]

DISGUISE AND THE RAGOUT METAPHOR

In praising the simple and the natural, some authors, among them Bonnefons, condemned what they referred to as "disguise"—the idea that mixtures of ingredients and strong spices concealed the real taste of the food. In his poem "La salade" (1560), the French poet Pierre de Ronsard praised salad, a simple dish he prepared with plants that he gathered from the meadow, cleansed in fountain water, and seasoned with salt, vinegar, and olive oil from Provence. He contrasted this with the hundreds of dishes served at court, where people ate without *goût.* The court represented the opposite of nature; it was a place of falseness, lies, and flattery. Ronsard did not say that the food at court was disguised but rather that the people's faces were.[20] This form of criticism was repeated around 1600 in an anonymous satire on court manners in which the author wrote that nothing natural had any value at court. He complained that the foods served at court were so disguised that they were unrecognizable; even the salads had so many ingredients that it was difficult to distinguish them.[21]

There are several examples of attacks on "disguised" food from the seventeenth century. In his study of England during the Restoration, "the masquerading age," John Spurr observed how popular masquerades were at the time and what unwelcome surprises they could lead to. He quoted from a seventeenth-century comedy: "A woman masked, like a covered dish, gives a man curiosity and appetite, when, it may be, uncovered, 'twould turn his stomach."[22] The English philosopher John Locke complained about disguised dishes in the 1660s, and in *Some Thoughts Concerning Education* (1693), he urged young people to eat frugally and not indulge in sauces, ragouts, and food masked by the art of cooking.[23] There was no coincidence that Locke chose ragout as his culprit, because this dish was attacked from many quarters in the 1690s.

Ragout was a dish that appeared in French cuisine in the early seventeenth century, and it consisted of meat cut into small pieces, stewed in a sauce with vegetables, and highly seasoned. The first recipes for ragout were printed in the 1650s. In a French book from 1654, it is said that "all the dishes in a good meal are almost all sauces and ragouts."[24] In the 1690s, the French pedagogue and archbishop François Fénélon published *Les aventures de Télémaque,* which recommended a noble and sober simplicity. He too denounced the ragout: "What a shame that the most advanced people let their greatness consist of ragouts, which weaken the soul and imperceptibly ruin the health of their bodies."[25] By 1691, the attacks had become so common that François Massialot felt he had to defend the dish in his popular cookbook *Le cuisinier royal et bourgeois,* which mentioned people who wanted to blame man's short lifespan on the fact that the simple and frugal food of the ancients had been replaced by "la multitude des ragoûts & assaisonnemens." But the author of the preface was not willing to accept this judgment. He argued that if an excess of ragouts possibly contributed to the corruption of the body, there was reason to believe that the variety in diet these ragouts represented could also strengthen and support the body.[26]

The attacks on ragout continued in the eighteenth century. In the great French *Encyclopédie, ou Dictionnaire raisonné des sciences et des métiers,* for example, which contained articles by many different specialists of the Enlightenment period, a long list of cookbooks was singled out as responsible for the development of a complicated cuisine and for popularizing all the inventions and changes that were used to disguise ingredients.[27] The *Encyclopédie* instead praised the simple food eaten by the first humans: milk, honey, fruit, vegetables, and bread. These are exactly the same products Rousseau mentioned when he praised simple, rustic food in his works He used almost identical expressions to describe the preferences of Émile and Julie, the protagonists of two of his most famous novels: Émile did not like fine ragouts at all, and Julie did not like meat, ragouts, or salt.[28]

Why did ragout receive this sort of criticism? A possible explanation is that the name of the dish comes from the French verb *ragoûter,* which means "to waken the appetite." Moralists believed that there was no reason to stimulate the appetite if a person was not hungry and that one should not spend extra time preparing a dish that involved multiple steps. Some cookbooks repeated moralist arguments. In *The English Housewife,* Gervase Markham emphasized that food should not "revive the appetites" and that one should avoid "the strangeness and rarity" of dishes from other countries.[29] But there were also cookbook authors who took great pride in the fact that their recipes excited the appetite. Nicolas de Bonnefons stated that he wanted his dishes to "revive the appetites bored by ordinary food."[30] The food historian Florent Quellier has noted the difference between La Varenne, who wrote about health, and Pierre de Lune, who wrote that his ragouts would awaken the appetite, and he argued that this shift gave a new meaning to the word *gourmandise.*[31] A German author declared that the recipes in his 1689 cookbook would appeal to food lovers not only by increasing their hunger but also by reviving their appetites.[32] In the nineteenth century, the Czech housewife Magdalena Rettigová proudly claimed that her recipes would whet the appetite because of the variations in preparation.[33]

COOKING AND ART

Ragout was also used as a metaphorical concept in theories about art during the eighteenth century, at the time when aesthetic considerations and discussions were coalescing into a critical discipline. The metaphor entered cookbooks; it can be found, for example, in the prefaces of two cookbooks by François Marin, published three years apart. The 1739 *Les dons de Comus* had a long and intellectual preface, which was anonymous but obviously by a professional writer.[34] The author gave a historical overview of French cuisine and claimed that it had finally stopped becoming increasingly complex and had now started to evolve into something more simple and scientific. He called modern French cuisine a sort of chemistry, explaining that the cook's science now consisted of analyzing food and then breaking it down to find its very essence. Cooks must extract the nourishing and light juices from ingredients, mix and blend them so that nothing dominates, and finally give them the same kind of unity that painters give colors and make them so homogeneous that from all the different flavors, only one taste is the result, a harmony of all the tastes.[35]

A few years later, in 1742, Marin published a three-volume continuation of *Les dons de Comus,* with another preface.[36] The author, again anonymous, picked up the theme from the 1739 preface, writing that he would compare two fields people find very far from each other: painting and cuisine. He noted that he personally had not found a better example to make his ideas understood: "The unity and rupture of colors that create the beauty of hues represent rather well in my opinion the blend of the juices and ingredients from which the Cook composes his ragouts.

It is necessary that the ingredients and the juices are drowned and melted the same way painters melt the colors and that the same harmony that in a picture draws attention from the connoisseur is felt by the fine palates tasting a sauce."[37]

Eighteenth-century philosophers also used the comparison between food and art in discussions about the concept of "delicacy." In his article about taste (*goût*) in the *Encyclopédie*, Montesquieu introduced *la délicatesse* as one important aspect. He distinguished between people who were *délicats*, who let one idea or taste be associated with others, and people who were *grossiers*, who were course and vulgar and added nothing to what nature provided. Those who judged creative works of art with taste would have an infinite number of impressions (*sensations*) that other people wouldn't have. He gave Apicius as an example of one of these people with taste, explaining that the Roman put things on the table that were unknown to "us ordinary eaters."[38] Montesquieu considered variety and novelty to be important values.[39]

A prominent British Enlightenment writer, Dr. Samuel Johnson, demonstrated a similar attitude in *A Dictionary of the English Language* (1755). He listed nine different meanings for the word "delicacy," and the first was: "Daintiness, fineness in eating." He also began his definition of the word "taste" by referring to eating; the meanings "distinguish intellectually" and "relish intellectually" followed as the third and fourth points.[40]

German philosophers, such as Kant and Hegel, took great care in distinguishing between the artistic values of different senses. According to Kant, taste and smell were subjective senses, whereas sight and hearing were objective senses.[41] Hegel believed that hearing and sight were "theoretical" senses, in that they were able to appreciate art in a way that the "material" senses—taste, smell, and touch—could not. He thought that what the eyes saw and the ears heard created an abstract image within the mind. The sensual (*der Sinnliche*) in art was spiritualized (*vergeistigt*).[42]

Such attitudes were ignored or criticized by the writers of "gastronomic literature," which had been established by Grimod de la Reynière and Brillat-Savarin. They were highly aware of "taste" in the context of food as well as art. One of these writers, Marcel Rouff, expressed it this way: "Cooking is the art of taste, as painting is the art of sight and music the art of hearing."[43] This view was shared by many of the nineteenth-century French novelists, such as Guy de Maupassant, who explained that a person was a gourmand in the same way that a person was an artist or a poet: "Taste is a delicate organ, perfect and respectable, like the eye and the ear."[44]

How do gastronomes apply this view when they write about the taste of a dish? It seems that no adequate language has been established in this field, as it has in the study of wine. This is probably why many gastronomic writers resort to metaphors or comparisons with art. Marcel Rouff, for example, used paintings in his analysis of a soup he praised as a masterpiece: "[The soup] had a kind of oldish charm à la Greuze but still contained a brutality à la Ribera and also some unexpected tenderness à la

Vinci."[45] Many cookbook authors compare art and food as well, such as Pellegrino Artusi: "Why does a man who enjoys a beautiful picture or a beautiful symphony have a higher reputation than someone who enjoys an excellent meal?"[46]

In response, many art critics would agree with Kenneth Clark's contention that "art must do something more than give pleasure."[47] In discussions about food and art, it is important to distinguish between the work done by the cook or the artist and the pleasure their works give the consumers. Critic Elizabeth Telfer has claimed that although a dish can be appreciated as a pleasure and even described in aesthetic terms, it can't transmit emotions, provoke, or produce reflections the way other arts can.[48] There are many who would disagree with this, however, among them readers of Marcel Proust's descriptions of emotions and reflections evoked by a modest madeleine.

A MEAL FOR ALL THE SENSES, AND
THE FUTURIST SOLUTION

Although this study will not delve into a broader or more profound analysis of food as art, it will discuss several writers who—ignoring the philosophy of art and the hierarchy of the senses—emphasized that a meal ought to please all the senses. It is an interesting paradox that two rather puritanical sixteenth-century philosophers—Erasmus and his friend Thomas More—wrote about meals in this way. A character in one of Erasmus's dialogues says that meals are meant for pleasure, they should feed the eyes, refresh the nose, and restore the mind, and he calls this pleasure *voluptas honestas,* as Platina did.[49] In his 1516 book, More wrote that on the (fictional) island of Utopia, no evening meal was without music, the burning of incense, and the sprinkling of ointments.[50] In the eighteenth century, the French philosopher Voltaire—who was in no way a puritan—in his controversial satirical poem about Jeanne d'Arc, *La pucelle d'Orléans,* praised twenty ragouts that charmed "the nose, the palate, and the eyes."[51]

The idea that meals should please the senses was repeated over and over in cookbooks. The court cook Marx Rumpolt included a chapter about how to arrange a banquet for princes and lords in his cookbook, and he mentioned music, plays, and fragrant smoke.[52] In 1698, another German author wrote about how a meal should give pleasure for the three senses of sight, taste, and smell,[53] but in a 1657 handbook on carving, the scholar and literary critic Georg Philipp Harsdörffer explained in detail that all the five senses should be satisfied during a meal. He wrote that the ears should be amused by charming music, poetry, and songs; the brain (which was thought to be the center of smell) should be fortified by fragrant perfumes and incenses; the mouth should be pleased with good food and sweet drinks; the hands should be occupied with selecting the best morsels; and the sight should enjoy the ingenious *entremets.*[54]

The pioneer of modern gastronomic literature, Grimod de la Reynière, wrote in his *Almanach des gourmands* that to be a gourmand, a person required more than just a fastidious palate; he needed all of his senses to be in constant agreement with his taste so that he could consider and evaluate food even before he brought it to his lips. In other words, his eyes needed to be penetrating, his ears vigilant, his touch exquisite, and his tongue perceptive.[55] With these requirements, Grimod seemed to have anticipated the beliefs of the leading personality within the futurist movement, Marinetti, author of *La cucina futurista*. Marinetti wanted to abolish the use of forks and knives so that diners would be able to enjoy a "tactile prelabial pleasure" (*piacere tattile prelabiale*).[56] Grimod's idea of agreement between the senses corresponds to what the futurists called *simultaneità* (simultaneity), which was a popular concept in the early twentieth century. If the goal of a meal was to satisfy all the senses at the same time, this implied that it was not adequate to serve a plate of food that only pleased the two senses of sight and taste. Marinetti therefore invented an instrument to be placed by every plate: a small box with velvet on one side and sandpaper on the other. The guest was supposed to touch the soft and the coarse surfaces while eating and simultaneously listen to music and inhale the smell of cologne that was sprayed into the room by one of the waiters.

The futurists elaborated a theory of culinary art that had the same concepts and categories as poetry, sculpture, painting, and other arts. Form—pleasing the eye— was important, and the interest the futurists showed in science, technology, and industry led to a fascination with geometrical figures. Circles, squares, cylinders, cones, cubes, and spheres were frequently used in futurist paintings and sculptures, and they also inspired new ways to design and decorate dishes. Even the futurist admiration for speed and modern means of transportation (such as cars and airplanes) influenced the movement's ideas about cuisine, resulting in several "aerodishes" and recipes, such as Digestive Landing and Libyan Aeroplane. War and violence were glorified by the use of "bombs" and "bombardments" in dish names—for example, Bombe à la Marinetti. Speed and violence were even combined in a dish called Car Crash.

The revolutionary break the futurists wanted to make with history and art traditions had to be implemented in cuisine as well, where they promoted the abolishment of established ideas about culinary taste and pleasure. They advocated abandoning the established syntax of poetry, and translating this idea to cuisine meant doing away with standard menu—culinary syntax, so to speak. They changed the sequence of dishes, and not every dish needed to be tasted. They tried out new combinations of dishes and tastes; a banana and an anchovy could be put on the same plate.

Bizarre food combinations were tried out in other settings as well. The French poet Apollinaire, for instance, wrote about a *dîner astronomique* in May 1912, around the same time the first futurist soirées took place, where a totally new cuisine was introduced. Guests were served destemmed violets sprinkled with lemon juice, burbot boiled in a decoction of eucalyptus leaves, and a sirloin steak cooked rare and seasoned not with salt and pepper but with tobacco. The main dish was quail, meticulously barded and then cooked in a licorice juice prepared from licorice sticks dissolved in chicken broth over a low fire.

Apollinaire described the meal in a short article called "Le cubisme culinaire."[57] He wanted to introduce cubist ideas into poetry, and his solution was *simultaneité*—like the *simultaneità* of the futurists, although he claimed to have invented the concept—because in a cubist picture it was possible to paint a face or another object so that two or more sides of it could be seen at the same time. The meal described above was not a cubist dinner—Apollinaire called it an example of *gastro-astronomisme*—but neither of these dinners was as successful in the field of gastronomy as the cuisine of the futurists, at least for a time.[58]

The same can be said of Salvador Dalí's surrealist cookbook, *Les dîners de Gala*. Dalí explained that he assigned essential aesthetic and moral values to all kinds of food, but he also emphasized that he liked only foods that had "a distinct form" comprehensible for the intelligence (une forme claire et compréhensible pour l'intelligence). He hated what he called horrible, disgraceful, and amorphous vegetables, such as spinach. The opposite of spinach was armor: "I adore eating armor, in fact everything that has shells" (tout ce qui est crustacé).[59] But the recipes were not his own; they were by prominent French cooks and represented a rather traditional cuisine when they were published in 1973, considering the reputation and status of the French nouvelle cuisine at this time. It is the framework, the illustrations, and the exhibitionist presentation that make this book special, not an aesthetic modernism in the elaboration of the dishes.

More down to earth than modern artists are the modern chefs who, as briefly noted in chapter 1, have launched culinary experiments in a search for new and more refined taste experiences. Helped and inspired by scientific research based on physics and chemistry, these chefs have discovered more exact methods of satisfying the palate, and by adventurously using new ingredients and unexpected combinations, they have managed to surprise restaurant guests and people reading their books. A statement on "new cookery," mentioned in chapter 1, was written in 2006 by chefs Ferran Adrià of El Bulli, Heston Blumenthal of the Fat Duck, Thomas Keller of the French Laundry and Per Se, and writer Harold McGee. They pointed to new possibilities for innovation as a result of excellent ingredients from all around the world, a greater understanding of cooking processes, and access to new technology. They stated that they are aware of the "narrow definitions and expectations embodied in local tradition" but want to build their new approach on the best that tradition has to offer. And—as so many have done before them—they realize that the act of eating engages all the senses as well as the mind. Blumenthal has, for example, relaunched the idea of simultaneity in his multisensory cooking: he once gave headphones to his guests so they could listen to the sounds of their own eating.

One of these chefs, Ferran Adrià, has even been approached as an artist, in the contemporary sense of the word, not just a mechanical artist. In 2007, he received an invitation from Documenta, the exhibition of modern and contemporary art that takes place in Kassel, Germany, every five years. The event's organizer, Roger Buergel, asked Adrià to participate because he saw the chef's work as a new artistic discipline, one that proved cuisine should be considered an art form. Creating a new cooking technique is, according to Buergel, just as complicated and challenging as creating a great painting.[60]

19

Gender in Cookbooks and Household Books

The difference in status and salary between professional male cooks and female cooks was discussed in chapters 1 and 2. But the question of gender and gender equality is something that concerns every household consisting of a man and a woman. Gender disparity can be seen in cookbooks and household books through the centuries. In ancient Greece, so-called economic literature contained a sort of management philosophy concerning household production, administration, and living conditions. Aristotle placed economics between ethics (rules for the individual) and politics (rule for the society). He believed that a household depended on three relationships: between husband and wife, between father and children, and between master and slaves.[1] Such thinking became the basis of the political theory of the French Renaissance philosopher Jean Bodin, who argued for the absolute authority of the sovereign of a state. He compared this authority to the one a husband had in a family, where a wife was expected to show obedience as well as reverence.[2] The idea spread quickly. In a speech to parliament in 1609, King James I of England declared that the king was the father of his people (*parens patriae*): "As for the father of a familie, they had of olde under the Law of Nature *Patriam Potestam,* which was *Potestam vitae & necis* [power over life and death] over their children and familie."[3] These patriarchal ideas were repeated in household works written in the early modern era.

HOUSEHOLD ENCYCLOPEDIAS

In the Italian book *Il padre di famiglia* (The father of the family), the famous Renaissance poet Torquato Tasso compared the responsibility the husband/father/

master of an estate had for his family and employees to the responsibility an emperor had for his empire and subjects.[4] Johann Coler, a German writer of economic literature, called the household a monarchy (which literally means "the rule of one"), where only one person, the husband, is master of the house and rules and governs.[5] A main theme in all such treatises is the subordination of women, who, in the words of the French physician and author Charles Estienne, ought to be diligent, peaceful, obliging, and obedient to God and their husbands and not quarrelsome, bad-tempered, talkative, or lazy.[6] The same attitudes are found in *Domostroi* (House order), a Russian household book from the sixteenth century, which emphasized the absolute authority of the tsar, the church, and the husband. A wife was expected to serve and obey: "Every day a wife should ask and consult her husband on all important matters and remember this."[7] However, this did not mean that a housewife was without responsibilities or even power; she was, in fact, often the one who directed work on the estate in her husband's absence. And according to a study of Tudor women, when he was at home, she "sat by his side after the meal, discussed the management of the entire estate with him, and was both companion and business partner."[8]

Typical for the medieval and early modern European estate was that daily social life was shared not only by the parents and children but also by other dependent relatives and the servants. In towns and cities, when the new affluent bourgeoisie set up their households in big homes on large properties, their apprentices were also included. The household rather than the family was "considered the basic urban social unit," according to the scholar Alexander Cowan: "More urban inhabitants belonged to households than to any other group within society."[9]

In these households, the housewife was in charge of the provisions for the kitchen and the cellar, but she also supervised childbirth and the health of all the people who lived on the estate. In some of the early household books—or "books of husbandry," as they were called in England—there were short chapters about "housewifery," which described the wide range of activities women were responsible for. But the first detailed account of a housewife's duties appeared in one of the most commercially successful English books of this genre, *Country Contentments*, written in 1615 by the gentleman Gervase Markham, who was the author and translator of several treatises on agriculture. The work was divided into two parts. The first was "The Husbandmans Recreations," and it gave instruction in horse breeding, hunting, hawking, shooting, and even some sports, such as tennis and bowling. The second was called "The English Housewife," and it was later printed separately. In his opening words, Markham referred to the first part of the book, intended for the master of the estate, who had outside duties, and then wrote that he would now "descend . . . to the office of our English housewife" and to the employment within the house.[10] "Descend!" There is certainly no doubt that the housewife's tasks were considered to be a step down in the hierarchy of household work. Describing the virtues and character of the ideal housewife and her behavior toward her husband, Markham wrote that she should be modest, "coveting less to direct than to be directed, appearing ever unto him pleasant, amiable, and delightful."

But within the household, the housewife had the authority to direct the cooking, brewing, and baking, the production of butter and cheese, the making of malt, the distillation of household waters, the preserving of wines, the supervision of the garden, the management of medicines (physical surgery), and the production and dyeing of textiles made from wool and hemp.

In Germany, the difference in the duties of the husband and the housewife is best illustrated by two five-volume household works published at the end of the eighteenth century: *Der Hausvater in systematischer Ordnung* (The husband in systematic order) and *Die Hausmutter in allen ihren Geschäften* (The housewife in all her businesses). The book for the husband was basically about agriculture, while the text for the housewife was an encyclopedic collection of all sorts of household duties and activities.[11]

NEW BOOKS FOR WOMEN: POETICIZING HOUSEWORK

In the eighteenth century, it was evident that a change was underway. There was an ever sharper division of labor between husband and housewife, not only on big country estates but also in the growing number of middle-class households. This can be seen in the new types of books that started replacing older encyclopedic works. Some of these new books combined information about cooking with other activities. One of these combinations was cooking and gardening, known already in the seventeenth century. The French author Nicolas de Bonnefons presented his cookbook as the continuation of his garden book, which had been published three years earlier.[12] The first vegetable cookbook in Germany was originally printed as an appendix to a famous work by the gardener at the court of the Prince of Brunswick.[13] In Denmark, Holland, and England, books were published with instructions for both gardening and cooking. John Evelyn's book about salads, *Acetaria*, is another example of this combination.

One important reason for this shift was that gardening was gradually breaking away from the other branches of agriculture and increasingly becoming a woman's domain. Bonnefons's books were "dédié aux femmes" (dedicated to the women), and this trend continued in the following centuries. But the real revolution began at the end of the nineteenth century and the beginning of the twentieth, when it became popular for middle-class homes in suburban areas to have orchards and herbal gardens. At the same time, sugar became cheaper and accessible to a broader public, and a flood of cookbooks were published with recipes for all sorts of sweet jams, juices, drinks, soups, and puddings based on fruits and berries that could be grown in home gardens.

Decorative works in small format containing recipes for medicines, cosmetics confectioneries, and food, described in chapter 12, were another type of combined book for women. These were popular as early as the sixteenth century and were followed in the seventeenth century by books that contained instructions for cooking and advice about proper manners and social behavior, the first of which was *The Gentlewoman's Companion,* published in 1673. "Thus the men's and the women's books catered to different audiences and the gap between the two groups would widen in the eighteenth century,"[14] wrote the scholar Gilly Lehmann, who also observed another change. Markham opened his early seventeenth-century book with words about the religious virtues and practical duties of a housewife, but in the next century, books that equated cooking with female duty "were now much less acceptable to the mistress." This can be seen in changes to book titles: *The Whole Duty of Woman* (1737), for example, was renamed *The Lady's Companion* (1740).[15]

The historian James Sharpe quoted a conduct book for women, *The Ladies' Calling* (1725), in which economy and household management is called "the most proper feminine business." According to Sharpe, male writers of conduct books in England between 1550 and 1760 "were envisaging a division of labour and responsibilities in the middle-class household which in some respects seems to have presaged the 'separate spheres' ideology of the Victorian period."[16] This nineteenth-century ideology implied a clear division between the genders that placed the active man in the public sphere and the passive woman in the domestic one. "Man for the field and woman for the hearth," Alfred Tennyson wrote in 1847, while England was governed by Queen Victoria, who soon would name him poet laureate. But men were not all in the fields anymore. Urbanization and industrialization had forced them into offices, shops, banks, factories, city halls, and parliament. This meant that the housewives were left to run the homes. Mary Randolph, an American cookbook author, now saw her responsibility the same way the husband did in the Italian poet Tasso's book: "The government of a family, bears a Liliputian resemblance to the government of a nation." And the main task was to keep the budget: "The contents of the Treasury must be known, and great care taken to keep the expenditures from being equal to the receipts."[17] In her classic Victorian cookbook, Isabella Beeton compared the mistress of the house to the commander of an army or the leader of an enterprise, but she also asserted that a good housewife was the best gift to a man.[18]

The division of labor was accompanied by a division of power. Tennyson echoed Markham in his poem "The Princess": "Man to command and woman to obey." The busy man lived and commanded in a world of capitalist competition and political strife. In this context, the home was idyllically described as a safe

FIGURE 31. Illustration from the nineteenth-century Danish cookbook *Illustreret kogebog for by og land* (Illustrated cookbook for the town and the country), by Laura Adeler.

sanctuary, where the housewife was "The Angel of the House" and represented compassionate values and qualities (figure 31).

To strengthen this image of women, young upper- and upper-middle class girls were given education in music, painting, poetry, foreign languages, and embroidery. But there was a problem with this development. Even if it was possible for the most affluent women to pursue such a life because they would have butlers and house-keepers and all sorts of domestic staff to help them, they were still expected to be responsible for managing their own households. As Lehmann pointed out, "there was a yawning gulf between the theory . . . and the daily reality of women's lives, which meant they were often obliged to take an active role in the kitchen and in the still-room, as they had in previous centuries."[19] Many authors of cookbooks and household books expressed a strong skepticism as to what some of them considered dilettante artistic activities, which they found to be a useless and pointless pastime.[20] A Russian cookbook writer, for example, suggested what she felt was a better alternative: she wished to raise the "artistic" status of household duties, including cooking. "Domestic economy," she wrote, "provides the means of poeticizing, so to speak, the most prosaic objects, such as the kitchen and household tasks."[21]

COOKBOOKS FOR GIRLS—FUTURE HOUSEWIVES

A form of "poeticizing" may be evident in a new branch of the cookbook genre that appeared in northern Europe in the mid-nineteenth century: cookbooks for children (figure 32). The first of these books were published in Denmark and Germany, but in both countries, the authors found it difficult to convince publishers to believe in this new idea. Once published, however, the books became very successful.[22]

The first German book was printed in Nuremberg, a center for the production of modern dollhouses. Dollhouses had existed in Germany since the seventeenth century, but they were exclusive and expensive toys for children in aristocratic or very affluent families. In the early nineteenth century, dollhouses were developed with kitchens that had spirit stoves, so it was actually possible to cook in them.[23] One of the early German cookbooks for children had the title *Puppenköchin Anna* (The doll cook Anna).[24]

A motive behind the new cookbooks was to amuse and entertain young girls, but the doll's kitchens and cookbooks were still not available for all social classes. The price of the dollhouses, books, and selection of foodstuffs required excluded the greater part of the population. The subtitle of one of the Danish books was "Amusing pastime for well-bred girls from 6 to 12 years."[25] "Well-bred" (*dannede*) did not allude to politeness or education but to social position. These books were for children who lived in homes with domestic servants, something that is clear from the prefaces: "When the maid has a day off, would it not be interesting for you to cook?"[26] This would be a completely inconceivable idea in a working-class or peasant home, where children took part in housework from an early age and the work was hardly considered a form of amusement.

Apart from the social aspect, there was the question of gender. These cookbooks were not for all children but specifically for *girls*. This was evident from many of the titles, but it was also emphasized in the prefaces. "Girls," one German cookbook stated, "are not attracted by the noisy games of their brothers."[27] The preface of a Swedish cookbook from 1875 admitted that boys in the family may occasionally help out in the kitchen, but this was followed by a warning: "By all means, don't let them touch a dough."[28] Even though some cookbooks acknowledged that a girl may want an education or a professional career—for example, as a photographer, clerk, or teacher—she was still bound by traditional gender roles: all girls needed to learn to cook, "because one day Mother may be ill or out of the house, and the daughter would need to cook for her father."[29]

FIGURE 32. Illustration from *Barnas Kokebok* (Children's cookbook), probably published by a weekly family magazine in the early twentieth century.

The books were meant to be a form of entertainment, but they obviously also had another agenda: they introduced the characteristics of a perfect housewife. The preface of the first children's cookbook, published in 1847, encouraged girls to embrace cleanliness, order, aesthetic sense, and a respect for the servants.[30] A German book printed in 1865 proudly declared: "We find among small girls born cooks and housewives."[31] Henriette Davidis, a prolific German author of cookbooks and advice books for housewives and young girls, expressed her hope of teaching them the most important of all female arts: cooking.[32] But her interest was wider. Her first cookbook, *Puppenköchin Anna,* was followed by *Puppenmut-*

ter Anna (The doll mother Anna), which aimed at "arousing the sense for domestic duties and household work among girls." In another book, she wrote that a "morally and practically raised daughter will in due time be a caring wife."[33]

It is rather interesting that there are few early children's cookbooks in the Mediterranean countries. One of them, the French *Bébé Cordon Bleu,* published in 1888, seemed to be less concerned with promoting the role of "housewife" than the role of "hostess." The book taught little girls to serve a simple dinner, but one based on the rules of the art of cooking, and it assured readers that everyone would admire the "delicate and appetizing food."[34] Compared to Germany and England, countries such as France and Italy produced more cookbooks than general household books for women. In Italy, most household books provided information for administrators of courts or practical instructions for agricultural work on country estates.

CLEANLINESS AND COZINESS

Cookbooks for girls constituted only a small part of a wider market for cookbooks in the nineteenth century. Particularly in Great Britain and northern Europe, increased literacy and better living conditions for more people created a new demand for cookbooks for smaller families. These households had perhaps only one domestic servant, who had to wash, clean, cook, and do whatever else was demanded.[35] In these homes, the housewife could not just give orders; she also had to take an active part in the work. To succeed in this, many qualities were necessary, such as industry, tidiness, and frugality. A cookbook from 1860 launched the phrase "the three domestic spices" that young housewives should have, which were characteristically given "From a father to a daughter." The "spices" were a snow-white tablecloth, meals at set times, and a mild and friendly face. The point about the tablecloth had the following commentary: "Even the most simple food will get an extra taste when the eyes dwell with pleasure on the white cloth, the shining porcelain and the bright glasses—the immediate association is 'a clever housewife.'"[36]

The tablecloth represented the virtue of cleanliness. This was nothing new in household literature, as discussed in chapter 1. In Torquato Tasso's household book, mentioned above, it was recommended that floor, walls, and ceilings be cleaned so they shone like mirrors. This of course had to do with hygiene, but for Tasso, there was also an aesthetic aspect to it and even a social one. He felt that cleanliness was pleasing to the eye but also that it conferred dignity. A similar point of view was detectable in the dominant bourgeois ideals of the nineteenth century. Cleanliness became a social distinction. The growing middle class wanted to distance itself from the working class, and one of the ways it did so was by keeping the home clean and tidy. As the Swedish sociologist Boel Berner observed: "The struggle against the dust becomes a struggle against the 'lower' classes, against ugliness and poverty, and this struggle has almost religious dimensions."[37]

This did not mean that the women of the working classes lacked the desire to maintain clean homes, but it was more difficult for them to do so. First of all, they had no domestic servants; on the contrary, they often took jobs outside the home as servants or workers themselves to improve the family economy. Many working-class homes did not have separate kitchens or running water. This is the context we need to understand the intellectual avant-gardists and Komsomol activists in the early stages of the new Soviet Union. They protested against the virtue of cleanliness and condemned it as a bourgeois ideal. In his 1918 satirical drama *Mystery-Bouffe*, Vladimir Mayakovsky contrasted the bourgeoisie, "the clean," with the proletariat, "the dirty."[38] But this distinction was abandoned in later Soviet household and advice literature, in which cleanliness was described as "the essential of a cultural life."[39]

Serving meals at set times was emphasized from early on as a duty for good housewives, because husbands did not like to come home and find that their food was not ready. In a Dutch cookbook from the beginning of the seventeenth century, housewives were warned that if they were late with dinner, their husbands would be angry and use harsh words.[40] The Russian author Elena Molokhovets mentioned that a housewife who was inexperienced in the art of cooking could expect a discontented family.[41] The German Mary Hahn stressed the value of cleanliness and punctuality for a good family life, but she also pointed to the importance of proper cooking: "An oversalted soup or a burnt roast are often the small reasons for a failed marriage."[42]

Many authors emphasized that the husband and his needs should always be put first. A wife must support her husband, a Swedish household catechism instructed, because a woman was after all the reason that he was cast out of Paradise.[43] A German book recommended that women suppress their own wishes in general, and also at dinner: "If you don't have enough money to prepare a dinner with meat for both of you, then renounce it yourself, but prepare it for your husband."[44] The title of a cookbook published in Germany during the Weimar period revealed its purpose: *Wie mache ich meinen Mann glücklich?* (How do I make my husband happy?).[45]

Because serving meals at the proper time was so important, some books included the preparation time in the recipes. A nineteenth-century English book assured readers in the preface: "The time which is required to cook each dish, is also laid down, so that the good wife can tell how long before the husband's dinner she should commence her cooking, so that she will always be able to have her meals ready at the appropriate time."[46]

Many books recommended creating a cozy home, explaining that this and a good meal would encourage the husband to go straight home after work and not yield to other temptations on the way.[47] The importance of saving the husband from drunkenness and other vices is found in books from several countries in northern Europe. One Norwegian author claimed that many clever housewives had prevented their husbands from becoming drunkards by serving them good dinners and maintaining cozy homes.[48] The 1914 edition of Molokhovets's classic cookbook includes a series of letters praising the author. A group of ladies from a society in Smolensk wrote that the cookbook, with its advice about how to create a cozy home, had "saved many families that otherwise would have been destroyed by drunkenness and loose living."[49]

DOMESTIC SCIENCE

These attitudes were part of the larger idea that the housewife was the guardian of moral values. But at the same time, moral concerns were not to in any way reduce the efficiency of executing daily duties. One of the most systematic approaches to household efficiency was laid out in *The American Woman's Home*, written by two American sisters, the pedagogue and cookbook author Catherine Beecher and the professional writer Harriet Beecher Stowe. The introduction stated: "The authors of this volume, while they sympathize with every honest effort to relieve the disabilities and sufferings of their sex, are confident that the chief cause of these evils is the fact that the honor and duties of the family state are not duly appreciated, that women are not trained for their trades and professions, and that, as the consequence, family labor is poorly done, poorly paid, and regarded as menial and disgraceful."[50]

The sisters did not promote ideas about women's rights and equality between men and women, but they did want to promote more respect for household work, which they called "woman's true profession." They believed that women needed a more professional education to prepare themselves to become housewives, just as men needed if they were to become lawyers or doctors. To elevate the professionalization of household work, Catherine Beecher suggested using the term "domestic economist" instead of "housewife." Expressions such as "domestic economy" and "domestic science" were later substituted by "home economics," inspired by the pioneer female scientist Ellen Richards, author of *The Chemistry of Cooking and Cleaning* (1882). She was a proponent of applying scientific knowledge to various forms of work in the home, and she believed that because women were responsible for this work, they ought to get a scientific education. Home economics became a key expression in new institutions, not only in the United States but also in Germany, Great Britain, and other parts of Europe from the mid- and late nineteenth century. The earlier cooking schools were transformed into household schools, and separate household classes for girls were introduced in primary schools. Order and cleanliness were still important, but they were supplemented with bookkeeping, nutritional theory, and technical knowledge. Industrialization had changed household work. More and more foodstuffs were sold ready to put into pots and pans. Culinary preparation had become simpler in many ways, but housewives were now required to master new stoves and kitchen machines. In the twentieth century, electric appliances were invented. All these changes were reflected in household books.[51]

The next stage came in the late twentieth century, when most women were working outside the home. Cookbooks took this into consideration and demonstrated that it was possible to make simple meals quickly and without too much preparation. Some of the books, however, expressed a nostalgia for the old days: "When Mother and Grandmother lived, the daughters still learned how to cook and manage a household."[52] But this stage was also characterized by education reform; classes in cooking and household management were not any longer exclusively for girls, but for pupils of both sexes. There has recently been an increased interest in cooking among men—which previously was lacking for all but professional cooks. However, there is still not full equality between men and women when it comes to household duties, although cooking is more popular among men than other tasks, at least in the more affluent and well-educated parts of the population in Western countries. So a relevant question is: As more men become interested in cooking, will cookbook publishers consider new and different approaches to appeal to them?

Epilogue

Cookbooks and the Future

The future of the cookbook is part of a broader question: What is the future of the book? When the cook Martino and the writer Platina met in the fifteenth century, the Gutenberg era had just begun. What will happen to the physical book as more and more information and texts of all kinds can be accessed via other media? According to the scholar David Greetham, we don't know yet if this shift "from the printed book to hypertext is of a different order from previous shifts in medium (for example from manuscript to print, from roll to codex, from oral transmission to the written word)."[1] It is possible that the primacy of print will be totally undermined by new technologies in the long run, but this does not necessarily signify the death of the book. Historians David Finkelstein and Alistair McCleery point out that, "in fact, some have argued that new media has the potential to extend the life of the book through individual engagement with written texts."[2]

Printed cookbooks are still flooding the market, but more and more people are turning to the Internet to look for recipes. Is it only a matter of time before cookbooks follow the same path as reference works, with exclusively electronic editions? Or do cookbooks have other functions and needs than most reference works? The history of the cookbook dates back to the manuscript age, when single recipes were recorded; over time, these were compiled into recipe collections. After the introduction of modern printing, individuals continued to put together their own cookbooks made up of material from friends as well as recipes found in printed books. Some printed cookbooks even included blank pages so readers could write down their personal recipes. In the nineteenth century, recipes were printed in magazines, which meant that instead of copying recipes by hand, housewives (and perhaps some men) could cut them out and paste them into their private cookbooks, still a common activity today. Some publishers even invented new alternative forms for collecting recipes, such as systems with each recipe printed on a separate card or a separate sheet that could be put into a box or a ring binder.[3]

In other words, cookbooks have a long tradition of being considered dynamic literature. In this context, using the Internet to search for and view recipes is just another step in the same direction. It is now possible to compile a personal electronic recipe collection and make the most of the new features this medium offers, such as hypertext and searchability. The Internet makes it possible to watch video clips of recipes being prepared, and recipes can also be introduced through the new medium of television cooking shows.

Illustrations have been printed in cookbooks since the incunabula era, but they were rarely pedagogically effective. Television brought a new type of approach, one that in many ways mimics the scenario in which a mother teaches her daughter or a master cook instructs his apprentice: words are followed by acts, or better, acts are explained by words. Normally, this is a one-way communication, from the television cook to the audience, but it is sometimes a dialogue between two people in a television studio. How is the host's language created in this new setting? Are the sentences planned and drilled—in other words, are they written texts learned by heart? Is this a false orality compared to the original teacher-pupil scenario? Or is all teaching based on a certain degree of performance and therefore dependent on training? At any rate, modern television cooks most certainly have reminiscences of all the cookbooks they have read and all the cooking teachers they have listened to. The scholar Walter Ong has called this new orality a secondary orality: "This new orality has striking resemblances to the old in participatory mystique, its fostering of a communal sense, its concentration on the present moment, and even its use of formulas. But it is essentially a more deliberate and self-conscious orality, based permanently on the use of writing and print."[4]

Most people watch television cooking shows as a form of entertainment. The writer Neil Postman observed in 1984 that television transformed part of Western culture into an arena of show business; education became an "amusing activity."[5] But practical professions are learned not only by listening and watching but also by doing. This means that television kitchen shows are only superficially similar to the original mother-daughter and master-apprentice scenarios because the daughter and apprentice actually had to repeat the acts demonstrated by their teachers. This may change through the use of new electronic media, such as personal blogs, which allow for interactivity.

Despite their popularity, television shows and blogs have not made books superfluous. Some of the hosts of these programs have become celebrity chefs, and the recipes from their shows have been collected and published as books, many of which have become bestsellers. Today, the same is happening with food blogs, many of which have also been turned into popular cookbooks. The Internet has become a steppingstone to producing a printed work. This has brought about changes to the editorial process. Traditionally, at least since the early twentieth century, publishers had ideas for cookbooks, contacted qualified individuals, made marketing analyses, and so on. Now, much of this work is done on social media. At the same time, technological advances have opened the gates for self-publishing. The Mexican intellectual Gabriel Zaid warned that the number of books increases geometrically, while the number of readers increases arithmetically; so, if the passion for writing continues like this, we are heading toward a world with more authors than readers.[6]

To answer the question of whether a cookbook is really necessary in this environment, we must begin with a discussion of function. Many television shows are available on the Internet, which means that the recipes can be watched repeatedly on a computer screen, but is this practical in the kitchen? There are still fumes and smoke in many kitchens, which can make electronic devices difficult or unsuitable to use. But even if these problems were to be solved, cookbooks would still be popular. The reason is that they don't need to be read for practical purposes. When the great French poet Baudelaire complained about the lack of good restaurants in Belgium, he found comfort in reading a cookbook.[7] That kind of pleasure is even more obvious today with the introduction of modern food design in the illustrations of beautiful editions of cookbooks in coffee-table format. The recipes in these books are meant to be leafed through and read sitting in a sofa or an easy chair rather than followed step by step over the kitchen stove. In this context, it is possible to see cookbooks as show business. When Postman refers to what he calls "television-oriented print media," he mentions magazines such as *People* and *US*, but there is a similar interchange between television cooking shows and food blogs and coffee-table cookbooks.[8]

As Angus Phillips has pointed out, books are also important for the authors themselves: "For an author, appearing in print remains better than being published on the Web. There is an affirmation of one's worth as a writer, and receiving a beautifully printed hardback of one's work is an undeniable pleasure."[9] This is particularly important if an author wants to be considered for prizes and awards, such as the annual Gourmand World Cookbook Award. Celebrity chefs can use their cookbooks to promote themselves, and cookbooks can be used to promote special products, foods, and kitchen appliances.

Finally, many cookbooks are conceived and written within the framework of a lifestyle ideology, representing new (and old) moral attitudes and practices. They are part of a self-help and self-development literature, to be studied mainly outside of the kitchen.

To predict what will happen to the cookbook is no easy task, and it is risky to start with preconceived ideas and make general conclusions based on situations in one historical period, such as the social anthropologist Jack Goody did in the 1970s when he wanted to prove his theory that the written form was more socially prestigious than the oral form. He referred to a small Italian restaurant in London that had no printed menu; instead, a waiter informed customers of the few dishes of the day.[10] But today, the snob values have been turned upside down. At many fashionable gourmet restaurants, waiters tell diners about the dishes the chef has chosen to prepare that day, and printed menus are not expected.

Today, the whole idea of print on paper is at stake. But fashion and trends shift in ways that are very difficult to predict. Historical development is a dynamic process that depends on factors that will often appear clearly only in retrospect. The interpretation of these factors in the future will, in turn, depend on solid knowledge and understanding of the history of the book. My hope is that this study of the life of cookbooks over seven centuries will be a small contribution to this history.

PROLOGUE

1. The biographical information in the following paragraphs is based on Bruno Laurioux's magisterial study of Platina's life and work. See Laurioux 2006b. Biographical material in English can be found in Milham 1998, pp. 1–59; and S. Bauer 2006, pp. 3–84.

2. Laurioux 1996b, pp. 44–45; Laurioux 2006b, p. 524. This does not mean that Martino had invented all his dishes. Several of them are similar to recipes in earlier manuscripts, but they were adapted and developed to new circumstances. See also Scully 2000, pp. 18–21 for a discussion of Martino's sources.

3. Laurioux 1997, p. 215.

4. Riley 2005.

5. Melozzo da Forli, *Papa Sisto IV nomina Bartolomeo Platina, prefetto della Biblioteca Apostolica Vaticana,* fresco, ca. 1477. It was later transferred to canvas and can now be found in the Vatican Museum (Pinacoteca Vaticana).

6. One early example: In the 1520s, when the Spaniard Francisco Delicado wrote his popular story about la Lozana Andaluza in Rome, he named Platina and Apicius as proponents of the most elaborate cuisine. See Delicado, *Retrato de la Loçana andaluza* (Venice, 1528), fol. 3 verso.

7. Vehling 1941. The German-born cook and book collector Joseph D. Vehling found the manuscript in an antiquarian bookshop in Italy, and he later sold it to A. W. Bitting, who gave it to the Library of Congress.

8. Platina's book was probably printed in Rome around 1470, but the edition does not give the name of the printer, place, or year. Therefore, references to Platina's work in this study are to the first dated edition, printed in Venice in 1475. This edition is without pagination and foliation, so the references are to chapter (called *liber,* i.e., "book") and the name of

the recipe. The English translation of the title is the one used by Mary Ella Milham in her critical edition and translation. See Milham 1998.

1. THE COOK

1. In his book about cooks and cooking, Michael Symons wrote that "cooks have always been in the background—both ever present and unnoticed." Symons 2000, p. x.

2. About the differences between guilds, see Christopher R. Friedrichs, *The Early Modern City* (London, 1995), p. 145; James R. Farr, *Artisans in Europe 1300–1914* (Cambridge, 2000), p. 113; Scully 1995, p. 239; and Christopher Hibbert, *The Rise and Fall of the House of Medici* (Harmondsworth, 1987), p. 25.

3. Aristotle, *Ta Politika*, 1256b 23; Niccolò Machiavelli, *Il principe* (Florence, 1532), chap. 14.

4. Nimb 1900, p. 450.

5. From a fifteenth-century manuscript, *Divers Makyng*, MS Beineke 163, Yale University, printed in Hieatt 1988, p. 91 (recipe 140).

6. In classical Rome, professional cooks were slaves and had no religious obligations. See Wilkins 2000, p. 369; and Dalby 2003, pp. 102–103.

7. Rambourg 2010, p. 11. This dualism brings to mind how fire in literature is the "contradictory, paradoxical symbol par excellence." See Karin Becker, "La symbolique du feu et de la flamme dans la littérature," *Linguæ &: Revista di lingue et culture moderne* 15, no. 1 (2016): pp. 9–28.

8. Carême 1847, vol. 2, p. xx; Grimod de la Reynière 2012, pp. 218–220.

9. Martínez Montiño 1611, fol. 1 verso; Czerniecki 1682, p. 10.

10. Geoffrey Chaucer, "The General Prologue," *Canterbury Tales;* Hieatt 1996, pp. 138–139.

11. Liberati 1668, p. 88.

12. Sebastian Brant, *Das Narrenschiff* (Basel, 1499), fol. 109.

13. Rossetti 1584, quoted in Albala 2007, p. 143.

14. Plato, *Gorgias* 518b; Plato, *Seventh Letter* 326b; Plato, *Politeia,* 372b–373b. In translations of the *Republic, opson* has been called *obsonium* (Latin), "relish" (English), *Zukost* (German), *mets* (French), *manjares* (Spanish), *companatico* (Italian), and *poklebka* (Russian).

15. Plato, *Gorgias* 462d, 463b.

16. Cicero, *De officiis* 150. Cicero also used the low social status of cooks in a pun; see Mary Beard, *Laughter in Ancient Rome* (Berkeley, 2015), p. 99.

17. Bauer 1987, p. 127.

18. Brant, *Narrenschiff,* fol. 110.

19. Raoul de Houdenc, *Le songe d'Enfer* (Paris, 1908), pp. 89–90.

20. Henisch 2009, p. 2.

21. Vincent-Cassy 1993, pp. 18–30.

22. Gerhard B. Winkler, *Bernardus claraevallensis: Sämtliche Werke,* vol. 2 (Innsbruck, 1992), pp. 92–98, 181; Eloy d'Amerval, *La grande diablerie,* (Paris, 1495), quoted in Sauzet 1982, p. 248; Taillevent 1486, fol. c7. At the time, the term *viandier* referred to a man who was responsible for provisions.

23. Henisch 2009, p. 12.

24. Elias 1939. Elias has been criticized for using conduct books as sources more often than observations from real life, but later research has supported most of his conclusions.

25. Burke 2009, p. 172. Carnival has been considered subversive by some scholars, but its function was mainly to relieve pressure for a while before society returned to the established order.

26. Wilkins 2000.

27. Platina 1475, book 1, De quoco; book 6, Cibaria alba.

28. See, for example, Willan 1977, p. 25; Laurioux 1997a, p. 213; and Faccioli 1992, p. xii.

29. Letter to Jacopo Ammannati Piccolomini, referred to in Milham 1998, p. 16.

30. "C'est un Newton dans l'art de la marmite / Un vrai César en fait de lechefrite." Frederick II, *Oeuvres de Frédéric le Grand,* ed. Johann David Erdmann Preuss (Berlin, 1846–1856), 13:101.

31. Platina 1475, book 8, Torta sambucea, Torta ex anguillis; book 9, Ova in veru.

32. Martino, printed in Faccioli 1992, p. 138.

33. Platina 1475, book 6, Ut pavo.

34. Laurioux 2006b, p. 17.

35. Milham 1998, p. 53.

36. Wilkins 2000, p. 46.

37. Henisch 2009, p. 15.

38. Willich 1563, fols. p4 verso–p5 recto.

39. An interesting parallel to this is that the local language of Dutch colonists in South Africa, before it became established under the name Afrikaans, was considered "a patois derided as Kitchen Dutch." André Brink, *A Fork in the Road* (London, 2009), p. 182. About *Küchenlatein,* see Pfeiffer 1931, pp. 455–459. Teofilo Folengo explains in *Liber Macaronices* (Venice, 1517) that "macaronic art" refers to macaroni, which he describes as gross, course, and rustic.

40. Burke 2000, pp. 82–85; Becker 2012, pp. 21–24.

41. Hernández de Maceras 1607, fol. ¶3 verso.

42. Evelyn 1699, fol. a4 verso.

43. Biographical information from C. Driver 1997.

44. Quoted in Patricia Storace, "Seduced by the Food on Your Plate," *New York Review of Books,* December 18, 2014.

45. Norman Bryson, *Looking at the Overlooked* (Cambridge, MA, 1990), pp. 14, 8.

46. Becker 2012; Rumpolt 1581, fol. XXXVI verso; Carter 1730, fol. [π]4 verso; Verral 1759, preface.

47. Bühler 1993, p. 540.

48. Poulain and Neirinck 2004, pp. 57–58; Pitte 1991, p. 157; Rambourg 2010, pp. 185–202.

49. Laurioux 1997a, p. 230.

50. Stefani 1662, pp. 9–11.

51. Buchinger 1671, fol. *2 verso.

52. Thorstein Veblen, *The Theory of the Leisure Class* (New York, 1905), p. 79.

53. Laurioux 1997a, p. 233; Liberati 1668, p. 87.

54. Rumpolt 1581, fol.)(4.

55. Capatti and Montanari 2002, p. xiv.

56. Deborah Simonton, "Gender," in *A Companion to Eighteenth Century Europe*, edited by Peter H. Wilson (Oxford, 2008), p. 36.

57. P. Ferguson 2006, p. 135.

58. A document from 1702 about servants in Lyon's aristocratic households lists a total of 264 registered servants, including 67 *femmes de chambre* and 54 *cuisinières*. See Maurice Garden, *Lyon et les lyonnais au XVIIIe siècle* (Paris, 1970), p. 250.

59. Rambourg 2010, p. 136.

60. Acton 1855, pp. xxiii–xxiv; G. Lehmann 2003, pp. 155–157.

61. Menon 1746.

62. Rumohr 1822, pp. 164–165.

63. P. Chr. Asbjørnsen, *Chemisk Koge- og Husholdningsbog* (Christiania, 1859), p. xv. This is a Norwegian translation of Klencke 1857.

64. Article by Philéas Gilbert, in the journal *L'art culinaire* 1 (1883): p. 124, quoted in Aron 1973, pp. 329–330.

65. Tamburini 1900. About the background of the author and her attitude to gender, see Salvatori 1998, pp. 905–906.

66. Quoted in Wiedemann 1993, p. 560.

67. Czerniecki 1682, p. 10; Rossetti 1584, chap. 13; Berchoux 1803, p. 49. In an anthology of gastronomic literature from 1855, *serviteur* was changed to *artiste*; see Justin Améro, *Les classiques de la table* (Paris, 1855), 2:355.

68. Martial, *Epigrammaton*, 14.220, "Cocus."

69. *Cuoco napolitano*, printed in Scully 2000, p. 83.

70. Scappi 1570. See, for example, fol. 74 verso (recipe 193), fol. 363 (recipe 107), fol. 374 (recipe 159). In other instances, Scappi used the expression *secondo il gusto* (according to taste); see fol. 354 (recipe 250). The popes Scappi served, Pius IV and Pius V, were not known as gourmets, but Scappi's earlier patrons were cardinals with a passion for good food.

71. Luraschi 1853, p. 1.

72. Le Goullon 1829, p. 110.

73. About freelance cooks in France around 1700, see Wheaton 1983, p. 151–153.

74. Huizinga 1919, p. 310. This situation is explained by the distinction between *artes mechanicae* and *artes liberales*, referred to earlier in this chapter.

75. Guerzoni 2008, p. 69; Jacques Barzun, *From Dawn to Decadence* (New York, 2001), p. 75, 81; Burke 1999, p. 2.

76. Burke 1999, p. 81.

77. Guerzoni 2008, p. 69.

78. Burke 1999, p. 77.

79. Norbert Elias, *Mozart: Zur Soziologie eines Genies* (Frankfurt am Main, 1991), p. 21.

80. W. A. Mozart, *Briefe und Aufzeichnungen*, edited by Wilhelm A. Bauer and O. E. Deutsch (Kassel, 1963), 3:98.

81. Joseph Haydn, *Gesammelte Briefe und Aufzeichnungen*, edited by Dénes Bartha (Kassel, 1965), pp. 227–242; Blanning 2002, p. 182.

82. Habermas 1969, p. 51.

83. Aron 1973, p. 221.

84. Beauvilliers 1814, preface.

85. Quoted in Gigante 2005, p. 120.

86. Grimod de la Reynière 2012, pp. 29–30, 153, 547.

87. Grimod de la Reynière 1808, pp. 122–123.

88. Grimod de la Reynière 2012, p. 951.

89. Morris 1975, pp. 206, 1; Soyer 1860, p. 4.

90. Drouard 2008, p. 14.

91. Escoffier 2011, p. 29.

92. P. Ferguson and S. Zukin 1998, pp. 92–120. This article refers to a study of the recruitment and career of American star chefs.

93. Paul Bocuse, in conversation with the author, September 1978, Paris, France.

94. P. Ferguson 2006, p. 167.

95. Ferran Adrià, Heston Blumenthal, Thomas Keller, and Harold McGee, "Statement on the 'New Cookery,'" *Guardian,* December 10, 2006, www.theguardian.com/uk/2006 /dec/10/foodanddrink.obsfoodmonthly.

96. Drouard 2008, p. 135–138. For an analysis of cooks and waiters in Belgium in the nineteenth and twentieth centuries, see Peter Scholliers 2004, pp. 137–165. See also the articles about labor relations in hotels and restaurants in Western Europe and the United States in *Food and History* 11, no. 2 (2013): pp. 197–377.

2. WRITER AND AUTHOR

1. Platina may have heard of the two German printers, Arnold Pannartz and Konrad Sweinheim, who had set up an office in the Benedictine monastery in Subiaco in 1464.

2. Parkes 1991, pp. 58–59.

3. Barthes 2002, p. 544.

4. Roberts and Robinson 2010, p. xi.

5. Bartolomeo Platina, *De honesta voluptate et valetudine,* MS 734, Biblioteca Trivulziana, Milan.

6. About the various reasons for errors by scribes, see Parkes 2008, pp. 67–68.

7. *Daz Buoch von guoter Spise,* 2°Cod., MS 731 (Cim 4), Universitätsbibliothek, Munich, printed in Hajek 1958, recipe 7; Wiswe 1970, pp. 14–15.

8. Pascale Bargain, "L'édition des manuscrits," in Martin 1983–86, 1; 50–52.

9. Parkes 1991, p. 69.

10. "What is *mouvance?*" last modified September 9, 2014,www.southampton.ac .uk/~wpwt/mouvance/mouvance.htm.

11. Ory 2011, p. 7. It is necessary to distinguish between people who could not read or write and people who were literate but had secretaries do their writing for them. Dictating texts was a common practice all the way into the twentieth century, and it did not end until the introduction of the personal computer.

12. Laurioux 1997a, p. 307; Laurioux 2006b, 524n419.

13. Baurmeister 2001, pp. 373–377; Hyman and Hyman 2002; Laurioux 1997a; François Villon, *Le grant testament Villon et le petit* (Paris, 1489), fol. e1 verso.

14. Hieatt and Butler 1985, p. 20.

15. Trude Ehlert, "Das Kochbuch des Meister Hans: Kulturhistorische Würdigung," in Ehlert 1996, pp. 331–343.

16. Brereton and Ferrier 1981, p. lii; Laurioux 1997a, pp. 148–158.

17. "Nul livres ouz escriptz faysans de cecy mencion ne memoyre." *Du fait de cuysine,* MS S 103, Médiathèque Valais, Sion, fol. 11 verso.

18. Eisenstein 1979, pp. 242–243.

19. Rontzier 1598, fol. [π]3.

20. Manfred Lemmer called the language a mix (*Mischsprache*) and theorized that the scribe spoke Low German and did not have full proficiency in High German. Lemmer 1979, pp. 8, 30.

21. Schino and Luccichenti 2007, pp. 13, 18–19.

22. Examples in Notaker 2010, entries 912–916.

23. Czerniecki 1682.

24. Hajek 1958, p. 7; Ruge-Schatz 1987, p. 218.

25. Deckhardt 1611, preface. Deckhardt was cook for the prince-elector of Saxony.

26. Hagger 1718, preface.

27. Le Goullon 1829, p. 107; Agnoletti 1832–34, 1:xii.

28. Molokhovets 1901, pt. 1, p. ii.

29. Fink 1995, pp. 17–18.

30. Menon 1755, "Avertissement."

31. Lebas 1738, "Epître dédicatoire."

32. Takats 2011, pp. 81–86.

33. Lehmann 2003, p. 63.

34. Elizabeth Cleland, Mrs. Frazer, and Susanna McIver in Edinburgh and Ann Cook, Susanna Kellet, and Elizabeth Marshall in Newcastle. See MacLean 1981.

35. *Vollständiges Nürnbergisches Koch-Buch* 1691, probably written by Anna Juliana Endter; Catharina van Zierikhoven, *Volkomen neerlandsche kookkundig wordenboek* (Leeuwarden, 1772), see Witteveen 1986, p. 281; Inga Olsen, *Kogebog for Hvermand* (Christiania, 1887).

36. Simmons 1796, p. [49].

37. Rayford W. Logan, ed., *Memoirs of a Monticello Slave as Dictated to Charles Campbell in the 1840s by Isaac, One of Thomas Jefferson's Slaves* (Charlottesville, VA, 1951), chap. 1.

38. In the preface to her cookbook, Abby Fisher explained that both she and her husband were illiterate (Fisher 1881, p. 3); see also Theophano 2003, pp. 52–68. One of the first books published in the United States by an African American was *The House Servant's Directory* (Boston, 1827), by the butler Robert Roberts, but this was not a cookbook, even if it did include a few recipes for drinks.

39. The Italian cookbook *Manuale di cucina* (Graz, 1893) was a translation of *Die Süddeutsche Küche,* written by the Austrian Katharina Prato.

40. Biographies of these cooks can be found in Poulain and Neirinck 2004.

41. *Du fait de cuysine,* fol. 11 recto; Laurioux 1997a, p. 182.

42. Rontzier 1598, fol. [π]3. The duke's printing office was Fürstliche Druckerey (Oficina Typographica Principalis Brunsvicensis).

43. Robert 1982; Ruberto 1529.

44. T. Gloning 2002, pp. 517–550.

45. *Le pastissier françois* (Paris, 1653), "Au lecteur."

46. Scappi 1570, fol. 67; La Varenne 1651, fol. Ã2 verso.

47. Rabisha 1682, fol. A4.

48. *Néo-physiologie du goût* (Paris, 1866), p. i. According to Georges Vicaire, the author was in fact Maurice Cousin, Comte de Courchamps, a distinguished gourmet (Vicaire 1890, col. 622).

49. Wheaton 1983, p. 113.

50. Susan Coultrap-McQuinn named several authors who pointed out this economic motive (Coultrap-McQuinn 1990).

51. Notaker 2001, p. 39.

52. Vilhelm Bergsøe, *Studenterleben og studentliv* (Copenhagen, 1903), p. 22; Anne Marie Mangor, *Kogebog for smaa Huusholdninger,* ([Copenhagen?], 1837).

53. Eliot and Rose 2009, pp. 229, 294; Finkelstein and McCleery 2013, pp. 67, 85.

54. Notaker 2010, pp. 56, 39, 33, 279, 343, 35.

55. Eisenstein 1979, pp. 153–154.

56. Hirsch 1967, p. 27.

57. Quoted by Wittmann 1991, p. 50.

58. For more details, see Notaker 2010, pp. 246–251. A French example is the tradition started by the Parisian bookseller Pierre Sergent in the 1530s, see Hyman and Hyman 1996, p. 650; and Albala and Tomasik 2015, introduction.

59. Sebastian 1581; Cooper 1654; Giovane [1530?]. See also Notaker 2010, p. 245; Richardson and Isabell 1984, pp. 40- 53; and Laurioux 1997a, p. 215.

60. Notaker 2010, pp. 215, 217.

61. Notaker 2001, p. 192.

62. Artusi 1911, "La storia di un libro."

63. Witteveen 1993, p. 24.

64. Review in *Aftonbladet* (Stockholm), September 19, 1871, p. 3.

65. Genette 1987, p. 42.

66. Rumohr 1822, p. iv. Rumohr's authorship was revealed in the second edition (1832).

67. Eleonora 1697.

68. Schellhammer 1692, 1697, 1699.

69. Egerin 1745; Elzberg 1751; Smith 1758; Glasse 1747.

70. This trend was later picked up in the United States, where books were authored "By an American Lady," "By a Boston Housekeeper," "By an American Physician," etc.

71. Raven 2003, p. 145.

72. Quoted in Ezell 2003, p. 63.

73. Mayr 1579, preface.

74. Markham 1615, fol. Q1 verso. About the sources, see Best 1998, pp. xvii–xxii, lvii. In *The Widowes Treasurie* (London, 1582), John Partridge admitted that the recipes came from a gentlewoman.

75. James Boswell, *Life of Johnson,* note, April 15, 1778.

76. M. P. Moroni Salvatori,"Premessa," in *La cucina bolognese* (Bologna, 1990). *Il cuoco bolognese* was originally published in 1843 with the title *Cucina economica moderna.*

77. Ticklecloth 1860.

78. Horace Raisson, *Code gourmand* (Paris, 1827); Mlle Marguerite, *Le Cordon Bleu, ou Nouvelle cuisinière bourgeoise* (Paris, 1827); Regine Hofmann, *Das Hausbuch* (Grimma, 1835); Laura Adeler, *Ny kogebog* (Copenhagen, 1897); Marie Larsen, *Kogebog for husmødre i by og bygd* (Kristiania, 1896).

79. Rehnberg 1978, p. 130.

80. Aleksandr Kravetskii, "Tainaia kukhnia Eleny Molokhovets," September 22, 2014, www.kommersant.ru/doc/2558138.

81. Burke 2000, pp. 82–85.

82. Voltaire to Marie Louise Denis, May 22, 1752, printed in Voltaire, *The Complete Works of Voltaire* (Geneva, 1971), 97:58.

83. Johann Georg Heinzmann, quoted in McCarthy 2010, pp. 148–149.

84. See, for example, DiMeo and Pennell 2013.

3. ORIGIN AND EARLY DEVELOPMENT OF MODERN COOKBOOKS

1. An inventory of most of these manuscripts is given in Lambert 1992, pp. 321–362.

2. These tablets are known as the "Yale culinary tablets." See Bottéro 1995 for a translation and description.

3. Some of the medical texts recorded on Egyptian papyrus from the second millennium BCE contain recipes that are very similar to culinary recipes, prescribing herbs and plants mixed with milk, oil, beer, water, etc. See B. Ebbell and Leon Banov Jr., eds., *Papyrus Eber* (Copenhagen, 1937), pp. 30–68.

4. Athenaeus referenced cookbook authors and short prose fragments. His quotations from a poetic culinary work by Archestratos have been edited and translated in Wilkins and Hill 1994 and in Olson and Sens 2000.

5. There is one copy at the New York Academy of Medicine and one beautifully illustrated copy at the Biblioteca Apostolica Vaticana, Vatican City. A selection of similar recipes, known as *Apici excerpta a Vinidario uiro inlustri,* can be found in an eighth-century manuscript: *Codex salasianus,* Codex Parisinus Latinus 10318, Bibliothèque nationale de France, Paris. See Grocock and Grainger 2006 for translations, descriptions, and a discussion of these manuscripts.

6. See, for example, Columella, *Res rustica,* particularly chap. 12; and Cato, *De agri cultura,* chaps. 116–121, also bread and porridges, chaps. 74–86.

7. Melitta Weiss-Amer (1992, pp. 69–80) considered the works an example of how physicians contributed to the spread of culinary recipes, but the editors of *Du manuscrit à la table* excluded them from their inventory because they consider them to belong to a different field of medieval literature. See Lambert 1992, pp. 317–318.

8. Particularly in chapters 9, 10, and 12. The book was first printed in a Latin translation in Venice in 1538; the first printed Greek edition was published in Basel in 1539. See Dalby 2011.

9. De' Crescenzi's book was first printed in Augsburg in 1471 as *Petri de Crescentiis ruralium commodorum libri duodecimo.*

10. Laurioux 1997a, p. 217.

11. Laurioux 1997b, pp. 27–28; Rosenberger 1996, p. 345–365; M. Marin 2004, pp. 35–52. For medieval Arab texts, see *Medieval Arab Cookery,* by A. J. Arberry, Charles Perry, and Maxime Rodinson (Totnes, 2001). For early Arab recipes in Europe, see Rudolf Grewe, "Hispano-Arabic Cuisine in the Twelfth Century," in Lambert 1992, pp. 141–148.

12. Olson 2013, p. 24; Kallendorf 2013, p. 49; Brown 2009, p. 179.

13. *Forme of Cury,* Bühler 36, Pierpont Morgan Library, New York; *Forme of Cury,* Add. 5016, British Library, London; *Viandier,* S 108, Médiathèque Valais, Sion.

14. Laurioux 1997a, p. 331.

15. Hieatt 1992, pp. 15–21; Lambert 1992, p. 318; Ehlert 2002, pp. 135–136.

16. Wheaton 1983, p. xxi; Santich 1984, pp. 131–140; Scully 1995, p. 197; Mennell 1996, pp. 49, 54; Ehlert 2002, p. 132; G. Lehmann 2003, 22n10.

17. Clanchy 1979.

18. Stock 1983, p. 9.

19. Briggs 2010, p. 499.

20. Giesecke 1991, p. 32.

21. Parkes 1991, pp. 278–282; Clanchy 1979, p. 1; Briggs 2010, pp. 488, 499, 502.

22. Roberts and Robinson 2010, p. xxii; Clanchy 2009, pp. 194, 204; Parkes 1991, p. 286; Finkelstein and McCleery 2013, p. 68; Parkes 2008, p. 39.

23. Wolfgang Wegner, "Entstehung und Überlieferung," in Haage and Wegner 2007, p. 50.

24. Georges Duby and Robert Mandrou, *Histoire de la civilisation française* (Paris, 1968), p. 184.

25. Ehlert 2002, p. 125.

26. Wegner, "Entstehung und Überlieferung," p. 52.

27. Mostert and Adamska 2014; Clanchy 2009, p. 205.

28. Briggs 2010, p. 188; Clanchy 2009, pp. 195–199.

29. Parkes 1991, p. 274.

30. Clanchy 2009, pp. 203–204.

31. Finkelstein and McCleery 2013, p. 68.

32. Giesecke 1991; Eis 1967. Laurel Braswell distinguished between theoretical, practical, prognostical, and occult literature (Braswell 1984, p. 338).

33. Eis 1967, p. 58.

34. Plato, *Phaidros,* 275d–276a.

35. Winsnes 1845, preface.

36. *The True Way* (London, 1695), fol. A3.

37. Crosby 1998, pp. 8, 9.

38. Giesecke 1983, p. 171.

39. Anna Maria Busse Berger, "The Evolution of Rhythmic Notation," in *The Cambridge History of Western Music Theory,* ed. Thomas Christensen (Cambridge, 2002), p. 628.

40. Lévi-Strauss 1964; Wrangham 2009.

41. Thomas Hobbes, *Leviathan* (London, 1651), p. 12 (orthography as in original).

42. Goody 1977, p. 78.

43. Bakhtin 1986, pp. 60–102.

44. Peter Koch and Wulf Oesterreicher, cited in Ehlert 1997, pp. 73–85.

45. Bakhtin 1986, p. 91.

46. Laurioux 2006a, pp. 223–238.

47. Fox 2000, p. 24.

48. Voigts 1984, p. 317.

49. Thomas Tusser, *A Hundred Good Points of Husbandry* (London, 1557); MS Pepys 1047, Magdalene College, Cambridge, printed in Gerald A. J. Hodgett, *Stere Htt Well* (London, 1972).

50. Laurioux 1997a, p. 249.

51. Stiennon 1973, pp. 146–149; Lalou 1992.

52. Robson 2009, pp. 70–81; Bottéro 1995; Finkelstein and McCleery 2013, p. 30.

53. Roemer 2009, p. 85; Small 1997, p. 182.

54. Athenaeus, *Deipnosofistae* 2:49 d.

55. Roemer 2009, pp. 85, 87.

56. Brown 2009, p. 179.

57. Saenger 1999, p. 127.

58. Laurioux 1997b, p. 29; *Enseignements,* MS Lat. 7131, Bibliothèque nationale de France, Paris, printed in Lozinski 1933, pp. 181–187, line 223.

59. "Vederle loro fare, domandarnegli, impararle, e tenerle a mente." Pandolfini 1734, pp. 54–55.

60. [Sabina Welserin's cookbook], MS 4° Cod. 137, Augsburg Staats- und Stadtbibliothek, printed in Stopp 1980, p. 148.

61. Eliot and Rose 2009, p. 3.

62. Menon 1739, preface.

63. Camporesi 1993, p. 84.

64. Ong 2002, pp. 24, 41. See also Goody 1977, p. 37.

65. Aebischer 1953, pp. 76–77; Hieatt and Butler 1985, pp. 9–11; Laurioux 1997a, pp. 40–43; Ehlert 2002, 247n8.

66. Hellinga 2009, p. 207.

67. Eisenstein 1979, pp. 73–74.

68. Febvre and Martin 1958, pp. 277–278.

69. For details, see Notaker 2010, entries 901, 902, 905, 701.

70. McKitterick 2003, p. 12. See also J. Crick and A. Walsham, "Introduction: Script, Print and History," in Crick and Walsham 2004, pp. 1–26.

71. Colclough 2009, p. 57.

72. Harris 2013, p. 212.

73. Stopp 1980; Spurling 1986.

74. John Evelyn's recipes can be found in *Receipts Medicinal,* a folio volume kept at the British Library, London; John Locke's recipes can be found in various parts of, MS Locke, Bodleian Library, Oxford; Kenelm Digby's notes were edited and printed after his death as *The Closet of the Eminently Learned Sir Kenelme Digby Kt. Opened,* see Digby (1669) 1997.

75. Levshin 1795–97, 5:40.

76. T. Gloning 2000, p. 359.

77. *Helle Schrøders Kaagebaag,* MS 8° 1547, Nasjonalbiblioteket, Oslo.

78. One manuscript is labeled *J. Lindberg,* and can be found in the Statsarkivet, Bergen. The other, which doesn't have a title, is in Stavanger Bibliotek and is printed in Hans Eyvind Naess, *Den Kiellandske Kogebog* (Stavanger, 1977). *En Høyfornemme Madames Kaagebog* (Copenhagen, 1703).

79. Fægri 1984, pp. 108–121.

80. Heiles 2011, pp. 501–504; Ehlert 2010, introduction.

81. H. Leeming, "A Seventeenth Century Polish Cookery Book and its Russian Manuscript Translation," *Slavonic and East European Review* 52, no. 129 (1974): 500–513.

82. The German book was the third edition of *Ein new Kochbuch,* by Marx Rumpolt, published in 1604. János Keszei translated it for Prince Mihály Apafi I and his wife, Anna

Bornemissza. A printed version was published by Krierion Könyvkiado in Bucharest in 1983 with the title *Bornemissza Anna Szakácskönyve 1680-ból.*

83. The manuscript cookbook is *Moda bardzo dobra smażenia różnych konfektów i innych słodkości,* printed in 2011 as part of the series Monumenta Poloniae Culinaria, edited by Jarosław Dumanowski and Rafal Jankowski. The Austrian book is *Ein Koch- und Artzney-Buch* (Graz, 1686).

84. Magdalena Schnellen, *Kunstbog 1656,* Hedmark Museum, Hamar, Norway, based on Rontzier 1598.

85. The title of this periodical was *Grundliche Nachrichten von allem ersinnlichen Koch-und Backwerck.*

86. Ernst Barlach, "Das Kochbuch," in *Das dichterische Werk in drei Bänden* (Munich, 1958) 2:198.

4. PRINTED COOKBOOKS

1. For more details about early cookbook production, see Notaker 2010.

2. Martínez Montiño 1611, fol. 4 verso; Rumpolt 1581, fol.)(4.

3. Georges Duby and Robert Mandrou, *Histoire de la civilisation française* (Paris, 1968), p. 270. For a discussion of the Italian influence on French culinary language, see Vollenweider 1963, pp. 59–88.

4. Tichá 1975, p. 12.

5. *Cock bouck,* MS 240 (B 79834), Stadsbibliotheek, Antwerp, printed in W.L. Braekman, *Een Antwerps kookboek voor leckertonghen* (Antwerp, 1995), recipe 67. See also E. Stols, "De Iberische wereld en de opbloei van de voedingscultuur in de Zuidelijke Nederlanden," in *Europa aan tafel,* ed. Francine De Nave and Carl Depauw (Antwerp, 1993), pp. 33–39.

6. Murrell 1638.

7. *Ouverture de cuisine,* by Lancelot de Casteau, was published in French in 1604, but in Liège, which at the time was ruled by Bavarian princes.

8. Vincent La Chapelle was a special case. He was French, but his book, *The Modern Cook* (London, 1733), was originally published in English. The French edition, *Le cuisinier moderne,* was published in The Hague in 1735, but much of the book was actually plagiarized from Massialot. See Hyman and Hyman 1979, pp. 44–54; 1981, pp. 35–40.

9. The report from a colloquium titled Modèle culinaire français, held in Tours in 2014, will be published in the autumn of 2017.

10. Rigaud 1780. The biographical information given here is based on the preface of his book.

11. *Il cuoco piemontese perfezionato in Parigi* (Turin, 1766), based on Menon 1746; *L'economia della città e della campagna ovvero il nuovo cuoco italiano secondo il gusto francese* (Florence, 1773), based on Liger 1714 or later editions.

12. Ludvig Holberg, *Jean de France* (Copenhagen, 1723), act 2, scene 1.

13. Denis Fonvizin, *Brigadir,* act 1, scene 1. Fonvizin wrote the play in 1766–67.

14. Alexander Pushkin, *Eugeny Onegin,* chap. 1, stanza 16, and chap. 7, stanza 4.

15. Levshin 1795–97; V. Levshin, *Poslanie ruskago k frantsuzoliubtsam* (Moscow, 1807). For a discussion of French influence in Russia, see Pokhlebkin 1978, pp. 8–9.

16. Peter von Polenz, *Deutsche Sprachgeschichte* (Berlin, 1994), 2:66.

17. May 1660, fol. A4 verso. It seems more correct to describe May's outlook as international rather than French; see G. Lehmann 2003, p. 45.

18. Glasse 1747, p. 2.

19. Beauvilliers 1814, p. viij.

20. *The School for Good Living* (London, 1814), preface.

21. Dods 1829, p. 328. The first edition, published in 1826, does not have a separate chapter about French cuisine.

22. John Ruskin, *The Ethics of the Dust* (London, 1866), p. 138.

23. Notaker 1991.

24. For more details about how these attitudes developed during the nationalist movements of the eighteenth and nineteenth centuries, see chapter 16.

25. For information about culinary development in these areas, see *Food and History* 10, no. 2 (2012).

26. E. Smith, *The Compleat Housewife* (Williamsburg, 1742), first published in London in 1727.

27. Susannah Carter, *The Frugal Housewife* (Boston, 1772), first published in London in 1765; Richard Briggs, *The New Art of Cookery* (Philadelphia, 1791), first published in London in 1788 as *The English Art of Cookery*.

28. Casper and Rubin 2013, p. 688.

29. Lowenstein 1972, pp. 2–4.

30. Simmons 1796.

31. Fleming 2013, p. 674. According to Ken Albala, *La cuisinière canadienne* is very consciously antiquated, with many dishes drawn indirectly from late medieval and early modern cookbooks. See Albala's article in Charlene Elliot, ed., *How Canadians Communicate about Food* (Edmonton, 2016).

32. E. Driver 2003, pp. 19–39.

33. Roldán Vera 2013, p. 662.

34. Corona 2013. Cookbooks followed first in two islands that were still Spanish colonies, Cuba (1858) and Puerto Rico (1859), and then in Chile and Peru (1867).

35. The two printers were the brothers Eduardo and Henrique Laemmert.

36. A facsimile edition of *The English and Australian Cookery Book* was published in Hobart in 2014 by the Culinary Historians of Tasmania with a companion volume containing articles by Barbara Santich, Michael Symons, and others.

37. Information based on Witteveen and Cuperus 1998.

38. Coetzee 1984, pp. 105–116. Witteveen and Cuperus 1998, vol. 1, entry 1508.

39. Platina 1475, book 10, De stirione, Lacteolini, Leo Marinus.

40. Martino, quoted in Faccioli 1992, p. 141; Platina 1475, book 6, Lucanicae. The Dutch version of the recipe can be found in Coeck-Indestege 1971, p. 126; the German version is in Platina Cremonensis 1542, fol. 49.

41. *Platine en françoys* (Lyon, 1505), fol. l4 verso–l5 recto. For details, see Flandrin and Serventi 2003; and Tomasik 2007.

42. Magirus 1612.

43. Statistics and a concordance ("Concordatietabel") with indications of which recipes were translated literally and which were more or less reworked by Magirus can be found in Schildermans, Sels, and Willebrands 2007, pp. 15, 212–217.

44. Granado 1599.

45. Allard 1987, pp. 35–41. Allard was the first to point out the link between Scappi and Granado.

46. Dods 1829, p. 330.

47. I checked Vladimir Dal, *Tolkovyi slovar' zhivogo velikarusskogo iazyka,* 4 vols. (Moscow, 1914); and Vasilii Il'ich Chernyshev, ed., *Slovar' sovremennogo russkogo literaturnogo iazyka* (Moscow, 1948).

48. Loofft 1758; Corrado 1786 (explanations on p. 231); Babilon 1989.

49. Wurm 2007.

50. See also Chartier 2014, p. 91: "Paul Zumthor affirmait ainsi que la traduction révèle bien plus l'identité de celui qui la propose que la littéralité du texte qu'il traduit."

51. Saxegaard 1953, preface; Dunham 1933, preface.

52. Stead 1983.

53. Of the 400 recipes in Vorselmann's cookbook, 133 were taken from Platina's book, 31 from Taillevent's *Le viandier,* and 115 from the first printed Dutch cookbook, *Een notabel Boecxken van Cokeryen* (Brussels, ca. 1514). For details, see Cockx-Indestege 1971, pp. 14–69.

54. Erken 1914b, preface.

55. Nimb 1900, pp. 5–6, preface of the 1888 edition.

56. Hughes 2006, pp. 214, 190.

57. *A Queen's Delight* (London, 1671), p. 5.

58. White 2004a, p. 81. A "rotten" cloth seems like a strange remedy; a better alternative would probably be a "cotton" cloth. But "rotten" appeared in the original 1655 edition Eileen White referred to, as well as in later editions published in 1658 and 1671. This may have been an error by a scribe or a printer who did not have relevant knowledge.

59. Stead 1983, p. 28; Glasse 1747, p. 53.

60. Theophano 2003, p. 45.

61. [Sabina Welserin's cookbook], MS 4° Cod 137, Augsburg Staats- und Stadtbibliothek, printed in Stopp 1980, pp. 148, 110, 56.

62. Staindl von Dillingen 1569, fol. 25 verso.

63. *Kucharzka* 1542, pt. 3, fol. 1.

64. *A Booke of Cookerie* (London, 1597), fol. 12; *The Compleat Cook* (London, 1671), p. 99.

65. Artusi 1911, recipe 551 (*gelato di banana*); Capatti 2009, p. 27.

66. Scappi 1570; Granado 1599; Magirus 1612; Notaker 2002, pp. 59–60; Schildermans and Sels 2003.

67. Notaker 2010, p. 34.

68. Acton 1855, p. xxi.

69. Rettigová 1831, p. iv, preface from the 1826 edition.

70. Quoted in Kelly 2001, p. xxiv.

71. Gouffé 1867, p. ii.

72. Josef Wiel, *Diätetisches Koch Buch* (Konstanz, 1871), quoted in Artelt 1976, p. 380.

73. Examples of this in Notaker 2010, p. 8.

74. About the various editions of *Von allen Speisen,* see Notaker 2010, entry 701; Platina Cremonensis 1542, fol. 45 verso; Rumpolt 1581, fol. 4.

75. Simon Schama, *Power of Art* (London, 2006), p. 190. The painting is *Saint Roch intercède la Vierge pour la guérison des pestiférés* (1780).

76. David's answer is cited in Antonia Fraser, *Marie Antoinette: The Journey* (London, 2002), p. 306.

77. Bouwsma 2000, p. 250; Ben Jonson, *Timber, or Discoveries; Made upon Men and Matter* (London 1641), p. 127.

78. Lehmann 1996, pp. [21–27].

79. Seidelin 1801, preface.

80. Davidis 1845, preface.

81. H. Gloning 1997, pp. 830–831.

82. Gilly Lehmann, e-mail message to the author November 12, 2012.

83. Beauvilliers 1814, "Discours préliminaire."

84. Martínez Montiño 1611, fol. 100 verso.

85. Camporesi 1995, p. xxxix.

86. 1914 edition, quoted in Toomre 1992, p. 11.

5. ORGANIZING THE COOKBOOK

1. "Femmes en sont maitresses, et chascun le sçait faire." *Le viandier Taillevent,* MS Regin. Lat. 776, Biblioteca Apostolica Vaticana, Vatican City, printed in Pichon and Vicaire 1892, p. 249. This may be a topos, as the same phrase is found in *Hortus sanitatis,* published by Jacob Meydenbach in Mainz in 1485: "alle luten wolbekant."

2. Staindl von Dillingen 1569, fol. 1.

3. There are also examples of cases in which a recipe was dropped because it was considered too difficult for most people. See Acton 1855, p. 390.

4. Messisbugo 1557, fol. 39 verso.

5. Pérez Samper 1998, p. 49.

6. "Satisfaire au vouloir & affection de plusieurs gentils personnaiges, mesmes au sexe feminine, qui continuellement est cupide de sçauoir & entendre chose de nouelleté." Nostradamus 1555, fol. 37 verso.

7. Quoted in Gonzague Saint-Bris, *François Ier et la renaissance* (Paris, 2008), pp. 55–56.

8. Robert Burton, *The Anatomy of Melancholy* (London, 1638), partition I, section 2, member 4, subsection 5 (orthography as in original).

9. Burke 2009, pp. 230–231.

10. In the seventeenth century, the terms "mode" and "modern" meant "contemporary."

11. Eisenstein 1979, p. 123.

12. Burke 2000, p. 114.

13. For example, *Le cuisinier moderne* (1735), *Das allerneueste Pariser Kochbuch* (1752), *L'apicio moderno* (1790), *The New System of Cookery* (1753), and *De nieuwe welervarene utrechtsche keuken-meid* (1769).

14. For example, the Swedish *Ny och fullkomlig kok-bok* (1737), the Portuguese *Cozinheiro moderno* (1780), the Danish *Ny fuldstændig kaage-bog* (1755), the Spanish *Nuevo arte de cocina* (1767), and the Czech *Nowá wýborná knjžka kuchařska* (1821).

15. La Chapelle 1735, pp. 1–2.

16. Carter 1730, fol. [π]3, "To the Reader."

17. Brillat-Savarin 1826, 1:x.

18. Dubois 1889, preface. There were, of course, still writers who, from a moral point of view, criticized cooks who gave priority to novelty. The German art and food critic Karl von Rumohr considered the obsession with new dishes to be a continuation of the art of cooking as it was described in the Roman cookbook attributed to Apicius, and he called it decadent: "Entartung der Kochkunst." Rumohr 1822, p. 21.

19. Escoffier 1903, p. vi.

20. David 1979, p. 8.

21. Flandrin, Hyman, and Hyman 1983, pp. 16–39; G. Lehmann 2003, pp. 36, 37; Mennell 1996, pp. 312–313.

22. "Ho adottato anch'io, nella mia cucina, questo stramento che risparmia la fatica di tritare col coltello e pester nel mortaio la carne." Pellegrino Artusi, quoted in Capatti 2009, p. 22.

23. "Se non avete il tritacarne, tritatela ben fine prima col coltella poi colla lunetta." Artusi 1911, recipe 303.

24. Glasse 1747; Stephanie Alexander, *The Cook's Companion* (Ringwood, VIC, 1996).

25. Santich 2010, pp. 304–305.

26. The Columbian Exchange went in the other direction as well, with products going from Europe to America, including traditional harvests such as wheat, olives, and wine grapes and important domesticated animals, such as pigs, sheep, chicken, and cattle.

27. Scappi 1570, fols. 59 (misnumbered 61), 127, 141; Rumpolt 1581, fol. LXVI.

28. Quellier 2007, p. 197.

29. Durante 1602, p. 372.

30. Latini 1692, p. 444.

31. Information in this paragraph from Grewe 1987, pp. 67–82.

32. Molokhovets, 1861; Elena Molokhovets, *Padarok molodym khaziaikam,* 4th ed. (St. Petersburg, 1869); Molokhovets 1901.

33. Hagdahl 1896, p. 630.

34. Blom 1888, pp. 168, 171.

35. Olaug Løken, *Matstel og husstel* (Kristiania, 1912), pp. 247, 59.

36. Dumas 1873, s.v. "banane."

37. "Un grosso baccello simile, in apparenza, ad un cetriuolo di buccia verde, ma liscia, triangolare e falcate." Artusi 1911, recipe 766.

38. Hedwig Heyl, *ABC der Küche* (Berlin, 1913), p. 592, cited in Thoms 1993, p. 15.

39. Lincoln 1884, p. 392; Farmer 1896, various examples, pp. 303–475.

40. Camporesi (1993, p. 99) referred to a proverb from Romagna: "L'erba u la ia de magner al bes-ciu" (grass is for animals); Asbjørnsen (1864, p. 17) referred to terms used by Norwegian peasants: *græs* (grass) and *ku- og grisemad* (cow and pig food).

41. Wall 2011, p. 167.

42. *Liber utilis coquinario,* MS Sloane 468, British Library, London, printed in Hieatt and Butler 1985, pp. 83–91; Carroll 1999, p. 28.

43. "Commence des poissons de mer et d'eve douche." *Enseignements,* MS Latin 7131, Bibliothèque nationale de France, Paris, printed in Lozinski 1933, pp. 181–187, line 125.

44. *Doctrina preparationis cibarum,* MS Palatino Latino 1179, Biblioteca Apostolica Vaticana, Vatican City; Laurioux 1997a, p. 35.

45. *Daz buoch von guoter spise*, printed in Hajek 1958, pp. 15–16 (recipes 3–5); Wiswe 1970, p. 16.

46. Dawson 1596–97, pt. 1, fol. [39].

47. Burke 2009, p. 106.

48. Hamel 2013, p. 64.

49. For details about this development, see Brian W. Ogilvie, *The Science of Describing: Natural Science in Renaissance Europe* (Chicago, 2006).

50. La Varenne 1651, p. 219.

51. Stefani 1662.

52. Sandra Sherman, review of *Reading and Writing Recipe Books 155–1800*, edited by M. DeMeo and S. Pennell, *Reviews in History*, November 2013, www.history.ac.uk/reviews /review/1507.

53. "Von allerhand Gekochten, Gebratenen, Gebackenen." Egerin 1745. See, for example, *A Booke of Cokery* (London, 1620).

54. Rumpolt 1581. The chapters about baking, pastry, vinegar, and wine were placed after the chapters about foodstuffs.

55. For a discussion of such books published in Germany, see Merta 2015, pp. 339–354.

56. Czerniecki 1682.

57. Briggs 2010, p. 498; Gilmont 2010, p. 135.

58. Mary Rouse and Richard H. Rouse, "La naissance des index," in Martin 1983–86, p. 78.

59. Notaker 2010, entry 701.

60. MS 255, Biblioteca Casanatense, Rome, printed in Faccioli 1992, pp. 73–97.

61. *Utaf adeligh öfningh een liten hand-book* (Stockholm, 1695), which included material from Nicolás de Bonnefons, *Les delices de la campagne*, first published in Paris, 1654.

62. Levshin 1795–97, which included material from French and German books; Notaker 1991, p. 7.

63. *Neues Lexikon der Französischen, Sächsischen, Österreichischen und Böhmischen Kochkunst* (Prague, 1785).

64. *The Cook's Own Book* (Boston, 1832).

65. MS Germ. fol. 244, Staatsbibliothek, Berlin, with incipit "Wiltu machen," printed in T. Gloning 1998, pp. 28–29.

66. "Se vos volez fere galantine a luis, prenez . . ."; "Por blanc mengier—Se vos volez fere blanc mengier . . ." *Enseignements*, printed in Lozinski 1933, pp. 181–187, line 141, line 119.

67. MS 1035, with incipit "Desen Bouc leert," Rijkuniversiteit te Gent Centrale Bibliotheek, Ghent.

68. Martino, cited in Faccioli 1992, p. 140, 152; *Forme of Cury*, MS Add. 5016, British Library, London, printed in Hieatt and Butler 1985, pp. 133 (recipe 158), 143 (recipe 200).

69. Carroll 2010, p. 64.

70. *Küchenmeisterei* [1490?], fol. [π]3.

71. Rumpolt 1581; Rontzier 1598; Latini 1692.

6. NAMING THE RECIPES

1. Hernández de Maceras 1607, p. 56.

2. Scappi 1570, fol. 156.

3. Rumpolt 1581, fol. LXXXII verso, recipe 16.

4. Plato, *Cratylus* 385e.

5. Taillevent 1486, fol. D5 verso; Molokhovets 1901, p. 396.

6. *Daz buoch von guoter spise,* printed in Hajek 1958, p. 35 (recipe 69); *Forme of Cury,* printed in Hieatt and Butler 1985, p. 138 (recipe 178); Ruberto 1529, fol. 28.

7. Rodovský z Hustiřan 1975, p. 92; *Koge Bog* 1616, recipe 79.

8. *Sopa dorada* in Scappi 1570, fol. 158 verso; *torta biancha* in *Cuoco napoletano,* MS 19, Pierpont Morgan Library, New York, printed in Scully 2000, no. 125; *hwitmoos* in *Libellus de arte coquinaria,* MS Ny Saml. 66, 8vo, Det Kongelige Bibliotek, Copenhagen, printed in Molbech 1826, p. 157 (recipe 15), see also Grewe and Hieatt 2001, p. 34; *saulce verte* in Taillevent ca. 1486, fol. E1; black caps in Dods 1826, p. 295.

9. *Le viandier Taillevent,* MS Regin. Lat. 776, Biblioteca Apostolica Vaticana, Vatican City, printed in Pichon and Vicaire 1892, p. 238; Rosenberger 1996, p. 362–365; Laurioux 1996a, p. 463.

10. La Varenne 1651, pp. 103, 235.

11. *Le viandier Taillevent,* printed in Pichon and Vicaire 1892, p. 268.

12. Le Grand d'Aussy 1999, p. 418.

13. The expression *à la,* still common today, is an abbreviation of *à la manière.* This is the reason for the feminine grammatical gender; the names *fermière, jardinière, paysanne,* etc. do not refer to women.

14. For a discussion of recipe names in Apicius, see Grocock and Grainger 2006, pp. 369–372.

15. "Pultem Punicam sic coquito." Marcus Porcius Cato, *De agri cultura,* chapter 85.

16. "French puffins," A. W., *A Book of Cookerye* (London, 1591), fol. 33; "karper Hoogh-Duytsche," *De verstandige kock* 1667, fol. H4 verso; "losos po polsku," Rodovský z Hustiřan 1975, p. 80; "mleko gdanskie," Czerniecki 1682, p. 85; "welsch Würst," *Ein sehr künstlich und fürtrefflichs Kochbuch* 1559, fol. E1; "Bohemische Erbsen," Coler 1593, p. 129; "piatto all'olandese," Latini 1692, p. 405; "Höcht auff ungerisch," Mayr 1579, fol. 16; "conejos a la portuguesa," Hernández de Maceras 1607, p. 42; "albergínies a la morisca," Robert 1982, p. 56; "riso turchesco," Messisbugo 1557, fol. 77.

17. Capatti and Montanari 2002, p. ix.

18. Baptized Muslims and their descendants, who kept certain old traditions, were called *moriscos* (Moors). This term was also used in the Spanish version of the Catalan cookbook by Robert; see Ruberto 1529, fol. 26.

19. Loofft 1758, p. 286; see also Rumpolt 1581, fol. CVII verso; Wecker 1598, p. 245; and *Ein Koch- und Artzney-Buch* 1686, p. 102.

20. Egerin 1745, p. 114; Schellhammer 1723, p. 78; Deckhardt 1611, pp. 91–92; Donacher 1627, p. 52.

21. Czerniecki 1682, pt. 2, recipe 56.

22. Messisbugo 1557, fol. 107; Rodovský z Hustiřan 1975, p. 63; Rumpolt 1581, fol. XCVII verso, fol. CVI verso; Coler 1593, p. 111; Casteau 1604, p. 23; Schellhammer 1723; p. 92; Deckhardt 1611, p. 94. There are also dishes called "Polish" with meat as the main ingredient; see, for example, Messisbugo 1557, p. 92; Rumpolt 1581, fol. IX; Coler 1593, p. 174; and Schellhammer 1723, p. 206. And there are sweet dishes with milk, cream, eggs, butter, sugar, etc., called "Hungarian"; see, for example, Messisbugo 1557, p. 81; Casteau 1604, p. 136; and May 1685, p. 82.

23. "Ég lév" (jelly); "hal fekete level" (fish in black sauce). *Szakáts mesterségnek könyvet-skéje* 1698, pp. 105, 121.

24. The Fáy manuscript, printed in Hermann 1887, p. 133.

25. Kucharzka 1542, pt. 2, fol. 8.

26. Artusi 1911, recipes 360, 636, 300, 277, 356, 320, 83.

27. Hugh Plat, *Delightes for Ladies* (London, 1611), recipe 14.

28. Toomre 1992, pp. 127, 194, 199.

29. *Skandinavisk illustreret kogebog,* Chicago 1884, p. 119.

30. Grimod de la Reynière 2012, p. 176; Brillat-Savarin 1826, 2:204.

31. Ritzerow 1868, p. 162.

32. Hommer 1858, p. 403.

33. Helena von Molochowetz, *Geschenk für junge Hausfrauen,* Leipzig 1877, p. 212. The recipe is not in the 1869 edition, so it must have been printed for the first time in the fifth (1871), sixth (1872), or seventh (1875) editions, which I have not been able to access.

34. Farmer 1896, p. 178; Fannie Farmer, *The Boston Cooking-School Cook Book* (Boston, 1923), p. 239.

35. Artusi 1911, recipe 604.

36. Höfler 1996.

37. Hagdahl 1896, p. 59; Malortie 1878, p. 13; Dubois 1856, p. 1. For information about the French system, see Cobbi and Flandrin 1999; and Flandrin 2007.

38. For examples of menus in different countries, see Malortie 1878; Patrick Rambourg, *À table . . . le menu!* (Paris, 2013); Livio Cerini de Castegnate, *I menu famos*i (Milan, 1988); and Henry Notaker, *Den norske menyen* (Oslo, 1991).

39. Dawson 1596–97, pt. 1, fol. A2.

40. Stefani 1662, p. 133.

41. Ranhofer 1894, pp. 1073–1138.

42. Poulain 1985, pp. 20–24.

43. Escoffier 1903.

44. "C'est s'ennoblir en consommant les attributs, les aliments emblématiques d'un des plus grand de la noblesse." Poulain 1985, p. 21

45. Aron 1973, pp. 177–179; see also Becker 2000, pp. 286–288.

46. Grimod de la Reynière 2012, p. 360.

47. Ude 1822, p. xxii.

48. *Le maître d'hôtel français* (Paris, 1822), 1:40–41.

49. The dish in *Le cuisinier gascon* is actually called *veau en crotte d'âne roulé à la Neuteau.*

50. Gouffé 1867, p. iv.

51. Escoffier 2011, pp. 31–32.

52. Malortie 1878, p. 80.

53. Henri Bergson, *Time and Free Will,* trans. F. L. Pogson (London, 1910), originally published as *Essai sur les données immédiates de la conscience* (Paris, 1889).

54. Capatti and Montanari 2002, p. 201.

55. Bocuse 1980.

56. David 1986, p. 40.

57. Blumenthal 2008, p. 23.

58. Ott 2011; Manguell 1997, pp. 170–171; Vollenweider 1963; Quellier 2013, pp. 131–132.

59. Michel de Montaigne, "De l'experience," in *Essais,* vol. 3, chap. 13, and "Des noms," in *Essais,* vol. 1, chap. 46.

60. Letters to Charles Augustin Feriol, Comte d'Argental, June 27, 1977, and August 4, 1777, printed in Voltaire, *The Complete Works of Voltaire,* vol. 128, *Correspondence and Related Documents* (Geneve, 1976), pp. 293, 330.

61. Honoré de Balzac, *Oeuvres complètes* (Paris, 1879), 22:236–237.

62. Marcel Proust, *À la recherche du temps perdu,* Bibliothèque de la Pleiade 100 (Paris, 1987–1989), 2:792, 3:546. Pampille was the pseudonym of Martha Daudet, née Allard, author of *Les bons plats de France* (Paris, 1913).

63. Proust, *Temps perdu,* 4:612.

64. The word "satire" itself has a culinary etymology.

65. *Satyres chrestiennes de la cuisine papale* (Geneva, 1560), pp. 48–49.

66. John Calvin and Philippe de Marnix de Sainte-Aldegonde quoted in Vollenweider 1963, p. 72. *Capilotade* was later used to refer to a collection of songs arranged alphabetically. See Fritz Nies, *Genres mineurs* (Munich, 1978), pp. 54–55.

67. *Critical Review,* no. 8 (1759), pp. 284–289.

68. *A Learned Dissertation on Dumpling* (London, 1726), pp. 1, 4, 21.

69. For more examples, see G. Lehmann 2003, p. 284.

70. Letter to Louis René Caradeuc de la Chalotais, July 11, 1762, printed in Voltaire, *The Complete Works of Voltaire,* vol. 109, *Correspondence and Related Documents* (Geneve, 1973), p. 96.

71. Anton Chekhov, *Sochineniia* (Moscow, 1974), 1:143–158.

72. Chekhov gives Molokhovets's first name as Olga instead of Elena, but this may have been be to avoid accusations of libel. There is no doubt that readers would think of Molokhovets's cookbook, which had already been printed in nine editions by 1882.

73. Molokhovets 1901, pt. 2, pp. 79–83.

7. PEDAGOGICAL AND DIDACTIC APPROACHES

1. Fisher 1881, p. 3.

2. Michael Joseph Oakeshott, *Rationalism in Politics, and Other Essays* (London, 1962), p. 119.

3. Laurioux 1997a, pp. 151, 253.

4. *Liber de coquina,* MS Latin 7131, Bibliothèque nationale de France, Paris, fol. 67 verso.

5. Bradley 1756, p. 32; Scheibler 1861, preface.

6. Quellier 2007, p. 212.

7. La Varenne 1651, pp. 1, 67, 251.

8. Scappi 1570, fol. 415.

9. Kitchiner 1817, preface, fol. b2 verso; Blom 1888, preface.

10. Thomas Gloning, e-mail to the author, November 7, 2012.

11. Warg 1755, p. 534, see also pp. 505, 537.

12. Raffald 1782, p. 267.

13. Kitchiner 1817, recipe 553.

14. Acton 1845, p. x. She also referred to "the exact proportion of each, and the precise time required to dress the whole. "

15. Particularly in chapter 4, which was about baked goods. See Rumohr 1822, p. 102. According to Caroline Nyvang (2010, p. 158), a Danish cookbook from the 1820s also listed ingredients at the top of the recipes

16. Marie Schandri, *Regensburger Kochbuch* (Regensburg, 1866).

17. Carroll 2010, p. 68.

18. Beeton 1861, p. 55; Acton 1855, p. 67; David 1988, p. 32.

19. Valerie Mars observed this system in an 1899 British cookbook. See Valerie Mars, "Beyond Beeton," in White 2004a, p. 191.

20. Carroll 2010, pp. 64–66.

21. Menon 1739.

22. Barthes 1984, p. 67.

23. Bocuse 1980, p. 7.

24. Kitchiner 1817, fols. a5 verso–a6 recto.

25. *Forme of Cury,* printed in Hieatt and Butler 1985, p. 133 (recipe 159).

26. Crosby 1998, p. 40.

27. Molbech 1826, p. 155 (recipe 6); see also Grewe and Hieatt 2001, p. 30.

28. *Libro per cuoco,* MS 225, Biblioteca Casanatense, Rome, printed in Faccioli 1992, p. 73.

29. Rumpolt 1581, fol. XLII. The attitude to exact measures may have had to do with the intended audience of a book. According to Karin Becker, medieval dietetic literature was more liberal and generous toward a noble public. Becker, e-mail to the author, April 13, 2015.

30. For an example, see Henry Notaker, "Printed Cookbooks: Food History, Book History, and Literature," *Food and History* 10, no. 2 (2012): 138.

31. Baeza 1592, vol. 2, chap. 20.

32. Laurioux 1997a, p. 338.

33. *A Queen's Delight* (London, 1671), p. 102.

34. Spiller 2010, pp. 57–58.

35. Dawson 1596–97, pt. 1, fol. 46.

36. Glasse 1747, p. 1; "ein Schilling aufgelösten gest," Hommer 1858, p. 851; "1/4 frantsuskoj 5 kop. bulki," Molokhovets 1901, p. 174; "ocho maravedis de especias," Hernández de Maceras 1607, p. 24.

37. Murrell 1638, p. 96; "tolshchina v dva tselkovykh," Molokhovets 1901, pt. 2, p. 32.

38. *Rigaisches Kochbuch* (Riga, 1880), p. 196.

39. Casteau 1604, pp. 21, 67.

40. Marin 1739, quoted in Fink 1995, p. 29.

41. Warg 1755, fol. [π]6 verso.

42. Kitchiner 1817, fol. b9.

43. Beeton 1861, p. 30

44. Farmer 1896, p. 27.

45. Raymond Sokolov, "Measure for Measure," *Natural History* 97 (July 1988).

46. Molokhovets 1901, pt. 1, p. ii.

47. Adrià 2011.

48. When the Metre Convention was signed in 1875, only Great Britain, Russia, and a few other European countries still used older systems.

49. Traugott Hammerl, *Norddeutsches Kochbuch* (Wismar, 1898), pp. 178, 201.

50. Taillevent 1486, fol. 8 verso; *De verstandige Kock* 1667, fol. I2; Raffald 1782, p. 56; La Varenne 1651, p. 11.

51. Faccioli 1992, p. 172. Scappi did the same; see Scappi 1570, fols. 392–393.

52. Glasse 1747, p. 129.

53. *Ein sehr Künstlichs vnnd Fürtrefflichs Kochbuch* (Augsburg, 1559), fol. 12.

54. Nostradamus 1555, fol. 71 verso.

55. Digby 1997, p. 109.

56. See *Libro per cuoco*, printed in Faccioli 1992, p. 95; Casteau 1604, p. 108; and Robert 1982, p. 51.

57. Martino, quoted in Faccioli 1992, pp. 149, 157, 195; Platina 1475, book 6, Iusculum croceum, book 7, Esicium ex carne, book 9, Ova in viru.

58. Carlo M. Cipolla, *Clocks and Culture* (London, 1967); David S. Landes, *Revolution in Time: Clocks and the Making of the Modern World* (London, 2000).

59. Lorna Weatherill, *Consumer Behaviour and Material Culture in Britain 1660–1760* (London, 1988), pp. 25–28.

60. Raffald 1782, p. 5.

61. Gouffé 1867, p. iii.

62. Athenaeus, *Deipnosofistae* 7:278a; Wilkins and Hill 1994, p. 73.

63. *Goud kokery*, MS Harley 2378, British Library, London, printed in Hieatt and Butler 1985, p. 150 (recipe 11); Scappi 1570, fol. 74.

64. Warg 1755, pp. 490, 506; Davidis 1845, p. 234.

65. Winsnes 1845, pp. 361, 353.

66. This 2002, p. 31.

67. May 1685, fol. A4.

68. *The Queen-Like Closet* (London, 1670), title page.

69. Tillinghast 1690, title page, fol. a1. She was referring to female scholars.

70. For example, Robert 1982, introduction; Hernández de Maceras 1607, fol. [π]4 verso; La Varenne 1651, fol. ã4.

71. Hagger 1718, vol. 1, fol. XX verso.

72. Rodovský z Hustiřan 1975, p. 27.

73. Pandolfini 1734, p. 55.

74. Hull 1982, p. 138.

75. Rettigová 1837, preface.

76. Winsnes 1845, p. [2].

77. Beauvilliers 1814, p. xj.

78. Carême 1847, 1:lvij. This condescending comment about novels (Carême's German contemporary Karl von Rumohr made a similar remark) was in line with warnings by moralists, who feared that novels were a bad influence for sensitive young women.

79. Camporesi 1995, 12n1.

80. Hyman and Hyman 2002, p. [5].

81. For more about the words "blaunchen" and "whiten," see Carroll 1999, p. 32.

82. Bergner 1858, p. xi. A similar approach can be found in Hommer 1858. See also Beeton 1861, pp. 44–46: "Explanation of French terms used in modern household cookery."

Pellegrino Artusi's cookbook did not have a list of French words but rather a list of words in the local Tuscan dialect that not all Italians would understand (although some of these words are admittedly of French origin). See Camporesi 1995, pp. 26–29.

83. Taillevent 1486, fol. d3.

84. Hernández de Maceras 1607, p. 129.

85. Warg 1755, p. 265. Note that in Sweden, *fricadeller* are boiled meatballs, whereas in Denmark, the term is used for fried meatballs.

86. Flandrin, Hyman, and Hyman 1983, p. 330

87. Soyer 1851, p. 110 (recipe 191).

88. This 2009, p. 15, 37.

89. Richard Sennett, *The Craftsman* (London, 2008), pp. 185–186.

90. Ibid., 185.

91. Hagger 1718, vol. 1, preface.

92. Bradley 1756, title page.

93. Kurth 1879, p. iv.

94. D. Shaw 2009, p. 222.

95. Eisenstein 1979, p. 85; Steinberg 1996, p. 71; Houston 1995, p. 162.

96. The German names of the fish are *Hausen, Huechen* (*Huchen*), *Karpfen,* and *Nerffling* (*Aland*). See Rumpolt 1581, fol. XCVI verso, fol. CI verso, fol. CXII verso, fol. CXVIII recto.

97. Benker 1986, p. 267.

98. Gheeraert Vorselmann, *Eenen nyeuwen Coock Boeck* (Antwerp, 1556); *Küchenmeisterei.* Franfurt am Main 1539.

99. Day 2004, pp. 98–150.

8. PARATEXTS IN COOKBOOKS

1. Genette 1987, p. 7.

2. W. H. Sherman 2007, p. 68.

3. This chapter will discuss a selection of cookbook titles, dedicatory epistles, and prefaces, but it has no ambition of giving a complete analysis of how paratexts function in cookbooks. Authors' names, indexes, and illustrations are discussed in chapters 2, 5, and 7.

4. Genette 1987, p. 73.

5. *Ocios de dispéptico y ensueños de famélico* (Berri, 1936); Marin 1739 (Comus is the Greek god of festivity and the son of Bacchus); Anton Hüppmann, *Der elegante Gaumen* (Pest, 1835); *Poesia nascosta* (Florence, 1931); Lina Dunlap, *Out of the Blue Grass* (Lexington, KY, 1910).

6. P. Lehmann 1949.

7. The short title of this book is *Vollständiges Nürnbergisches Koch-Buch.*

8. Bergengruen 1960, p. 17.

9. Eugenia Cheng, *How to Bake Pi* (New York, 2015).

10. Genette 1987, p. 87; G. E. Lessing, *Hamburgische Dramaturgie* (Hamburg, 1767), p. 162; Umberto Eco, *Postille a il nome della rosa* (Milan, 1984), p. 8.

11. Quoted in Salvatori 1990, p. 909n.

12. Bergengruen 1960, pp. 13–14.

13. Vicaire 1890, columns 541–543.

14. Weiss 1996, entries 3363–3366.
15. Vegenfeldt 1978, entries 456–457.
16. Genette 1987, pp. 121–122.
17. La Varenne 1651, fol. ã3.
18. Murrell 1638, fol. a3 recto and verso.
19. Platina ([1470?]) 1498, dedicatory epistle; Rodovský z Hustiřan 1975, dedicatory epistle, p. 25; Latini 1692, fol. [π]2 recto and verso; Evelyn 1699, fol. A1–8, fol. a1–2.
20. Fink 1995, pp. 89, 92.
21. Quoted in Capatti and Montanari 2002, p. 200.
22. Carême 1847, vol. 1, pp. v, vij.
23. Genette 1987, p. 150.
24. Ibid., p. 158.
25. Marin 1742, pp. j–liij.
26. *Daz buoch von guoter spise,* printed in Hajek 1958, p. 14; *Von Speisen* (Frankfurt am Main, 1531).
27. Schellhammer 1692, preface. During the twenty years before 1692, one cookbook was published every year in Germany (on average), and twelve of them were new titles. The quote from Solomon is from Ecclesiastes 12:12.
28. "Quoi! dira-t-on peut-être, encore un ouvrage sur la cuisine?" Menon 1759, preface.
29. "Noch ein Kochbuch! wird das Publikum ausrufen." *Neues Lexikon* 1785, preface.
30. E. Smith 1758, preface.
31. L. S. R 1674, pp. 4–5.
32. *The Cook's Guide* (London, 1861), pp. iv–v.
33. "Klarheit, Eindeutigkeit und Genauigkeit der Aussage." Eis 1967, p. 53.
34. "Nuditas enim animi, ut olim corporis, innocentiae et simplicitatis comes est." Francis Bacon, "Distributio operis," in *Novum organum* (London, 1620).
35. "Não sou literato." Mata 1876, preface.
36. Hagger 1718, vol. 1, preface; *Das Allerneueste Pariser Kochbuch* 1752, preface.
37. Egerin 1745, fol.)(2 verso.
38. Hannah Woolley, quoted by Hobby 1988, p. 170.
39. Warg 1755, preface. She may have read Alexander Pope: "Words are like leaves, and where they most abound / Much fruit of sense beneath is rarely found."
40. Stefani 1662, p. 7. This may have been an established pun; it was used some years later by Latini (1692, fol. A1 verso).
41. Dubois 1889, preface.
42. *Universal-Lexikon der Kochkunst* 1878, preface.
43. The references to Curtius are from Curtius 1969, pp. 93–95.
44. Hagger 1718, vol. 1, preface.
45. Nimb 1900, preface.
46. Genette 1987, p. 193.
47. Hagger 1718, vol. 1, preface. See also Menon 1759; *Neues deutsches Kochbuch* [1870?].
48. Muro 1982, preface.
49. Preface of the 1713 edition, quoted in G. Lehmann 2003, p. 92.
50. Lehmann 2003, p. 92.
51. Raffald 1782, p. i.

52. Hagger 1718, vol. 1, preface; May 1665, preface; La Varenne 1651, fol. ā4. See also Lebas 1738, preface.

53. Schuppe 1698, preface.

54. Albano 2001, pp. 7–39; G. Lehmann 2003, pp. 48 51; Notaker 2010, p. 110.

55. Maren E. Bang, *Huusholdningsbog* (Fredrikshald, 1842), preface.

56. Rettigová 1831, pp. xi–xvi. The first edition of Rettigová's book was published in 1826. The other book, *Nowá wyborná knjžka kuchařská*, was printed in 1821; the name of the author on the title page was Antonin Kuperyus, although Rettigová said no such person existed and claimed that it was an invented name.

57. Marivaux, *La voiture embourbée* (1714), quoted in Genette 1987, p. 213.

58. Smith 1758, preface.

59. Dods 1829, "Advertisement to Fourth Edition."

60. Cervantes, *Don Quijote,* "Prólogo."

61. Latini 1692, fols. A2–a3 verso.

62. Corrado 1786, fols. A3–a4 verso.

63. Camporesi 1995, pp. 22–24.

64. May 1685, fols. A6–A8 verso; Rabisha 1661, fols. A5 verso–A6 recto.

65. Audiger 1692, printed on four pages before the dedicatory letter.

66. *A Supplement to The Queen-Like Closet* (London, 1674), fol. A8.

9. THE RECIPE FORM

1. *Liber de coquina,* printed in Faccioli 1992, p. 22. The word "recipe" appeared in an English translation of a medical book around 1400, but only once, as an exception to the regular use of "take": "Recipe litargium as myche as þou wolt." Lanfranco of Milan, *Science of Cirurgie* (New York, 1894).

2. Montefiore 1846; Acton 1845. See also Dods 1826 (Scotland) and Rutledge 1847 (United States).

3. According to the *Oxford English Dictionary* (2nd ed.), "receipt" comes from Latin *recepta,* from *recipĕre,* to receive.

4. Among the exceptions are συνταγή (Greek), *opskrift,* (Danish), *oppskrift* (Norwegian), and *uppskrift* (Icelandic). The word *recept* (and similar forms) is also used to refer to a medical "recipe" in many European languages, but other languages use different terms, for example, "prescription" in English, *ordonnance* in French, and *lyfseðill* in Icelandic.

5. The Danish, Norwegian, and Icelandic words refer to something written.

6. Several examples in Athenaeus and Galen. See also *First Alcibiades* 117c (attributed to Plato).

7. Platina 1475, book 1, De ficis. Platina copied not only the term but also the contents from Pliny the Elder, *Historia naturalis,* 23.149.

8. Favre 1905; Marinetti and Fillià 1932.

9. Geoffrey Chaucer, "The Chanouns Yemannes Tale," *Canterbury Tales.*

10. *Le menagier de Paris,* MS 12477 Fonds français, Bibliothèque nationale de France, Paris, printed in Brereton and Ferrier 1981, p. 279.

11. Valentin Boltz, *Illuminierbuch* (Frankfurt am Main,, 1578), fol. 19 verso.

12. Laurioux 1997a, p. 255.

13. Furnivall 1867, p. 33; Laurioux 1997a, p. 256.

14. Laurioux 1997a, 1997b; Wolańska-Köller 2010, pp. 8–14.

15. Adrià 2011.

16. Bocuse 1980. For a more detailed structure (preparation, application, evaluation, and so on), see Alonso-Almeida 2013, pp. 68–92.

17. *A Booke of Cookerie* (London, 1597), fol. B3 verso.

18. Acton 1855, p. 350; *The Compleat Cook* (London, 1671), p. 53; Raffald 1782, pp. 89–90.

19. Raffald 1782, p. 181; Rabisha 1682, p. 119; Farmer 1896, p. 228; David 1983, p. 52; "puis seruez auec jus de citron," Taillevent 1486, p. 95; "e puo' li colorare, e fare Verdi con erbe peste," *Libro della cocina,* MS 158, Biblioteca Universitaria di Bologna, printed in Faccioli 1992, p. 54; "& açucar & canela," Ruberto 1529, fols. 17, 19 verso, 21, 21 verso, and others.

20. Smith 1758, p. 73; Acton 1855, p. 119.

21. "Kindbetterin und Aderlasser," Staindl von Dillingen 1569, fol. 13; "ein Kriegsmann zu Felde liegt," Rumpolt 1581, fol. LIX

22. Simmons 1796, p. 17.

23. "& sera ottimo," Messisbugo 1557, p. 83; "so wirdt es wolgeschmack vnd gut," Rumpolt 1581, fol. XXVII verso; "is een goede Saus," *De verstandige Kock* 1667, fol. I4.

24. Murrell 1638, p. 46; *Libro della cocina,* printed in Faccioli 1992, p. 52; *Daz buoch von guoter spise,* in Hajek 1958, e.g., recipes 3, 4, 5; La Varenne 1651, e.g., pp. 5, 6, 7; Rodovský z Hustiřan 1975, e.g., p. 35, 41, 46.

25. Carroll 1999, p. 33. The morality added to old fables could be considered another example of a formulaic feature.

26. Dawson 1596–97, pt. 2, p. 9; "prima farai la tua pasta . . . poi fa," Messisbugo 1557, fol. 43.

27. "Om honan intet gör det fett nog, så hav litet smor deri." *Een lijten kockebok* (Stockholm, 1650), quoted in Rogström 2000, p. 12.

28. "Que en culinaria se llama *gratin*." Muro 1982, p. 79.

29. Dods 1829, recipe 736.

30. For a far more detailed classification of nouns, see Wolańska-Köller 2010, pp. 211–212.

31. Dawson 1596–97, pt. 2, p. 14; La Varenne 1651, p. 159; *Kökerye* (Lübeck, 1570), fol. A5 verso; Rosnack 1845, p. 33; E. Smith 1758, p. 224.

32. Roden 1985, pp. 189, 444, 268.

33. Glasse 1747, pp. 77, 92; Murrell 1638, p. 91; La Varenne 1651, p. 158.

34. Farmer 1896, p. 126.

35. Dawson 1596–97, pt. 1, fol. 28 verso.

36. Farmer 1896, p. 64.

37. Culy 1996, p. 98.

38. Robaschik 1988, p. 112.

39. The Belgian linguist Annick Englebert has interpreted the form *prenez* as an indicative and not an imperative, as the forms are the same in second person plural. See Englebert, *Mange! L'impératif français, du mythe à la réalité* (Bruxelles, 2009).

40. Austin 1975, pp. 76–77.

41. Greimas 1983, pp. 159–160.

42. See, for example, MS 1213 Helmst, with incipit "Wyltu maken," Herzog August Bibliothek, Wolffenbüttel, printed in Wiswe 1956, p. 29; *Libro per cuoco,* MS 255 in Biblioteca

Casanatense, Rome, printed in Faccioli 1992, p. 74; and *Sent soví*, MS 68 in Biblioteca Universitat de Barcelona, printed in Grewe 1979, p. 133. For a discussion of the hypothetical recipe opening, see Haage 1982, pp. 363–370.

43. T. Gloning 2002, p. 528. More detailed examples of different forms in Ehlert 1987, p. 276; and Wolańska-Köller 2010, pp. 312–313. For a discussion of the different verbal forms used in Apicius and other texts from antiquity, see Grocock and Grainger 2006, p. 99.

44. *Man* in German and Scandinavian languages, *men* in Dutch.

45. *Libellus de arte coquinaria*, MS Ny Saml. 66, 8vo, Det Kongelige Bibliotek, Copenhagen, printed in Molbech 1826, pp. 154–160. See also Grewe and Hieatt 2001, pp. 28–39.

46. Wolańska-Köller 2010, p. 345.

47. Wiedemann 1993, p. 562; Becker 2012, p. 73.

48. Torttila and Hakkarainen 1990, pp. 31–42; Glaser 2002, pp.165–183; Wolańska-Köller 2010.

49. Anna Widmer, *Kochbuch der Privat-Kochschule Widmer Zürich* (Zürich, 1923), quoted in Glaser 2002, p. 169.

50. Hödl 1999, pp. 63–64. This is based on a study of seven books published from 1974 to 1996.

51. Robaschik 1988, p. 110.

52. Ehlert 1987, p. 275.

53. Glaser 2002, p. 165.

54. Jäderberg 1995, pp. 93–119.

55. This shift has also been documented in other genres. See Anward 1994.

56. Czech philology scholar Roar Lishaugen, e-mail to the author, January 17, 2017.

57. Francatelli 1846, pp. 1, 190; Francatelli 1847, pp. 18, 19.

58. *Tractatus*, MS Lat. 7131, Bibliothèque nationale de France, Paris; *Küchenmeisterei* [1490?].

59. Scappi 1570, fol. 56 verso.

60. Warnes 2010, pp. 52–71.

61. Sheila Ferguson, *Soul Food* (New York, 1989), quoted in Warnes 2010, pp. 54–55.

62. Rogström 2000, pp. 3–4, quoting Marianne Nordman, *Minilekter* (Vasa, 1994).

63. Mattheier 1993, p. 249.

64. T. Gloning 2002, p. 524.

65. Norrick 1983, pp. 173–182; Görlach 2004 (first printed in 1992); Carroll 1999, p. 38. See also the discussion of medieval recipes in Griffin 2013, pp. 135–149.

66. Goody 1977, pp. 108, 136.

67. See the presentation of the project, "POLIMA: Le pouvoir des listes au Moyen Âge," last modified March 30, 2015, www.dypac.uvsq.fr/polima-le-pouvoir-des-listes-aumoyen-age-351370.kjsp?RH=1354726198736.

68. Found in various manuscripts, for example, *Divers Makyng*, Yale Beinecke MS 163, Yale University, New Haven, printed in Hieatt 1988, p. 59, no. 72.

69. Umberto Eco, *Vertigine della lista* (Milan, 2009), chap. 7.

70. Alexander Pope, *An Essay on Criticism* (London, 1711), p. 9; Gillian Riley, review of *The Opera of Bartolomeo Scappi*, by Terence Scully, *PPC* no. 88 (2009), p. 106; Camporesi 1995, p. liii.

71. Eis 1967, p. 53.

72. B. D. Haage, "Textsorten," in Haage and Wegner 2007, p. 37.

73. Wiswe 1970, p. 24; Görlach 2004, p. 129.

74. "Ein scherzhaftes Intermezzo in dem sonst so nüchtern-sachlichen Buch." Wiswe 1970, p. 23.

75. B. D. Haage, "Textsorten," in Haage and Wegner 2007, p. 39.

76. "D'abord bien cuire vous les faites, / Dans un léger ragoût vous les passez, / Qu'avec ris de veau vous ferez, / Des truffes, champignons, des crêtes." Lebas 1738, p. 92.

77. Tore Wretman, "Le festin joyeux: Det glada gästabudet," *Gastronomisk kalender* (1986): p. 81.

78. Allum 1833; Henry Notaker, "Poetiske oppskrifter," *Vinduet,* no. 2 (1991).

79. "Saa altså Husets Moder / kan synge efter Noder." Sax, *Kogebog for musikalske hus-mødre* (Copenhagen, 1895), p. 3.

80. "Bigosu smak przedziwny, kolor i woń cudną." Adam Mickiewicz, *Pan Tadeusz* (Paris, 1834), book 4.

81. "Versez goutte à gouttelette / Votre mousse en ces puits, puis / Que ces puits / Passent au four, et, blondines, / Sortant en gais troupelets, / Ce sont les / Tartelettes amandines!" Edmond Rostand, *Cyrano de Bergerac,* act 2, scene 4. The play was first performed in Paris in 1897.

82. "Y del ajo español dos cachos mondo." Muro 1982, p. 102.

83. Acton 1855, p. 135. Eliza Acton did not publish her own recipes in verse, but rather sent them to her sister.

84. Wolańska-Köller 2010, pp. 327–329, 350–353.

85. "Mandeln erstlich, rat' ich dir, / Nimm drei Pfunde, besser vier." Eduard Mörike, *Sämtliche Werke,* vol. 2 (Munich, 1985), p. 384.

86. Steinmetz 1977, pp. 84–85.

87. "Nun aber bringe das Gebrodel / In eine Schüssel (der Poet, / Weil ihm der Reim vor allem geht, / Will schlechterdings hier einen Model)." Steinmetz 1977, p. 384.

88. See, for example, "Schweinekopfsülze," by Günter Grass, and "Pfannkuchenrezept," by Günter Eich.

89. Laurioux 2006b, p. 29.

90. *Bolshoi akademicheskii slovar' russkogo jazika,* vol 2 (Moscow 2005).

91. Jacob Laugesen Borch, *Ordsamling fraa Vesteraalen 1698* (Oslo, 1956).

92. Guillaume de Rondelet, *Histoire des poissons* (Lyon, 1558), quoted in Ferrières 2007, p. 77.

93. Elizabeth Romer, *The Tuscan Year* (London, 1984), "April."

94. J. M. Simmel, *Es muss nicht immer Kaviar sein* (Zurich, 1960); Laura Esquivel, *Como agua para chocolate* (Madrid, 1989).

95. Kurt Vonnegut, *Deadeye Dick* (London, 1983), p. 7. The first edition was published in New York in 1982.

96. Wheaton 1984, pp. 66–67.

97. Quoted in Davidson 1988, p. 310. More crazy recipes can be found in the Danish cookbook *Den forkeerte Kaage-Bog* (Copenhagen, 1782).

98. Burke 2009, pp. 170–171. In this text, "geneva" refers to "gin."

99. Görlach 2004, p. 126.

100. Ladies of Des Moines, *A Collection of Choice Recipes* (Des Moines, 1903), quoted in Davidson 1988, p. 308.

101. Interview with Mathews in *Paris Review,* no. 19 (2009).

102. *The Court and Kitchin of Elizabeth* 1983, p. 73.

103. Ibid., p. 75.

104. Griffin 2013, p. 147.

10. THE COOKBOOK GENRE

1. Laurioux 1997b, p. 13. The question of how to define a cookbook is discussed in Notaker 2010, pp. 1–2.

2. For example, medical, pharmaceutical, codicological (on book production), agricultural, technical, etc.

3. Monique Chastanet has pointed out the affinity between meteorological, agricultural, and culinary proverbs in such publications. See Chastenet, "Dictons, saisons et alimentation paysanne," in Becker, Moriniaux, and Tabeaud 2015, pp. 105–126.

4. There are in fact cookbooks with one recipe on each page, printed like poems in many books of poetry, within large white margins, "grandes marges de silence" as Paul Éluard called them. See Éluard, "L'évidence poétique," in *Oeuvres complètes* (Paris, 1968), 1:515.

5. Hoey 2001, p. 75.

6. Laurioux 1997b, pp. 18–23.

7. Notaker 2010.

8. Torquato Tasso, "Discorso dell'arte del dialogo," in *Prose* (Milan, 1959), pp. 335–336. For examples of didactic manuscripts in dialogue form in Middle English literature, see Keiser 2004, p. 233.

9. "Wie? Kan man Essig brauwen? / Ja, wisset ihr das nicht?" Maius 1647, p. 44.

10. See, for example, Christopher Polhem, *Samtal mellan en svärmoder och en son-hustru om allahanda hushållsförrättningar* (Stockholm, 1745); *Neues lehrreiches und vollständiges Magazin vor junges Frauenzimmer* (Karlsruhe, 1771); and the anonymous seventeenth-century manuscript cookbook *Cocho bergamasco alla casalenga,* quoted in Capatti and Montanari 2002, p. 208.

11. Written by the engineer John Bourne and published in London 1847.

12. Marlov 1799; Rücherschöld 1800; Seidelin 1801.

13. Soyer 1860, p. 15.

14. Kübler 1850.

15. Ueding 1976, p. 177.

16. Andrew Maunsell, *The Second Parte of the Catalogue of Printed Bookes* (London, 1595), p. 6.

17. *Libellus de arte coquinaria,* MS Ny Saml. 66, 8vo, Det Kongelige Bibliotek, Copenhagen.

18. Laurioux 1997a, pp. 311–314, 359.

19. Aichholzer 1999, pp. 19–20.

20. Eis 1950, p. 269.

21. Haage and Wegner 2007, p. 161.

22. Irmintraut Richarz, ed., *Haushalten in Geschichte und Gegenwart* (Göttingen, 1994).

23. Coler 1593, recipes on pp. 103–207.

24. Wolf Helmhard von Hohberg, *Georgica curiosa* (Nürnberg, 1682), 5th ed., with recipes, published 1715–16. The publisher of the book was Martin Endter.

25. Otto Brunner, *Neue Wege der Verfassungs- und Sozialgeschichte* (Göttingen, 1968), p. 103.

26. "Schaugerichte und alchemistische tricks." Wiedemann 1993, p. 558.

27. *Oeconomia Nova paa Danske* (Copenhagen, 1648).

28. Alessio Piemontese, *Secreti* (Venice, 1662). First edition published in Venice in 1555.

29. Robert Clavell, *A Catalogue of All the Books Published in England. . . .* (London, 1680).

30. A. A. Schleiermacher, *Bibliographisches System der gesammter Wissenschaftskunde* (Brunswick, 1847).

31. Melvyl Dewey, *Classification and Subject Index for Cataloguing* (Hartford, 1876).

32. Willem Jonckbloet, quoted in Jansen-Sieben 1989, p. 543.

33. Braswell 1984; Jansen-Sieben 1989; Mattheier 1993, p. 251.

34. Glaisyer and Pennell 2003, pp. 10–14.

35. Tebeaux 1993.

36. Wellek and Warren 1949, p. 22.

37. One interesting example is the Belorussian Svetlana Alexievich, who was awarded the Nobel Prize for Literature in 2015.

38. In recent years, German and Scandinavian scholars have introduced the term *Sachprosa/sakprosa*, which has been translated into English as "subject-oriented texts." See Johan L. Tønnesson and Kjell Lars Berge, "Forskningen om sakens prosa," *Sakprosa* 1, no. 1 (2010); Boel Englund and Per Ledin, eds., *Teoretiska perspektiv på sakprosa* (Lund, 2003); and Kjell Lars Berge, "The Rhetoric of Science in Practice: Experiences from Nordic Research on Subject-Oriented Texts and Text Cultures," in *Language and Discipline Perspectives on Academic Discourse*, ed. Kjersti Fløttum (Cambridge, 2007).

39. *Catalog der Kochbücher-Sammlung von Theodor Drexel* (Frankfurt am Main, 1885); Carl Georg, *Verzeichnis der Litteratur über Speise und Trank* (Hanover, 1888). The expression "food and drink" has since been used in book auction catalogs as a heading or title.

40. Vicaire 1890, "Avertissement." Note the use of *ouvrage* instead of *oeuvre*. Both are used to refer to a "work," but the latter puts more emphasis on the artistic quality.

41. André L. Simon, *Bibliotheca gastronomica* (repr., London, 1954), introduction.

42. Berchoux 1803.

43. Athenaeus (*Deipnosofistae*, 1.4e) refers to *Gastronomia* as one of the titles of Archestratus's famous text from the fifth century BCE. According to Françoise Hache-Bissette and Denis Saillard, this was also mentioned in a French work from 1623. See Hache-Bissette and Saillard 2009, 9n2.

44. Grimod de la Reynière 2012; Brillat-Savarin 1826.

45. Barthes 1975; Revel 1979; Revel 1982; Mennell 1996; Ory 2009; Gigante 2005, introduction.

46. Revel 1979, pp. 238- 241.

47. Gillet 1993, pp. 5, 39.

48. Quoted in Jean-Claude Bonnet, "Préface," in Grimod de la Reynière 2012, p. 11.

49. Grimod de la Reynière 2012, p. 529.

50. Brillat-Savarin 1826, 1:322. Brillat-Savarin explained his use of "we" in the preface: "When I write of ME in the singular, I gossip with my reader, he may examine, discuss, doubt or laugh; but when I say WE I am a professor, and all must bow to me." (Quand j'écris et parle de moi, au singulier, cela suppose une confabulation avec le lecteur; il peut examiner, discuter, douter et même rire. Mais quand je m'arme du redoutable nous, je professe; il

faut se soumettre). Brillat Savarin, *The Physiology of Taste,* trans. Fayette Robinson (Philadelphia, 1854), p. 45.

51. Grimod de la Reynière 2012, p. 607.

52. Brillat-Savarin 1826, 2:259–261.

53. Ibid., 1:97–98.

54. Ibid., 2:411–412.

55. Rumohr 1822, p. vii.

56. Pennell 1903, introduction.

57. Auden 1973.

58. Ude 1822, pp. xx–xxi.

59. Antonin Carême, *Le cuisinier parisien* (Paris, 1828), pp. 30–31. Carême had more positive words later in life, when he discovered that cooks had been praised by Grimod. See Carême 1847, 1:x.

60. Mennell 1996, pp. 270–271.

61. Gigante 2005, p. xix.

62. Grimod de la Reynière 2012, p. 261; Brillat-Savarin 1826, 1:269.

63. Becker 2000, pp. 259–278.

64. The first translations were into Spanish in 1852 (Mexico), into English in 1854 (United States), and into German in 1865 (Germany).

65. Anthus 2006.

66. Hegel's *Vorlesungen über die Ästhetik* were held in the late 1820s and printed in 1835.

67. Anthus 2006, p. 17.

68. Denise Gigante, *Taste: A Literary History* (New Haven, 2005), Kindle ebook loc. 2568–70.

69. Vaerst 1851, p. vii.

70. Rajberti 1850–51, vol. 1, chap. 6.

71. "Kak kvas, pet' nektar blagodatnoj / A trjufel' est' kak ogurets." Filimonov 1837, p. 33. See also Chamberlain 1983, pp. 31–38.

72. Mennell 1996, p. 271.

73. Gigante 2005, p. 58.

74. Beeton 1861, p. iii.

75. Honoré de Balzac, *Oeuvres complètes* (Paris, 1879), 22:234.

76. Gigante 2005, pp. xvii–xviii.

77. Barthes 1975, p. 28.

78. Revel 1979, p. 243n.

79. Ory 2009, p. 49.

80. Gigante 2005, pp. xxxiv–xxxv.

81. Fragments of Matro from Athenaeus's *Deipnosofistae* collected and translated in S. Douglas Olson and Alexander Sens, *Matro of Pitane and the Tradition of Epic Parody in the Fourth Century BCE* (Atlanta, 1999); Petronius's *Satyricon,* with the description of Trimalchio's dinner, has been printed in many editions and translations, and Federico Fellini even made a movie based on it, the 1969 *Satyricon.*

82. Grimod de la Reynière 2012, p. 201.

83. Rajberti 1850–51, "Prefazione."

84. Camba 1962, pp. 589, 569, 600.

85. First editions: Hagdahl 1879; Artusi 1891; Muro 1894.

86. Capatti 2009, p. 24.

87. Camporesi 1995, p. xlix.

88. Salvatori 1998, p. 909.

89. Aron 1973, p. 325.

90. Becker 2000, p. 264. For a discussion of food and gastronomy in relation to *Sexualität, Erotik,* and *Frauenbild,* see Becker 2000, pp. 48, 663, 676.

91. Balzli 1931, p. 20.

92. Walter Scott, who was highly respected for his poetry, published his Waverley novels anonymously, but the public soon recognized his style, and they suspected that he also was the author of *Cook and Household's Manual,* which had in fact been written by Johnstone. Arnold 1993, pp. 7–10.

93. Ian Duncan, *Scott's Shadow: The Novel in Romantic Edinburgh* (Princeton, 2007), p. 288. Duncan gives an analysis of Johnstone's work and also describes the differences between the early editions of the cookbook.

94. Dods 1829, "Advertisement to Fourth Edition." The other work she mentioned was *The French Cook,* by Louis E. Ude.

95. Becker 2000, p. 269.

96. Mennell 1996, p. 271.

97. Umberto Eco, *Vertigine della lista* (Milan, 2009), chap. 20.

98. Laurioux 1997a, p. 281; Hyman and Hyman 1996, p. 643.

99. Quoted in Becker 2000, p. 258.

100. This conclusion is from Laurioux 1997a, p. 248.

11. COOKBOOKS FOR THE RICH AND THE POOR

1. Friedrich Engels, *Die Lage der arbeitenden Klasse in England* (Leipzig, 1845), p. 95.

2. First editions of Soyer's four cookbooks were published the following years: 1846, 1848, 1849, 1854.

3. Winsnes 1845, 1862, 1857.

4. Winsnes 1857, p. 180.

5. A relevant association here is another work from 1845, Benjamin Disraeli's novel *Sybil, or The Two Nations,* in which "the rich and the poor" are described as inhabitants of different planets, "fed by a different food."

6. Finnur Jónsson, ed., *De gamle Eddadigte* (Copenhagen, 1932), p. 158.

7. A. C. Cawley, "The Grotesque Feast in Prima Pastorum," *Speculum* 30, no. 2 (1955): pp. 213–217; George Fenwick Jones, "The Function of Food in Medieval German Literature," *Speculum* 35, no. 1 (1960): pp. 78–86; Giulio Cesare dalla Croce, *Le sottilissime astutie di Bertoldo* (Vicenza, 1620), p. 88.

8. Edith Ennen, *Frauen in Mittelalter* (Munich, 1985), p. 224.

9. Laurioux 1989, p. 28.

10. Rumpolt 1581, fols. 11–41.

11. Sumptuary law enacted May 31, 1517.

12. "Forordning om klædedragt, brylluper, barseler og giestebude, 13.3.1683," in *Kgl. forordninger 1670–1683* (Copenhagen, 1683), p. 892.

13. *Kongl. Maij:tz Stadga och Påbudh, Öfwer åthskillige Excessers och Oordningars aff-skaffande widh Rijksens Borgerskaps Troolofningar, Gästebudh, Barndoop och Begrafningar, sampt Klädedrächter* (Gothenburg, 1664).

14. *Ordnung der Stadt Leipzig 1661*, quoted in Hansen 1968, p. 155.

15. Serres 1600, pt. 8, chap. 1; Ferrières 2007, pp. 15–16. *Piquette* was originally the name of a drink made from skin and pits from grapes after winemaking, refermented in water, but the word is also used to refer to a wine of inferior quality.

16. Rodovský z Hustiřan 1975, p. 115; Tichá 1975, p. 20.

17. Kelly 2001, p. 143; Toomre 1992, p. 49.

18. Kelly 2001, p. 169. She refers to a 1909 book by Sophia Dragomirova.

19. Elena Molokhovets, *Podarok molodym khaziaikam* (St. Petersburg, 1869), p. 470.

20. Molokhovets 1901, pt. 2, p. 97.

21. Ibid., pt. 1, pp. 45, 93. For Easter and other holidays, Molokhovets proposed richer meals.

22. Arseny Tarkovsky, "Elena Molokhovets," in *Stikhotvoreniia* (Ekaterinburg, 2004), pp. 157–158.

23. Winsnes 1845, pp. 262, 58, 52, 219.

24. Flandrin 1986, pp. 34, 58.

25. Wilson 1991, pp. 34, 58.

26. Adolph von Knigge, *Über den Umgang mit Menschen* (Hanover, 1788), quoted in Eda Sagarra, *A Social History of Germany 1648–1914* (New York, 1977), p. 383.

27. *Boke of Cokery* (London, 1500), fol. A2.

28. Ruberto 1529, title page.

29. Messisbugo 1557, title page.

30. Massialot 1691, fol. A5.

31. G. Lehmann 2003, pp. 90–91.

32. Francatelli 1846, 1847.

33. Cauderlier 1861, 1863.

34. Rettigová 1831; M. D. Rettigová, *Dobrá rada slowanským wenkowankám* (Prague, 1838).

35. Elena Molokhovets, *Prostaia obshchedostupnaia kuhnia* (St. Petersburg, 1883).

36. Camporesi 1995, p. 15.

37. Laurioux 1997a, pp. 305–306.

38. Burke 2009, p. 106.

39. Notaker 2010, p. 4.

40. H. G. Koenigsberger, George L. Mosse, and G. Q. Bowler, *Europe in the Sixteenth Century* (Harlow, Essex, 1989), p. 80.

41. Rondo Cameron, *A Concise Economic History of the World* (Oxford, 1997), p. 220.

42. Bernard Comrie, Gerald Stone, and Maria Polinsky, *The Russian Language in the Twentieth Century* (Oxford, 2003), p. 8.

43. In Sweden and Denmark, scientists and academics started the switch to roman type in the eighteenth century, and the process was gradual. In Germany, gothic had been kept mainly as an example of national identity, although scholars favored roman, but in 1941, Hitler declared that it was a Jewish invention and imposed the use of Antiqua.

44. For example, John Murrell (see Notaker 2010, pp. 72–76) and Henriette Schønberg Erken (see Notaker 2001, p. 12).

45. Lüchou 1968, p. 167.

46. Jacques Dubois, *Conseil très-utile contre la famine* (Paris, 1546).

47. Houston 1995, pp. 185–186.

48. Carolina Weltzin, *Anwisning till tarfwelig matredning* (Stockholm, 1805), preface.

49. Ibid., preface; Mademoiselle Marianne, *La cuisine facile pour tout le monde* (Paris, 1861), preface.

50. Menon 1746, p. 28.

51. Erken 1914a; Erken 1914b. A similar contrast can be found in two Swedish books, Hagdahl 1896 and A. H., *Husmanskost* (Stockholm, 1896).

52. The observations in this paragraph are based on a comparative study of the three books. See Toomre 1983, pp. 48–65.

53. "Si grossière que j'ay regret d'y employer le temps et le papier." Bonnefons 1655, p. 103: *Rave de Limousin* is a type of white turnip.

54. L. S. R. 1674, p. 7.

55. Pardo Bazán 1913, p. 205.

56. Pérez Samper 1998, p. 81.

57. Robert Burns, "Address to a Haggis," first printed in the *Caledonian Mercury* in 1786; Dods 1826, p. 49.

58. Nikolai Gogol, *Mertvye dushi* (Moscow, 1842), chap. 5; Osipov 1790.

59. For example, in Belgium, Gouy 1895, p. 127; in Denmark, Suhr 1909, p. 78; in Norway, Erken 1905, p. 94.

60. Weiss-Adamson 2002, pp. 163–164.

61. Menon 1746, p. 147; Menon 1755, 2:340–349.

62. See, for example, P. B. Munsche, *Gentlemen and Poachers: The English Game Laws 1671–1831* (Cambridge, 1981), p. 22. The aristocracy also had special privileges that gave them the right to catch fish in lakes and rivers and even, in certain cases, the sea. Piero Camporesi (1993, p. 97) pointed out that in the Ravenna region in Italy, the landowners had the right to seafood caught up to "the third wave," which was generally twenty to thirty meters from the shore.

63. *La nouvelle cuisinière bourgeoise* (Paris, 1815), p. 62.

64. Artusi 1911, recipe 281; Hagdahl 1896, p. 419; Erken 1914b, p. 179; Prato 1873, p. 220; Rettigová 1831, p. 79.

65. May 1685, p. 121.

66. Pepys's diary, January 6, 1660.

67. Hannah Glasse's *The Art of Cookery,* according to Wilson 1984, p. 204.

68. Rumpolt 1581, fols. III, VI, XVI, XXXIX, VIII, XI, XXVIII, V, XI.

69. Messisbugo 1557, fol. 39.

70. Ferrières 2007, p. 449.

71. Marc-André Wagner, *Le cheval dans les croyances germaniques* (Paris, 2005), p. 468.

72. Rumpolt 1581, fol. LVI.

73. Waverley Root, *Food* (New York, 1980), s.v. "Horse."

74. Lesniczak 2003, p. 164.

75. *Tatarskaia kukhnia* (Kazan, 1985), pp. 30–33; Prato 1873, p. 175.

76. Erken 1905.

77. Destaminil, n.d.; *La cuisinière assiégée* 1871.

78. *La cuisinière assiégée* 1871, p. 13.

79. Robert 1982, p. 77; Ruberto 1529, fol. 42.

80. Victor Hugo, *Choses vues 1870–1875* (Paris, 1972), pp. 114, 126.

81. Ibid., pp. 117–118.

82. "Menu: 25 Décembre 1870," accessed July 18, 2016, https://en.wikipedia.org/wiki/Siege_of_Paris_(1870%E2%80%9371)#/media/File:Menu-siegedeparis.jpg.

83. *La cuisinière assiégée* 1871, p. 13.

84. D. Richter 1984; Müller 1984; Camporesi 1996, pp. 52–88; Quellier 2013, pp. 41–60.

12. HEALTH AND MEDICINE IN COOKBOOKS

1. *Diuersa Servicia,* MS Douce 257, Bodleian Library, Oxford, printed in Hieatt and Butler 1985, p. 79.

2. *Küchenmeisterei* [1490?], fol. [π]1 verso.

3. La Varenne 1651, fol. Ã7 verso.

4. Martino, quoted in Faccioli 1992, p. 164; Platina 1475, book 7, Cibarium croceum.

5. Scappi 1570, fols. 391–436.

6. Wecker 1598.

7. *Een notabel boecxken van cokeryen* (Brussels, [1514?]), fol. D3 verso, fol. F3 recto.

8. Rumpolt 1581, fol. CXLV.

9. Platina 1475, book 1, Diligendus locus ad habitandum.

10. Geoffrey Chaucer, "The Prologue," *Canterbury Tales.*

11. *Forme of Cury,* printed in Hieatt and Butler 1985, p. 20.

12. Boorde 1542, chap. 18.

13. Lemmer 1980, p. 12.

14. Nicolas de Chesnaye, *La condamnation de banquet* (Geneva, 1991).

15. Eamon 1996, p. 86.

16. Boorde 1542, chap. 16.

17. Hernández de Maceras 1607, pp. 52, 80.

18. Hildegard von Bingen, *Physica* (Strasbourg, 1533), p. 33. See Thomas Gloning, ed., *Physica,* (Berlin, 2010).

19. Boorde 1542, chap. 18.

20. Some of the versions are written as simple rhymes in a Latin that was close to vernacular Italian. See "Flos medicinae," in *Collectio salernitana,* vol. 5, edited by Salvatore de Renzi, G. E. T. Henschel, and C. Daremberg (Naples, 1859).

21. They were called *res non naturales,* because humans were able to influence or direct them, something they could not do with nature. In the first chapter of his book, Platina also built on this model.

22. Weiss-Amer 1992, pp. 69–78.

23. Laurioux 2006a, pp. 223–238.

24. Magnino from Milan, *Regimen sanitatis,* (Strasbourg, 1503), chapter 18, De piscibus (About fish).

25. MS A. N. V. 12, Öffentliche Bibliothek der Universität, Basel, printed in Ehlert 1996, p. 310.

26. Jansen-Sieben 1994, p. 262.

27. Pisanelli 1583, pp. 96–97.

28. Eleonora Maria Rosalia 1697.

29. *Le pâtissier françois* (Paris, 1653); *Ein Koch- und Artzney-Buch* (Graz, 1686).

30. *A Closet for Ladies and Gentlewomen* (London, 1608), title page.

31. Baeza 1592, bk. 1, chap. 1.

32. Nostradamus 1555, fol. 64.

33. Ryff 1544, fol. B1–2.

34. Platina 1475, book 2, De saccharo.

35. G. Lehmann 2003, p. 33.

36. Nicholas Culpepper, *The Complete Herbal* (London, 1653).

37. Wilkins 2000, p. 399.

38. Eamon 1996, pp. 4–5. For details about English books of secrets, see Ferguson 1981; more recent studies of this genre can be found in Leong and Rankin 2011.

39. Alessio Piemontese 1562, "Ai lettori." The English translation is by William Warde, 1558. It is believed that Girolamo Ruscelli published the book under the pseudonym Alessio Piemontese.

40. Liza Picard, *Restoration London* (London, 2001), p. 80.

41. Burke 2009, p. 371.

42. *A Closet for Ladies and Gentlewomen* (London, 1636), fol. [D1], verso.

43. John Hale, *The Civilization in Europe in the Renaissance* (London, 1993), p. 545.

44. Alessio Piemontese 1562, "Ai lettori."

45. Roy Porter, *The Greatest Benefit to Mankind* (London, 1999), pp. 282–283.

46. Albala 2002.

47. Scappi 1570, e.g., fols. 337, 338, 338 verso, 339, and others.

48. Scully 1993, p. 11.

49. Miguel de Cervantes, *Don Quijote,* pt. 2, chap. 47.

50. Shakespeare, *The Taming of the Shrew,* act 4, sc. 3.

51. Albala 2002, p. 36.

52. Menon 1789, p. 115.

53. F. Marin 1742, 1:xxj.

54. Gentilcore 2016, chap. 2.

55. Acton 1855, p. xix.

56. McGee 1986, p. 76.

57. Klencke 1857.

13. RECIPES FOR FAT DAYS AND LEAN DAYS

1. *Küchenmeisterei* [1490?].

2. 1 Timothy 4:4. About the role of fasting in the early Christian Church, see Grimm 1996; and T. Shaw 1998.

3. *Regula benedicti,* chap. 39: "De mensura cibus."

4. Chevalier 1982, p. 194.

5. Quoted in Harvolk 1993, p. 582.

6. Harvolk 1993, p. 583.

7. Ehlert 1996, p. 267.

8. Rambourg 2010, pp. 100–102.

9. Hommer 1858, p. 853.

10. *Postnaia povarikha* (Kostroma, 1793).

11. Levshin 1816, p. 43.

12. Martino, quoted in Faccioli 1992, p. 184; Platina 1475, book 8, Butyrum fictum.

13. MS A. N. V. 12, Öffentliche Bibliothek der Universität, Basel, printed in Ehlert 1996, p. 235.

14. MS 1213 Helmst., Herzog August Bibliothek, Wolffenbüttel, printed in Wiswe 1956, p. 32 (recipe 10).

15. *Le menagier de Paris*, MS 12477 fonds français, Bibliothèque nationale de France, Paris, printed in Brereton and Ferrier 1981, p. 250. The similarity between "milt" and "milk" and *laitance* and *lait* is also found in other languages, for example, Spanish (*lecha/leche*), Russian (*moloki/moloko*), Swedish (*mjölke/mjölk*), and German (*Milch*, for both).

16. MS Germ. 244, Staatsbibliothek, Berlin, printed in T. Gloning 1998, p. 26.

17. Furnivall 1867, p. 37.

18. MS A. N. V. 12, Öffentliche Bibliothek der Universität, Basel, printed in Ehlert 1996, p. 318.

19. *Küchenmeisterei* [1490?], fol. A5.

20. Rumpolt 1581, fol. LX verso.

21. Prato 1873, p. 307. There is the question of whether these strange dishes were actually prepared and eaten and not simply riffs on the popular bestiaries or part of a jocular tradition. But most of them are documented in other sources, and the practical recipes in several cookbooks seem to be meant as serious information.

22. Grimod de la Reynière 2012, p. 117.

23. Pierre Belon, *L'histoire naturelle des estranges poissons marins* (Paris, 1551), p. xiii, quoted in Ferrières 2007, p. 416.

24. Menon 1789, p. 479.

25. Grimod de la Reynière 2012, pp. 47-48.

26. "Folaghe in umido." Artusi 1911, recipe 275.

27. Hernández de Maceras 1607, pp. 60-72.

28. Santiago Gómez Laguna, ed., *Domingo Hernández de Maceras: Libro del arte de cozina* (Salamanca, 1999), p. 294.

29. Voltaire, *Questions sur l'encyclopédie: Troisième partie* (Paris, 1770), p. 202.

30. *Kucharzka* 1542, fols. v1-z4, fol. aa 1-4.

31. Rodovský z Hustiřan 1975.

32. Murrell 1638, title page.

33. The word "ember" comes from the Anglo-Saxon *ymbren* (circuit), which refers to the annual cycle of the year.

34. The Greek term is *megale tessarakoste* or *sarakoste*. More examples are the Russian *velikii post*, the Polish *wielki post*, and the Norwegian *langfasten*.

35. La Varenne 1651, pp. 303-309.

36. *Krapfen* is a type of doughnut. The German buns are probably *Heisse Wecken* (hot wicks). In a cookbook published in Hamburg (a Lutheran area), the buns are called *Fastnacht-National-Weissbrot* (Shrove Tuesday national white bread). See Hommer 1858, p. 848.

37. See Albala and Eden 2011.

38. Ulrich Zwingli, *Von Erkiesen und Freyhait der Speisen* (Basel, 1522).

39. Martin Luther, *An den Christlichen Adel deutscher Nation* (Wittenberg, 1520), fol. J1 recto.

40. Jean Calvin, *Institutio christianae religionis* (Geneva, 1559), 5:230.

41. Desiderius Erasmus, "Convivium profanum," in *Colloquia familiaria* (Magdeburg, 1536).

42. Scappi 1570, fols. 313–314.

43. Walter Benjamin, "Denkbilder," in *Gesammelte Schriften* (Munich, 1972), 4:376.

44. Sale 1664, p. 103.

45. *Koge Bog* 1616, recipes 55, 56.

46. Rettigová 1831, pp. 210–211.

47. *Vollständiges Nürnbergisches Koch-Buch* 1691.

48. *De volmaakte Hollandsche Keuken-Meid* 1761; *Het Hollands* 1724.

49. May 1685, fol. B8 verso.

50. *A Lenten Cookery Book* (London, 1876) became *Maigre Cookery* (London, 1884); *Meatless Fare and Lenten Cookery* (London, 1909) became *Meals without Meat, or Meatless Fare Cookery* (London, 1915–17).

51. J. de San Luis, *Cocina de cuaresma* (Barcelona, 1908); *La mejor cocina de cuaresma* (Barcelona, 1914).

52. Artusi 1911, recipes 67, 81, 506.

53. Takats 2011, p. 111.

54. See Watts 2011.

55. Voltaire, *Dictionnaire philosophique,* in *Oeuvres de Voltaire,* vol. 27, edited by M. Beuchot (Paris, 1829), p. 452.

56. Carême 1847, 3:23.

57. Around the same time Dumas's book was published, a collection of recipes for Lenten dishes was printed: De Latreille and Henry Palmé, *La cuisine de Carême et des jours d'abstinence* (Paris, 1872).

14. VEGETARIAN COOKBOOKS

1. Plutarch, *Moralia* 993b. The translation is taken from Howard Williams, *The Ethics of Diet* (London, 1883), p. 41.

2. F. Marin 1742, pp. vi–x.

3. Corrado 1786, p. 125. Several works on the Pythagorean diet (*vitto Pitagorico*) were published in Italy in the 1740s and '50s; see Westbury 1963, pp. 30, 49–50, 179.

4. Benjamin Franklin, *The Art of Eating* (Princeton, 1958), p. 7.

5. Thomas Tryon, "Bill of Fare," *PPC,* no. 74 (2003): p. 53.

6. Tryon 1694, p. 10.

7. John Ray, quoted in Evelyn 1699, pp. 171–172.

8. The second edition was published in 1803 with the title *On Food*. Both books printed in "Poughill near Ludlow."

9. Percy Bysshe Shelley, *Queen Mab,* stanza 8.

10. Shelley's *A Vindication of Natural Diet* (London, 1813) is well known.

11. Nicholson 1832, pp. 45–46.

12. Haber 2002, pp. 9–19.

13. Nicholson 1832, pp. 47–48.

14. Struve 1869.

15. Weilshäuser 1896.

16. Barlösius 1998, p. 287.

17. Ebmeyer 1878.

18. For a history of Italian vegetarianism, see Alberto Capatti, "La nascita delle associazione vegetariane in Italia," *Food and History* 2, no. 1 (2004): pp. 167–190.

19. As a student in London, Gandhi published a series of articles about vegetarianism in which he stated that Indians "don't believe in plain boiled vegetables, but must have them flavoured with plenty of condiments, e.g., pepper, salt, cloves, turmeric, mustard seed, and various other things." M. K. Gandhi, "Indian Vegetarians," pt. 2, *Vegetarian* (February 14, 1891).

20. Kellogg 1893, p. 32.

21. Kellogg 1904, p. 398.

22. Kellogg 1904, pp. 398, 409, 415, 402, 405.

23. J. Smith 1866; Baltzer 1903.

24. Farmer 1896, p. 252. For example, in Germany, Davidis 1845, p. 62; in Scotland, Dods 1826, p. 142; in Denmark, Suhr 1909, p. 151; in Norway, Blom 1888, p. 5; in Russia, Molokhovets, see Toomre 1992, p. 243.

25. Arnold Frank Hills, *Vital Food* (London, 1892).

26. Alice Bircher, *Diätetische Speisezettel und fleischlose Kochrezepte* (Berlin, 1906); Bertha Brupbacher-Bircher, *Das Wendepunkt-Kochbuch* (Zurich, 1927).

27. Molokhovets 1901, pt. 1, pp. 681–695.

28. Zelenkova 1909.

29. The information about Nordman is from Goldstein 1997, pp. 109–117.

15. JEWISH COOKBOOKS

1. *Kochbuch für den jüdischen Haushalt und Grossbetriebe* [1935?], p. 4.

2. *Kochbuch für die jüdische Küche* 1926, p. iii.

3. Genesis 9:3–4.

4. Kauders 1886, p. 171.

5. Joseph Stoltz, *Kochbuch f. Israeliten, oder praktische Anweisung, wie man nach den jüdischen Religionsgründen alle Gattungen der feinsten Speisen kauscher bereitet* (Karlsruhe, 1815).

6. Aschmann 1835.

7. The legal commentaries, known collectively as the Talmud, were compiled in the sixth century in Babylonia.

8. Exodus 23:19 and 34:26; Deuteronomy 14:21.

9. Aschmann 1835, p. 1.

10. Kauders 1886, p. 172.

11. Wolf 1853, preface.

12. Acton 1855, p. 606.

13. Kafka wrote the letter in 1919, but his father never received it. It was published in 1952.

14. Kauders 1886, p. 107.

15. The information in the following paragraphs is from Kirschenblatt-Gimblett 1986–87, pp. 51–89; Raphael 1985, pp. 7–30; S. Sherman 2002, pp. 72–94.

16. S. Sherman 2002, pp. 76–77.

17. Stanley Weintraub, *Disraeli: A Biography* (New York, 1993).

18. Kirschenblatt-Gimblett 1986–87, p. 56.

19. For details, see Abigail Green, *Moses Montefiore* (London, 2010).

20. Montefiore 1846, p. 11.

21. Ibid., pp. v–vi.

22. Wolf 1853, preface.

23. Curriel 1915, p. 5.

24. S. Sherman 2002, p. 74.

25. Montefiore 1846, pp. 19, 25, 19.

26. Ibid., p. 32.

27. Ibid., p. 52.

28. Ibid., pp. xiii, 62.

29. *The Little Book of Jewish Cookery* (London, [1912]); Kirschenblatt-Gimblett 1986–87, p. 66.

30. Richard I. Cohen, "Urban Visibility and Biblical Visions," in *Cultures of the Jews*, ed. David Beale (New York, 2002), 3:736.

31. Ibid., p. 738.

32. *Nayes follshtendiges kokhbukh fir di yidishe kikhe: Ayn unentbehrlikhes handbukh fir yidishe froyen und tökhter nebst forshrift fon flaysh kosher makhen und khale nehmen, iber-hoypt iberraynlikhkayt und kashrut* (Vienna, 1854).

33. Bloshteyn 1898.

34. Kirschenblatt-Gimblett 2007.

35. According to the 2000 census, the number of Yiddish speakers in the United States today is about 180,000, but it may be higher.

36. Levy 1871; Kirschenblatt-Gimblett 1986–87.

37. Levy 1871, p. 3.

38. Kirschenblatt-Gimblett 1990, pp. 75–105. This article discusses the place of a kosher diet and many other aspects of Jewish cookbooks and Jewish cuisine in the United States in the twentieth century.

39. Kramer 1889.

40. Kirschenblatt-Gimblett 1990, p. 79.

41. The printer's mark of Bloch's company may also give an indication: it is a Star of David with "B & Co" in the center.

42. Kander 1901.

43. Sara Vos, *Oorspronkelijk Israëlitisch Kookboek* (Amsterdam, 1894).

44. Verbond voor Liberaal-Religieuze Joden in Nederland.

45. Malvine Glück and E. Bramson-Brest, *Geillustreerd ritueel kookboek* (Amsterdam, 1932).

46. *Poesia nascosta: Seicento ricette di cucina ebraica in Italia* (Florence, 1931).

47. *Kochbuch für die jüdische Küche* 1926, p. x.

48. *Kochbuch für den jüdischen Haushalt und Grossbetriebe* [1935?], pp. 121–124.

49. Richard J. Evans, *The Third Reich in Power* (London, 2006), p. 555.

50. Theophano 2003, pp. 79–80.

51. Cara de Silva, *In Memory's Kitchen: A Legacy from the Women of Terezin* (Northvale, NJ, 1996).

52. German 2011, pp. 137–154.

53. For more about the history of Jewish cookbooks, see Kirschenblatt-Gimblett 2007.

54. Roden 1981, p. 112.

16. COOKBOOKS AND ASPECTS OF NATIONALISM

1. Benedict Anderson, *Imagined Communities: Reflections on the Origin and Spread of Nationalism* (London, 1983).

2. Artusi 1911, recipe 235.

3. *Oxford English Dictionary*, 2nd ed., s.v. "national," 1.a, 2.a.

4. Rumpolt 1581, fol. XXV (recipe 13).

5. Bouwsma 2000, p. 1.

6. Anthony D. Smith, *National Identity* (London, 1991), p. 75.

7. Capatti and Montanari 2002, p. viii; (italics in original). See also Annie Hubert, "Cuisine et politique: Le plat national existe-t-il?" *Revue des sciences sociales,* no. 27 (2000), www.revue-des-sciences-sociales.com/pdf/rss27hubert.pdf.

8. Nyvang 2010, p. 156; Francis Collingwood and John Woollams, *The Universal Cook* (London, 1792), published in Danish as *Nye og fuldstændig huusholdningsbog for driftige huusmødre* (Copenhagen, 1796).

9. Gustafwa Björklund, *Kokbok* (Stockholm, 1847), preface.

10. Simmons 1796, p. 12.

11. Artusi 1911, recipe 427.

12. X. Marcel Boulestin, *Simple French Cooking for English Homes* (London, 1923); Henriette Davidis, *German National Cookery for American Kitchens* (Milwaukie, WI, 1901); J. L. Cuniberti, *Practical Italian Recipes for American Kitchens* (Janeville, WI, 1917).

13. Johann Wolfgang von Goethe, "Kampagne in Frankreich," in *Goethes Werke,* vol. 10 (Hamburg, 1960), p. 257.

14. "Vor Nationalret Faaremelk og Æblegrød," O. M. Mynster, *Pharmakologie I* (Copenhagen, 1810), p. 427; Mason 2002, pp. 179–180.

15. Dods 1826, pp. 48, 61, 82; Dods 1829, p. 328.

16. Acton 1855, pp. 605–622, 35.

17. Dubois 1872.

18. Csergo 1996, p. 838.

19. Dose 1988, p. 245.

20. Revel 1979, p. 220.

21. Quellier 2007, p. 230.

22. Camporesi 1993, pp. 78, 85, see also pp. 162, 176.

23. *Le cuisinier méridional d'après la méthode provençale et languedocienne* (Avignon, 1835). In the preface, the author complains about the northern dominance in contemporary French cookbooks.

24. Lesniczak 2003, pp. 134–135.

25. Prato 1873, preface.

26. Ritzerow 1868, p. 3.

27. Bergner 1858, p. iii.

28. Weiss 1996, p. 482.

29. Nicolas de Bonnefons, *Le jardinier françois* (Paris, 1651), fol. Ã3 verso.

30. See Weiss 1996, entries 519, 718, 994, 3137.

31. Merta 2015, p. 347.

32. For example, Hedwig von Hohenwald, *Illustriertes Victoria-Kochbuch der nord- und süd-deutsche Küche* (Oranienburg, 1891). There are older cookbooks, published in the early nineteenth century, with "German" in their titles, but they did not have any nationalist tendency.

33. *De belgische keukenmeyd* (Ghent, 1838) was a modern edition of *De volmaakte hollandsche keukenmeid* (first printed in Amsterdam in 1746). *Nationaal kookboek voor vlaamsche vrouwen* (published in Leuven around 1908) was the fifth edition of A. G. L. Westenberg's *Nationaal kookboek samengesteld door nederlandse vrouwen,* which was first published in Leiden in 1893. For details, see Witteveen and Cuperus 1998.

34. For the Norwegian titles and more details, see Notaker 2001.

35. For a full discussion of these cookbooks in the context of nineteenth-century nationalism, see Notaker 2002.

36. Gustava Schartau, *Hywäntahtoisia neuwoja katowuosina* (Helsinki, 1834), originally published as *Wälmenta råd i missvextår* (Stockholm, 1831).

37. The information about Finland is from Lüchou 1968, pp. 147–193.

38. Stephensen 1800; Nikólína 1858; see also Notaker 1990; Gísladóttir 1999.

39. Ólafsson 1792, pp. 173–215.

40. Η μαγειρική (Cooking) was published in 1828 in Hermopolis, on the island Syros, one of the important locations for early printing outside of Athens. The title page states that the book is a translation from Italian but does not identify the original.

41. A. Gogué, Τα μυστήρια της γαλλικης μαγειρικης (Athens, 1860), originally published as *Les secrets de la cuisine française* (Paris, 1856).

42. Anna Matthaiou, "Brillat-Savarin et le poisson de l'amiral Canaris: Les livres de cuisine en Grèce au XIXe siècle." Typed manuscript, January 2001.

43. On Turkish cookbooks, see Kut 1990, pp. 29–48.

44. Sapounaki-Dracaki 2003, p. 198.

45. The book, *200 rețete cercate* (200 exquisite recipes), was first published (in Cyrillic script) in Iași by the writer Kostache (Costache, Constantin) Negruzzi and the historian and statesman Mihail Kogălniceanu, who on the title page were identified only as K.N.-M.K.

46. For a more detailed account of this cookbook and its background, see Notaker 1990b.

47. Jan Babilon, *Prvá kuchárska kniha v slovenskej reči* (Pest, 1870).

48. For more details of the Slovak book, see Ivanová-Šalingova 1989; and Notaker 2002.

49. Also the author of the first printed Croatian cookbook from 1813, the Zagreb canon Ivan Birling, explains that he has used German culinary terms because they give a better understanding. See Jelena Ivanišević, "Traditional Cuisine: The First Croation Cookbook," *Iće and Piće,* no. 34 (April 2013), www.iceipice.hr/en/article/200-years-of-written-culinary-history.

50. Simmons 1796.

51. Mary Tolford Wilson, "The First American Cookbook," in *The First American Cookbook* (New York, 1984), pp. vii–xxiv.

52. This is based on Brown and Brown 1996.

53. *Svensk-amerikansk kokbok* (Stockholm, 1882); *Ny norsk-dansk og amerikansk kogebog* (Chicago, 1905); *Suomalais-amerikalainen keittokirja* (New York, 1914).

54. Johann Georg Krünitz, *Ökonomisch-technologische Encyklopädie* (Berlin, 1806).

55. Quoted in Kelly 2001, p. 123.

56. Hulda Garborg, *Heimestell* (Kristiania, 1899).

57. Karthaus 1937, p. 12. See also Ida Klein, *Neuzeitliche Küche* (Hamburg, 1941); *Gut backen im eigenen Herd* (Leipzig, 1942).

58. Zühlke 1934, p. 48.

59. Goetze 1936, preface.

60. Köstlin 1986, p. 222.

61. For more details on this period, see Notaker 2008, pp. 67–92; Gerhard 2015.

62. "Der Nationalsozialismus ist eine gute deutsche Hausmannskost, ein Eintopfgericht." Quoted in Christian Zentner and Friedemann Bedürftig, eds., *Das grosse Lexikon des dritten Reiches* (Munich, 1985).

63. Bettónica 1982, pp. 138–140.

64. Randi 1942. According to Moroni Salvatori (1998, p. 922), Randi took recipes from other cookbooks, many from Artusi's *La scienza in cucina e l'arte di mangiar bene,* and these recipes were very far from adhering to the strict economy she recommended in the preface.

65. Marinetti and Fillià 1932.

66. "La guerra porta al maximo di tensione tutte le energie umane." *La dottrina del fascismo,* 1935. See www.polyarchy.org/basta/documenti/fascismo.1932.html.

67. Marinetti and Fillià 1932, pp. 71–77.

68. Scipione Maffei, *Il raguet,* act 3, sc. 2. The French names are *ragoût, farci, gateau, côtelette, croquante, fricandeau, canard,* and *beignet.*

69. Gianfranco Lotti, *L'avventurosa storia della lingua italiana* (Milan, 2000), p. 120.

70. Camporesi 1995, p. xi.

71. Artusi 1911, recipe 455.

72. Camporesi 1995, p. xvi.

73. Capatti 2009, pp. 19–28.

74. Ernst Lössnitzer, *Verdeutschungs-Wörterbuch für Speisekarte und Küche* (Leipzig, 1888), p. iii. For editions published after 1900, the title was changed to *Deutsche Speisekarte.*

75. Brenneke 1914.

76. Ernst Lössnitzer, *Deutsche Speisekarte* (Berlin, 1921), p. 12.

77. Gottl. Weisser, "Fremdländische Namensbezeichnungen auf Speisekarten," *Die Küche* 39, no. 11 (1933): p. 260.

78. "Schafft fremdwortfreie Speisekarten," *Die Küche* 42, no. 1 (1938): p. 23.

79. See, for example, Wilhelm Schmidt, *Geschichte der deutschen Sprache* (Stuttgart, 1993), p. 142.

80. *Hitler's Table Talks,* translated and presented by Hugh Trevor-Roper (London, 1953), p. 612.

81. "Vore tappre Soldater." Mangor 1864, p. 3.

82. A food riot actually broke out in Richmond in the same year the Confederate cookbook was published. See Nancy Isenberg, *White Trash* (New York, 2016), pp. 166, 285.

83. Ida Keller, *Neues Kohlrüben-Kriegskochbuch* (Chemnitz, [1917]), referred to in Thoms 1993, p. 27.

84. Petrali Cicognara and Merli 1941.

85. Wiedermann 1915, preface.

86. Mrs. Robert S. Bradley, *Cook Book: Helpful Recipes for War Time* (Manchester-by-the-Sea, 1917), pp. 4–5.

87. Amy L. Handy, *War Food* (Boston, 1917), pp. vii–viii. See also C. Houston Goudiss, *Foods That Will Win the War and How to Cook Them* (New York, 1918), all the recipes in which had "been endorsed by the U.S. Food Administration."

88. Randi 1942, p. 19.

89. See, for example, Erna Horn, *Der neuzeitliche Haushalt* (Feldkirchen bei Munich, 1934); and Cläre Meichsner, *Mehr Milch—Mehr Volkskraft* (Cologne, 1934).

90. Scholtz-Klink 1943, preface.

91. Bergmann 1940, p. 102.

92. Herrmannsdorfer 1917.

93. Heyl 1914.

94. "Drum, liebe Hausfrau, halte stand / Hilf retten unser Vaterland!" Heinlen 1915.

95. Quotes in this paragraph from Kingsbury 2010, pp. 92–94.

96. Vázquez Montalbán 1982, pp. 134–135.

97. Scholtz-Klink 1937, p. 6.

98. Slogan on the cover of the journal *Vita: Quindicinale di politica, igiene e propaganda alimentare* 1, no. 1 (April 21, 1940).

99. Doddridge 1918, pp. 98–101.

100. Harrison and Harrison 1916.

101. Harrison and Harrison 1918, preface.

17. DECORATION, ILLUSION, AND ENTERTAINMENT

1. Visser 1987, p. 14. For an interesting analysis of the Spanish *tapeo*—the eating of tapas—as a scenography of the terrace, see Anne-Claire Yemsi-Pallissé, "Cuisine et manière de table en Espagne: Le tapas en terrasse, un dispositif à l'épreuve du temps," in Becker, Moriniaux, and Tabeaud 2015, pp. 355–365.

2. Wolfgang Wegner, "Hofkünste (Theatrica)," in Haage and Wegner 2007, pp. 256–257.

3. For a description of the culinary elements of court festivals, see Wheaton 1983, pp. 129–130.

4. Peter Burke, *The Fabrication of Louis XIV* (New Haven, 1992). See also Jean-Marie Apostolides, *Le roi-machine: Spectacle et politique au temps de Louis XIV* (Paris, 1981).

5. Elias 1979, p. 71.

6. Latini 1692, p. 213. For more information about Latini, see Astarita and Latini 2014.

7. Bradley 1756, p. 69.

8. Martino, quoted in Faccioli 1992, p. 138; Platina 1475, book 6, Ut pavo; "Pekok rostyd," in MS Sloane 7, British Library, London, printed in Hieatt 1988, p. 109.

9. Molokhovets 1901, pt. 1, p. 345 (recipe 983); pt. 2, p. 206 (recipe 4114).

10. F. Marin 1742, p. 137.

11. For details about *service à la française,* see Cobbi and Flandrin 1999; and Flandrin 2007.

12. Juvenal, *Satire XI.*

13. Antonio Contreras Mas and Joan Miralles, "Com tayllaràs devant un senyor," www.sciencia.cat/biblioteca/documents/ContrerasMiralles_Comtayllaras.pdf; Grewe 1979, pp. 74–84; Robert 1982, pp. 25–33; Ruberto 1529, fols. 3–6; Henrique de Aragon, *Arte cisoria, o Tratato del arte del cortar del cuchillo* (Madrid, 1766), printed from a manuscript from 1423.

14. *Boke of Kervinge* (London, 1508).

15. Cervio 1593; The carving guide was added to editions of Scappi's *Opera* published in 1605, 1610, and 1622, all printed in Venice.

16. Giegher 1639; titles of badly produced copies in Day 2004, 148n4. An exception is John Trusler's *The Honour of the Table* (London, 1788); see Day 2004, p. 128. A hundred years earlier, also in Padua, Andreas Vesalius became famous for his descriptions of anatomy and dissection—another form of carving—illustrated in detailed copper engravings, which Giegher's publisher may have been familiar with. See Andreas Vesalius, *De humani corporis fabrica* (Basel, 1543).

17. Klett 1700, p. 4.

18. Cervio 1593, p. 113; Cesare Evitascandalo, quoted in Albala 2007, p. 156; Klett 1700, p. 4; Latini 1692, p. 37.

19. *Meister Hanssen,* MS A.N.V. 12, Öffentliche Bibliothek der Universität, Basel, printed in Ehlert 1996, p. 305; Staindl von Dillingen 1544, fol. 26.

20. *Le viandier Taillevent,* MS Regin. Lat. 776, Biblioteca Apostolica Vaticana, Vatican City, printed in Pichon and Vicaire 1892, p. 239; Hernández de Maceras 1607, p. 34; Dods 1829, p. 442; A. de Herrera, *Obra de agricultura* (Madrid, 1818; originally printed in Alcalá de Henares, 1513), 1:198.

21. *Vivendier,* 4° MS Med 1, Gesamthochschul-Bibliothek Kassel, Landesbibliothek und Murhardsche Bibliothek der Stadt Kassel, printed in Laurioux 1997a, p. 372, (recipe [15]); Rumpolt 1581, fol. XXIX verso, fol. LXXX verso; MS A.N.V 12, Öffentliche Bibliothek der Universität, Basel, printed in Ehlert 1996, pp. 315, 316.

22. Found in Dutch, German, French, English, Czech, Portuguese, and Danish books. See Notaker 2015, p. 16.

23. The dish was called "cockagrys." See *Forme of Cury,* printed in Hieatt and Butler 1985, p. 139.

24. Recipes for pie with birds can be found in *Liber de coquina,* MS Latin 7131, Bibliothèque nationale de France, Paris, printed in Faccioli 1992, p. 28; *Epulario* (Venice, 1518), fol. 5; and *Epulario, or The Italian Banquet* (London, 1598). A recipe for pie with hare can be found in Rumpolt 1581, fol. 14 verso.

25. MS A.N.V. 12, Öffentliche Bibliothek der Universität, Basel, printed in Ehlert 1996, p. 304; La Varenne 1651, p. 64.

26. "Solches ist eine schöne lust fürs Frawenzimmer" (This is a nice pleasure for the ladies). Rontzier 1598, p. 183.

27. Apicius, 9.13.1, 4.2.12; Petronius, *Satyricon;* Philoxenus, quoted in Plutarch, *Moralia* 14e.

28. MS Cosin v.iii.11, Durham University Library, printed in Hieatt and Butler 1985, p. 39; *Boke of Cokery* (London, 1500), fol. A2.

29. Markham 1615, pt. 2, p. 78.

30. Hansen and Bauer 1968, p. 173.

31. Geoffrey Chaucer, "The Persones Tale," *Canterbury Tales.*

32. Bruyère-Champier, *De re cibaria* (Lyon, 1560); Hansen and Bauer 1968, p. 175.

33. Messisbugo 1557, fol. 12 verso, fol. 7 verso.

34. Huizinga 1919, p. 114.

35. Huizinga 1939, p. 289.

36. Wheaton 1983, p. 9.

37. Burke 2009, p. 52; Dimmock and Hadfield 2009.

38. Bouwsma 2000, p. 131. For a recent discussion of humor in different periods and contexts, see Mary Beard, *Laughter in Ancient Rome* (Berkeley, 2015), pp. 49–69.

39. Schellhammer 1723, p. 15.

40. Hagger 1718, pt. 2, bk. 2, p. 51–56. In England, edible architecture was made with "stiff flummery" (made from almonds, sugar, and calf's foot stock). See, for example, the recipe for Solomon's Temple in many bold colors in Raffald 1782, p. 204.

41. Schellhammer 1699, p. 4.

42. Hommer 1858, p. 827; Suhr 1909, pp. 308–311.

43. Prato 1873, pp. 475, 479; Hagdahl 1896, p. 794; Erken 1914b, p. 629.

44. Thomas Mann, "Lübeck als geistige Lebensraum," in *Über mich selbst: Autobiographische Schriften* (Frankfurt am Main, 1983), pp. 43–44.

45. Le Sieur Gilliers, *Le cannameliste françois* (Nancy, 1751); Vincenzo Corrado, *Il credenziere di buon gusto* (Naples, 1778); Joseph Bell, *A Treatise of Confectionary* (Newcastle, 1817); William Jarrin, *The Italian Confectioner* (London, 1820). See also L. Mason, "William Alexis Jarrin and The Italian Confectioner," in White 2004a, pp. 151–174.

46. Grimod de la Reynière 2012, pp. 527, 124.

47. Ibid., p. 168.

48. *Le pâtissier pittoresque* (Paris, 1815), quoted in Rambourg 2010, p. 219. Carême also wrote books about city architecture that included projects for Paris and St. Petersburg.

49. Day 1999.

50. Ferrières 2007, pp. 346–347.

51. Gouffé 1867, pp. 334–336.

52. Michael Maurer, "Geschichte und gesellschaftliche Strukturen des 17. Jahrhundert," in Meier 1999, p. 72.

53. Schellhammer 1692, plate VIII.

54. Steffen Martus, "Sprachtheorien," in Meier 1999, pp. 142–143.

55. Lucas 1995, p. 683.

56. Beeton 1861; Molokhovets 1901; Luraschi 1853.

57. Rumohr 1822, p. 191.

58. Malortie 1878, pp. 9–10.

59. Romagnoli 1996, p. 511.

60. Giovanni Boccaccio, *Decamerone*, giornata 1 (day 1), novela 5 (story 5).

61. Beeton 1861, p. 13.

62. Hagdahl 1896, p. 46.

63. Muro 1982, p. 700.

64. Grimod de la Reynière 2012, p. 197.

65. Pisanelli 1583; Henry Buttes, *Dyets Dry Dinner* (London, 1599).

66. Rumohr 1822, p. 170.

67. Klett 1700; Greflinger 1674; Ulfsparre 1620; *Halffandet hundrede artige riim om lev-erne* 1689; Peter Neumann, "Nachwort," in Klett 1700.

18. TASTE AND PLEASURE

1. Platina 1475, book 1. It is worth mentioning that the word Platina used for "cook" was not *coquus,* a term that he reserved for the great chef Martino, but *popinarius,* which referred to people who ran a *popina,* low-class eating houses or cooking shops. *Oxford Latin Dictionary,* edited by P. G. W. Glare, (Oxford, 1996).

2. Dante Alighieri, *Inferno,* canto 10, canto 4.

3. Platina blamed Metrodorus of Lampsacus and Hieronimus of Rhodes, both of whom had been strongly criticized by Cicero. For a discussion of Epicurus and his position at the time of Platina, see Laurioux 2006b, pp. 199-254.

4. Artusi 1911, preface.

5. Evelyn 1699, fol. A4 verso.

6. Latini 1692, fol. [*]2 verso.

7. *Le menagier de Paris,* printed in Brereton and Ferrier 1981, p. 36. The five branches of gluttony can be sumed up in these Latin expressions: *prae-propere* (too often), *laute* (expensive), *nimis* (too much), *ardenter* (too eagerly), and *studiose* (exquisite). It should be added that the moral arguments against gluttony were often supported by social arguments made by medieval theologians as well as by Renaissance thinkers such as Erasmus and Calvin.

8. Desiderius Erasmus, "Epicureus," in *Colloquia familiaria* (Magdeburg, 1536).

9. Escoffier 2011, pp. 218-219.

10. Hagdahl 1896, p. 45.

11. Desiderius Erasmus, "Polydaitia: Dispar convivium," in *Colloquia familiaria.* The character who refers to Ars Poetica is called Apicius.

12. Scappi 1570, fol. 1 verso.

13. Simon Schama, *Power of Art* (London, 2006), p. 30.

14. L. S. R. 1674, pp. 1-2.

15. Nicolas Boileau, *Oeuvres poétiques* (Tours, 1870), 1:81.

16. Nicolas Boileau, *L'art poétique* (Paris, 1674) "Chant III," verses 411-414.

17. Boileau, *Oeuvres poétiques,* 1:83.

18. L. S. R. 1674, pp. 136-137.

19. Voltaire, *Le temple du goût* (Geneva, 1953), p. 144; Voltaire, *Dictionnaire Philosophique,* in *Oeuvres de Voltaire,* vol. 30, edited by M. Beuchot (Paris, 1829), p. 74. These theoretical statements seem to contradict much of Voltaire's lifestyle.

20. Pierre de Ronsard, *Poésies choisies* (Paris, 1959), pp. 192-195.

21. Claude-Gilbert Dubois, ed., *L'isle des hermaphrodites* (Geneva, 1996), pp. 146, 144. This work is attributed to Artus Thomas and was first printed in 1605.

22. John Spurr, *England in the 1670s: The Masquerading Age* (Oxford, 2000), p. 112.

23. H. R. Fox Bourne, *The Life of John Locke* (London 1876), 1:104-105; John Locke, *Some Thoughts Concerning Education* (Oxford, 1989), p. 106.

24. César Pellenc, *Les plaisirs de la vie,* quoted in Rambourg 2010, p. 119.

25. François Fénélon, *Les aventures de Télémaque* (Paris, 1920), pp. 267–268.

26. Massialot 1691, fols. ã2–3.

27. Diderot and d'Alembert 1751–80, s.v. "cuisine."

28. Jean-Jacques Rousseau, *Oeuvres complètes* (Paris, 1959–95), 1:72, 4:465, 2:453.

29. Markham 1615, pt. 2, p. 4.

30. Bonnefons 1655, fol. A7.

31. Quellier 2013, p. 137.

32. J. S. V. Z., *Neues alamodisches Kochbuch* (Frankfurt am Main, 1689), title page.

33. Rettigová 1837, p. xvi.

34. The anonymous preface has been attributed to the two Jesuits Pierre Brumoy and Guillaume-Hyacinthe Bougeant, but according to Marie-Renée Morin, it may have been written by Anne-Gabriel Meusnier de Querlon. See Morin, *Livres en bouche* (Paris, 2001), p. 205.

35. F. Marin 1739, pp. xii–xiv.

36. The preface was anonymous, but it was probably written by Anne-Gabriel Meusnier de Querlon.

37. F. Marin 1742, p. xx.

38. Diderot and d'Alembert 1751–80, s.v. "goût."

39. Also worth mentioning in the era of Enlightenment is Le Grand d'Aussy's work, *Histoire de la vie privée des français depuis l'origine de la nation jusqu'à nos jours,* first published in Paris in 1782. As Julia Csergo observed, "Le Grand d'Aussy tente, pour la première fois, une histoire du goût." Csergo 1999, p. 15.

40. Samuel Johnson, *A Dictionary of the English Language* (London, 1755). It is interesting from a historical perspective to observe that in the revised editions of the dictionary published after Johnson's death, the references to food are given far less importance. It is no surprise then that the editors of the sixth edition of the *Encyclopedia Britannica* (1823) dismissed cooking as a topic, stating that it did not deserve consideration "in a work of this nature." See Symons 2000, p. x.

41. Immanuel Kant, *Anthropologie in pragmatischer Hinsicht* (Hamburg, 2000), §20, §§64–68.

42. G. W. F. Hegel, *Vorlesungen über die Ästhetik,* in *Werke,* vol. 13 (Frankfurt am Main, 1975), p. 61.

43. Rouff 1995, p. 10.

44. Quoted in Karin Becker, "Für eine Literaturgeschichte des Essens: Die 'gastronomie' im französichen Roman des 19. Jahrhundert," *Food and History* 1, no. 1 (2003): p. 142. On Balzac, Flaubert, and Zola, see Becker 2000.

45. Marcel Rouff, *La vie et la passion de Dodin-Bouffant* (Paris, 1984), pp. 100–101.

46. Camporesi 1995, p. 11. Artusi was quoting from a letter sent to him by the poet Lorenzo Stecchetti.

47. Kenneth Clark, *Looking at Pictures* (London 1972,).

48. Telfer 1996, pp. 41–60.

49. Desiderius Erasmus, "Convivium religiosum," in *Colloquia familiaria.*

50. Thomas More, *Utopia* (Antwerp, 1516), fol. g2 verso.

51. Voltaire, *La pucelle d'Orléans,* in *The Complete Works of Voltaire,* vol. 7 (Geneve, 1970), p. 265.

52. Rumpolt 1581, fols. 8 verso–9 recto.

53. Schuppe 1698, preface.

54. Harsdörffer 1657, p. 140.

55. Grimod de la Reynière 2012, p. 261.

56. Marinetti and Fillià 1932, p. 32. The book *La cucina futurista* was a collection of manifests, reports, and texts by members of the futurist movement, edited by F. T. Marinetti and the artist Fillià (Luigi Colombo).

57. Guillaume Apollinaire, "Le cubisme culinaire," in Apollinaire 1965, 1:453–455.

58. A continuation of futurist food experiments can be detected in the visual and scenic art of Eat Art. See Deville 2008 and Gasperi 2010.

59. Dalí 1973, p. 10

60. "Retrospective: Documenta 12," accessed January 5, 2016, ww.documenta.de/en /retrospective/documenta_12#.

19. GENDER IN COOKBOOKS AND HOUSEHOLD BOOKS

1. Aristotle, *Ta politika* 1253b.

2. Jean Bodin, *Six livres de la république* (Paris, 1576), bk. 1, chap. 3.

3. Charles H. McIlwain, ed., *The Political Works of James I* (Cambridge, 1918; repr. of the 1616 ed.), pp. 307–308.

4. Torquato Tasso, *Il padre di famiglia* (Venice, 1580). The first English translation had the title *The Housholders Philosophie* (London, 1588).

5. Coler 1593, bk. 1, chap. 5.

6. Estienne 1570, fol. 14 verso.

7. Kolesov 1991, p. 59.

8. Pearl Hogrefe, *Tudor Women* (Ames, 1975), quoted in Tebeaux 1993, p. 187. See also Teuteberg 2004, p. 120.

9. Alexander Cowan, *Urban Europe 1500–1700* (London, 1998), p. 70.

10. Markham 1615, pt. 1, p. 1.

11. The books were written by Otto von Münchhausen, an educated landowner and bailiff, but they were published under the pseudonym Christian Friedrich Germershausen. The work was reprinted four times and translated into Russian.

12. Nicolas de Bonnefons, *Le jardinier françois* (Paris, 1651); Nicolas de Bonnefons, *Les délices de la campagne* (Paris, 1654).

13. Johann Boyer, *Beschreibung* (Halberstadt, 1648).

14. G. Lehmann 2003, p. 56.

15. Ibid., pp. 104–105. According to Hans Teuteberg (2004, p. 107), German books in the nineteenth century also dropped the *Tugendpredigte* (sermons on virtue).

16. Sharpe 1997, p. 202.

17. Mary Randolph, *The Virginia Housewife* (Washington, DC, 1824), p. ix.

18. Beeton 1861, p. 1.

19. G. Lehmann 1996, p. [16].

20. Wilz 1998a, p. 92.

21. Ekaterina Avdeeva, quoted in Kelly 2001, p. 123.

22. Mangor 1847; Bimbach 1854; Riedl 1854.

23. Stille 1988, p. 13.

24. Henriette Davidis, *Puppenköchin Anna* (Dortmund, 1856).

25. *Alle smaapigers kogebog* (Copenhagen, 1855).

26. Fru Constantin, *Smaapigernes kogebog* (Copenhagen, 1906), p. 9.

27. Kübler 1850, p. 1.

28. *Småherrskapets kokbok* (Stockholm, 1875), p. 4.

29. A. M. Frederiksen, *Smaapigernes Kogebog* (Helsingør, 1905), p. 1.

30. Mangor 1847, preface.

31. Krebs 1865.

32. Henriette Davidis, *Puppenmutter Anna* (Dortmund, 1858); Davidis and Heine 1898; Stille 1988, p. 48.

33. Davidis, quoted in Sierck 1998, p. 357.

34. Brandès 1888, p. vi.

35. This was also mirrored in cookbooks. See, for example, A. E. Congreve, *The One Maid Book of Cookery* (New York, 1913).

36. Anne Marie Mangor, *Fortsættelse af Kogebog for smaa huusholdninger*, 7th ed. (Copenhagen, 1860), quoted in Vegenfeldt and Kornerup 1978, p. 24.

37. Boel Berner, *Sakernas tillstånd* (Stockholm, 1996), quoted in Mårdsjö 2001, p. 311.

38. Vladimir Mayakovsky, *Polnoe sobranie sochinenii* (Moscow, 1956), p. 245.

39. Kelly 2001, pp. 283–285.

40. "Sy worden korsel / gram / sy spreken haestich." Magirus 1612, fol. (:)6 verso.

41. Elena Molokhovets, *Podarok molodym khaziaikam* (St. Petersburg, 1869), p. 1.

42. Mary Hahn, *Volkskochbuch für die einfache Küche* (Berlin, 1939), p. 3. The first edition was published around 1910.

43. Rücherschiöld 1800, p. 3–4.

44. Wilz 1998b, p. 32.

45. Elsa Herzog, *Wie mache ich meinen Mann glücklich?* (Berlin, 1930).

46. *Cheap, Nice, and Nourishing Cookery* (London, [1841?]), p. iii.

47. Nyvang 2010, p. 191. Nyvang refers to coziness with the Danish word *hygge*, a term that entered the *Collins English Dictionary* in 2016 after a flood of cookbooks and household books were printed in Great Britain with *hygge* in the titles.

48. Marie Landmark, *Kogebog for land og by* (Bergen, 1920), p. 11.

49. Toomre 1992, p. 12.

50. *The American Woman's Home* (Hartford, 1998), p. 13.

51. For an analysis of how such books functioned, see Sonja Petersen, "Das elektrische Kochen: Die vollelektrische Küche als Leitbild moderner Haushaltsführung," *Food and History* 11, no. 1 (2013): pp. 75–106.

52. Wilz 1998a, p. 91.

EPILOGUE

1. Greetham 2009, p. 25.

2. Finkelstein and McCleery 2013, p. 27.

3. See, for example, Helen I. Borrowman, *Card Text System of Cookery for School and Home Use* (Milwaukie, [1923?]).

4. Ong 2002, pp. 133–134.

5. Neil Postman, *Amusing Ourselves to Death* (London, 1987), p. 146.

6. Zaid 2010.

7. Charles Baudelaire, "Pauvre Belgique," in *Oeuvres complètes* (Paris, 1966), 3:1010.

8. Postman, *Amusing Ourselves to Death,* pp. 113–115.

9. Phillips 2009, p. 557.

10. Goody 1977, p. 135.

REFERENCES

The bibliographical list below contains books and articles referred to in the notes. The list is limited to important cookbooks, works describing or analyzing culinary literature and food history, and studies of literary theory, book history, and cultural topics. Works of fiction, reference works, general works on history, and special studies of nonculinary subjects are referred to in full in the notes and not included here.

The works of classical authors from antiquity (Plato, Athenaeus, etc.) and later (Boccaccio, Shakespeare, Pushkin, etc.) are known in many editions and referred to in the notes according to established traditions or by act, part, chapter, etc. Unless otherwise noted, translations of foreign texts are my own. The German letter *ß* has been transcribed *ss*. European towns and cities are referred to by their English names. Christiania/Kristiania was the name of Norway's capital, Oslo, between 1624 and 1924. The English journal *Petits Propos Culinaires* is abbreviated as *PPC*.

Acton, Eliza. 1845. *Modern Cookery for Private Families.* London.
———. 1855. *Modern Cookery for Private Families.* 14th ed., London.
Adrià, Ferran. 2011. *La comida de la familia.* Barcelona.
Aebischer, P. 1953. "Un manuscrit valaisan de *Viandier* attribué à Taillevent." *Vallesia,* no. 8: 73–100.
Agnoletti, Vincenzo. 1832–34. *Manuale del cuoco e del pasticciere.* 3 vols. Pesaro.
Aichholzer, D. 1999. *Wildu machen ayn guet essen: Drei mittelhochdeutsche Kochbücher.* Berne.
Albala, Ken. 2002. *Eating Right in the Renaissance.* Berkeley.
———. 2007. *The Banquet.* Urbana, IL.
Albala, Ken, and Trudy Eden, eds. 2011. *Food and Faith in Christian Culture.* New York.
Albala, Ken, and Timothy J. Tomasik, eds. 2015. *The Most Excellent Book of Cookery.* Totnes.
Albano, C. 2001. "Introduction." In *The Gentlewoman's Companion,* by Hannah Woolley, 7–39. Totnes.

Alessio Piemontese. 1562. *Secreti.* New ed., Venice. First edition published in Venice, 1555.

Allard, Jeanne. 1987. "Diego Granado Maldonado." *PPC,* no. 25: 35–41.

The Allied Book of Recipes. 1914. Dublin.

Allum, H. 1833. *Den norske Huusmoder i sit Kjøkken og Spisekammer.* Christiania.

Alonso–Almeida, Francisco. 2013. "Genre Conventions in English Recipes 1600–1800." In DiMeo and Pennell 2013, 68–92.

Anthus, Antonius [Gustav Blumröder]. 2006. *Vorlesungen über die Esskunst.* Frankfurt am Main. Reprint of first edition, published in Leipzig, 1838.

Anward, Jan. 1994. "Från potatisen kokas till koka potatisen." In *Språkbruk, grammatik och språkförändring: En festskrift till Ulf Teleman,* by Ulf Teleman et al., 351–362. Lund.

Apollinaire, Guillaume. 1965–66. *Oeuvres complètes.* 4 vols. Paris.

Arnold, Rose. 1993. "Meg Dods: A Character and a Cookery Book." *PPC,* no. 44: 7–10.

Aron, Jean-Paul. 1973. *Le mangeur du XIXe siècle.* Paris.

Artelt, W. 1976. "Die deutsche Kochbuchliteratur des 19. Jahrhunderts." In Heischkel-Artelt 1976, 350–385.

Artusi, Pellegrino. 1911. *La scienza in cucina e l'arte di mangiar bene.* 15th ed., Turin. First published in Florence, 1891.

Asbjørnsen, P. Chr. [Clemens Bonifacius]. 1864. *Fornuftigt Madstel.* Christiania.

Aschmann, Rahel. 1835. *Geprüftes Kochbuch für Israeliten.* Quedlinburg.

Astarita, Tommaso, and Antonio Latini. 2014. *The Italian Baroque Table.* Tempe, AZ.

Auden, W. H. 1973. "The Kitchen of Life." In *Forewords and Afterwords,* 484–491. London.

Audiger. 1692. *La maison reglée.* Paris.

Austin, J. L. 1975. *How to Do Things with Words.* Oxford.

Babilon, Jan. 1989. *Prvá kuchárska kniha v slovenskej rei.* Bratislava. Reprint of the first edition, published in Pest, 1870.

Baeza, Miguel de. 1592. *Los quatro libros del arte de la confitería.* Alcalá de Henares.

Bakhtin, M. M. 1986. *Speech Genres and Other Late Essays.* Translated by Vern W. McGee. Austin.

Baltzer, Eduard. 1903. *Vegetarianisches Kochbuch.* 15th ed., Leipzig.

Balzli, Hans. 1931. *Gastrosophie.* Stuttgart.

Barlösius, Eva. 1998. "Vegetarische Kochbücher." In Framke 1998, 287–291.

Baron, Sabrina Alcorn, Eric N. Lindquist, and Eleanor F. Shevlin, eds. 2007. *Agent of Change: Print Culture Studies after Elizabeth L. Eisenstein.* Amherst, MA.

Barthes, Roland, ed. 1975. *Physiologie du goût.* By Jean Anthelme Brillat-Savarin. Paris.

———. 1984. *Le bruissement de la langue.* Paris.

———. 2002. "L'ancienne rhétorique." In *Oeuvres complètes,* vol. 3, 527–601. Paris.

Bauer, Gerd. 1987. "In Teufels Küche." In Bitsch, Ehlert, von Ertzdorff, and Schulz 1987, 127–142.

Bauer, Stefan. 2006. *The Censorship and Fortuna of Platina's Lives of the Popes in the Sixteenth Century.* Turnhout.

Baurmeister, Ursula. 2001. "À propos de Taillevent." *Bulletin du bibliophile,* no. 2: 273–277.

Beauvilliers, Antoine. 1814. *L'art de cuisinier.* Paris.

Becker, Karin. 2000. *Der Gourmand, der Bourgeois und der Romancier.* Frankfurt am Main.

———. 2012. *Le lyrisme d'Eustache Deschamp: Entre poésie et pragmatisme.* Paris.

Becker, Karin, Vincent Moriniaux, and Martine Tabeaud, eds. 2015. *L'alimentation et le temps qu'il fait: Essen und Wetter—Food and Weather.* Paris.

Beeton, Isabella. 1861. *Book of Household Management*. London.

Benker, Gertrud. 1986. "Illustrationen früher Kochbücher." In *Populäre Bildmedien,* edited by Rolf Wilhelm Brednich and Andreas Hartmann, 263–273. Göttingen.

Berchoux, Joseph. 1803. *La Gastronomie.* 2nd ed., Paris.

Bergengruen, Werner. 1960. *Titulus.* Zurich.

Bergmann, Edith-Sylvia. 1940. *Gut gekocht—gern gegessen.* Berlin.

Bergner, Anna. 1858. *Pfälzer Kochbuch.* Mannheim.

Best, Michael R., ed. 1998. *The English Housewife.* Montreal.

Bettónica, Luis. 1982. "Desde el plato único a la nueva cocina." In UIMP 1982, 137–152.

Bierlaire, Franz. 1982. "Erasme, la table et les manières de table." In Margolin and Sauzet 1982, 147–160.

Bimbach, Julie. 1854. *Kochbüchlein für die Puppenküche.* Nuremberg.

Bitsch, I., T. Ehlert, X. von Ertzdorff, and R. Schultz., eds. 1987. *Essen und Trinken in Mittelalter und Neuzeit.* Sigmaringen.

Blanning, T. C. W. 2002. *The Culture of Power and the Power of Culture.* Oxford.

Blom, Marie. 1888. *Husholdningsbog for By og Land.* Kristiania.

Bloshṭeyn, Oyzer. 1898. *Ḳokh-bukh far Yudishe froyen.* 2nd ed., New York.

Blumenthal, Heston. 2008. *The Big Fat Duck Cookbook.* London.

Blumröder, Gustav. *See* Anthus, Antonius.

Bober, Phyllis P. 1999. *Art, Culture, and Cuisine.* Chicago.

Bocuse, Paul. 1980. *La cuisine du marché.* Paris.

Bonnefons, Nicolas de. 1655. *Les delices de la campagne.* New ed., Amsterdam.

Boorde, Andrew. 1542. *Dyetary of Health.* London.

Bottéro, Jean. 1995. *Textes culinaires mésopotamiens.* Winona Lake, IN.

Bouwsma, William J. 2000. *The Waning of the Renaissance.* New Haven.

Bradley, Martha. 1756. *The British Housewife.* London.

Brandès, Mary. 1888. *Bébé Cordon Bleu.* Paris.

Braswell, Laurel. 1984. "Utilitarian and Scientific Prose." In Edwards 1984, 337–387.

Brenneke, Rosa. 1914. *Erstes rein deutsches Koch-Lehrbuch unter vermeidung sämtlicher Fremdwörter: Ein Beitrag zur Linderung der Kriegsnot.* Leipzig.

Brereton, Georgine E., and Janet M. Ferrier, eds. 1981. *Le menagier de Paris.* Oxford.

Briggs, C. F. 2010. "Literacy, Reading, and Writing in the Medieval West." In *The History of the Book in the West: 400 AD–1455,* edited by J. Roberts and P. Robinson, 481–404. Farnham.

Brillat-Savarin, Jean Anthelme. 1826. *Physiologie du goût.* Paris.

Brown, Michelle P. 2009. "The Triumph of the Codex: The Manuscript Book before 1100." In Eliot and Rose 2009, 179–193.

Brown, Eleanor, and Bob Brown. 1996. *Culinary Americana.* Reprint, New York.

Bruegel, M., and B. Laurioux, eds. 2002. *Histoire et identités alimentaires en Europe.* Paris.

Buchinger, B. 1671. *Koch-Buch für geistliche als auch weltliche Haushaltungen.* Molsheim.

Bühler, Susanne. 1993. "Koch und Köchin: Arbeitsplatz Küche." In Zischka 1993, 539–545.

Burke, Peter. 1999. *The Italian Renaissance: Culture and Society in Italy.* Oxford.

———. 2000. *A Social History of Knowledge.* Cambridge.

———. 2009. *Popular Culture in Early Modern Europe.* 3rd ed., Farnham.

Camba, Julio. 1962. *Obras.* Vol. 1. Barcelona.

Camporesi, Piero. 1993. *The Magic Harvest.* Translated by J. K. Hall. Cambridge.

———, ed. 1995. *La scienza in cucina e l'arte di mangiar bene.* By Pellegrino Artusi. Turin.

———. 1996. *The Land of Hunger.* Translated by T. Croft-Murray. Cambridge.

Capatti, A., and M. Montanari. 2002. *La cucina Italiana.* 2nd ed., Rome.

Capatti, Alberto. 2009. "Pellegrino Artusi editore casalingo." In *Storia della lingua e storia della cucina,* edited by Cecilia Robustelli and Giovanna Frosini, 19–28. Florence.

Carême, Antonin. 1847. *L'art de la cuisine française au XIXeme siècle.* 5 vols. Paris.

Carroll, Ruth. 1999. "The Middle English Recipe as a Text-Type." *Neuphilologische Mitteilungen,* no. 100: 27–42.

———. 2010. "The Visual Language of the Recipe: A Brief Historical Survey." In *Food and Language,* edited by Richard Hosking, 62–72. Totnes.

Carter, Charles. 1730. *The Complete Practical Cook.* London.

Casper, S. E., and J. S. Rubin. 2013. "The History of the Book in America." In Suarez and Woudhuysen 2013, 682–709.

Casteau, Lancelot de. 1604. *Ouverture de cuisine.* Liège.

Cauderlier, Philippe-Édouard. 1861. *L'économie culinaire.* Ghent.

———. 1863. *La cuisinière.* Ghent.

Cervio, Vincenzo. 1593. *Il trinciante.* Rome.

Chamberlain, Lesley. 1983. "Filimonov: A Russian Brillat-Savarin?" *PPC,* no. 14: 31–38.

Chartier, Roger. 2014. *L'œuvre, l'atelier et la scène.* Paris.

Chevalier, B. 1982. "L'alimentation carnée à la fin du XVe siècle." In Margolin and Sauzet 1982, 193–199.

Clanchy, M. T. 1979. *From Memory to Written Record: England 1066–1307.* London.

———. 2009. "Parchment and Paper: Manuscript Culture 1100–1500." In Eliot and Rose 2009, 194–206.

Cobbi, Jane, and Jean-Louis Flandrin, eds. 1999. *Tables d'hier, tables d'ailleurs.* Paris.

Cockx-Indestege, Elly, ed. 1971. *Eenen nyeuwen Coock Boeck.* By Gheeraert Vorselmann. Reprint of Vorselmann 1560. Wiesbaden.

Coetzee, Renata. 1984. *The South African Culinary Tradition.* Cape Town.

Colclough, Stephen. 2009. "Readers, Books, and Biography." In Eliot and Rose 2009, 50–62.

Coler, Johann. 1593. *Oeconomia oder Hausbuch.* Wittenberg.

Cooper, Jos. 1654. *The Art of Cookery.* London.

Coron, Sabine, ed. 2001. *Livres en bouche: Cinq siècles d'art culinaire français.* Paris.

Corona, Sarah Bak-Geller. 2013. *Narrativas deleitosas de la nación: Los primeros libros de cocina en México (1830–1890).* Mexico City.

Corrado, Vincenzo. 1786. *Il cuoco galante.* Naples.

Coultrap-McQuinn, Susan. 1990. *Doing Literary Business.* London.

The Court and Kitchin of Elizabeth. 1664. London.

Crick, J., and A. Walsham, eds. 2004. *The Uses of Script and Print 1300–1700.* Cambridge.

Crosby, Alfred W. 1998. *The Measure of Reality.* Cambridge.

Csergo, Julia. 1996. "L'émergences des cuisines régionales." In Flandrin and Montanari 1996, 823–841.

———. 1999. "Avant-propos." In Le Grand d'Aussy 1999, 11–25.

La cuisinière assiégée. 1871. Paris.

Le cuisinier gascon. 1740. Amsterdam.

Le cuisinier méridional d'après la méthode provençale et languedocienne. 1835. Avignon.

Culy, C. 1996. "Null Objects in English Recipes." *Language, Variation and Change*, no. 8: 91–124.

Curriel, S. 1915. *Fru Curriels Kogebog: Jødiske Opskrifter fra Fortid og Nutid*. Copenhagen.

Curtius, E. R. 1969. *Europäische Literatur und Lateinisches Mittelalter*. Berne.

Czerniecki, Stanislaw. 1682. *Compendium ferculorum, albo Zebranie potraw*. Kraków.

Dalby, Andrew. 2003. *Food in the Ancient World from A to Z*. London.

———. 2011. *Geoponika: Farm Work*. Totnes.

Dalí, Salvador. 1973. *Les dîners de Gala*. Paris.

Das Allerneueste Pariser Kochbuch. 1752. Strasburg.

David, Elizabeth. 1979. "Hunt the Ice Cream." *PPC*, no. 1: 8–13.

———. 1983. *Mediterranean Food*. London.

———. 1986. *An Omelette and a Glass of Wine*. London.

———. 1988. "The Excellence of Eliza Acton." In Davidson 1988, 32–34.

Davidis, Henriette. 1845. *Zuverlässige und selbstgeprüfte Recepte*. Osnabrück. New ed. published in 1847 with the title *Praktisches Kochbuch*.

———. 1861. *Die Hausfrau*. Leipzig.

———. 1892. *Der Beruf der Jungfrau*. Leipzig.

Davidis, H., and E. Heine. 1898. *Praktisches Kochbuch für kleine und grosse Mädchen*. Leipzig.

Davidson, Alan, ed. 1988. *On Fasting and Feasting*. London.

———, ed. 1999. *The Oxford Companion to Food*. Oxford.

Dawson, Thomas. 1596–97. The *Good Huswifes Iewell*. 2 vols. London.

Day, Ivan. 1999. "Sculpture for the 18th Century Garden Dessert." In *Food in the Arts*, edited by Harlan Walker, 57–66. Totnes.

———. 2004. "From Murrell to Jarrin: Illustrations in British Cookery Books." In White 2004a, 98–150.

Deckhardt, Johann. 1611. *New kunstreich und nützliches Kochbuch*. Leipzig.

Destaminil. n.d. *La cuisine pendant la siège*. Paris.

De verstandige kock. 1667. Amsterdam.

Deville, Michel. 2008. *Food, Poetry, and the Aesthetics of Consumption*. New York.

De volmaakte hollandsche keuken-meid. 1761. Amsterdam.

Diderot, Denis, and Jean le Rond d'Alembert, eds. *Encyclopédie, ou Dictionnaire raisonné des sciences et des métiers*. 1751–80. Paris.

Digby, Kenelme. 1997. *The Closet of the Eminently Learned Sir Kenelme Digby Kt. Opened*. London. Reprint of the first edition, published in 1669.

DiMeo, Michelle, and Sara Pennell, eds. 2013. *Reading and Writing Recipe Books 1550–1800*. Manchester.

Dimmock, Matthew, and Andrew Hadfield, eds. 2009. *Literature and Popular Culture in Early Modern England*. Farnham.

Doddridge, Amelia. 1918. *Liberty Recipes*. Cincinnati, OH.

Dods, Margaret [C. I. Johnstone]. 1826. *The Cook and Housewife's Manual*. Edinburgh.

———. 1829. *The Cook and Housewife's Manual*. 4th ed., Edinburgh.

Donacher, Jacob. 1627. *Ein schönes nutzliches Hauss- und Kunstbüchlein*. Augsburg.

Dose, Hanna. 1988. "Die Geschichte des Kochbuchs." In Framke and Marenk 1988, 51–70.

———. 1998. "Die regionale Küche und ihre Kochbücher." In Framke 1998, 241–245.

Driver, Christopher. 1997. *John Evelyn: Cook*. Totnes.

Driver, Elizabeth. 2003. "Canadian Cookbooks (1825–1949)." *PPC*, no. 72: 19–39.

Drouard, Alain. 2008. *Geschichte der Köche in Frankreich*. Stuttgart.

Dubois, Urbain. 1856. *La cuisine classique*. Paris.

———. 1872. *Cuisine de tous les pays*. Paris.

———. 1889. *La cuisine d'aujourd'hui*. Paris.

Duhart, Frédéric. 2009. "Une certaine image de la France." In Hache-Bissette and Saillard 2009, 163–174.

Dumas, Alexandre. 1873. *Grand Dictionnaire de Cuisine*. Paris.

Dunham, Edith. 1933. *Palatable Patter*. Chicago.

Durante, Castor. 1602. *Herbario nuovo*. New ed., Venice.

Eamon, William. 1996. *Science and the Secrets of Nature*. Princeton.

Ebmeyer, Ottilie. 1878. *Die gute vegetarische Küche*. Zürich.

Edwards, A. S. G., ed. 1984. *Middle English Prose*. New Brunswick, NJ.

———, ed. 2004. *A Companion to Middle English Prose*. Cambridge.

Egerin, Susanna. 1745. *Leipziger Koch-Buch*. Rev. ed., Leipzig.

Ehlert, Trude. 1987. "Nehmet ein junges Hun, ertränkets mit Essig: Zur Syntax spätmittelalterlicher; Kochbücher." In Bitsch, Ehlert, von Ertzdorff, and Schulz 1987, 261–276.

———, ed. 1996. *Maister Hanssen des von Wirtenberg Koch*. Frankfurt am Main.

———. 1997. "Indikatoren für Mündlichkeit und Schriftlichkeit in der deutschsprachigen Fachliteratur am Beispiel der Kochbuchüberlieferung." In *Durch aubenteuer muess man wogen vil*, edited by Wernfried Hofmeister and Bernd Steinbauer, 73–85. Innsbruck.

———. 2002. "Les manuscrits culinaires médiévaux témoignent-ils d'un modèle alimentaire allemand?" In Bruegel and Laurioux 2002, 121–136.

———, ed. 2010. *Küchenmeisterei: Edition, Übersetzung und Kommentar zweier Kochbuch-Handschriften des 15. Jahrhunderts*. Frankfurt am Main

Ein Koch- und Artzney-Buch. 1686. Graz.

Ein sehr künstlichs und fürtrefflichs Kochbuch. 1559. Augsburg.

Eis, Gerhard. 1950. "Die sieben Eigenkünste und ihre altdeutsche literaturdenkmäler." *Forschungen und Fortschritte* 26: 269–271.

———. 1967. *Mittelalterliche Fachliteratur*. Stuttgart.

Eisenstein, Elizabeth. 1979. *The Printing Press as an Agent of Change*. Cambridge.

Eleonora Maria Rosalia, Duchess of Troppau and Jägerndorff. 1697. *Freiwillig auffgesprungener Granat-Apffel, dess Christlichen Samaritans*. Vienna.

Elias, Norbert. 1939. *Über den Prozess der Zivilisation*. Basel.

———. 1979. *Die höfische Gesellschaft*. Reprint, Darmstadt.

Eliot, S., and J. Rose, eds. 2009. *A Companion to the History of the Book*. Oxford.

Elzberg, Margareta. 1751. *Försök til en pålitelig Matrednings-Bok*. Stockholm.

Erken, Henriette Schønberg. 1905. *Kogebog for sparsommelige husmødre i by og bygd*. Kristiania.

———. 1914a. *Billig mad*. Kristiania.

———. 1914b. *Stor kokebok*. Kristiania.

Escoffier, Auguste. 1903. *Le guide culinaire*. Paris.

———. 2011. *Souvenirs culinaires*. Edited by Pascal Ory. Paris.

Estienne, Charles. 1570. *L'agriculture et maison rustique*. New ed., Paris.

Evelyn, John. 1699. *Acetaria*. London.

Ezell, Margaret J. M. 2003. "By a Lady: The Make of the Feminine in Restoration, Early Eighteenth Century Print Culture." In *The Faces of Anonymity,* edited by Robert J. Griffin, 63–79. New York.

Faccioli, Emilio. 1992. *L'arte della cucina in Italia.* 2nd ed., Turin.

Fægri, Knut. 1984. "Oppskriftsamlingen fra Ledaal." *Maal og Minne,* nos. 1–2: 108–121.

Farmer, Fannie Merritt. 1896. *The Boston Cooking-School Cook Book.* Boston.

Favre, Joseph. 1891. *Dictionnaire universel de cuisine.* Paris.

———. 1905. *Dictionnaire universel de cuisine pratique.* Paris.

Febvre, Lucien, and Henri-Jean Martin. 1958. *L'apparition du livre.* Paris.

Ferguson, John. 1981. *Bibliographical notes on Histories of Inventions and Books of Secrets.* Reprint, London.

Ferguson, P. Parkhurst. 2006. *Accounting for Taste: The Triumph of French Cuisine.* Chicago.

Ferguson, P. Parkhurst, and Sharon Zukin. 1998. "The Careers of Chefs." In *Eating Culture,* edited by Ron Scapp and Brian Seitz, 92–111. Albany.

Ferrières, Madeleine. 2007. *Nourritures canailles.* Paris.

Filimonov, V. 1837. *Obed. Poema.* St. Petersburg.

Fink, Beatrice. 1995. *Les liaisons savoureuses.* Saint-Étienne.

Finkelstein, D., and A. McCleery. 2013. *An Introduction to Book History.* London.

Fischer, Ludwig, Knut Hicketier, and Karl Riha, eds. 1976. *Gebrauchsliteratur: Methodische Überlegungen und Beispielanalysen.* Stuttgart.

Fisher, Abby. 1881. *What Mrs. Fisher Knows about Old Southern Cooking.* San Francisco.

Fisher, M. F. K. 2004. *The Art of Eating.* Hoboken, NJ.

Flandrin, Jean-Louis. 1986. "La distinction par le goût." In *Histoire de la vie privée,* vol. 3, edited by Philippe Ariès and Georges Duby, 267–309. Paris.

———. 2007. *Arranging the Meal.* Berkeley.

Flandrin, Jean-Louis, Philip Hyman, and Mary Hyman. 1983. *Le cuisinier françois.* Paris.

Flandrin, Jean-Louis, and Massimo Montanari, eds. 1996. *L'histoire de l'alimentation.* Paris.

Flandrin, Jean-Louis, and Silvano Serventi. 2003. *Le Platyne en françois.* Paris.

Fleming, P. Lockhart. 2013. "The History of the Book in Canada." In Suarez and Woudhuysen 2013, 671–681.

Floyd, Janet, and Laurel Forster, eds. 2010. *The Recipe Reader.* London.

Fox, Adam. 2000. *Oral and Literate Culture in England 1500–1700.* Oxford.

Framke, Gisela, ed. 1998. *Man nehme: Literatur für Küche und Haus.* Bielefeld.

Framke, Gisela, and Gisela Marenk, eds. 1988. *Beruf der Jungfrau.* Oberhausen.

Francatelli, Charles Elmé. 1846. *The Modern Cook.* London.

———. 1847. *Plain Cookery for the Working Classes.* London.

Furnivall, Frederick J., ed. 1867. *The Boke of Nurture by John Russell.* London.

Gasperi, C. 2010. "Towards an Ontology of the Food Artwork." In *Food and History* 8, no. 1: 199–212.

Genette, Gérard. 1987. *Seuils.* Paris.

Gentilcore, David. 2016. *Food and Health in Early Modern Europe: Diet, Medicine and Society 1450–1800.* London.

Gerhard, Gesine. 2015. *Nazi Hunger Politics.* Lanham, MD.

German, Kathleen M. 2011. "Memory, Identity, and Resistance: Recipes from the Women of Theresienstadt." In *Food as Communication: Communication as Food,* edited by Janet M. Cramer, Carlnita P. Greene, and Lynn M. Walters, 137–154. New York.

Giegher, Mattia. 1639. *Le tre trattati.* Padua.

Giesecke, Michael. 1983. "Überlegungen zur sozialen Funktion und zur Struktur handschriftlicher Rezepte im Mittelalter." *Zeitschrift für Literaturwissenschaft und Linguistik,* no. 13: 167–184.

———. 1991. *Der Buchdruck in der frühen Neuzeit.* Frankfurt am Main.

Gigante, Denise, ed. 2005. *Gusto.* New York.

Gillet, Philippe. 1993. *Le goût et les mots: Littérature et gastronomie XIVᵉ–XXᵉ siècle.* Paris.

Gilmont, Jean-François. 2010. "Printing at the Dawn of the Sixteenth Century." In *The History of the Book in the West 1455–1700,* edited by Ian Gadd, 131–141. Farnham.

Giovane, Maestro. [1530?] *Opera dignissima.* Milan.

Girard, Alain R. 1982. "Du manuscript à l'imprimé, le livre de cuisine en Europe au 15ᵉ et 16ᵉ siècles." In Margolin and Sauzet 1982, 107–117.

Gísladóttir, Hallgerður. 1999. *Íslensk matarhefð.* Reykjavik.

Glaisyer, N., and S. Pennell, eds. 2003. *Didactic Literature in England 1500–1800.* Aldershot.

Glaser, Elvira. 1996. "Die textuelle Struktur handschriftlicher und gedruckter Kochrezepte im Wandel: Zur Sprachgeschichte einer Textsorte." In Grosse and Wellmann 1996, 225–249.

———. 2002. "Fein gehackte Pinienkerne zugeben! Zum Infinitiv in Kochrezepten." In Restle and Zaefferer 2002, 165–183.

Glasse, Hannah. 1747. *The Art of Cookery.* London.

Gloning, Heike. 1997. "Handschriftliche Frauenkochbücher des 17. und 18. Jahrhunderts als Editions- und Forschungsaufgabe." In *Editionsdesiderate zur Frühen Neuzeit,* vol. 2, edited by H.-G. Roloff, 829–847. Amsterdam.

Gloning, Thomas, ed. 1998. *Rheinfränkisches Kochbuch.* Frankfurt am Main.

———. 2000. "Handschriftliche Rezeptnachträge in einem 'Göppinger Kochbuch' von 1790." In Richter, Riecke, and Schuster 2000, 353–372.

———. 2002. "Textgebrauch und sprachliche Gestalt älterer Kochrezepte (1350–1800): Ergebnisse und Aufgaben." In Simmler 2002, 517–550

Goetze, Elinor. 1936. *Kochtopf der Heimat.* Stuttgart.

Gogué, A. 1856. *Les secrets de la cuisine française.* Paris.

Goldstein, Darra. 1997. "Is Hay Only for Horses? Highlights of Russian Vegetarianism at the Turn of the Century." In *Food in Russian History and Culture,* edited by M. Glants & J. Toomre, 103–123. Bloomington, IN.

Goody, Jack. 1977. *The Domestication of the Savage Mind.* Cambridge.

Görlach, Manfred. 2004. "Text Types and Language History: The Cooking Recipe." In *Text Types and the History of English,* 121–140. Berlin.

Gouffé, Jules. 1867. *Le livre de cuisine.* Paris.

Gouy, Jean de. 1895. *La cuisine et la pâtisserie bourgeoises.* Brussels.

Granado Maldonado, Diego. 1599. *Libro del arte de cozina.* Madrid.

Greetham, David. 2009. "What Is Textual Scholarship?" In Eliot and Rose 2009, 21–32.

Greflinger, G. 1674. *Ethica Complementaria Das ist Complementier-Büchlein.* Copenhagen.

Greimas, A. J. 1983. "La soupe au pistou ou la construction d'un objet de valeur." In *Du sens II: Essais sémiotiques,* 157–169. Paris.

Grewe, Rudolf, ed. 1979. *Llibre de Sent Soví*. Barcelona.

———. 1987. "The Arrival of the Tomato in Spain and Italy: Early Recipes." *Journal of Gastronomy* 3, no. 2: 67–82.

Grewe, Rudolf, and C. B. Hieatt, eds. 2001. *Libellus de arte coquinaria*. Tempe, AZ.

Griffin, Carrie. 2013. "Reconsidering the Recipe: Materiality, Narrative and Text in Later Medieval Instructional Manuscripts and Collections." In *Manuscripts and Printed Books in Europe 1350–1550*, edited by E. Cayley and S. Powell, 135–149. Liverpool.

Grimm, Veronika E. 1996. *From Feasting to Fasting*. London.

Grimod de la Reynière, A. B. L. 1808. *Manuel des amphitryons*. Paris.

———. 2012. *Almanach des gourmands*. Chartres. Reprint of vols. 1–8, first published in Paris, 1803–12.

Grocock, C., and S. Grainger. 2006. "Introduction." In *Apicius: A Critical Edition*, edited by C. Grocock and S. Grainger, 13–123. Totnes.

Grosse, Rudolf, and Hans Wellmann, eds. 1996. *Textarten in Sprachwandel: Nach die Erfindung des Buchdrucks*. Heidelberg.

Guerzoni, G. 2008. "Between Rome and Ferrara: The Courtiers of the Este Cardinals in the Cinquecento." In *Art and Identity in Early Modern Rome*, edited by J. Burke and M. Bury, 59–77. Aldershot.

Haage, B. D. 1982. "Zur hypotetischen Rezepteingang im Arzneibuch des Erhart Hesel." In Keil 1982, 363–370.

Haage, B. D., and Wolfgang Wegner. 2007. *Deutsche Fachliteratur der Artes in Mittelalter und Früher Neuzeit*. Berlin.

Haber, Barbara. 2002. *From Hardtack to Home Fries*. New York.

Habermas, Jürgen. 1969. *Strukturwandel der Öffentlichkeit: Untersuchungen zu einer Kategorie der bürgerlichen Gesellschaft*. Neuwied.

Hache-Bissette, Françoise, and Denis Saillard, eds. 2009. *Gastronomie et identité culturelle française: Discours et représentations (XIXᵉ–XXᵉ siècles)*. Paris.

Hagdahl, Charles-Emil. 1896. *Kok-konsten som vetenskap och konst*. Rev. ed., Stockholm. First edition published in 1879.

Hagger, Conrad. 1718. *Neues Saltzburgisches Koch-Buch*. 4 vols. Augsburg.

Hahnemann, A., and D. Oels, eds. 2008. *Sachbuch und populäres Wissen im 20. Jahrhundert*. Frankfurt am Main.

Hajek, Hans, ed. 1958. *Daz Buoch von guoter Spise*. Berlin.

Halffandet Hundrede Artige Riim om Leverne. 1689. Copenhagen.

Hamel, Christopher de. 2013. "The European Medieval Book." In Suarez and Woudhuysen 2013, 59–79.

Hansen, Hans Jürgen, and Ingetrud Bauer, eds. 1968. *Kunstgeschichte des Backwerks*. Hamburg.

Harris, Michael. 2013. "Printed Ephemera." In Suarez and Woudhuysen 2013, 205–219.

Harrison, Grace Clergue, and Gertrude Clergue Harrison. 1916. *Allied Cookery*. New York. Translated into French as *La cuisine des Alliées*. (Paris, 1918).

Harsdörffer, G. Ph. 1657. *Vollständiges und von neuem vermehrtes Trincir-Buch*. Nuremberg.

Harvolk, Edgar. 1993. "Abstinenz und Fasten." In Zischka 1993, 591–585.

Heiles, Marco. 2011. "Der Solothurner Codex S 490: Eine 'Küchenmeisterei'-Abschrift." *Zeitschrift für deutsches Altertum und deutsche Literatur* 140: 501–504.

Heinlen, Luise. 1915. *Schwäbisches Kriegskochbuch*. Geislingen.

Heischkel-Artelt, E., ed. 1976. *Ernährung und Ernährungslehre im 19. Jahrhundert*. Göttingen.

Hellinga, Lotte. 2009. "The Gutenberg Revolutions." In Eliot and Rose 2009, 207–219.

Henisch, Bridget Ann. 2009. *The Medieval Cook*. Wadbridge.

Hermann, Ottó. 1887. *A magyar halászat könyve*. Budapest.

Hernández de Maceras, Domingo. 1607. *Libro del arte de cozina*. Salamanca.

Herrmannsdorfer, Caroline. 1917. *Haus und Herd in schwerer Zeit*. Munich.

Het Hollands, of Nederlands Kook-Boek, Beschreeven door een Rooms-gesinde. 1724. Leiden.

Heyl, Hedwig. 1914. *Kleines Kriegskochbuch*. Berlin.

Hieatt, Constance B., ed. 1988. *In Ordinance of Pottage*. London.

———. 1992. "Listing and Analysing the Medieval English Culinary Recipe Collections: A Project and Its Problems." In Lambert 1992, 295–296.

———. 1996 "A Cook of 14th-Century London: Chaucer's Hogge of Ware." In *Cooks and Other People*, edited by Harlan Walker, 138–143. London.

Hieatt, Constance B., and Sharon Butler, eds. 1985. *Curye on Inglysch: English culinary manuscripts of the 14th century*. Oxford.

Hietala, Marjatta, and Tanja Vahtikari, eds. 2003. *The Landscapes of Food*. Helsinki.

Hirsch, Rudolf. 1967. *Printing, Selling and Reading 1450–1550*. Wiesbaden.

Hobby, Elaine. 1988. *Virtue of Necessity*. London.

Hödl, Nicola. 1999. "Vertextungskonventionen des Kochrezepts vom Mittelalter in die Moderne." In *Kontrastive Textologie*, edited by Eva Martha Eckkrammer, Nicola Hödl, and Wolfgang Pöckl, 47–76. Vienna.

Hoey, Michael. 2001. *Textual Interaction*. London.

Höfler, Manfred. 1996. *Dictionnaire de l'art culinaire français*. Aix-en-Provence.

Hommer, Sophie Charlotte. 1858. *Neues Hamburger Kochbuch*. Hamburg.

Houston, R. A. 1995. *Literacy in Early Modern Europe*. London.

Hughes, Kathryn. 2006. *The Short Life and Long Times of Mrs. Beeton*. London.

Huizinga, J. 1919. *Herfsttij der Middeleeuwen*. Haarlem.

———. 1939. *Homo ludens*. Amsterdam.

Hull, S. 1982. *Chaste, Silent, and Obedient*. San Marino, CA.

Hunter, Alexander. 1804. *Culina famulatrix medicinae*. York.

Hyman, Philip, and Mary Hyman. 1979. "La Chapelle and Massialot." *PPC*, no. 2: 44–54.

———. 1981. "Vincent La Chapelle." *PPC*, no. 8: 35–40.

———. 1983. "Les cuisines régionales à travers des livres de recettes." *Dixhuitième Siècle*, no. 15: 65–74.

———. 1996. "Imprimer la cuisine: Les livres de cuisine en France entre le XVᵉ et le XIXᵉ siècle." In Flandrin and Montanari 1996, 643–655.

———. 2002. "Préface." In *Le cuisinier françois*, by La Varenne, edited by Silvano Serventi. Paris.

Ivanová-Šalingová, Mária. 1989. "'Stopät,' desiar rokov slovenskej odbornej reči." In Babilon 1989, 458–466.

Jäderberg, Lars. 1995. "Matrecept från tre sekel: En genrestudie." *Språk och stil: Tidskrift för svensk språkforskning*, no. 5: 93–119.

Jansen-Sieben, Ria. 1989. "La littérature utilitaire moyen-néerlandaise." *Revue Belge de Philologie et d'Histoire* 67, fasc. 3: 543–550.

———. 1994. "From Food Therapy to Cookery-Book." In *Medieval Dutch Literature in Its European Context*, edited by Erik Kooper, 261–279. Cambridge.

Jatsenkov, Nikolai. 1790–91. *Noveishaia i polnaia povarennaia kniga.* 4 vols. Moscow.

Johnstone, Christian Isobel. *See* Dods, Margaret.

Kallendorf, Craig. 2013. "The Ancient Book." In Suarez and Woudhuysen 2013, 39–53.

Kander, Lizzie Black. 1901. *The Settlement Cook Book.* Milwaukee, WI.

Karthaus, Elisabeth. 1937. *Gau-Kochbuch.* Frankfurt am Main.

Kauders, Marie. 1886. *Erstes israelitisches Kochbuch für böhmische Küche.* Prague.

Keil, Gundolf, ed. 1982. *Fachprosa-Studien: Beiträge zur mittelalterlichen Wissenschafs- und Geistesgeschichte.* Berlin.

Keil, Gundolf, and Peter Assion, eds. 1974. *Fachprosa-forschung.* Berlin.

Keiser, George. 2004. "Scientific, Medical, and Utilitarian Prose." In Edwards 2004, 231–247.

Kellogg, Ella Eaton. 1893. *Science in the Kitchen.* Battle Creek, MI.

———. 1904. Science in the Kitchen. 4th ed. Battle Creek, MI.

Kelly, Catriona. 2001. *Refining Russia.* Oxford.

Kingsbury, Celia M. 2010. "In Close Touch with Her Government: Women and the Domestic Science Movement in World War One Propaganda." In Floyd and Forster 2010, 88–101.

Kirschenblatt-Gimblett, Barbara. 1986–87. "The Kosher Gourmet in the Nineteenth Century Kitchen." *Journal of Gastronomy* 2, no. 4: 51–89.

———. 1990. "Kitchen Judaism." In *Getting Comfortable in New York,* edited by Susan L. Braunstein and Jenna Weissman Joselit, 75–105. New York.

———. 2007. "Jewish Cookbooks." In *Encyclopedia Judaica,* 2nd ed., vol. 3, edited by the Bureau of Jewish Education. London.

Kitchiner, William. 1817. *Apicius Redivivus, or The Cook's Oracle.* London.

Klencke, Herman. 1857. *Chemisches Haus- und Wirtschaftsbuch.* Leipzig.

Klett, Andreas. 1700. *Neu-vermehrt nützliches Trenchier-Buch.* Kunstburg.

Kochbuch für den jüdischen Haushalt und Grossbetriebe. [1935?] Berlin. This is a revised edition of *Kochbuch für die jüdische Küche,* published in 1926.

Kochbuch für die jüdische Küche. 1926. Düsseldorf.

Koge Bog. 1616. Copenhagen.

Kolesov, V. V., ed. 1991. *Domostroi.* Moscow.

Köstlin, Konrad. 1986. "Der Eintopf der Deutschen: Das zusammengekochte als Kultur." In *Tübingen Beiträge zur Volkskunde,* edited by Utz Jeggle, 220–241. Tübingen.

Kramer, Bertha. 1889. *Aunt Babette's Cook Book.* Cincinnati, OH.

Krebs, Marina. 1865. *Illustriertes Spielbuch für Mädchen.* Leipzig.

Krohn, Deborah L. 2015. *Food and Knowledge in Renaissance Italy.* Farnham.

Kübler, Marie Susanne. 1850. *Das Hauswesen nach seinem ganzen Umfange durchgestellt in Briefen an eine Freundin.* Stuttgart.

Kucharzka. 1542. Prague.

Küchenmeisterei. [1490?] Nuremberg.

Kurth, L. 1879. *Illustriertes Kochbuch.* 9th ed., Berlin.

Kut, Turgut. 1990. "A Bibliography of Turkish Cookery Books up to 1927." *PPC,* no. 36: 29–37.

La Chapelle, Vincent. 1735. *Le cuisinier moderne.* The Hague.

Lalou, É., ed. 1992. *Les tablettes à écrire de l'antiquité à l'époque moderne.* Turnhout.

Lambert, Carole, ed. 1992. *Du manuscrit à la table.* Montreal.

Latini, Antonio. 1692. *Lo scalco alla moderna.* Naples.

Laurioux, Bruno. 1989. *Le moyen âge à table.* Paris.

———. 1996a. "Cuisines médiévales." In Flandrin and Montanari, 459–477.

———. 1996b. "I libri di cucina italiani alla fine del medievo." *Archivio storico italiano,* no. 154: 33–58.

———. 1997a. *Le règne de Taillevent.* Paris.

———. 1997b. *Les livres de cuisine médiévaux.* Turnhout.

———. 2006a. "Cuisine et médecine au Moyen Age: Alliées ou ennemies?" In "La figure de Jules César au Moyen Âge et à la Renaissance," edited by Bruno Méniel et Bernard Ribémont, special issue, *Cahiers de Recherches Médiévales et Humanistes,* no. 13: 223–238.

———. 2006b. *Gastronomie, humanisme et société à Rome au milieu du XVe siècle: Autour du* De honesta voluptate *de Platina.* Florence.

La Varenne. 1651. *Le cuisinier françois.* Paris.

Lebas, J. 1738. *Festin joyeux, ou La cuisine en musique, en vers libres.* Paris.

Le Goullon, François. 1829. *Der neue Apicius.* Weimar.

Le Grand d'Aussy, P. J. B. 1999. *Histoire de la vie privée des français depuis l'origine de la nation jusqu'à nos jours.* Paris. Reprint of the first edition, published in 1782.

Lehmann, Gilly, ed. 1996. *The British Housewife.* Vol. 1. By Martha Bradley. Totnes. Facsimile.

———. 2003. *The British Housewife: Cookery Books, Cookery and Society in Eighteenth-Century Britain.* Totnes.

Lehmann, Paul. 1949. *Mittelalterliche Büchertitel.* Munich.

Lemmer, Manfred. 1979. "Kommentar." In *Kunstbuch von mancherlei Essen,* by Franz de Rontzier, facsimile of Rontzier 1598, 5–33. Munich.

———. 1980. "Nachwort." In *Ein new Kochbuch,* by Marx Rumpolt, facsimile of Rumpolt 1581, 3–17. New York.

Leong, Elaine, and Alisha Rankin, eds. 2011. *Secrets and Knowledge in Medicine and Science 1500–1800.* Farnham.

Lesniczak, Peter. 2003. *Alte Landschaftsküchen im Sog der Modernisierung.* Stuttgart.

Lévi-Strauss, Claude. 1964. *Le cru et le cuit.* Paris.

Levshin, V. A. 1795–97. *Slovar' povarennyi.* 6 vols. Moscow.

———. 1816. *Russkaia povarnia.* Moscow.

Levy, Esther. 1871. *Jewish Cookery Book.* Philadelpia.

Liberati, Francesco. 1668. *Il perfetto maestro della casa.* Rome. First edition pubished in 1658.

Liger, Louis. 1714. *Le ménage des champs et de la ville, ou Le nouveau cuisinier françois accomodé au goût du temps.* Paris.

Lincoln, M. J. 1884. *Mrs. Lincoln's Boston Cook Book.* Boston.

Loofft, Marcus. 1758. *Nieder-Sächsisches Koch-Buch.* 3rd ed., Altona.

Lowenstein, Eleanor. 1972. *Bibliography of American Cookery Books 1742–1860.* New York.

Lozinski, G., ed. 1933. *La bataille de caresme et de charnage.* Paris.

L. S. R. 1674. *L'art de bien traiter.* Paris.

Lucas, Corinne. 1995. "Le paraître et la table sous l'Ancien Régime." In *Dictionnaire raisonné de la politesse et du savoir-vivre,* edited by Alain Montandon, 655–688. Paris.

Lüchou, Marianne. 1968. "De första finlandssvenska kokböckerna." *Historiska och Litteraturhistoriska Studier,* no. 43: 147–193.

Luraschi, Giovanni Felice. 1853. *Nuovo cuoco milanese.* Milan.

MacLean, Virginia. 1981. *A Catalogue of Household and Cookery Books 1701–1800.* London.

Magirus, Antonius. 1612. *Koocboec oft familieren Kevkenboec.* Leuven.

Maius, Dietlevus. 1647. *Stockholmisch Koch Gesprächs Vortrab.* 2nd ed., Stockholm. First edition published in 1644.

Malortie, Ernst von. 1878. *Das Menu: Eine culinarische Studie.* Hanover.

Mangor, Anne Marie. 1847. *Kogebog for Smaapiger.* Copenhagen.

———. 1864. *Kogebog for Soldater i Felten.* Copenhagen.

Manguel, Alberto. 1997. *A History of Reading.* 2nd ed., London.

Mårdsjö, Karin. 2001. "Sparsamt, nyttig och effektivt." In *Verklighetens texter,* edited by Björn Melander and Björn Olsson, 305–321. Lund.

Margolin, J. C., and R. Sauzet, eds. 1982. *Pratiques et discours alimentaires à la renaissance.* Paris.

Marin, François. 1739. *Les dons de Comus, ou Les délices de la table.* Paris.

———. 1742. *Suite des dons de Comus, ou L'art de la cuisine réduit en pratique.* 3 vols. Paris.

Marin, Manuela. 2004. "From al-Andalus to Spain: Arab Traces in Spanish Cooking." *Food and History* 2, no. 2: 35–51.

Marinetti, F. T., and Fillià. 1932. *La cucina futurista.* Milan.

Markham, Gervase. 1615. *Countrey Contentments.* London.

Marlov, Sophie. 1799. *Catechismus der Kochkunst.* Leipzig.

Martin, Henri-Jean, ed. 1983–86. *Histoire de l'édition française.* 4 vols. Paris.

Martínez Montiño, Francisco. 1611. *Arte de cocina.* Madrid.

Martino, Maestro. 1992. *Libro de arte coquinaria.* In Faccioli 1992, pp. 131–218. This text is based on a manuscript in the Library of Congress: MS 153 "Rare Books."

Mason, Laura. 2002. "Les puddings et l'identité anglaise." In Bruegel and Laurioux 2002, 169–181.

Massialot, François 1691. *Le cuisinier royal et bourgeois.* Paris.

Mata, João da. 1876. *Arte de cosinha.* Lisbon.

Mattheier, Klaus J. 1993. "Das Essen und die Sprache: Umrisse einer Linguistik des Essen." In *Kulturthema Essen,* edited by Alois Wierlacher and Eva Barlösius, 245–254. Berlin.

May, Robert. 1685. *The Accomplisht Cook.* 5th ed., London. First edition published in 1660.

Mayr, Georgius. 1579. *Ein kunstreich und bewert Kochbuch.* Augsburg.

McCarthy, John A. 2010. "Rewriting the Role of the Writer." In *The History of the Book in the West 1700–1800,* edited by Eleanor F. Shevlin, 133–157. Farnham.

McGee, Harold. 1986. "Science and the Study of Food." In *Cookery, Science, Lore and Books,* edited by Tom Jaine, 73–80. London.

McKitterick, David. 2003. *Print, Manuscript and the Search for Order 1450–1830.* Cambridge.

Meier, Albert, ed. 1999. *Die literatur des 17. Jahrhunderts.* Munich.

Mennell, Stephen. 1996. *All Manners of Food.* 2nd ed., Chicago.

Menon. 1739. *Nouveau traité de la cuisine.* Paris.

———. 1746. *La cuisinière bourgeoise.* Paris.

———. 1755. *Les soupers de la cour.* Paris.

———. 1759. *Le manuel de l'officier de bouche.* Paris.

———. 1789. *La science du maître d'hôtel cuisinier.* Paris. First edition published in 1749.

Merta, S. 2015. "Saisonale Rezepte und Kochbücher um die Jahrhundertwende." In Becker, Moriniaux, and Tabeaud 2015, 339–354.

Messisbugo, Christofaro di. 1557. *Libro novo.* Venice. First edition published with the title *Banchetti* in Ferrara, 1549.

Milham, Mary Ella. 1998. *Platina: On Right Pleasure and Good Health.* Tempe, AZ.

Molbech, Christian, ed. 1826. *Henrik Harpestrengs danske Lægebog fra det trettende Aarhundrede.* Copenhagen.

Molokhovets, Elena. 1861. *Podarok molodym khoziaikam.* Kursk.

———. 1901. *Podarok molodym khoziaikam.* 22nd ed., St. Petersburg.

Montefiore, Judith. 1846. *The Jewish Manual.* London.

Morokhovtsev, K. K. 1901. *Polnyi podarok molodym khoziaikam.* Moscow.

Morris, Helen. 1975. *Portrait of a Chef.* Reprint, London.

Mostert, M., and A. Adamska, eds. 2014. *Uses of the Written Word in Medieval Towns.* Turnhout.

Müller, Martin. 1984. *Das Schlaraffenland.* Vienna.

Muro, Angel. 1982. *El practicón.* Barcelona. Corrected reprint of the 18th ed., printed in Madrid, 1903. First edition published in Madrid, 1894.

Murrell, John. 1638. *Two Books of Cookerie and Carving.* 5th ed., London.

N'Diaye, Catherine, ed. 1993. *La gourmandise: Délices d'un péché.* Paris.

Negruzzi, Costache, and Mihail Kogălniceanu. 1841. *200 rețete cercate.* Iași.

Neues deutsches Kochbuch. [1870?] Stuttgart.

Neues Lexikon der Französischen, Sächsischen, Österreichischen und Böhmischen Kochkunst. 1785. Prague.

Nicholson, Asenath. 1832. *Nature's Own Book.* New York.

Nikólína, Þora Andrea. 1858. *Ny matreiðslubók.* Akureyri.

Nimb, Louise. 1900. *Fru Nimbs Kogebog.* 3rd ed., Copenhagen. First edition published in 1888.

Nordman, Natalia. 1911. *Povarennaia kniga dlia golodaiushchikh.* St. Petersburg.

Norrick, Neal R. 1983. "Recipes as Texts: Technical Language in the Kitchen." In *Sprache, Diskurs und Text,* edited by R. Jongen, 173–183. Tübingen.

Nostradamus, Michael. 1555. *Le vray et parfaict embellissement.* Lyon.

Notaker, Henry. 1990. "Iceland's First Cookbook." *PPC,* no. 34: 13–17.

———. 1990b. "Romania: Cooking, Literature and Politics." *PPC,* no. 35: 7–22.

———. 1991. "Russian Cookbooks before 1800." *PPC,* no. 37: 7–20.

———. 2001. *Norwegian Cookbooks until 1951: History and Bibliography.* Oslo.

———. 2002. "En contrepoint: L'identité nationale à travers les livres de cuisine du XIXe siècle." In Bruegel and Laurioux 2002, 137–150.

———. 2008. "Cooking and Ideology in the Third Reich." *Food and History* 6, no. 1: 67–82.

———. 2010. *Printed Cookbooks in Europe, 1470–1700: A Bibliography of Early Modern Culinary Literature.* New Castle, DE.

———. 2015. "Nature in Cookbooks: Imitation, Control and Submission." In Becker, Moriniaux, and Tabeaud 2015, 15–24.

Nyvang, Caroline. 2010. "Medie og måltid: Danske kogebøger i 1800-tallet." In *Syn på mad og drikke i 1800-tallet,* edited by O. Hyldtoft, 145–230. Copenhagen.

Oeconomia nova paa Danske. 1648. Copenhagen.

Ólafsson, Ólafur. 1792. "Um Matar-tilbúning af mjólk, fiski og kiöti á íslandi." *Rit þess konungliga Islenska Lærdómslísta Félags* 12: 173–215.

Olson, Carl. 2013. "The Sacred Book." In Suarez and Woudhuysen 2013, 19–38.

Olson, S. Douglas, and Alexander Sens, eds. 2000. *Archestratos of Gela.* Oxford.

Ong, Walter J. 2002. *Orality and Literacy.* 2nd ed., London.

Ory, Pascal. 1998. *Le discours gastronomique français des origines à nos jours.* Paris.

———. 2009. "Brillat-Savarin dans l'histoire culturelle de son temps." In Hache-Bissette and Sailland 2009, 39–50.

———. 2011. "Preface." In Escoffier 2011, 7–20.

Osipov, Nikolai. 1790. *Starinnaia russkaia khoziaika kliuchnitsa i striapukha.* St. Petersburg.

Ott, Christine. 2011. *Feinschmecker und Buchfresser.* Munich.

Pandolfini, Agnolo. 1734. *Trattato del governo della famiglia.* Florence.

Pardo Bazán, Emilia. 1913. *La cocina española antigua.* Barcelona.

Parkes, M. B. 1991. *Scribes, Scripts and Readers.* London.

———. 2008. *Their Hands before Our Eyes: A Closer Look at Scribes.* Aldershot.

Pennell, Elizabeth Robins. 1903. *My Cookery Books.* Boston.

Pérez Samper, Maria Angeles. 1998. *La alimentación en la España del Siglo de Oro.* Huesca.

Petrali Cicognara, R., and A. Zuccardi Merli. 1941. *Cucina in tempo di guerra.* Rome.

Pfeiffer, R. 1931. "Küchenlatein." *Philologus: Zeitschrift für klassische Philologie,* no. 86: 455–459.

Phillips, Angus. 2009. "Does the Book Have a Future?" In Eliot and Rose 2009, 547–559.

Pichon, Jérôme, and Georges Vicaire, eds. 1892. *Supplément au Viandier de Taillevent.* Paris.

Pisanelli, Baldassare. 1583. *Trattato della natura de' cibi et del bere.* Rome.

Pitte, Jean-Robert. 1991. *Gastronomie française.* Paris.

Platina, Bartolomeo. 1475. *De honesta voluptate et valetudine.* Venice.

Platina Cremonensis, B. 1542. *Von der Eerlichen zimlichen auch erlaubten Wolust des Leibs.* Augsburg.

Pokhlebkin, V. V. 1978. *Natsional'nye kukhni nashikh narodov.* Moscow.

Postnaia povarikha. 1793. Kostroma.

Poulain, Jean-Pierre. 1985. "Sens et function des appellations culinaires au XIXe siècle." *Sociétés,* no. 6: 20–23.

Poulain, J.-P., and E. Neirinck. 2004. *Histoire de la cuisine et des cuisiniers.* Paris.

Prato, Katharina. 1873. *Die Süddeutsche Küche.* 9th ed., Graz.

Quellier, Florent. 2007. *La table des Français: Une histoire culturelle.* Rennes.

———. 2013. *Gourmandise: Histoire d'un péché capital.* 2nd ed., Paris.

Rabisha, William. 1682. *The Whole Body of Cookery.* 4th ed., London.

Raffald, Elizabeth. 1782. *The Experienced English House-Keeper.* 8th ed., London.

Rajberti, Giovanni. 1850–51. *L'arte di convitare spiegata al popolo.* 2 vols. Milan.

Rambourg, Patrick. 2010. *Histoire de la cuisine et de la gastronomie françaises.* Paris.

Randi, Elisabetta. 1942. *La cucina autarchica.* Florence.

Ranhofer, Charles. 1894. *The Epicurean.* New York.

Raphael, Chaim. 1985. "The History and the Mystery of *The Jewish Manual.*" In *The Jewish Manual,* by Judith Montefiore, 7–30. Facsimile, London.

Raven, James. 2003. "The Anonymous Novel in Britain and Ireland, 1750–1830." In *The Faces of Anonymity,* edited by Robert J. Griffin, 141–166. New York.

Rehnberg, Mats. 1978. "Matsedel och musikk." *Gastronomisk kalender:* 116–137.

Restle, David, and Dietmar Zaefferer, eds. 2002. *Sounds and Systems: Studies in Structure and Change.* Berlin.

Rettigová, M. D. 1831. *Domácý Kuchařka.* 2nd ed., Prague. First edition published in 1826. The author's surname is spelled Retikowa on the title page of these early editions.

Revel, Jean-François. 1979. *Un festin en paroles.* Paris.

————. 1982. "Brillat-Savarin et le style aimable." In *Physiologie du goût*, by Jean Anthelme Brillat-Savarin, pp. 5–15. Reprint, Paris.

Richardson, Louise A., and J. R. Isabell. 1984. "Joseph Cooper, Chief Cook to Charles I." *PPC*, no. 18: 40–53.

Richter, Dieter. 1984. *Schlaraffenland: Geschichte einer populären Phantasie*. Cologne.

Richter, Gerd, Jörg Riecke, and Britt-Marie Schuster, eds. 2000. *Raum, Zeit, Medium: Sprache und ihre Determinanten*. Darmstadt.

Riedl, Christine Charlotte. 1854. *Die kleine Köchin*. Lindau.

Rigaud, Lucas. 1780. *Cozinheiro moderno, ou Nova arte de cozinha*. Lisbon.

Riley, Gillian. 2005. "Renaissance in the Kitchen." In *Maestro Martino: Libro de arte coquinaria*. Oakland. CD-ROM.

Ritzerow, Frieda. 1868. *Mecklenburgisches Kochbuch*. Rostock.

Robaschik, Sigrid. 1988. "Russischsprachige Kochrezepte." In *Fachtext als Instrument und Resultatkommunikativer Tätigkeit*, edited by R. Glaser, 106–114. Leipzig.

Robert, Mestre. 1982. *Libre del coch*. Edited by Veronika Leimgruber. Barcelona. Reprint of the first edition, published in 1520.

Roberts, J., and P. Robinson. 2010. "The History of the Manuscript Book in the West 400 AD–1455: An Overview." In *The History of the Book in the West 400 AD–1455*, edited by J. Roberts and P. Robinson, xi–xxvi. Farnham.

Robson, E. 2009. "The Clay Tablet Book in Sumer, Assyria, and Babylonia." In Eliot and Rose 2009, 67–83.

Roden, Claudia. 1981. "Cooking in Israel: A Changing Mosaic." In *Oxford Symposium, 1981: National and Regional Styles of Cookery*, edited by Alan Davidson, 112–116. London.

————. 1985. *A New Book of Middle Eastern Food*. London.

Rodovský z Hustiřan, Bavor. 1975. *Kuchařství*. Reprint, Prague. First edition published in 1591.

Roemer, Cornelia. 2009. "The Papyrus Roll in Egypt, Greece, and Rome." In Eliot and Rose 2009, 84–94.

Rogström, Lena. 2000. *När blev receptet minilekt?* Meddelanden från institutionen för svenska språket, Göteborgs Universitet, 32. Göteborg.

Roldán Vera, Eugenia. 2013. "The History of the Book in Latin America." In Suarez and Woudhuysen 2013, 656–670.

Romagnoli, Daniela. 1996. "Guarda no sii vilan: Les bonnes manières à table." In Flandrin and Montanari 1996, 511–523.

Romoli, Domenico. 1560. *La singolare dottrina*. Venice.

Rontzier, Franz de. 1598. *Kunstbuch von mancherlei Essen*. Wolffenbüttel.

Rosenberger, Bernard. 1996. "La cuisine arabe et son apport à la cuisine européenne." In Flandrin and Montanari 1996, 345–365.

Rosnack, Marie. 1845. *Stettiner Koch-Buch*. Stettin.

Rossetti, Giovanni Battista. 1584. *Dello scalco*. Ferrara.

Rouff, Marcel. 1995. *La vie et la passion de Dodin-Bouffant, gourmet*. Paris.

Royer, Johann. 1648. *Beschreibung des ganzen Fürstlichen Braunschweigischen Gartens zu Hessem*. Halberstadt.

Ruberto de Nola. 1529. *Libro de cozina*. Logroño. First edition pubished in Toledo, 1525.

Rücherschöld, Anna Maria. 1800. *Försök till en liten Hushålls-Cateches*. Stockholm.

————. 1801. *Den Nya och Fullständiga Kok-Boken*. Stockholm.

Ruge-Schatz, Angelika. 1987. "Von der Rezeptsammlungen zum Kochbuch: Einige sozial-historische Überlegungen über Autoren und Benutzer." In Bitsch, Ehlert, von Ertzdorff and Schultz 1987, 217–244.

Rumohr, Karl Friedrich von. 1822. *Geist der Kochkunst*. Stuttgart.

————. 1832. *Geist der Kochkunst*. 2nd ed., Stuttgart.

Rumpolt, Marx. 1581. *Ein new Kochbuch*. Frankfurt am Main.

Rutledge, Sarah. 1847. *The Carolina Housewife*. Charleston.

Ryff, Walther. 1544. *Confect-Büchlin und Hauss Apoteck*. Frankfurt am Main.

Saenger, Paul. 2003. "Reading in the Middle Ages." In *A History of Reading in the West*, edited by Guglielmo Cavallo and Roger Chartier, 120–148. Oxford.

Sale, Romble. 1664. *Then Frantzöske-Kocken och Pasteybakaren*. Stockholm.

Salvatori, M P. Moroni. 1998. "Ragguaglio bibliografico sui ricettari del primo Novecento." In *Storia d'Italia*, vol. 13: *L'alimentazione*, edited by A. Capatti, A. De Bernardi, and A. Varni, 887–925. Turin.

Santich, Barbara. 1984. "L'influence italienne sur l'évolution de la cuisine médiéval catalane." In *Manger et boire au Moyen Âge*, edited by Centre d'études médiévales de Nice, 131–140. Paris.

————. 2010. "Doing Words: The Evolution of Culinary Vocabulary." In *Food and Language*, edited by Richard Hosking, 301–310. Totnes.

Sapounaki-Dracaki, Lydia. 2003. "Modernizing the Traditional Greek Diet: The Role of Cookery Books 1833–1914." In Hietala and Vahtikari 2003, 198–212.

Sauzet, Robert. 1982. "Discours cléricaux sur la nourriture." In Margolin and Sauzet 1982, 247–55.

Saxegaard, Annik [Cara Mell, pseud.]. 1953. *Sleiven er mitt scepter*. Drammen.

Scappi, Bartolomeo. 1570. *Opera*. Venice.

Schartau, Gustava. *Franska Kocken*. 1825. Stockholm.

Scheibler, S. W. 1861. *Allgemeines Deutsches Kochbuch*. Leipzig.

Schellhammer, M. S. 1692. *Die wohl unterwiesene Köchin*. Helmstedt.

————. 1697. *Die wol unterwiesene Köchinn*. 2nd ed., Helmstedt.

————. 1699. *Der wohl unterwiesene Köchin Zufällige Confect-Tisch*. Brunswick.

————. 1723. *Das Brandenburgische Koch-Buch*. Berlin.

Schildermans, Jozef, and Hilde Sels. 2003. "A Dutch Translation of Bartolomeo Scappi's *Opera*." *PPC*, no. 74: 59–70.

Schildermans, J., H. Sels, and M. Willebrands, eds. 2007. *Lieve schat, wat vind je lekker?* Leuven.

Schino, June di, and Furio Luccichenti. 2007. *Il cuoco segreto dei papi*. Rome.

Scholliers, Peter. 2002. "L'invention d'une cuisine belge." In Bruegel and Laurioux 2002, 151–168.

————. 2004. "Anonymous Cooks and Waiters: Labour Markets and the Professional Status of Restaurant, Café and Hotel Personnel in Brussels 1840s–1900s." *Food and History* 2, no. 1: 137–165.

Scholtz-Klink, Gertrud. 1937. *Einsatz der Frau in der Nation*. Berlin.

————. 1943. *Was essen wir heute zum Abendbrot?* Leipzig.

Schuppe, Hans. 1698. *Traiteur à la mode*. Lübeck.

Scully, Terence. 1993. "Medieval Cookery and Medicine." *PPC*, no. 44: 11–20.

————. 1995. *The Art of Cookery in the Middle Ages*. Woodbridge.

————, ed. 2000. *The Neapolitan Recipe Collection*. Ann Arbor, MI.

Sebastian, Meister. 1581. *Koch und Kellermeisterei*. Frankfurt am Main.

Seidelin, K. H. 1801. *Den danske Husmoders Køkken-Katekismus*. Copenhagen.

Seleskowitz, Louise. 1880. *Wiener Kochbuch*. Vienna.

Serres, Olivier de. 1600. *Le théâtre de l'agriculture*. Paris.

Sharpe, J. A. 1997. *Early Modern England: A Social History 1550–1760*. London.

Shaw, David J. 2009. "The Book Trade Comes of Age." In Eliot and Rose 2009, 220–231.

Shaw, Teresa M. 1998. *The Burden of the Flesh*. Minneapolis.

Sherman, Sandra. 2002. "The Politics of Taste in *The Jewish Manual*." *PPC*, no. 71: 72–94.

Sherman, W. H. 2007. "On the Threshold: Architecture, Paratext, and Early Print Culture." In *Agent of Change: Print Culture Studies after Elizabeth L. Eisenstein*, edited by S. A. Baron, E. N. Lindquist, and E. F. Shevlin, 67–81. Amherst, MA.

Sierck, Bettina. 1998. "Wegweiser zum häuslichen Glück für Mädchen." In Framke 1998, 357–363.

Simmler, Franz, ed. 2002. *Textsorten deutscher Prosa vom 12/13. bis 18. Jh. und ihre Merkmale*. Bern.

Simmons, Amelia. 1796. *American Cookery*. Hartford.

Skandinavisk illustreret kogebog: Udarbeidet for skandinaviske housholdninger i Amerika. 1884. Chicago.

Small, Jocelyn Penny. 1997. *Wax Tablets of the Mind*. London.

Smith, E. 1758. *The Compleat Housewife*. 16th ed., London.

Smith, John. 1866. *Vegetable Cookery*. London.

Soyer, Alexis. 1846. *The Gastronomic Regenerator*. London.

————. 1848. *Charitable Cookery, or The Poor Man's Regenerator*. London.

————. 1851. *The Modern Housewife*. Reprint, London. First edition published in 1849.

————. 1860. *A Shilling Cookery for the People*. Reprint, London. First edition published in 1854.

Spiller, Elizabeth. 2010. "Recipes for Knowledge." In *Renaissance Food from Rabelais to Shakespeare*, edited by Joan Fitzpatrick, 55–72. Burlington, VT.

Spurling, Hilary, ed. 1986. *Elinor Fettiplace's Receipt Book*. London.

Staindl von Dillingen, Balthasar. 1569. *Ein künstlich und nutzlichs Kochbuch*. Augsburg. First edition published in 1544.

Stead, J. 1983. "Quizzing Glasse: Or Hannah Scrutinized." Pts. 1 and 2. *PPC*, no. 13: 9–24; no. 14: 17–30.

Stefani, Bartolomeo. 1662. *L'arte di ben cucinare*. Mantua.

Steinberg, S. H. 1996. *Five Hundred Years of Printing*. Rev. ed., London.

Steinmetz, Horst. 1977. "Textverarbeitung und Interpretation." *Jahrbuch Deutsch als Fremdsprache* 3: 81–93.

Stephensen, Marta María. 1800. *Einfaldt Matreiðslu Vasa-Qver*. Leira.

Stiennon, Jacques. 1973. *Paléographie du Moyen Âge*. Paris.

Stille, Eva. 1988. "Puppenküchen." In Framke and Marenk 1988, 143–150.

Stock, Brian. 1983. *The Implications of Literacy*. Princeton.

Stopp, Hugo, ed. 1980. *Das Kochbuch der Sabina Welserin*. Heidelberg.

Struve, G. von. 1869. *Pflanzenkost, die Grundlage einer neuen Weltanschauung*. Stuttgart.

Suarez, Michael F., and H. R. Woudhuysen, eds. 2013. *The Book: A Global History.* Oxford.

Suhr, Ingeborg. 1909. *Mad.* Copenhagen.

Symons, Michael. 2000. *A History of Cooks and Cooking.* Urbana, IL.

Szakáts mesterségnek könyvetskéje. 1698. 2nd ed., Kolozsvár.

Taillevent. 1486. *Le Viandier.* Paris.

Takats, Sean. 2011. *The Expert Cook in Enlightenment France.* Baltimore.

Tamburini, Giulia Ferraris. 1900. *Come posso mangiar bene?* Milan.

Tebeaux, Elizabeth. 1993. "Technical Writing for Women of the English Renaissance." *Written Communication* 10, no. 2: 164–199.

Telfer, Elizabeth. 1996. *Food for Thought: Philosophy and Food.* London.

Teuteberg, Hans J. 2004. "Von der Hausmutter zur Hausfrau." In *Die Revolution am Esstisch,* edited by Hans J. Teuteberg, 101–128. Stuttgart.

Teuteberg, Hans J., and Günter Wiegelmann. 1986. *Unsere tägliche Kost.* Münster.

Theophano, Janet. 2003. *Eat My Word: Reading Women's Lives through the Cookbooks They Wrote.* New York.

This, Hervé. 2002. *Molecular Gastronomy.* New York.

———. 2009. *Building a Meal: From Molecular Gastronomy to Culinary Constructivism.* New York.

Thoms, Ulrike. 1993. "Kochbücher und Haushaltslehren als ernährungshistorische Quellen." In *Neue Wege zur Ernährungsgeschichte,* edited by D. Reinhardt, U. Spiekermann, and U. Thoms, 9–50. Frankfurt am Main.

Tichá, Zdeňka. 1975. "Předmluva." In Rodovský z Hustiřan 1975, 9–22.

Ticklecloth, Tabitha. 1860. *The Dinner Question.* London.

Tillinghast, Mary. 1690. *Rare and Excellent Receipts.* New ed., London.

Tomasik, Timothy J. 2007. "Translating Taste in the Vernacular Editions of Platina's *De honesta voluptate.*" In *At the Table,* edited by T. J. Tomasik and J. M. Vitullo, 189–210. Turnhout.

Toomre, Joyce. 1983. "Soyer's Soups." *PPC,* no. 13: 48–65.

———. 1992. *Classic Russian Cooking.* Bloomington, IN.

Torttila, Minna, and Heikki J. Hakkarainen. 1990. "Zum Satzbau der deutschen Kochrezepte des 20. Jahrhunderts." *Zeitschrift für germanistische Linguistik,* no. 18: 31–42.

Tryon, Thomas. 1694. *A Pocket-Companion.* London.

Turquet, Theodore. 1658. *Archimagirus anglo-gallicus.* London.

Ude, Louis E. 1822. *The French Cook.* 7th ed., London.

Ueding, Gert. 1976. "Vom Stil der Kochkunst." In Fischer, Hickethier, and Riha. 1976, 170–181.

UIMP (Universidad Internacional Menéndez y Pelayo). 1982. *Conferencias culinarias.* Barcelona.

Ulfsparre, C. I. 1620. *Några bordrim höfligit och lustigt, så wäl andeligen som wärdsligen.* Stockholm.

Universal-Lexikon der Kochkunst. 1878. Leipzig.

Vaerst, Eugen von. 1851. *Gastrosophie, oder Die Lehre von den Freuden der Tafel.* Leipzig.

Vázquez Montalbán, Manuel. 1982. "Una interpretación de la autarquía en la cocina española." In UIMP 1982, 123–136.

Vegenfeldt, Regina, and Lilian Kornerup. 1978. *Danske kogebøger 1616–1974.* 2nd ed., Odense.

Vehling, Joseph. 1941. *Platina and the Rebirth of Man.* Chicago.

Verral, William. 1759. *A Complete System of Cookery.* London.

Vicaire, Georges. 1890. *Bibliographie gastronomique.* Paris.

Vincent-Cassy, Mireille. 1993. "Un péché capital." In N'Diaye 1993, 18–30.

Visser, Margaret. 1987. *Much Depends on Dinner.* Toronto.

Voigts, Linda Ehrsam. 1984. "Medical Prose." In Edwards 1984, 315–335.

Vollenweider, Alice. 1963. "Der Einfluss der italienischen auf die französische Kochkunst im Spiegel der Sprache." *Vox Romanica* 22: 59–88.

Vollständiges Nürnbergisches Koch-Buch. 1691. Nuremberg.

Vorselmann, Gheeraert. 1560. *Eenen nyeuwen Coock Boeck.* Antwerp. First edition published in 1556.

Wall, Wendy. 2011. "Reading the Home: The Case of *The English Housewife.*" In *Renaissance Paratexts,* edited by H. Smith and L. Wilson, 165–184. Cambridge.

Warg, Cajsa. 1755. *Hjelpreda i Hushållningen för Unga Fruentimber.* Stockholm.

Warner, Richard. 1791. *Antiquitates culinariæ.* London.

Warnes, Andrew. 2010. "Talking Recipes, What Mrs. Fisher Knows and the African-American Tradition." In Floyd and Forster 2010, 52–71.

Watts, Sydney. 2011. "Enlightened Fasting: Religious Conviction, Scientific Inquiry, and Medical Knowledge in Early Modern France." In Albala and Eden 2011, pp. 105–124.

Wecker, Anna. 1598. *Ein Köstlich new Kochbuch.* 2nd ed., Amberg. First edition published in 1597.

Weilshäuser, Emil. 1896. *Illustriertes vegetarisches Kochbuch.* Leipzig.

Weiss, Hans U. 1996. *Gastronomia.* Zurich.

Weiss-Adamson, Melitta. 2002. "Medieval Germany." In *Regional Cuisines in Medieval Europe,* edited by Melitta Weiss-Adamson, 153–196. New York.

Weiss-Amer, Melitta. 1992. "The Role of Medieval Physicians in the Diffusion of Culinary Recipes and Cooking Practices." In Lambert 1992, 69–80.

Wellek, René, and Austin Warren. 1949. *Theory of Literature.* London.

Westbury, Lord. 1963. *Handlist of Italian Cookery Books.* Florence.

Wheaton, Barbara Ketcham. 1983. *Savouring the Past.* London.

———. 1984. "No hoax." *PPC,* no. 16: 66–68.

White, Eileen, ed. 2004a. *The English Cookery Book.* Totnes.

———. 2004b. "Domestic English Cookery and Cookery Books, 1575–1675." In White 2004a, 72–97.

Wiedemann, Inga. 1993. "Kochen und schreiben." In Zischka 1993, 557–562.

Wiedermann, E. 1915. *Das Kriegskochbuch des Vaterländischen Frauenvereins.* Berlin.

Wilkins, John. 2000. *The Boastful Chef.* Oxford.

Wilkins, John, and Shaun Hill, eds. 1994. *Archestratus: The Life of Luxury.* Totnes.

Willan, Anne. 1977. *Great Cooks and Their Recipes.* London.

Willich, Jodoc. 1563. *Ars Magirica.* Zurich.

Wilson, C. Anne. 1984. *Food and Drink in Britain.* New ed., Harmondsworth.

———, ed. 1991. *The Appetite and the Eye.* Edinburgh.

Wilz, Annemarie. 1998a. "Allgemeine Kochbücher." In Framke 1998, 87–93.

———. 1998b. "Haushaltsratgeber." In Framke 1998, 27–85.

Winsnes, Hanna. 1845. *Lærebog i de forskjellige Grene af Huusholdningen.* Christiania.

———. 1862. *Husholdningsbog for tarvelige Familier i By og Bygd.* Christiania.

———. 1957. "For fattige Husmødre." *Folkevennen,* no. 6: 163–188.

Wiswe, Hans. 1956. "Ein mittelniederdeutsches Kochbuch des 15. Jahrhunderts." *Braunschweigisches Jahrbuch,* no. 37: 19–55.

———. 1970. *Kulturgeschichte der Kochkunst.* Munich.

Witteveen, Joop. 1986. "Aaltje and Her Publishers." *Quaerendo* 16, no. 4: 281–296.

———. 1993. "Sterbeeck and His Theatrum Fungorum." *PPC,* no. 43: 22–31.

Witteveen, Joop, and Bart Cuperus. 1998. *Bibliotheca Gastronomica: Eten en drinken in Nederland en België 1474–1960.* 2 vols. Amsterdam.

Wittmann, Reinhard. 1991. *Geschichte des deutschen Buchhandels.* Munich.

Wolańska-Köller, Anna. 2010. *Funktionaler Textaufbau und sprachliche Mittel in Kochrezepten des 19. und 20. Jahrhunderts.* Stuttgart.

Wolf, Rebekka. 1933. *Kochbuch für Israelitische Frauen.* 14th ed., Frankfurt am Main.

Wrangham, Richard. 2009. *Catching Fire: How Cooking Made Us Human.* London.

Wurm, Andrea. 2007. *Translatorische Wirkung.* Frankfurt am Main.

Zaid, Gabriel. 2010. *Los demasiados libros.* Barcelona.

Zelenkova, Olga [Vegetarianka, pseud.]. 1909. *Ja nikogo ne em.* St. Petersburg.

Zischka, Ulrike. 1993. *Die Anständige Lust: Von Esskultur und Tafelsitten.* Munich.

Zühlke, Anna. 1934. *Frauenaufgabe, Frauenarbeit in Dritten Reich.* Leipzig.